THE

HISTORY OF BOXFORD,

ESSEX COUNTY, MASSACHUSETTS,

FROM THE EARLIEST SETTLEMENT KNOWN TO THE
PRESENT TIME

𝔄 𝔓𝔢𝔯𝔦𝔬𝔡 𝔬𝔣 𝔞𝔟𝔬𝔲𝔱 𝔗𝔴𝔬 ℌ𝔲𝔫𝔡𝔯𝔢𝔡 𝔞𝔫𝔡 𝔗𝔥𝔦𝔯𝔱𝔶 𝔜𝔢𝔞𝔯𝔰.

BY

SIDNEY PERLEY,

MEMBER OF THE NEW-ENGLAND HISTORIC-GENEALOGICAL SOCIETY, MEMBER OF
ESSEX INSTITUTE, ETC

ILLUSTRATED

" Remember the days of old, consider the years of many generations " — DEUT xxxii. 7

BOXFORD, MASS.:
PUBLISHED BY THE AUTHOR.
1880.

Franklin Press:
Rand, Avery, & Company,
117 Franklin Street,
Boston.

PREFACE.

—————•❖•—————

N O literary productions are so interesting to most people as those relating to the place of their nativity; and, although most of the work may be made up of homely facts and local incidents, uninteresting to the stranger, it will be highly prized by him who loves the home of his birth, and who can discern upon its pages the part that his fathers played in the history of the past. Perhaps this interest has been the sole cause of the production of this volume. The work was commenced in the fall of 1875, — when the author was seventeen years of age,* — merely to gratify a longing to know about the past ; but, the notes becoming voluminous, the idea of preparing a history presented itself, and was indulged to such an extent that the result is before us.

In the preparation of this work thousands of volumes have been read and referred to; much travel, inquiry and correspondence have been necessary; and considerable money, and month after month of time, have been given it. Some estimate of the amount of work may be made by learning the following facts: Our own local public records have demanded the expenditure of much time upon their examination. The town records consist of about twenty-five volumes, generally of foolscap size, and containing two or three hundred pages each ; the records of the two parishes are contained in fifteen volumes

* Sidney Perley was son of Humphrey and Eunice (Peabody) Perley, and was born in Boxford, March 6, 1858.

of foolscap size, and aggregating more than three thousand pages; the records of the two churches take up six volumes of a smaller size : these, together with the innumerable scattering private volumes and loose sheets found in all portions of the town, have been read and thoroughly conned. The records of the neighboring towns, parishes, and churches have been read and examined as necessity required. These together with the records of the probate registry, registry of deeds, and court records of the county of Essex, and those in the State Archives, comprise the public records which have been examined. Many town histories, genealogies, biographies, and other printed works have also been perused.

The illustrations are all original, and have been engraved, at a considerable expense, expressly for this volume.

In the compilation of this volume, our thanks are due to all those who have aided in any degree, by forwarding information or correcting errors ; to the custodians of the public records, for their courtesy ; and to all others who have expressed their interest in, and given encouragement to, the work. The pecuniary help which the town has rendered is gratefully acknowledged.

As we present our work to the public, we would remind them, if they find within its pages any thing seemingly not just or equitable, not to judge too hastily, but to remember the times in which the participants lived, and to make that allowance due to an imperfect age. And, while we derive instruction from their deeds, be they honorable or ignoble, let us regard them as beacon-lights, located along the banks of the river of life to warn us of the shoals and quicksands that endanger our voyage, and to show us where the current runs deep, and the voyager can majestically float down the stream to the ocean of eternity.

THE AUTHOR.

BOXFORD, 6th of 3d mo., 1879.

INDEX OF PRINCIPAL SUBJECTS.

HISTORY OF BOXFORD.

CHAPTER I.

TOPOGRAPHICAL DESCRIPTION.

LOCATION. — TERRITORY. — SOIL. — PLAINS. — HILLS. — PONDS. —
BROOKS. — MINERALS. — PLANTS. — ANIMALS.

HE territory of the present town of Boxford occupies a central position in the county of Essex, and a north-easterly one in the old Bay State. Both easterly and southerly, only seven and a half miles intervene between the most easterly and southerly points of the town and the ocean. The nearest part of the Atlantic coast in an easterly direction is Ipswich Beach, located on Ipswich Bay. The same is also true of Salem Harbor in a southerly direction. The marshes which lie along the coast are in such close proximity, that most of the farmers in the town avail themselves of gathering, for fodder for cattle and other purposes, the salt hay which they produce. From the most north-western point of the town to the dividing-line between the States of Massachusetts and New Hampshire, the distance is but three miles, Salem being the nearest New-Hampshire town. Merrimac River, on the north, flows within one hundred and twenty-five rods of the most north-western point of the town's boundaries The southerly part of the town bounds, for a considerable distance, upon a smaller stream, known as Ipswich River. The cities of Boston, Salem, Lynn, Gloucester, Lowell, Lawrence, Haverhill, and Newburyport, in Massachusetts, and Nashua, Exeter, and other important places, in New Hampshire, lie less than twenty-five miles away. The location of the town, geographically, is 71° 1' west longitude, and 42° 25' north latitude

Boxford occupies an area of 11,459 acres, or nearly eighteen square miles. Its shape, as viewed from the north-east, appears like a side-view of a shoe, with the toe pointing to the north-west. The entire length of the town is eight and three-fourths miles ; the greatest breadth, which occurs between the Middleton and Rowley boundary lines, is five miles About one-tenth of the area consists of English mowing, one-sixteenth of meadow land, one-half of pasturage, one-ninth of woodland, one-fifth of land unimproved, and about four hundred acres of unimprovable area, consisting mostly of that portion taken up by the watershed.

The surface consists of hills and valleys, with the exception of two or three quite extensive plains All the varied varieties of soil known to our New-England region, from the rocky, barren hillside to the rich alluvial land, are found here. The best farming-lands lie together in the valleys, separated from others of equal quality by the hills and ridges, on whose slopes, where they are not taken up by the wood-growth, the cattle graze. The soil of the plain land is of a poor nature; but by assiduous cultivation, and application of manure, some portions are very productive.

The plains most worthy of mention are three in number. The largest of these, containing about four hundred acres, forms the site of the East Parish village. This was known as " The Plain " from the earliest settlement of the town. The second in size is the " Old Camp Ground." This contains about three hundred acres, and is noted as the camp-ing-ground of some regiments of the Massachusetts soldiers during the Rebellion.* The third in size is that south of the old burial-ground in the West Parish, containing about two hundred and fifty acres. This plain was mentioned as early as 1652.

There are numerous eminences in town, though but few are denominated by a name. Long and Bald † Hills are the only noticeable ones in the East Parish. The hills in the West Parish afford some grand landscape views, while from their summits the neighboring country can be seen for miles around ; the gentle-flowing Merrimac, which has often inspired the Muse's pen, can be traced in its meandering course for miles away. Stiles' is the only hill in the West Parish to which the map-makers have thought fit to give a name.

The ponds in Boxford afford fine fishing and pleasant sailing. There are several quite extensive sheets of water, whose number has been increased by the artificial forming of mill-ponds by flowing some of the lowlands, and the power thus gained utilized for manufacturing purposes. Of this last class Lowe's and Hayward's mill-ponds are examples. Hovey's Pond, more recently known as Mitchell's Pond, ‡ is a beautiful sheet of water, containing thirty-six acres. This has its outlet through a brook into Johnson's Pond, § which is a large lake of about two hundred acres in area, situated partly in Groveland, and partly in Boxford.

* This plain has also been used since the Rebellion for the parade and drill of a part of the Massachusetts militia at their annual muster. In ante-Revolutionary times the town militia held their annual trainings there, at one of which Samuel Symonds, who belonged to the Andover and Boxford Cavalry, fell from his horse, and was killed, July 29, 1775, at the age of twenty-two years : so says tradition.

† This hill was known as Bald Hill, probably on account of its bare summit, as early as 1670.

‡ This pond has recently been stocked with fish by some gentlemen residing in the vicinity.

§ This was known by the same name as early as 1666.

From this point, through a brook, the waters flow to the
Merrimac River, and from thence to the ocean. Fowler's
Pond * is a small sheet of about a dozen acres, and has its
outlet through Hazzeltine Brook and Parker River. Reyner
Pond,† of fifty-four acres, with an outlet through Pen
Brook to Parker River, is one of the pleasantest lakes in
the county. Stetson's Pond, known half a century ago as
Wood Pond, contains twenty-two acres. This has its
outlet through a brook into Four-mile Pond. It was
mentioned as early as 1652 as Five-mile Pond. Four-mile
Pond covers an area of forty-two acres, and has its outlet
through Pye Brook and Ipswich River. Stevens' Pond,
near by, contains thirteen acres, and also has its outlet by
way of Pye Brook. This was known half a century ago by
the name of the occupant of the residence which stood
near by (Spofford). Stiles' Pond, at the base of Stiles'
Hill, is a sheet of water covering an area of sixty acres,
entirely hid from the traveller's view, with the exception of
a single glance at its placid waters obtainable near the
residence of the late Mr. Ephraim F. Cole. This pond has
its outlet through Fish Brook into Ipswich River. Cedar
Pond, known as early as 1666 as Humphrey's Pond, contains thirteen acres, and has its outlet as above. Kimball's
Pond, the pond at the match-factory, and a pond at the
east base of Bald Hill, known for nearly two centuries as
Crooked Pond, are also quite extensive sheets of water.

Hazzeltine, Pye, and Fish are the three largest brooks in
the town. Hazzeltine Brook is the beginning of Parker
(known two centuries ago as Falls) River. The meadow

---

* Fowler's Pond, lately known as Hovey's Pond, was called, a century
and a half ago, Rush Pond, probably on account of the many rushes that
grew upon the water's edge. It has also recently been called Chadwick
Pond.

† Reyner Pond, lately known as Perley's Pond, was called Elder's Pond
as early as 1666. It was also called, at the same period, Baldpate Pond,
because of its close proximity to the eminence of that name.

on its edges was laid out to the Hazzeltines of Bradford prior to 1666, from which fact the brook derived its name. Pye Brook has been called by the same name for two hundred and twenty-eight years. It serves to drain Stetson's, Four-mile, and Stevens' Ponds, and through Ipswich River forms their connection with the ocean. Fish Brook, known as early as 1652 as Fishing Brook, rises between Clay Pit and Woodchuck Hills in North Andover, and through Ipswich River flows to the ocean. By means of its tributaries it forms the outlet of Stiles', Cedar, and Crooked Ponds.

Many specimens of the various kinds of metals, such as silver, lead, antimony, zinc, and iron, have been found here. Arsenic, sulphur, and other minerals, are found. The rock is calcareous gneiss and sienite. Ledges are common. During the mining excitement of 1875–77 several shafts were opened in the town at an expense of many thousands of dollars. The expensive work was soon abandoned for something more profitable, however. Mr. Daniel F. Harriman, on the land of Misses Sarah P. and Lucy A. Perley, opened a shaft to the depth of forty-three feet, through a solid ledge the entire distance. A hoisting engine and apparatus were employed, and for several months business was carried on very briskly. After abandoning this place, he worked for a season in his pasture in the West Parish, and, for the purpose of ascertaining the result of his work, erected smelting-works near his residence, at a large expense. Mr. Nathan K. Fowler, near his residence in the West Parish, opened a shaft to the depth of about fifty feet. He now uses it for a well.

The flora of Boxford is rich and varied. Most of the families are represented. Among the curious plants are two species of *Drosera* (sun-dew), a curious plant lately found by actual experiment to digest animal food. The order *Compositæ* is, of course, largely represented. The

Epigœa repens (trailing arbutus), two species of *Azalea* (one, the beautiful white, surpassing in beauty and fragrance many of our cultivated shrubs), and the *Cuscuta Gronovii* (dodder), a remarkable parasitic plant, being almost the only known flowering genus having no cotyledons (seed-leaves), are found. In stagnant water can be found the curious *Utricularia cornuta* (horned bladderwort), order *Lentibulaceæ*, with its leafless stems and fibrous roots, the latter bearing little bladders.

The wolf and bear, which were so dangerous to our early settlers, have long since been forgotten. The wildcat, also a formidable enemy, has not been met with for a century. The moose, red deer, and beaver were quite numerous ; but they, too, have passed away. The red fox (*Canis vulpes*) is still shot by the sportsman. The porcupine, which is now so scarce in our neighborhood, has recently been killed in town. The raccoon (*Procyon lotor*) and otter now and then appear in some sequestered places. The mink and muskrat are found on the margin of the streams ; the woodchuck and polecat (*Viverra mephitis*), in the fields ; the striped, red, and gray squirrel, and the rabbit, in the forests. The flying-squirrel and the ferret are occasionally taken. The most mischievous of these denizens of the field and forest is the woodchuck, which is very prolific, and by night, as well as by day, destroys the tender vegetables of the farm and garden. Of birds, we have scores of varieties, among which are hawks, owls, crows, blue-jays, chickadees, larks, blackbirds, bobolinks, robins (*Turdus migratorius*), pewits, bluebirds, thrushes, wrens, sparrows, woodpeckers, swallows, humming-birds, and many others. The whippoorwill (*Caprimulgus vociferus*) may be heard almost every evening during the summer season. The partridge (*Tetrao umbellus*), though much hunted, is still found. The ponds contain pickerel, perch, and other common varieties of fish ; and Boxford has enjoyed the privilege of furnishing anglers from the city with very good fishing. The town has lately passed a vote authorizing the selectmen to stock whatever ponds in the town they think proper with useful fish.

As a whole, Boxford is a fine old farming-town; pleasant to live in, healthy, and the many natural beauties of her landscapes, with the sweet warbling of the native songsters, that inhabit the glades, and the exquisite ferns in the spring unrolling from their woolly blankets, the cardinal-flowers of the late summer, the golden-rod and asters of the autumn, and all the lovely sisterhood of flowers which adorn our hills and meadows, give a continual glow of pleasure to the heart which loves the truly beautiful and the wonders of creation.

CHAPTER II.

FIRST SETTLEMENT BY THE ENGLISH.

EARLY NEIGHBORING SETTLEMENTS. — ROWLEY SETTLED — THE
ABORIGINES — TERRITORY OF ROWLEY VILLAGE. — ZACCHEUS
GOULD. — ENDICOTT'S FARM — ABRAHAM REDINGTON — "OLD
ANDOVER ROAD." — EARLY SETTLERS, 1650–65. — TWO THOU-
SAND ACRES OF LAND LAID OUT IN THE "PLAIN." — "VIL-
LAGE LANDS" LAID OUT. — ROWLEY'S THREE THOUSAND ACRES.
— JOHN SPOFFORD.

N 1620 the Pilgrims landed at Plymouth, Mass.,
and commenced the first permanent settlement in
New England. From this place, as a centre, new
sites were settled on the south, west, and north,
during the immediate following years. In 1624 the Dorchester Company in England was formed, and sent over
persons to found a fishing and planting station at Cape
Ann. In 1625 Roger Conant was chosen to superintend
affairs there. The following year the settlement was
broken up; and Conant removed to Salem, and, as he as-
serts, was the first person who had a house there. Two
years later (1628) Gov. John Endicott, with his company,
came to Salem, and formed the first permanent settlement
in Essex County. The second place where a settlement
was begun was at Ipswich, in 1633, by John Winthrop, son
of the governor. The bounds of Salem extended six
miles into the country, Ipswich included all that area
north of Salem bounds, as far as the Merrimac River, and
from the ocean west as far as the line which divides Box-

ford and North Andover. By the General Court, 4 March, 1634-35, it was

"Ordered that the land aboute Cochichowicke [Andover] shalbe reserved for an inland plantaçon, & that whosoeuer will goe to inhabite there shall haue three years imunity from all taxes, levyes, publique charges & services whatsoeuer (millitary dissipline onely excepted)."

A settlement at Andover had already been begun by Newton people; and under the care of Esquires John Winthrop, Richard Bellingham, and William Coddington, of Boston, the settlement prospered. 6 May, 1635, the General Court order as follows :

"Wessacūcon is allowed by the Court to be a plantaçon, & it is referd to Mr Humfry, Mr Endicott, Capt Turner, & Capt Traske, or any three of them, to sett out the bounds of Ipswch & Wessacūcon, or soe much thereof as they can, & the name of the said plantaçon is changed, & hereafter to be called Neweberry."

The Newbury settlement was begun on the southerly side of the Merrimac River, in the present town of Newbury. The line, above ordered to be laid out, cut the town of Ipswich into two nearly equal parts ; and *thus* the dividing line remained for three years.

Early in the winter of 1638-39 a company of emigrants, numbering about twenty families, with Rev. Ezekiel Rogers as their guide, left Yorkshire, Eng., and came to Salem, Mass., where they spent the winter, — it being then too late in the season to proceed further in their investigations. While in Salem their number was increased to sixty families. When spring opened they removed to a location which they had chosen half-way between the towns of Ipswich and Newbury. They purchased of these two towns, for eight hundred pounds, an extensive tract of land now comprising the towns of Rowley, Boxford, Bradford, Groveland, Georgetown, and parts of two or three others. The site of their settlement is the site of Rowley village at

the present time. This place was probably selected on
account of its pleasantness, its nearness to a river, and the
abundance of thatch that grew upon the river-banks, with
which they could cover the roofs of their humble dwellings,
and apply it to many other useful purposes in their primitive arts.   Under the name of Rowley they obtained a
town-charter, or an " Act of Incorporation," 4 Sept., 1639.
They held their lands, and labored in common, for nearly
five years, when they laid out to each family a house-lot,
&c.   The colony lived and throve in spite of the many dis-
advantages that accrue to such positions, and soon became
a prominent colonial town   Their harvests were mostly
abundant, their log-cottages warm, and every thing appeared
as cheerful and pleasant as could be expected.   What a
curiosity it would be to us if we could for a half-hour turn
the current of time back to the years of its early history,
and quietly "drop in" upon one of these families as its
members were seated around the open fireplace some
winter evening! the aged grandfather with his silver locks,
and the boys and girls in their homespun garments — the
founders and originators of our Union.

The south-western portion of the town (Rowley), which
is now known as the town of Boxford, and whose history
forms the subject of this work, remained unsettled by the
white man for several years.   From time immemorial the
only occupants had been of the tribe of North-American
Indians called the *Agawams*, — a sub-tribe, probably, of
the *Massachusetts*.   The number of the Indians had been
greatly diminished by a fatal disease three years anterior
to the arrival of the Pilgrims, which made the settlement of
the country easier than had it been otherwise.   The Indians
usually selected the most beautiful ponds, waterfalls, and
valleys for their villages, and supported themselves by
hunting, by raising a little Indian corn, a few beans and
squashes, and by the nuts and berries which the wil-

derness spontaneously produced. Their implements were made of hard wood, stone or bone, or sea-shells. They dwelt in wigwams rudely made, and used for money wampum, which consisted of shell-beads strung upon a belt. When kindly treated by the English, they, for the most part, exhibited a friendly spirit in return. Many Indians resided here previous to the coming of the white man, evidences of which fact are often found. About 1830, several bodies and great numbers of arrow-heads, together with a stone mortar and pestle, were dug up.* Arrow-heads are frequently unearthed by the ploughshare. In a field belonging to Mr. Samuel Killam has been discovered a regular aboriginal workshop. Last year the plough turned up a bed of arrow-heads, sinkers, pestles, and spear-heads, — some were perfect, others broken in the making, — and a great many chips from the implements. The stone is foreign, none said to be found nearer than the eastern portion of Maine. From the great quantity of relics in all conditions of perfection, it is reasonable to believe that here was a manufactory of Indian supplies, and quite extensively carried on. Not uninteresting, though perhaps sad, is the thought that in this place where we now reside once dwelt a different race of men. Here they hunted, here they fished, here they had their council-fires, but now, supplanted by us, they have forever passed away.

The territory of the *Agawams* comprised the original town of Ipswich. In 1638 their sachem, Masconnomet, conveyed by deed to John Winthrop, son of the governor of Massachusetts, all his right to the land then within the bounds of Ipswich, in consideration of twenty pounds. This chieftain who surrendered, for such a pittance, his princely domain, became a poor dependent on the colonists, and died and was buried, about 1658, upon Sagamore Hill, in Hamilton. In 1667, nine years later, a man was prose-

* *Essex Memorial*, p. 68.

cuted for digging up his bones and carrying his skull on a
pole.

Rowley Village, as Boxford was originally termed, was
much more extensive in its area than at the present time.
The bounds also included a part of the present towns of
Groveland, Georgetown, Topsfield, and Middleton. The
line between Boxford and Bradford at the present time
also divided "Rowley Village" from "Rowley Village by
the Merrimac" (Bradford), in early days. From Mr.
Elijah Stiles' the line ran across Johnson's Pond to Pen-
tucket Pond, — now in Georgetown, — and from the pond
the line ran in the vicinity of Pen Brook, probably to
where Mr. T. B. Masury resides, and then following the
present line between Boxford and Rowley, and Boxford
and Ipswich, straight to where the towns of Boxford and
Topsfield now meet, in front of Mrs. Isaac Hale's residence.
Between this point and Ipswich River the line was indefinitely stated, which fact caused much trouble afterwards.
It was intended to run, probably, straight to Ipswich River,
passing on the east side of Lake's Hill (now in Topsfield).
From this point Ipswich River formed the boundary for
about four miles. Near Indian Bridge, in Middleton, the
line left the river, and ran in a straight line in the rear
of the present Middleton church to Pout Pond ; from which
place the line extended in a northerly direction on the east
side of Major-Gen. Dennison's grant, — which he sold, in
1663, to Thomas Fuller of Woburn, — to the north-easterly
corner of said grant, which was about half a mile south of
Bald Hill. From this point, proceeding westward, the line
formed the northern boundary for the grants of Dennison
and Bellingham, and proceeding about a mile through
"wild land" reached the present corner bounds of Boxford,
Middleton, and North Andover. The boundary-line of Andover and Boxford was nearly the same as that now existing between Boxford and North Andover. The original

territory of Rowley Village comprised about seventeen thousand acres, or twenty-six square miles.

Capt. Patrick received a grant of three hundred acres from the General Court, which he sold to Mr. William Paine. In 1640 this was laid out on the north of Ipswich River, and east of Fish Brook. Paine sold this land to Zaccheus Gould,* an emigrant, for one hundred pounds; and Gould built himself a dwelling-house upon it before Nov. 14, 1652, when the sale was confirmed. At a town-meeting, Feb. 23, 1658, in Topsfield, Mr. Gould "joined himself and estate to Topsfield for seven years, or term of his life, or until a minister was settled in Rowley Village." At a meeting of the selectmen of Topsfield, March 10, 1661–62, he "gives his farm into Topsfield forever, with all the privileges and appurtenances thereunto belonging." This made the change in the line which is now seen on the map.

Across the brook (Fish Brook) from the above grant, five hundred and fifty acres were laid out to Gov. Endicott in 1640 This included the southern portion of the present town of Boxford, and the farms of G. and S Killam, T. Sawyer, and the late Francis Curtis. As this farm, after being laid out, was found to lie within the town of Rowley, the General Court granted Rowley as much more common land bounding on the river, and lying north of Salem bounds. This was the reason that that strip of land, which originally followed on the banks of Ipswich River down to Salem bounds, was a part of Rowley Village.

* Zaccheus Gould was son of Richard Gould of Bovington, Eng., and born in 1589. He resided at Hemel Hempsted and Great Missenden in England, and came to New England about 1638, and settled in Rowley Village, as above. He died about 1670 By his wife Phebe, who died Sept. 20, 1663, he had the following children (all born in England) · Phebe, Mary, Martha, Priscilla, and John, who was the ancestor of the several Gould families who have resided and do reside in Boxford The site of the old Gould mansion is on the south side of Lake's Hill in Topsfield, which homestead has continued in the ownership of the Gould family for nearly two centuries and a half. See *Gould Genealogy*, by B. A. GOULD, 1872.

The first settler of the present town of Boxford was,
undoubtedly, Abraham Redington. His name is first met
with in 1645, his first child being born that year.   His
birth and parentage are unknown.   He was, probably,
brother of John Redington of Topsfield, who was born in
1620.   The residence of Mr. D S Gillis is situated, undoubtedly, on the site of Mr. Redington's house   The
present house was probably built by his son Thomas some
time toward the end of the seventeenth or the beginning
of the eighteenth century, as the house is evidently very
ancient, although the care which has been taken of it hides
much of its antiquated appearance   On the mantelpiece
in one of the rooms is cut out with a jackknife the name,
" Thomas Redington."   He owned a large tract of land
around his residence, the ancient cemetery being a part of
his territory.   On his death in 1697 the land was equally
divided between his two sons, Thomas and Abraham, the
dividing-line running south to Fish Brook, on the west side
of the burial-ground   Abraham had the east, and Thomas
the west part.   By their father's will, the daughters received forty pounds each.   Mr. Redington was the leading
spirit of the Village, and wealthiest of the early settlers.
When the Village became a town, his name led the rest of
the petitioners', and he was the chosen bearer of the petition to the General Court   He was held in much esteem,
as the following extract from the Topsfield (where our
early settlers attended church) town records show   " The
Town has manifested by voat that thay doe defier Abraham Redington fen^r to come and fite in y^s fore feeate,
and old Goodman Nickles in ye feckond feeate" (6 March,
1682–83).   Mr. Redington, being aged and " sick of body,"
made his will — which he signed with his mark : ⑬ —
14 Oct, 1693, and which was proved 8 Nov., 1697, he
having died on the preceding Sept 12th.   By his wife
Margaret he had the following children : 1. Elizabeth,[2]

b 18 Feb., 1645 ; m. —— Prescott. 2. Abraham,[2] b 25 Nov., 1647 3 Thomas,[2] b 25 July, 1649. 4. Sarah,[2] b. 15 March, 1654 ; m , as his second wife, John Rowe of Gloucester, September, 1684; and died 15 Feb., 1701, having given birth to four children. 5. Isaac,[2] b. 27 June, 1657; d. 4 May, 1659. 6. Benjamin,[2] b. 19 April, 1661, who probably died young. Abraham [2] settled in the Village, where he was a valuable citizen, and deacon of the First Church for several years. He was made a freeman March 22, 1689–90 , married Martha —— (who died Feb. 3, 1695) , and died Dec. 22, 1713 Thomas [2] was made a freeman March 22, 1689–90 ; settled in the Village ; and died Jan. 7, 1702–03. He married Mary, daughter of Thomas Kimball of Bradford, March 22, 1682–83, by whom he had five daughters and one son, Thomas,[3] who married Hepzibah Perley, by whom he had nine children, and settled on his father's place One of his sons, only, Abraham,[4] resided here He married Sarah Kimball, and became the father of seven children. About 1771, the family removed to Waterville, Me., and helped to settle that locality. Abraham's [4] son Samuel [5] was for many years an efficient and highly-esteemed member of the Massachusetts and Maine legislatures. A son of Samuel [5] was Adjutant-General of Maine, and mayor of the city of Augusta. His nephew, Judge Asa [5] Redington, was Law Reporter for that State Abraham [4] was the last of the name that resided in Boxford.

In 1652, for the convenience of Andover, Ipswich, and the other towns mentioned, the General Court ordered that a highway should be laid out from Ipswich to Andover, and from Andover to Newbury, passing over the Village lands. The following spring, Richard Barker of Andover, Thomas Hale of Newbury, James Howe of Ipswich, and John Pickard of Rowley, the committee appointed for the work, laid out the road from Andover to Ipswich, as follows, viz. : —

"Begininge at the south end of Andevour, contynuing it in the cart way neere halfe a mile vnto a hill at the foot of the hill called Bare Hill, as it is marked with trees, then cominge into the beaten way which leadeth over a playne belonginge to Rowley, so leading on the southwest of a pond called Fiuemile Pond, & then contynuinge the cartway vnto a pond, called Mr Bakers Pond leauing the pond on the south, & so passinge ouer a little strip of meddow, & so on the cart way to Mr Winthrops playne, & so still the cartway on the south side of Capt. Turners hill, & from thence the beaten way to Ipswich."

This was the first road ever laid out in Boxford, and has always been known, even to the present day, as the "Old Andover Road." This passes the houses of Capt. Enoch Wood, the late Edward Batchelder, John Hale, and others, and passing on the north-east side of Hood's Pond, in Topsfield, continues its way to Ipswich. The road from Andover to Rowley and Newbury (mentioned in the above order) continues in the "Old Andover Road" within "half a mile of Five Mile Pond," then "goeinge in the beaten way of the south side of the Bald Hills, & contynuinge the beaten way untill it come to the vppermost Falls Riuer, then by marked trees," &c. This is the highway that leads from Mrs. J. E. Foster's residence, past Mr. Daisy's house, and over Spofford's Hill in Georgetown. Boxford was at this time an almost untraversed forest, Mr. Redington's being probably the only family that lived here. Communication between these several towns demanded as good a road as possible; and no doubt, even in its infancy, it was better than we are apt to suppose.

From 1650 to 1665 several new families took up tracts of land here, and most of them were originators of an interesting and extensive posterity. The first of these was

ROBERT ANDREWS, a native of Boxford in England. He emigrated to New England, and settled in Boxford about 1656, his family then consisting of himself and wife and six children. He purchased two hundred acres of land of John Lambert of Rowley (which sale was con-

firmed July, 1661), lying on the west side of Pye Brook, in
the vicinity of Mr. Joseph H. Janes' residence, on which
he erected a dwelling-house, and fenced and improved a
portion of his purchase. He also purchased several other
tracts of land in the Village and in Topsfield. He bought
of Zaccheus Gould a lot of land on Fish Brook. His
house was destroyed in some way, probably, before 1668
(when this is called the " Seller Lot "), and he erected a
new dwelling, — probably the old Andrews house, lately
situated below the late Mr. Nathaniel Smith's house, on
the same road, — which was bequeathed (in his will), with
the homestead adjoining, to his eldest son, Thomas. Mr.
Andrews was an extensive cultivator of the soil, having at
the time of his death (May, 1668), twenty-five acres of corn
planted. Among numerous other things mentioned in the
inventory of his estate, are two muskets and a rest, which
probably constituted his armory, a mare and colt, four
cows, four young cattle, four steers, sheep, lambs, a calf,
twelve bushels of malt ; and the mention made in his will
of " the new ship-saw, and other carpenter's tools," proves
him to have had some mechanical genius in the joiner's
art. Mr. Andrews died May 29, 1668. His will was
dated May 16, 1668 ; and proved, 1st of 5 mo., 1668. His
widow Grace, whom he married about 1636, survived him,
and continued in a single state until her death, which
occurred Dec. 25, 1700 (?). Her will is dated Sept. 4,
1699, and was proved Jan. 4, 1702–03. To her will she
placed her mark : J. They were both interred in the cemetery at Topsfield, probably, as he requested to be in his
will. Their children, a part of whom were probably born
in England, were as follows, viz. : 1. Mary,[2] b. about
1638 ; m. Isaac Cummings of Topsfield, Nov. 27, 1659.
2. Hannah,[2] b about 1642 ; m. Capt John Peabody, one
of the early settlers of Boxford. 3. Elizabeth,[2] b. about
1643 ; m. Samuel Symonds, another of the early settlers of

Boxford. 4. Thomas,[2] * b about 1645 5. John,[2] b. 1648,
made a freeman October, 1690; m. Sarah, dau. of James and
Rebecca Dickinson of Rowley, 18 April, 1683 (or 1684),
and had eight children; lived in Boxford, where he was a
trustworthy citizen   6. Robert,[2] b. about 1651; probably

* The following is the line of descent of the present Andrews residents
of Boxford from Robert's son Thomas :—

Thomas[2] m. 1st, Martha, widow of Obadiah Antrum of Ipswich, June 22,
1670; m. 2d, Mary Belcher, 9 Feb, 1681; m. 3d, Rebecca ——, who d. 24
April, 1——. Ch. 1. Elizabeth,[3] b. 16 Jan, 1671; m. William Wilson of Ipswich, 19 April, 1693 2. Martha,[3] b 25 Dec, 1673. 3 Rebecca,[3] b. 14 April,
1686, d 21 May, 16— (169-?) 4 Lilborn,[3] b 1 Oct, 1688; d. 23 May, 16—.
5 Patience,[3] b. 29 March, 1689-90. 6. Esther,[3] b 16 Feb., 1692-93; m. John
Bixby of Boxford, 8 May, 1722. 7 Thomas,[3] b. 18 Dec, 1694, m Ruth Bixby,
1 March, 1721-22, and had eight children; lived in Boxford. 8. Robert,[3] b. 16
May, 16—.

Robert[3] m. Deborah Frye of Andover, 10 March, 1719-20. He d. 14
April, 1751. Lived on the old homestead. Ch. 1 James,[4] b 19 March,
1721; m. 1st, Ruth Wood, 18 Feb, 1746-47, who d. 7 April, 1764; m 2d,
Elizabeth Bryant, 16 April, 1765, had seven children, lived in Boxford.
2. Robert,[4] b 8 Nov, 1722; pub. to Lucy Bradstreet of Topsfield, 23 Jan, 1746.
3 Nathan,[4] b 25 May, 1726. 4 Deborah,[4] bapt. September, 1728, d. 4 June,
1737 5. Samuel,[4] b. 27 May, 1731 (A Dorman, Esq, says 1724)

Nathan[4] m. 1st, Mehitable Foster of Andover, 23 April, 1751, who d. 25
Jan, 1760; m. 2d, Sarah, widow of Joseph Symonds, 6 Feb, 1764. He d. 29
March, 1806 Lived on the old homestead. Ch.. 1 Deborah,[5] b. 19 Oct,
1752; m. Joshua Andrews, 11 June, 1778. 2 Nathan,[5] b 11 Nov, 1754.
3. Lydia,[5] b. 21 Oct., 1756. 4. Mehitable,[5] b. 23 Sept., 1759; m Jonathan
Knight, jun, of Middleton, $\left\{ \begin{smallmatrix} 23 \\ 28 \end{smallmatrix} \right\}$ May, 1782

Nathan[5] m. 1st, Esther Kimball, 20 May, 1783, who d. 11 Feb, 1791. He
m 2d, Eunice Kimball of Ipswich, (pub.) 12 Nov., 1792, who d. 28 Oct, 1845.
He d 17 June, 1844 Lived on the old homestead Ch . 1 Mehitable,[6] b 23
July, 1784; d 15 Sept., 1784 2 Robert,[6] b 31 July, 1785 3 Mehitable,[6] b.
13 June, 1788; d. unm. 3 Sept, 1870 4 Samuel,[6] b 18 Sept., 1793, d. unm.
9 April, 1879 5 Esther,[6] b 15 March, 1795, d. unm 29 Oct, 1868. 6.
Daniel,[6] b. 13 April, 1797; m Nancy, dau. of Moses and Anne (Mecum)
Gould, 15 Oct., 1844; no issue, d 26 April, 1879. 7. Dean,[6] b. 12 July, 1800
8 Eunice,[6] b 13 March, 1803; m. Abraham P Howe, 1871.

Dean[6] m. Harriet A, dau. of Henry and Hannah (Wood) Perley, 4 April,
1838. He d 1 March, 1869 Ch 1 Emily A,[7] b 25 July, 1845, m. Solomon
W., son of Edward and Mary Ann (Lowe) Howe, 16 Feb, 1870. 2. Harriet
E,[7] b. 12 April, 1852.

died unm. ; will dated 6 Dec., 1675. 7. Rebecca,[2] b. about
1654; m Samuel Marble. 8. Joseph,[2] b 18 Sept., 1657 ;
m. 1st, Sarah Perley, 1 Feb., 1681, who d. 15 Jan., 1693–94,
leaving four children ; m. 2d, Mary Dickinson of Rowley,
29 March, 1694, who d. 25 Feb., 1700 (?), leaving two infant
daughters; resided in Boxford. 9. Sarah,[2] b. about 1658 ;
m. Daniel Wood, an early settler of Boxford. 10. Ruth,[2] b.
27 May, 1664; m. Edward, son of Edward and Elizabeth
Phelps of Andover, March 19, 1683. Of his sons, Joseph[2]
was made a freeman March 22, 1689–90, and was the
great-great-grandfather of John A. Andrew, the twenty-first
governor of Massachusetts. Thomas[2] was made a freeman
March 22, 1689–90, settled on the old homestead, and
through him the name has been perpetuated here to the
present time. He, and his long line of descendants, have
been respected and honored citizens. This branch of the
wide-spread Andrews family well represented that true
patriotism and native strength characteristic of New-England principles.

ROBERT STILES, another early settler, was an emigrant
from Yorkshire, Eng. In 1659 we find him owning a
farm containing two hundred and fifty acres, with buildings
thereon, in Rowley Village. His residence was near the
East-Parish village. Dec. 16th of that year, he mortgages
his farm to Thomas Wasse of Ipswich. To write his name
was more than he was capable of doing. The next year,
4 Oct., 1660, he married Elizabeth, daughter of John and
Anna Frye of Andover, by whom he had the following
children, viz. : 1 John,[2] b. 30 Jan., 1661 ; made a freeman
October, 1690; m. Deliverance Town of Topsfield, 24 Nov.,
1684, who d. 16 May, 1700, and by whom he had several
children ; lived in Boxford, south side of Fish Brook. 2.
Elizabeth,[2] b. 15 March, 1662 ; m John Buswell, 8 July,
1700. 3. Sarah,[2] b. 31 Jan., 1664; d. 1 Feb., 1664. 4. Abigail,[2] b 15 Feb., 1666. 5. Ebenezer,[2] b. 20 Feb., 1669; m

Dorothy Dalton, 23 July, 1701, and d. 3 June, 1746; lived in Andover and Middleton. 6. Sarah,[2] b 20 Oct., 1672. 7. Robert,[2] b. 15 Nov., 1675; m Ruth Bridges, 10 Nov., 1699; resided in Boxford, and had issue. 8. Eunice.[2] 9. Timothy,[2] b. 1 Oct., 1678; m. Hannah, dau. of Ephraim and Hannah Foster of Andover, 5 March, 1701–02; d 7 Dec., 1751; lived in Boxford, and had issue. 10 Samuel,[2] b. 21 May, 1682; m Elizabeth Cary, 2 May, 1703; lived in Boxford, and had children. Robert Stiles, sen., died 30 July, 1690; and the administration of his estate was granted to his widow Elizabeth, a month later Descendants of this emigrant have ever since continued to reside in Boxford.

JOSEPH BIXBY was one of the leading men in Rowley Village, where he was living in 1661, having removed from Ipswich the preceding year. He was noted in being a soldier in King Philip's War in 1676 His residence in Boxford was north of the mills of S. W. Howe. He could not write his name, and made for his signature this character ; 𝒵. Is styled "Sergeant." He was made a freeman 22 March, 1689–90. 15th of tenth month, 1647, he made a marriage agreement with the widow of Luke Heard, then of Salisbury, — they having lived in Ipswich, — whose will was probated 28th of seventh month, 1647 Heard left two sons, John and Edmund, both under thirteen years of age He was young when his death occurred; and his widow, being also in youth, married, a few weeks later, Joseph Bixby. Her maiden name was Sarah Wyatt At the time of her marriage with Mr. Bixby her parents were both living, and her mother was owning land in Asington, County Suffolk, Eng. Joseph Bixby died, "being aged," 19 April, 1700 His will was made 11 Nov., 1699, and proved 6 March, 1703–04. His widow died at the age of eighty-four years, 3 June, 1704 (?) Their children were. 1. Joseph,[2] m., 29 March, 1682, Sarah, dau. of John and Sarah (Baker) Gould of Topsfield, and had eight children.

2. Sarah,[2] d. 18 Jan, 1657 3 Nathaniel,[2] d. 11 July, 1658. 4 Mary,[2] b 18 Feb., 1659, in Ipswich; m. —— Stone. 5. George.[2] * 6. Jonathan,[2] m. Sarah Smith of Topsfield, 2 Feb, 1692–93, by whom he had nine children; lived in Boxford, where his descendants resided for many years. 7. Daniel,[2] m Hannah Chandler of Andover, 2 Dec., 1674; lived in Andover, and had several children. 8 Benjamin,[2] m. Mary ——, lived in Topsfield, and had numerous descendants, one of whom, Mr. Daniel Bixby, now resides in Boxford. 9 Abigail.[2]

JOHN CUMMINGS resided near by the preceding settler (Joseph Bixby), in Rowley Village. He owned five hundred acres of land in the Village, and was taxed in 1661 ten shillings He probably settled here in 1658; was here in 1678–79, when he was a gatherer of a rate to procure powder and bullets; and was also living on the same place in May, 1699, which is the last we know of him. None of his children are again mentioned on the records — with the exception of the death of one in infancy — after the

* The following is the line of descent of the present Bixby residents of Boxford from Joseph's son George —

George[2] m Rebecca ——. He lived on land given to him by his father. Ch.: 1. Nathaniel,[3] b. 1 March, 1693 (?), d 9 March, 1702–03. 2 *Gideon*,[3] b 1 Sept, 1699.

Gideon[3] m. Rebecca, dau. of Timothy and Ruth (Andrews) Foster, 20 June, 1751 He d. 1754 or 1755, and she m 2d, Solomon Gould of Topsfield, 12 May, 1756 Ch. 1. *Gideon*,[4] b 15 June, 1752.

Gideon[4] m. Sarah Wood, 18 July, 1780, who d 9 Oct., 1837. He d 15 Feb, 1830 Ch : 1 Rebecca,[5] b 12 May, 1781; m. Ancill Kimball, 5 Jan, 1805 2. Sally,[5] b 6 Dec., 1783. 3. David,[5] b 20 April, 1786 4 George,[5] b 27 Dec, 1788. 5 Charles,[5] b 19 Oct, 1793; m Hannah French, 31 Dec, 1818; had issue 6. *Samuel*,[5] b 13 April, 1799

Deacon *Samuel*[5] m Eleanor E Johnson of Andover, 4 Feb., 1830 Ch.: 1. Sarah Ellen,[6] b 30 March, 1831; m Charles Foster. 2. Samuel Johnson,[6] b 4 Feb., 1833 3 George Loring,[6] b 25 Jan, 1835; d. 17 Jan, 1838 4 Stephen Augustus,[6] b 3 Dec, 1836. 5. George Loring,[6] b 11 July, 1839 6. Rebecca Kimball,[6] b. 17 March, 1841, m Charles N. Sargent, 1873 7 Mary Peabody,[6] b. 23 May, 1843. 8. Harriet E,[6] b. 17 Nov., 1844; m Gardner Kimball 9. Abbie M.,[6] b. 12 Dec., 1845.

date of their births, which are recorded at Salem. By his wife Sarah he had the following children: 1. Nathaniel,[2] b. 10 Sept., 1659. 2. Sarah,[2] b. 28 Jan., 1661. 3. William,[2] b. 5 Aug., 1671; d. 30 March, 1672. 4. Eliezer,[2] twin with the preceding, b. 5 Aug., 1671. 5. Benjamin,[2] b. 23 Feb., 1672. 6. Samuel,[2] b. 28 Dec., 1677.

ROBERT EAMES (spelled at the present time, *Ames*), another early inhabitant, probably came from Boxford, Eng. He undoubtedly resided near the Andover line, as several of the births of his oldest children are recorded on the Andover town records. We find no conveyances of property either to or from him; and for forty shillings his son Daniel (at his father's death) discharges to his brothers John and Robert all his right of dower in their father's estate: so that we conclude, from this and connecting circumstances, that this settler had little property. He married, about 1660, Rebecca, eldest daughter of George Blake of Gloucester, who afterwards removed to Boxford, and became an early settler. She was rather of a loose character, and in 1692 was arrested as a witch, and condemned; but was reprieved after seven months' imprisonment, and lived to be eighty-one years old, dying 8 May, 1721. She was imprisoned in August, 1692, reprieved in March, 1693; and her husband died 22 July following. Their children were: 1. Hannah,[2] b. 18 Dec., 1661; m. Ephraim Foster of Andover, about 1678. 2. Daniel,[2] b. 7 April, 1663. 3. Robert,[2] b. 1666 or 1667. 4. John,[2] b. 11 Oct., 1670. 5. Dorothy,[2] b. 20 Dec., 1674; m. Samuel Swan of Haverhill. 6. Jacob,[2] b. 20 July, 1677. 7. Joseph,[2] b. 9 Oct., 1681. 8. Nathaniel,[2] b. about 1685. Daniel,[2] the eldest son, m. Lydia Wheeler in Andover, 15 April, 1683, and settled in Boxford. In the beginning of the winter of 1693–94 he left his wife and six small children (the oldest being a daughter under ten years of age) in destitution. She applied to the selectmen for help; and John Peabody took the family to his home, and supplied them with the necessaries of life during the winter. We know no more of him. Robert,[2] jun., m. Bethiah Gatchell of Seekonk, 20 April, 1——, lived in Boxford, and had children. John[2] m. Priscilla Kimball of Bradford, — Nov., 1——, by whom he had seven children; lived in Boxford, where he was a worthy citizen. Joseph[2] m. Jemimah ——, and died 27 Dec., 1753, at the age of seventy-three years. Of his nine children, two of his sons, Jacob[3] and Jonathan,[3] settled here. The cellar over which stood the house in which Jonathan[3] lived is plainly visible on the road between the two parishes, not far from the corner near the residence of Capt. Enoch Wood. Jonathan's wife was Elizabeth Blunt of Andover. By her he had, among other children, a son Jonathan, who married a young wife, and resided with his parents in the above-mentioned house. After being married but a little while, the young bride very mysteriously and suddenly died, and was buried; but was exhumed, as murder by poisoning was suspected. The body was brought to the house, laid on a table, and every one who was present was requested to lay their hand on her face, as the belief then was, that when the guilty hand touched her flesh blood would issue forth. This Jonathan's mother refused to do; whereupon she was committed to jail, and in her sleep was heard to mutter: "Don't tell on me, Jonathan. If you do, I shall be hanged." The family were rich, and it is said that money saved her life. This occurred in 1769. The name has been extinct here for about a century; but there is a possible chance of its being re-established by the family of Mr. John C. Ames.

WILLIAM FOSTER, from Ipswich, settled in Rowley Village in 1661. The old house that stood, some years ago, on the site of the late residence of Mr. Dean Andrews, deceased, was undoubtedly his residence. The first town-meetings were held in his house; and in it was also kept, for several years after the incorporation of the town, a kind of tavern, called, in the language of those days, an *ordinary*. Mr. Foster was one of the principal men in the Village, as the numerous offices of trust of all kinds held by him fully prove. He was born in England in 1633, and was son of Reginald and Judith Foster, who emigrated (from Exeter, Devonshire, Eng., says tradition) to Ipswich, Mass., bringing William with them, he then being but five years of age. While of Ipswich, 15 May, 1661, he married Mary, daughter of William and Joanna Jackson of Rowley, who was born 8 Feb., 1639 He died 17 May, 1713, at the age of eighty years. Their children were: 1. Mary,[2] b. 16 March, 1661–62 ; m. Samuel Kilburn of Rowley, November, 1682. 2. Judith,[2] b. 19 June, 1664 ; m. John Platts of Rowley, 13 April, 1693. 3. Hannah ;[2] m. Theophilus Rix of Wenham, 11 May, 1710. 4. Jonathan,[2] * b. 6 March,

---

* The following is the line of descent of the present Foster residents of Boxford from William's son Jonathan · —

Jonathan[2] m. 14 Dec , 16—, Abigail, daughter of John and Sarah Kimball, — early settlers of Boxford, — and d. 21 May, 1730. Ch.: 1. *Jonathan*,[3] b. 15 Sept., 169–. 2. Abigail,[3] b. 22 Nov , 1697 ; m. Jacob Tyler of Andover, 13 July, 1727. 3. Zebadiah,[3] b. 28 Sept , 1702 ; m Margaret Tyler, 30 Jan., 1723-24 , lived in Boxford, and had nine children ; d. 21 Feb., 1772

Jonathan[3] m. Hannah, dau. of William and Hannah (Hale) Peabody of Boxford, who d. 1 June, 1769, a. 76. Ch.: 1. Oliver,[4] b. 17 Aug , 1719, in Boxford. 2. Hannah,[4] b. 15 Dec., 1721, in Boxford ; d. in Boxford, 22 Jan., 1760, unm. 3. *Jonathan*,[4] b. 11 Oct., 1727, in Haverhill. 4. William,[4] b. 9 Nov., 1729, in Haverhill. *Richard*,[4] b 20 Feb., 1732-33, in Boxford

Jonathan[4] m. Rebecca, dau. of John and Rebecca (Smith) Dorman of Boxford, 28 June, 1764, who d. 16 Oct., 1794, a. 62. He was a captain in the Revolution, and d. 28 July, 1813. Ch.: 1. Israel,[5] b. 16 March, 1765 ; m. Mehitable Carleton, 17 April, 1794 , lived in Boxford, and had children. 2. Charles,[5] b. 26 April, 1767 , m. Lucy Austin of Andover, $\left\{ {10 \atop 20} \right\}$ March, 1796 ; had children. 3 Betsey,[5] b 12 March, 1769. 4. Amasa,[5] b. 8 May, 1771 ; pub. to Betsy Poor of Rowley, 1 Oct , 1792. 5. *Jonathan*,[5] b. 3 Feb, 1774. 6. Phineas,[5] b. 27 July, 1776.

Richard[4] m. Elizabeth Kimball of Andover, 19 Nov., 1761. Ch · 1. Jedidiah,[5] b 25 Nov, 1762 2. Phineas,[5] b. 10 Aug., 1764. 3. *Asa*,[5] b. 29 April,

1667-68. 5. William,[2] b. 1670. 6. Timothy,[2] b. 1672. 7.
David,[2] b. 9 May, 1679. 8. Samuel,[2] b. 20 Feb., 1681-82.
9. Joseph,[2] b. 168-. William[2] married Sarah Kimball, sister
of his brother Jonathan's wife, and settled in Boxford. He
removed to Andover after the births of two of his children
Timothy[2] m. Mary Dorman and Ruth Andrews. He was
a worthy citizen of Boxford, where he had several children
born. David[2] m Mary Black, and in 1705 or 1706 removed
to Haverhill. Samuel[2] m. Mary Macoon of Cambridge,
and settled in Boxford, where two of his sons also lived.
This branch of the Foster family fully sustained the high
character of its ancestors and other branches.

ROBERT SMITH, another early settler, born in 1623 or
1626, was an inhabitant of Boxford as early as 1661. He
was a rather quiet man, and a friend to the advancement of
the settlement. He died 30 Aug , 1693, leaving an estate
valued at about two hundred pounds. He died intestate ;
and the administration of the estate was granted to his
son Samuel, 3 Oct., 1698. By his wife Mary, he had the

1766 4. Benjamin,[5] b 17 June, 1769. 5. Dorcas,[5] b. 3 Dec., 1772. 6. Betty,[5]
b. 11 June, 1775. 7. Hannah,[5] b. 2 Sept., 1777

Jonathan[5] m Mary Kimball, 24 Dec., 1800, and d. 17 Nov., 1856. Ch.: 1.
Mary,[6] b. 12 Oct, 1801. 2. Eleanor,[6] b 26 Feb., 1804. 3. Asa Kimball,[6] b 20
Feb., 1807 ; d 18 Nov , 1835. 4 Eliza Augusta,[6] b. — Nov., 1810 ; d. 6 May,
1835. 5. *Jonathan Edwards*,[6] b. 9 May, 1815. 6. George Noyes,[6] b. 31
March, 1817.

Asa[5] m. Dolly Morrill of Salisbury, 20 Jan , 1802 He d — Dec , 1831.
Ch : 1. Archelaus Morrill,[6] b 10 March, 1803 ; d. 24 March, 1827. 2. Asa,[6]
b 10 Nov., 1806 ; d. insane, 22 April, 1835. 3. *Richard Kimball*,[5] b. 21 Aug.,
1809.

Jonathan Edwards[6] m. Susan R., dau of Benjamin and Rachel (Hunting) Peabody of Boxford, 10 Jan., 1843. He died of small-pox, 28 Jan., 1867.
Ch.: 1. Thomas Peabody,[7] b. 30 Oct., 1843. 2. Reginald Dana,[7] b. 18 Feb.,
1848. 3. Eliza Edwards,[7] b. 23 Nov., 1850 4. Fannie Florence,[7] b. 3 Sept.,
1855 ; d. of consumption, 23 Aug , 1878.

Richard Kimball[6] m. Elizabeth Webb. Ch.: 1. Richard Allen,[7] b. 15
Nov., 1843. 2. Elizabeth A.,[7] b. 19 March, 1846 ; m. L. H Cheney. 3,
William Webb,[7] b. 24 Oct , 1848 ; d 1 May, 1849.

following children: 1 Phebe,[2] b. 26 Aug., 1661. 2. Ephraim,[2] b. 29 Oct., 1663. 3 Samuel,[2] b 26 Jan., 1666. 4 Amye,[2] b 16 Aug., 1668. 5 Sarah, b. 25 June, 1670, d 28 Aug., 1673. 6. Nathaniel,[2] b 7 Sept, 1672 7. Jacob,[2] * b. 26 Jan., 1674. 9 Mariah,[2] b. 18 Dec., 1677. Ephraim [2] m. Mary, dau. of John and Elizabeth (Perkins) Ramsdell, — early settlers of Boxford, — 6 Sept, 1694; by whom he had several children. He lived in Boxford, where also several generations of his posterity resided. Samuel [2] resided in Boxford, until he removed to Topsfield in 1693 or 1694, and married Phebe Howe of that town. He married, second, Rebecca Curtis of that place, of whom was born Samuel Smith, great-grandfather of Joseph Smith, the founder of the Mormon faith, who was born at Sharon, Vt, 26 Dec, 1805, lived at Palmyra and Manchester, N.Y., and Nauvoo, Ill, and was killed

---

* The following is the line of descent of the present Smith residents in Boxford from Robert's son Jacob: —

Jacob [2] m. Rebecca Symonds. Ch. 1. Rebecca,[3] b. 30 Jan., 1707–08, m John Dorman, 28 Jan, 1729–30. 2. Jacob,[3] b. 20 Oct., 1709 3 Joseph,[3] b. 23 May, 1713 4 Kezia,[3] b. 30 April, 1716, m Jacob Baker, 5 Aug, 1736. 5 Moses,[3] b. 13 June, 1718. 6 Ruth,[3] b 21 Sept., 1721 7. *Nathaniel*,[3] b. 5 Aug, 1724

Nathaniel [3] m. Sarah Burpee of Rowley, 23 May, 1751 Ch : 1. Anna,[4] b. 25 June, 1752 2. Jacob,[4] b 28 Nov., 1753; d 30 June, 1829. 3. Merriam,[4] b. 28 April, 1755 4 Nathaniel,[4] b 30 Dec, 1756; m. Mary Hood, 2 Feb, 1778. 5 Ruth,[4] b 25 April, 1758; d 5 Nov., 1759 6 Sarah,[4] b 28 Aug, 1759. 7. Ruth,[4] b. 20 April, 1761. 8 Ebenezer,[4] b 9 Jan, 1763 9. Rebecca,[4] b 17 Sept, 1764 10. Moses,[4] b 6 July, 1766. 11. Hepzibah,[4] b. 9 April, 1768 12 *Joseph*,[4] b. 27 Feb., 1771

Joseph [4] m 1st, Hepzibah Chapman, 24 Dec., 1799; m. 2d, Kezia Gould, 17 Dec, 1805, who d. 23 Aug, 1842. He d. 10 Dec, 1826 Ch, by 1st wife 1 Elizabeth Chapman,[5] b. 3 Dec, 1800 2. Charles,[5] b 6 May, 1802. By 2d wife : 3 Ruthy Ann,[5] b 4 Nov., 1806; m. Hiram Perley. 4 Nathaniel,[5] b. 24 June, 1808, m Martha Pearce, d. 17 April, 1879; no issue. 5 *Calvin*,[5] b 27 Aug, 1809

Calvin [5] m. Elizabeth Pearce, 1833, and d 18 Nov, 1870 Ch. 1. Elizabeth Matilda,[6] b. 7 April, 1834 2 George Cheever,[6] b 17 March, 1836. 3 Mary Priscilla,[6] b 5 July, 1838. 4 Joseph H II,[6] b 3 March, 1841. 5 William Arthur,[6] b. 18 Dec, 1844 6. Charles L,[6] b 2 July, 1846. 7. Josephine.[6] 8. Benjamin P,[6] b. 24 April, 1852. 9. Walter,[6] b. 19 Oct, 1855.

at Carthage, Ill , 27 June, 1844. The Smith residents in Boxford at the present time can claim kinship with the "prophet."

ZACCHEUS CURTIS lived first in Reading, then moved to Gloucester, where he had a daughter, Mary, born 12 May, 1659 He removed to Rowley Village (Boxford) shortly after , being of the village in 1663, 8 June, when Zaccheus Gould of Topsfield deeds to him a parcel of land lying on the south side of Fish Brook, and also gives said Curtis liberty to pasture as many cattle upon Gould's common-land as he (Curtis) could raise fodder enough on the bargained premises to "winter" from year to year, and also a highway for Curtis to go to Topsfield in on the east side of Robert Andrews' house, &c. Mr. Curtis' residence was about half a mile directly west from the residence of the late Francis Curtis, where the cellar is still pointed out. His wife was Joanna. His children, besides the above Mary (who m. Jonathan Look, 19 Nov., 1678 ; lived in Topsfield), were undoubtedly, Zaccheus,* Ephraim, Abigail,

* The following is the line of descent of the present Curtis residents in Boxford from Zaccheus' son Zaccheus : —

Zaccheus[2] m Mary, dau. of George and Dorothy Blake of Gloucester (afterwards early settlers of Boxford), 4 Dec., 1673, and died in the summer of 1712. Ch. 1. Mary,[3] b 10 Feb , 1674 , d 31 Dec., 1674 2. Sarah,[3] b. 27 Dec , 1675 ; m. James Scales (her cousin) of Rowley, 10 March, 1703-04. 3 Mary,[3] b. 11 Nov , 1677, d. 21 Oct., 1683 4 Zaccheus,[3] b. 4 Jan., 1679, d. 7 Nov., 1683. 5 James,[3] b. 12 Dec, 1681. 6. Abigail,[3] b 21 Oct., 1683. 7. Mary,[3] b 1 March, 1684-85. 8. Ruth,[3] b. 26 April, 1686. 9. Zachariah, b 26 July, 1688. 10. Prudence,[3] b 24 Sept , 1689 11 Joseph,[3] b 11 March, 1692. 12. Mercy,[3] b. — —, 1694 13 Deborah,[3] b 25 May, 1696.

James[3] m Eleanor, dau. of Francis Jafford of Casco Bay. Ch : 1, James, [4] b about 1712.

James[4] m. Sarah Buswell, (pub.) 1 Oct., 1731 Ch : 1. Sarah,[5] b 8 Oct , 1733 , m Ebenezer Ingalls of Andover, 29 Jan , 1765 2 Daniel,[5] b. 23 Jan , 1735-36 ; m Mary ——, and lived in Boxford. 3. Eleanor,[5] b 7 Aug 1738. 4. John,[5] b 20 April, 1741. 5. Asa,[5] b. 1744 6 Moses,[5] b 24 Feb , 1747. 7. Hannah,[5] b 11 Jan., 1750 ; m Pelatiah Day of New Salem, 14 Oct , 1773

John[5] m. Ruth Peabody of Middleton, 8 Oct., 1765, and d. 12 July,

Sarah, and perhaps John of Topsfield. Sarah m. James, son of William and Ann Scales of Rowley, 7 Nov., 1677, whose son (James) m. Sarah, daughter of Zaccheus Curtis, jun., and resided in Boxford. Ephraim married Elizabeth Kilburn of Rowley, by Mr. Payson, 6 Sept., 1693, and had several children, who continued to reside on the original homestead, — it having been bequeathed to Ephraim, after his mother's death, by his father's will, which was made upon his death-bed in 1682. Zaccheus, jun., built his house on the site now occupied by the late residence of Francis Curtis, deceased, who was a lineal descendant. April 12, 1682, the town of Topsfield voted to give Zaccheus Curtis enough clapboards and shingles to cover his house, &c., if it don't take over fifteen hundred: this was when he built his house probably

Capt. JOHN PEABODY was son of Lieut. Francis and Mary (Foster) Peabody, and was born in 1642. He was the first of the name born in America. In 1665 he took to himself a wife from the Village, having settled here two years previously. His house stood where the barn stands at the

1783 She m. 2d, Bartholomew Trask of Beverly, 2 May, 1796, and d. 22 March, 1829, a. 85 years. Ch.: 1 John,[6] b. 19 June, 1766; m Eunice Harris of Ipswich, (pub.) 25 June, 1785 2. Ruth,[6] b. 1 March, 1768. 3. Francis,[6] b. 11 Jan., 1770; d. y. 4. Sarah,[6] b 30 March, 1772. 5. James,[6] b. 25 Jan., 1774. 6. Peggy,[6] b. 7 Sept., 1775 7. *Francis*,[6] b. 6 Oct., 1777 8. Betty,[6] b. 1779. 9. Elizabeth,[6] b. 28 April, 1781. 10. Rebecca,[6] b. 26 March, 1783.

Francis[6] m. Mary Killam, 18 Jan., 1798, who d 31 Dec., 1847. He d. 11 Oct., 1829. Ch.: 1. Betsey,[7] b. 18 March, 1798. 2 Polly,[7] b 4 Nov., 1799; m. John Gould. 3. Cynthia,[7] b. 18 May, 1803. 4. *Francis*,[7] b. 21 April, 1805 5. John,[7] b. 25 Aug., 1814, lives in Middleton; m. —— Killam.

Francis[7] m. Lorintha Davis of Reading, Vt. He d. 11 Sept., 1878. Ch.: 1. Francis,[8] b. 11 July, 1836 2 George,[8] b. 28 Sept., 1837. 3. Oscar F.,[8] b. 2 Jan., 1839. 4 Lucy D,[8] b. 1841. 5. Marietta,[8] b. 8 July, 1843. 6. Francelia,[8] b. 16 April, 1845; m Daniel Fuller of Topsfield. 7. Irene W.,[8] b. 27 March, 1847; m Edward B. Lowe of Lynn, 9 June, 1872. 8. Christopher L.,[8] b. 22 Dec., 1851; d. 28 March, 1878. 9. *Justin*,[8] b. 23 June, 1855.

Justin[8] m. Ella M. Gould, 16 Dec., 1876. Ch: 1. Justin,[9] b 31 July, 1877. 2. Nellie Marietta,[9] b. 12 May, 1879.

summer residence of the late Hon. Julius A. Palmer, —
Mr Palmer's wife being a lineal descendant of Mr Peabody. The old house was standing until about fifteen
years ago, when it was razed to the ground by Mr. Palmer.
It was a large, two-story, square mansion, and, as was the
custom in early times, the walls were filled in with brick.
On the front the second story projected about a foot over
the lower story. While in the last days of its existence it
presented a most forlorn and dreary appearance. It stood
in an open field alone ; and in front, near the road, was an
old tumble-down wall over which the blackberry and other
vines had trailed themselves in labyrinthian texture. For
many years a selectman, and twenty-four years town-clerk,
he was the principal town officer. Most of the early town
records are in his handwriting, and, for those days, the
chirography is very good.
His autograph is here given,
as written by him in 1690
In the militia, he had attained
to the degree of captain, which appellation he bore till
his death. Among his descendants are the late George
Peabody, Esq., the well-known London banker ; Josiah
Greenough Peabody, mayor of Lowell, 1865 and 1866 ;
and many other noted persons. He married 1st, Hannah,
daughter of Robert and Grace Andrews — early settlers
of Boxford, — 23 Nov., 1665 ; who died 4 Dec., 1702, and
was buried in Malden, where her gravestone is yet preserved. He married, secondly, Sarah Mosely of Dorchester, 26 Nov., 1703 ; and died 5 July, 1720. His children
(all by first wife) were : 1. John,[2] b. 28 Aug., 1666 ; d.
unm. in Caess, Spain, 4 March, 169–. 2. Hannah,[2] b. 8
May, 1668 ; m. Joseph Buckman, 24 Feb., 1690. 3.
Thomas,[2] b. 22 July, 1670 ; d. in Boston (?) unm., 30
Nov., 170– 4 Mary,[2] b. 4 April, 1672 ; m. Richard Hazen.
5. Lydia,[2] b. 10 March, 1673–74 ; m. Jacob Perley, 6 Dec,

1696.   6   Francis,[2] b. 11 March, 1677 ; d in France, — Dec., 1704.   7. David,[2] * b. 12 July, 1678.   8. Elizabeth,[2] b. 13

* The following is the line of descent of the present Peabody residents in Boxford from John's son David —

David[2] m. Sarah Pope of Dartmouth, and d. 4 Sept., 1726. "Ensign" in the militia   Ch · 1 *Thomas*,[3] b 22 Sept, 1705   2 Hannah,[3] b. 14 Oct., 1707   3. Sarah,[3] b. 26 Sept., 1709, d. 18 May, 1788.   4. Marcy,[3] b 23 Jan., 1712-13; d. 26 Sept, 1798.   5 John,[3] b. 7 April, 1714; d. 27 April, 1765. 6. Deborah,[3] b. — Sept., 1716, d 21 Aug, 1736.   7. Rebecca,[3] b 8 Dec, 1718, d. 25 Feb., 1798.   8 Susanna,[3] b 27 July, 1721; d — Oct, 1794   9. David,[3] b. in Boxford 4 Oct., 1724, lived in Andover and Haverhill; m. Mary Gaines of Ipswich, Mass., who d. at Newburyport, — April, 1806, a 77, he d 16 Aug, 1774. [Thomas,[4] son of David,[3] b in Andover, 7 Sept., 1762; m Judith, dau of Jeremiah and Judith (Spofford) Dodge of Rowley, — Dec, 1788; lived in Haverhill and Danvers, d 13 May, 1811; she died at Lockport, N.Y., 22 June, 1830, a 60. Their son George,[5] the celebrated London banker, b. in Peabody, Mass, 18 Feb, 1795, and d. 4 Nov., 1868.]   10 Mary,[3] b. 1 Nov., 1726; d. in Ipswich, 2 Sept, 1736

Thomas[3] m. Ruth Osgood of Andover, 21 Nov., 1738, and d. 1 April, 1758   Ch : 1 Susanna,[4] b 7 Feb, 1738-39.   2. Thomas,[4] b. 28 Sept, 1740. 3. *Ebenezer*,[4] b. 7 Dec, 1742.   4 Sarah,[4] b 16 Dec., 1744; d 20 Oct, 1747. 5 Ruth,[4] b 9 Dec, 1746   6 Sarah,[4] b 5 Oct, 1748   7 Rebecca,[4] b 3 Jan., 1750-51   8 Seth,[4] b. 14 April, 1753   9 Nathan,[4] b 31 Aug, 1756, d. in Boston, 1798.

Lieut *Ebenezer*[4] m 1st, Elizabeth Pearl, 9 Feb, 1764, who d. 11 March, 1776, a. 32   He m 2d, Sarah Pearl, 18 March, 1780. He d — Jan., 1829. A Revolutionary officer, suffering the trials and privations of war during the entire seven years   Ch by 1st wife · 1. Lois,[5] b 6 Aug, 1764.   2 Ebenezer, b. 13 Feb., 1767   3 Thomas,[5] b. 4 Feb, 1769   4. Stephen,[5] b. 24 Aug, 1771.   5 Sarah,[5] b 20 Aug, 1773; d. 12 Feb, 1776   Ch by 2d wife 6. Seth,[5] b. 21 Feb, 1782.   7. Sarah,[5] b 11 Sept, 1783   8 Hannah,[5] b. 8 Dec, 1785.   9. Betsey,[5] b 6 Oct., 1787.   10 *Benjamin*,[5] b 2 Nov, 1789. 11. Isaac[5] b 14 March, 1791.   12. Daraxa,[5] b. 2 Dec, 1794; m John Bacon.

Benjamin[5] m Rachel Hunting of Boston, 26 March, 1815. He d. 10 April, 1879   Ch.: 1. Susan Rachel,[6] b. in Boston, 1 Feb, 1816; m Jonathan Edwards Foster.   2 Sarah Ann,[6] b in Boston, 16 Feb., 1818, m. John P Foster   3 Thomas Isaac,[6] b 29 Aug, 1820, was out in Boston Harbor, sailing with the boatman and twenty scholars of the Farm School there, of which he was teacher, when the boat was upset and all drowned, in 1842. 4. Caroline Amelia,[6] b 3 July, 1822, m S H Batchelder.   5. Eliza Osgood,[6] b. 8 Oct, 1824, m Isaac W. Andrew, brother to Gov. John A. Andrew; resides in Boxford   6 Louisa Jennette,[6] b 24 June, 1827   7. Benjamin Franklin,[6] b. 15 Jan, 1832.   8. Ada Byron,[6] b. 10 May, 1836, m. William P. Cleaveland

Aug, 1680; m. David Andrews, 12 Feb, 1702. 9. Nathan,[2] b. 21 July, 1682. 10. Ruth,[2] b 13 Nov., 1684; m. John Wood (father of Hon Aaron Wood). 11. Moses,[2] b 27 Feb., 1687; d. in Cocheco (now Dover, N. H.), 21 March, 170-. Several of his sons settled in Boxford, where many of their posterity were also worthy citizens.

SAMUEL SYMONDS was born in January, 1638; m. Elizabeth, daughter of Robert and Grace Andrews — early settlers of Boxford, — and settled here in 1663. He was made a freeman, 22 March, 1689-90. After serving the town as selectman, and many other ways, for several years, he died 14 Aug., 1722, at the age of eighty-four years and seven months. His widow died 17 March, 1725, aged eighty-three years. The residence of this settler was undoubtedly situated westerly of the dwelling-house of Mr. George W. Twitchel, where the ancient cellar is yet discerned. His children were: 1. Elizabeth,[2] b. 12 July, 1663. 2. Hannah,[2] b. 27 Dec, 1665.. 3. Grace,[2] b. 14 Oct., 1667; m. Zerubabel Endicott, an early settler of Boxford 4. Mary,[2] b. 26 Feb., 1669; m. Joseph Peabody of Ipswich, 1693–94. 5. Samuel,[2] b. 6 April, 1672. 6. John,[2] b. 29 March, 1674. 7. Ruth,[2] b. 24 Dec., 1676; m Andrew Elliot of Boston, 19 July, 170-. 8. Rebecca,[2] b. 31 May, 1679, m. Jacob Smith, and lived in Boxford. 9. Phebe,[2] b. 2 Oct., 1682; m. John Fuller of Salem, 9 June, 17—. 10 Joseph,[2] b. 24 May, 1685. 11. Nathaniel,[2] b. 26 Jan., 1687. Of these sons, Samuel[2] resided in that part of the town which was afterwards included in the town of Middleton. He was a deacon of the church in Middleton for many years. He married three wives, and, after being the father of more than a dozen children, died 7 July, 1755, at the age of eighty-four years. John[2] m. Hannah, dau. of Thomas and Mary (Howlett) Hazen, — early settlers of Boxford, and had a large family. He lived in Boxford, as also his brother Joseph,[2] who married Mary

Peabody, and settled on the old homestead, where his descendants have resided until within half a century. Nathaniel [2] also lived here, but was never married.

Before the land in the Village was laid out, Abraham Redington, Robert Stiles, Joseph Bixby, John Cummings, William Foster, and John Peabody, six of the early settlers of whom we have been speaking, bought of Joseph Jewett of Rowley, three thousand acres of the Village lands. . Soon after, the town of Rowley laid out twelve hundred acres of it to the several owners, which was bounded south by Fish Brook; east by "Abel Langley's farm;" * north by Northend's and Dickinson's farm, which was in the vicinity of Reyner Pond; and west by a tract of land belonging to Samuel Pickard of Rowley. This last line was probably in the vicinity of the match-factory. As will at once be recognized, these twelve hundred acres were laid out so as to enclose the plain on which the East Parish village is situated. Six house-lots of thirty acres each were laid out, on which the proprietors built their houses and settled down upon the plain, thus becoming the first residents of Rowley Village. A road was laid out from east to west, "as near Fish Brook as possible," and another highway, twelve rods in breadth, leading from this road to "the hills on the north side of the plain," for "the cattle to go and come in." The undivided land, lying in front of the post-office at the present time, was made common May 2, 1710, for the neighborhood to pasture their " cattle and other creatures " in. Also, on the side of the highway in the west part of this tract of land, as much land was left common as there was in the other common just mentioned, for the same purpose. Eight hundred acres more were laid out on the west of Pickard's farm, shortly afterward, in which high-

---

* This "farm," which merely means *land*, was situated on the west side of Pye Brook, and contained eighty acres. Langley belonged to Rowley.

ways were laid out for the cattle to go and come in, in 1710.*

Until 1666 or 1667, most of the land in the Village, with the exception of some of the tracts already mentioned, lay common. Then the town of Rowley appointed two men, — Ezekiel Northend and John Pickard, — who laid the land out to those who owned shares in these lands by right of purchase, and to owners of house-lots in Rowley. The size of the tracts granted to the last-named class was in proportion to the size of their house-lots; those owning a two-acre house-lot obtained two hundred acres, and a one-and-a-half-acre house-lot, only sixty-seven acres. Where other men obtained larger tracts, it was because of some business contract, or as in the case of John Pickard, who owned several house-lots. We insert a list of the several tracts, to whom laid out, size, &c.: —

"To Zacheus Gould, thirty-two hundred acres; bounded south by Ipswich river, west by the town line that runneth from the river to the eight-mile tree, north and east by Fishing brook and various persons' lands, including the John Endicott farm [see p. 21] of five hundred and fifty acres within its boundaries.

"To the town of Rowley, three thousand acres. The right to this land was sold by Zacheus Gould to Joseph Jewett, for the benefit of such as employed him to make the purchase, for which Jewett paid ninety pounds. Jewett, by agreement with the town, received in exchange nine hundred and sixty acres in the neck, by Merrimack river, and forty acres of meadow, in three pieces, in the village lands. The three thousand acres were bounded north by the line dividing the village lands from the Merrimack lands, east by the line which parts Rowley lands from village lands, south by the pond called Elder's or Baldpate pond, in part, and part by undivided lands.

"To Lieut. John Remington, eighty acres; bounded east by Topsfield line, west by Goodman Gould's land.

"To John Lambert, eighty acres; bounded west by Goodman

* Hundreds of plans of these tracts of land, highways, &c., have been made by the author. We have no doubt but that, if we had time, a very good map might be made of these ancient landmarks.

Gould, on other parts by various persons, touching upon Fishing brook and Wade's neck, so called.

"To Abel Longley, eighty acres; bounded south-east by said Lambert and Gould, south-west by Fishing brook. Also a hundred and twenty acres more, bounded north by Baker's meadow, on Pye brook, and by various persons.

"To Samuel Brocklebank, two hundred acres; bounded south-east by Topsfield line, north by Baker's meadow at Pye brook; on other parts by various persons.

"To Ezekiel Northend, three hundred acres, in two parcels; one parcel lying upon the Village plains, so called; the other piece is bounded north-westerly by Elder's pond, &c.

"To Thomas Dickenson, two hundred acres. adjoining the way to Andover on the north; the south side is by land belonging to Topsfield men, hereafter named.

"To John Pickard, four hundred acres; bounded north by the line between Rowley and the village land, by land of E. Northend, and Elder's pond; west by a highway six rods wide, running from the head of Elder's pond to Andover way. Also four hundred acres more, lying easterly of the above piece. Also a hundred acres more, lying easterly of the last piece. Also two hundred and fifty acres more, lying near Johnson's pond, and adjoining the line of Merrimack lands on the north. Bounded easterly by the line between the three thousand acres belonging to Rowley and the village lands.

"To Thomas Dickinson, a hundred acres; bounded north by the minister's farm; also bounded by the Great pond, and by Sedgy meadow.

"To the Topsfield men, Goodman Dorman, Goodman Peabody, and the rest, six in all, twelve hundred acres. Bounded south by the Fishing brook, west by John Pickard, north by Ezekiel Northend and others, east by Abel Longley.

"To Thomas Leaver, sixty-seven acres; bounded north by Johnson's pond, east by John Pickard [see p. 398].

"To John Sandys, in right of his father, Henry Sandys, two hundred acres; bounded north by the line of Merrimack and a pond, east by undivided land

"To Wm. Stickney, Wm. Tenny, Thos. Palmer, John Burbank, Peter Cooper, Wm. Scales, to all these sixty-seven acres each, or four hundred and two acres.

"To Richard Langhorn, a hundred acres. These seven have their land together. It lyeth on both sides the highway that goeth from Ipswich to Andover; that on the north of the highway, runneth from the highway at the head of Elder's pond, taking in the little pond and meadow around it, to land laid out to Mrs. Rogers, in right of her first husband, Thomas Barker. The part on the south side the Andover road is bounded east by Thomas Dickinson, by a line running near the five-mile pond; south by a line running near the north side of Humphrey's pond; west by land of Thomas Dorman, John Cummins, and Robert Stiles; north by said Andover road.

"To Thomas Dorman, John Cummins, and Robert Stiles, four hundred acres; bounded east by land of William Stickney and others; west by Andover line; north by a highway which separates it from Mrs. Rogers' land, in part, and part by other people's land; south with a line running straight from Andover line to a clump of trees on the north side of Humphrey's pond. These boundaries include a piece of meadow called Fry's meadow, before laid out to Mr. [Philip] Nelson.

"To Francis Peabody, Joseph Bixbie, Abraham Redington, and William Foster, eight hundred acres; bounded north by land of Dorman, Cummins, and Stiles; west by Andover line; south by Wade's brook, &c.; east by various lots of land.

"To Mrs. Mary Rogers, as the right of her former husband, Thomas Barker, a thousand acres; bounded east by the line of the three thousand acres, so called, of the town's land, and land of William Stickney and others; north by meadow * laid out to the Heseltines and to Hadley; west by John Johnson and others; south by the highway leading from Topsfield to Andover.

"To John Johnson, sixty-seven acres; bounded east by Mrs. Rogers, north by the Heseltine meadow.

"To Charles Brown, sixty-seven acres; bounded east by Johnson, north by Heseltine's meadow.

"To Richard Wicom, sixty-seven acres; bounded east by Brown, north by Heseltine's meadow, west by Andover line.

"To John Spofford, sixty-seven acres; bounded east by Wicom, west by Andover line.

"To Richard Swan, in right of Michael Hopkinson, sixty-seven acres; bounded by Andover line.

"To Joseph Chaplin, in right of his father, Hugh Chaplin, sixty-seven acres; bounded south-east by Hopkinson, west by Andover line.

"To John Dresser, Sen., sixty-seven acres; bounded south-east by Chaplin, west by Andover line.

* This meadow, by the change of town lines, is now included within the boundaries of the town of Georgetown.

"To Mr. [Philip] Nelson, two thousand acres; bounded by Andover line on the south-west; the line of the Merrimack land on the north-west, extending the last line to a marked tree at the south-west part of the Little pond, so called; north-west, part by John Sandys' land; south by John Dresser's land. This includes some meadow laid out to Joseph Jewett, with his land at the neck.

"To John Trumble, seventy acres, adjoining Johnson's Pond." *

The second lot — three thousand acres to the town of Rowley — comprised the western half of the present town of Georgetown. The following year, Rowley laid out a farm at the "Gravelle Plain, near the Bald Hills," in the three thousand acres. This farm was located upon what is now known as Spofford's Hill in Georgetown. The farm was leased for twenty-one years to John Spofford, who came from Yorkshire, Eng., with Mr. Rogers' company in 1638, and settled with them in Rowley, Mass., where he continued to reside until his removal to the farm, leased as above, in the spring of 1669 After the farm was laid out, and before it was leased, a clearing was made for a pasture on one of the hills, which was afterward known from this fact, probably, as Baldpate Hill. This removal of Mr. Spofford's was several miles into the almost unbroken wilderness He was the first settler of Georgetown, and was, beyond all reasonable doubt, as Dr. Spofford truly says, the progenitor of all the name in New England, New York, Pennsylvania, and Canada. For the first five years he was to pay as rent, three hundred feet of white-oak plank; and after that time ten pounds each year — one-half in English corn at price current, or Indian corn if he pleases; the other half in "fat cattel or leane," at price current. This lease was assigned over to his sons John and Samuel, 16 March, 1676, and the rent reduced to eight pounds, and to be wholly remitted "duringe the time of the Indian wars," and it was extended by agreement three-

* The above is a verbatim transcript from Gage's *History of Rowley.*

score years from the date thereof. At the expiration of the lease the farm reverted to the town. The northerly part of the farm was then leased for nine hundred and ninety-nine years; the southerly part continued to be let on seven-years' leases, till 1851, in which year it was sold to Mr. Sewell Spofford.

John Spofford m. Elizabeth ——, by whom he had the following children, viz.: 1. Elizabeth,[2] b. 15 Dec., 1646. 2. John,[2] b. 24 Oct., 1648; m Sarah Wheeler; lived on the old farm many years, and died 22 April, 1696. 3. Thomas,[2] b. 4 Nov., 1650; m. Abigail Hagget, 22 Sept, 1668. 4. Samuel,[2] b. 31 Jan., 1653; m Sarah Burkbee, lived on the old place, and d. 1 Jan., 1743, aged ninety-one years. [Samuel's[2] son Samuel[3] was the first of the name that settled in the present town of Boxford.] 5. Hannah,[2] b. 1655. 6. Mary,[2] b. 1656. 7. Sarah,[2] b. 15 Jan., 1658; d. 15 Feb., 1660. 8. Sarah,[2] b. 24 March, 1662; m. Richard Kimball 7. Francis,[2] b. 24 Sept., 1665; m Mary Leighton.

Among the descendants of John Spofford are many prominent men of several generations, who have made themselves public benefactors, have bravely led on the field of battle, taught religion in the pulpit, and have practised the healing art with good success. The educators and the educated have been honored by their company. Among these we have room to mention but two or three, viz , Gen Ira Spofford, Dr. Jeremiah Spofford, and Ainsworth R. Spofford, Librarian of Congress at the present time.

This " three thousand acres " continued to be within the limits of Rowley Village until the incorporation of the town of Boxford in 1685, when the line between the two towns was settled nearly as it is at the present time, thus annexing the "three thousand acres" to Rowley. This was afterwards a part of New Rowley (Georgetown), and in

1838, April 21, was incorporated, with other lands, as Georgetown. The settlement of the "three thousand acres" was not continued till the beginning of the eighteenth century, when the southern part of the tract was rapidly taken up by new settlers, the common land in that section having been laid out in plots of five acres each, and known by the letters of the alphabet, A, B, C, D, E, &c.

CHAPTER III.

1665–1685.

OPSFIELD was first settled in 1635. Preaching was first carried on there in 1641, by Rev. William Knight, a resident of Ipswich, which town paid him for his services. Mr. Knight died, as is supposed, in 1655, as in that year Rev. William Perkins came hither from Gloucester to preach the gospel. Mr. Perkins had been the spiritual guide of the little band of worshippers then living in Weymouth, and removed to Gloucester in 1646, where he continued in the ministry from 1650, for five years, when he came to Topsfield to take charge of spiritual matters there. To his preaching the earliest settlers of Rowley Village (Boxford) listened from sabbath to sabbath, and received the true essence of piety and holiness of life. Far from being an Antinomian or a Liberalist, he preached, whether his audience bore or forbore, the truth in a manner that would make our ministers of to-day, who claim to be orthodox, hide their faces

for shame.   It is said of him that he could pronounce the
word "damn" with greater emphasis than any other man.
Mr. Perkins was son of William Perkins, a merchant-tailor
of London, Eng., where, by his wife Catharine, William
was born, Aug. 25, 1607.   In 1633 we find him associated
with John Winthrop, jun., in the settlement of Ipswich
He was made a freeman in 1634.   He married Elizabeth
Wooton, at Roxbury, where he was then living, Aug. 30,
1636, by whom he had several children.   One of his
daughters married a son of Gov. Bradstreet, and thus became the ancestor of him who is now penning these lines.
In 1640 he revisited his native country, and after his return removed to Weymouth, which town he represented in
the General Court in 1644.   He was the leader of a military
company, and one of the Ancient and Honorable Artillery
Company.   It is not known that he was ever set apart
for the work of the ministry by ordination, or that he was
recognized by the ministers of his time as a fellow-laborer
of equal standing and authority in the vineyard of the
Lord.   He preached in Topsfield until Mr. Gilbert was
settled (in 1663), when Mr. Perkins turned farmer, and
spent the remainder of his days in that pursuit.*   He died
in Topsfield, May 21, 1682

The meeting-house in which our first-settlers worshipped
stood near the residence of the late Sylvanus Wildes, Esq.,
near the Newburyport turnpike, in the east part of Topsfield   It was without a pulpit, but was probably a very
good edifice for the times.   In 1663 the church was gathered in Topsfield, and Rev. Thomas Gilbert invited to
settle over it.   This Mr. Gilbert agreed to do if those of
Rowley Village would pay their share of his salary, &c.
This the Villagers agreed to if the Topsfield people would
move the meeting-house so as to be more convenient for

* Babson's *History of Gloucester*, pp. 193-195 ; Cleaveland's *Address*, pp.
33, 62.

them to attend divine service   The Topsfield people agreed to this, and accordingly moved the meeting-house into the south-east corner of what is now the cemetery, near the residence of Mr. Samuel Todd.

Nov. 4, 1663, Rev. Mr. Gilbert was installed as pastor of the little church in Topsfield. Besides the Rowley Villagers, the settlers of Linebrook Parish, Ipswich, also attended church there.   Mr. Gilbert, by birth a Scotchman, had been a clergyman of the Established Church at Chedlie and at Edling. in England.   He was one of the two thousand clergyman who were ejected from their benefices by the Act of Uniformity in 1662 ; so that he came almost directly from an English vicarage or curacy to minister to the spiritual wants of the incipient church in Topsfield.*

After the Village lands were laid out, several new settlers came here immediately, viz. : —

DANIEL BLACK, a Scotchman by birth, was in New England as early as 1660.   The first we know of him is from the court records, where we find that : " 1660, Sept., Daniel Blake is fined £5, and respited for £4, conditionally, for making love to Edmund Bridges' daughter, without her parents' consent." This daughter was Faith Bridges, whom he afterwards married.   In 1664 he complains of his wife. It does not appear that he owned land in Boxford ; he owned a small tract in Topsfield in 1663. A Black family lived easterly of the residence of Benjamin S Barnes, Esq, about a hundred and fifteen years ago, but the original settlement was probably near Fish Brook.   He was probably employed by the iron company here, as we find by the court records that he sued Henry Leonard for a debt of £5 12 s. 10 d., and received satisfaction by the court at Ipswich, in September, 1673. The following births of his children are recorded : 1. Daniel, born 24 Aug, 1667. 2. Mehitable, b. 10 March, 1671.

* Cleaveland's *Address*, p 33

3. John, b. 28 July, 1672. 4. Edmund, b. 6 Feb., 1674. He probably had another son, James, who married Abigail —— about 1700, and lived in Boxford, where his children and grandchildren also lived. This emigrant was poor, as the following extract from the town records of Boxford proves :—

"The 12th of June in [16]88 the Selact men of Boxford met to hear of the pooer & did order daniell Black Juner to help hif father af much af hee head need of in hay time & to give a Count of it to the Selact men."

Daniel, the father, died Dec. 5, 168-. Of the other children, except Daniel, we know nothing. Daniel was a weaver by trade, and married, first, Mary Cummings of Topsfield, July 14, 169-, who died Dec. 16, 169-. Then he married, secondly, Sarah Adams of York, Me., July 19, 1695, and immediately removed to York, where he was living the following May. Of his circumstances there, or of his posterity, nothing is known. For forty-two pounds, while of York, he deeds to Daniel Wood, sen., of Boxford, May 28, 1696, sixty-two acres of upland and meadow lying in Boxford. Twenty-eight acres of this land was in the vicinity of Stetson's Pond, and the remaining thirty-four acres across the Andover road from this piece. No living descendants of this emigrant are known to the writer. The name has been extinct in Boxford for a century.

MOSES TYLER, born in Andover, probably, in 1642, was undoubtedly son of Job and Mary Tyler of that place. He married in 1666, and probably settled here in that year. He lived where Capt. Enoch Wood now resides, a part of the present house being, tradition says, a part of the original mansion. His father's family, no doubt, settled here with Moses, as in the list of families in Rowley Village, in 1680, two Tyler families are named — "Old Goodman Tiler's," and "Moses Tiler's." Moses Tyler was made a freeman, October, 1690. He repeatedly served the town as selectman, committee-man, surveyor, &c. He was known as "Quartermaster" Tyler. He married, 6 July, 1666, Prudence, daughter of George and Dorothy Blake — early settlers of the town. She died 9 March, 1689. He was living in 1712. Their children were: 1. Moses,[2] born 16 Feb., 1667. 2. John,[2] b. 14 Sept., 1669. 3. Joseph,[2] b. 18 Sept., 1671. 4. Ebenezer,[2] b. 17 Dec., 1673. 5. Job,[2] b. 16 Dec., 1675. 6. Samuel,[2] b. 2 May, 1678 7. Nathaniel,[2] b. 14 Aug., 1680. 8. Joshua,[2] b 4 July, 1688. Mr. Tyler married 2d, Martha ——, who was born in 1649, and died 13 Feb., 1735, at the age of eighty-six years. Moses [2] m. 1st, Sarah ——, by whom he had a son Jacob, born 9 Jan., 169- He married 2d, Ruth Perley of Ipswich, 3 Jan , 1693-94, who survived him, and died in Andover (?) 10 May, 1738, aged sixty-two years. They removed just within the town of Andover about 1698 ; and he died, leaving several children, 11 Oct., 1732, aged sixty-five years. John [2] was a captain in the militia, which title he honorably bore to his death He probably settled on the old homestead, where his descendants have ever since resided. He married Anna Messenger of Boston, who was born in 1677, and died 11 Feb., 1745, aged sixty-nine years. Her husband survived her until 17 June, 1756, when he died at the age of eighty-seven years. A lineal descendant of the name, Miss Mercy Wood Tyler, aged eighty-six years, and her sister Mehitable (Mrs. Enoch Wood), now reside on the old place Ebenezer [2] m. Elizabeth ——, who was born in 1668, and died 9 April, 1745, aged seventy-seven years. He died 1 Dec., 1743. Their issue numbered eight, — several of whom resided in Boxford. Job [2] also resided here, and had by his wife Margaret several children. Tyler has always been a common name in Boxford, especially in the West Parish.

JOHN KIMBALL was an inhabitant of Boxford as early as 1669, — his first child being born here that year. 24 Aug.,

1665, Richard Hubbard, Gent., of Ipswich, confirmed to
Richard Kimball of Wenham his farm in Rowley Village,
which he purchased of Deacon William Goodhue, and the
said Goodhue purchased of Robert and Nicholas Wallis,
and which was confirmed to the Wallises by Joseph Bixby
(who purchased it of Joseph Jewett of Rowley, the original
owner), 1 July, 1661. On this land, probably, John Kimball settled The remains of the cellar of his residence
were unearthed a few years since near the residence of his
descendant, the late Moses Kimball. He was undoubtedly
son of Richard Kimball of Wenham, the owner of the land.
John Kimball was made a freeman 22 March, 1689–90.
He was styled " Corporal." He was a tax-collector for the
Village in 1675, and the frequency with which we meet
the name of " Corporal Kimball " upon the early records of
Boxford proves that he was prominent in his adopted town.
By his wife Sarah he had the following children, viz.. 1.
Sarah,[2] b. 19 Sept, 1669 ; m. William, son of William
Foster — an early settler. 2. Mary,[2] b. 15 Jan., 1671 ; m.
Benjamin Kimball of Ipswich, 16 Jan, 1694–95. 3. Rich-
ard,[2] * b. 28 Sept., 1673. 4. Abigail,[2] b. 29 April, 1677 ;

---

* The following is the line of descent of the present Kimballs in Boxford
from John's son Richard : —

Richard[2] m. Hannah, dau of Ephraim and Mary Dorman of Topsfield,
22 Feb , 1698–99. Their remains lie in the old cemetery near the residence
of Mr. Walter French. He d 22 April, 1753 She d. — March, 1748.
Ch. · 1. Jacob,[3] b. 9 June, 1700, m Sarah Hale, and settled in Boxford.
2. Hannah,[3] b. 30 June, 1702 ; m. John Andrews, 3d. 3. *Aaron*,[3] b. 17 Jan ,
1704–05 4 Amos,[3] b 8 Sept., 1707 ; m. 1st, Margaret Hale , 2d, widow
Abigail Sessions of Andover 5 Richard,[3] b. 18 June, 1710 , m 1st, Mercy
Kimball , 2d, Elizabeth Seeton of Lunenburgh. 6 John,[3] b 6 March, 1713 ;
m. 1st, Sarah Barker of Andover ; 2d, widow Hannah Andrews 7 Mary,[3]
b. 10 Feb , 1715–16. 8. Moses,[3] b 23 Aug., 1718, m Sarah Prichard 9.
Ephraim,[3] b. 11 April, 1721; m Elizabeth ——.

Deacon *Aaron*[3] m. 1st, Sarah Wood, (pub.) 13 May, 1733 ; m 2d, widow
Mehitable Kimball of Bradford, 7 Jan , 1767. He was deacon of the First
Church. Ch : 1 Lucy,[4] b. 30 April, 1734 ; m. Joseph Symonds of Middle-
ton. 2. Sarah,[4] b. 3 Dec., 1736 ; m Abraham Redington. 3. Rebecca,[4] b

m. Jonathan Foster, brother to her sister Sarah's husband.
5. Elizabeth,[2] b. 28 Sept., 1679; d. 24 June, 1708. 6.
Hannah,[2] b. 11 April, 1682; d 15 Aug., 1709. 7. John,[2] *

29 March, 1740; m Moses Putnam of Danvers. 4. David,[4] b 2 April,
1743; m. Rebecca Flint of Danvers. 5. *Samuel*,[4] bapt. 10 May, 1747.

Samuel[4] m. 1st, Eunice Upton of Reading, (pub.) 16 May, 1782; m. 2d,
Mrs. Mary Putnam (dau. of Gen. Mugford) of Marblehead, (pub.) 27 Dec.,
1799 She d. 28 April, 1847, aged seventy-nine years. Ch.: 1. *Samuel*,[5] b.
4 Jan, 1801. 2. Mary,[5] b. 11 April, 1802; d unmarried, 20 May, 1868.

Samuel[5] m Elizabeth, dau of John Sawyer of Boxford, 17 March,
1831. Lives in Boxford. Ch.. 1. Sarah Elizabeth,[6] b. 2 March, 1832;
m. Rev. David, son of William and Ellen Bremner, a native of Scotland,
20 Sept, 1854. 2 Mary Ann,[6] b. 8 March, 1834; m. Jacob P., son of Dea.
J. A. Palmer. 3. Samuel A,[6] b 13 Nov, 1845; d. — July, 1864.

* The following is the line of descent of the present Kimballs in Boxford
from John's son John: —

John[2] m. Elizabeth Chapman, 5 Dec., 1700 (?); and d. 10 May, 1760,
aged eighty years. Ch.: 1. *Nathan*,[3] b. 18 Nov., 1706. 2. Sarah.[3] 3.
Hannah;[3] m. Thomas Holt of Andover. 4. Mercy;[3] m. Richard Kimball,
jun. 5. Alice;[3] d. 14 June, 1751. 6 Mehitable;[3] m. Timothy Barker of
Andover. 7. Elizabeth.[3]

Nathan[3] m. Sarah Goodridge, (pub.) 1 Nov, 1730; and d. 9 Dec., 1784,
aged seventy-eight years. Ch.: 1. Sarah,[4] b 10 Feb, 1731. 2. Hannah,[4]
b. 27 Sept, 1734; m. Asa Carleton of Andover, 6 Jan., 1757. 3. John,[4] b.
18 Sept, 1737; d. 5 Dec, 1759. 4. *Moses*,[4] b. 16 April, 1740. 5. Mehitable,[4] b. 29 Oct, 1742; d. 9 Jan, 1785. 6. Eunice,[4] b. 3 May, 1746; m.
John Pearl. 7. Nathan,[4] b. 25 April, 1749; m Mary Poor, 12 July, 1770;
lived in Boxford, and had children. 8. Samuel,[4] b. 2 May, 1753; d. 30
Dec., 1762.

Moses[4] m Rebecca Poor, who was born in Newbury 25 Dec., 1742. Mr.
Kimball dying 16 or 18 Feb, 1795, she m 2d, John Runnells of Bradford, 26
Oct, 1797, and d. 3 Nov., 1821. Ch : 1. Samuel,[5] b. 18 Jan., 1767; m.
Susanna Kimball of Bradford; lived in Boxford, and had children. 2. *John*,[5]
b. 26 Sept, 1769 3. Hannah,[5] b 8 June, 1772 4. Sophia,[5] b 12 April, 1780

John[5] m Ruth Eastman of Haverhill, N H., (pub.) 17 Nov, 1792, who
d 8 July, 1830, aged fifty-nine years. He d. 24 April, 1850 Ch.: 1.
Almira,[6] b 24 Oct, 1795; d. in Byfield, 15 June, 1828. 2. *Moses*,[6] b. 8 Jan.,
1798. 3. Abigail Tyler,[6] b. 13 July, 1801; m. George Pearl. 4. Rebecca
Poor,[6] b 15 Jan, 1805 5. Dorcas Foster,[6] b. 1 Nov., 1808; d. 27 Nov.,
1829. 6. Horatio G.,[6] b. 10 March, 1811; d. 4 April, 1836. 7. Ruth,[6] b. 3
Oct., 1813; d. 1 Jan., 1817. 8 Ruth,[6] b 4 April, 1818; d 5. Sept, 1834.

Moses[6] m. Mary Stone, dau. of Rev. Peter Eaton, 20 Oct, 1833, who d.
23 March, 1846. Mr Kimball d. 8 June, 1879. Ch.: 1. Lucy Stone,[7] b 21
June, 1834

b. 7 Feb., 1685. His first wife dying, Corporal John
Kimball m. 2d, Hannah Burton, 29 Oct., 170–, who d.
27 July, 1706. The date of his death is unknown. John [2]
and Richard [2] settled here, where their lineal descendants
of the name still reside. Kimball is a name that has held
a prominent position upon the records of our town; and in
other places where the name has been known, thrift, virtue,
and education are also found.

In March, 1668–69, a highway was laid out from Topsfield to Merrimac River, at Haverhill. This road is that
which now leads from Mr. Samuel Todd's to S. D. Hood's
residence, both in Topsfield, where it joined the "Old
Andover Road" at the head of Prichard's Pond (then
called Baker's Pond, because Baker owned the meadows
near by on Pye Brook). It then followed in the "Old Andover Road" till it came near Stetson's Pond, when it left
the road, and, turning more northerly, passed on the east
side of Stetson's Pond, and, continuing in the road now
travelled past the residence of the late Capt. Aaron Spofford, so on the nearest way to Haverhill Bridge. The
following is the record of the laying-out of this highway as
recorded in Essex Registry of Deeds at Salem, Vol. VI.,
folio 305, Ipswich records : —

"A return of the highway from Topffield to Haverell fferry.

"Wee whofe names are under written being chofen by [the] refpec-
tive Townes of Rowley Topffield [and] Rowley Village by merrimack
To lay out a country high way betwixt Topffield and merrimack River,
we have agreed & detarmyned, That from Topffield meeting houfe,
along vnder the North East Syde of the Hill called bare Hill, along
as the trees are marked, over the brooke by Ephraim Dormans
Houfe, and so along the plaine, called the Pine plaine, trees being
marked, to the end of Bakers Pond, and over the brooke at the pond
end, by william Pritchetts houfe as the trees are marked, vnto the
high way y[t] comes betweene Andover and Ipfwich and so along that
High way, vntill we come near vnto a pond calle[d] y[e] five mile pond,
and then turneing of to the right hand, as the trees are marked, vntill
we come to the brooke called Hafelltines brooke, where they of Row-

ley Villiage, have made a bridge over it, neare the lower end of Robert Hafelltines meadow & foe along, as the high way now goeth to A place commonly called, the aptake, and at the top of that Hill leaveing the high way, that now is A little on the left hand, and soe as the trees are marked, to Johnfons Brooke, and over the brooke vntill it meet with the high way againe, as trees are marked, and so along that high way, to Robert Hafeltines, corner of his barne yard, and as the trees are marked on both sydes of the way, to Thomas Kimballs and soe along the high way to the fferry place, by Merrimack Riuer. This is our finall determination, This 16th of march 1668 or (69)

"SAMUEL BROCKLEBANKE,   EZEKIELL NORTHEND,
JOHN GOULD,   THOMAS BAKER,
JOSEPH PIKE,   JOHN GRIFFING."

When the Village lands were laid out in 1666, as we see by the second chapter, John Pickard of Rowley had a "farm" laid out to him in the north-easterly corner of the Village lands, lying south-easterly of Johnson's pond, and containing two hundred and fifty acres. Sept. 30, 1667, Pickard lets his "farm" to Edmond James of Rowley, agreeing * to "build and finish" a cellar twenty-four feet long, with a chimney in it, by the middle of the next April; also, John Pickard is to build upon the land a dwelling-house twenty-four feet long and sixteen feet wide, and to "cover and finish the house and cellar," excepting the clay-work and underpinning, which James is to do. The house was to be finished by the middle of April, 1669. Pickard was also to build near the house a barn forty-six feet long and eleven feet stud, with "grate doors so that a loaden cart may conveniently goe in, and little dores soe as an unloaden cart may goe out thereof." He was also to "board or clapboard" the sides, ends, and roof of the barn; James was to shingle and underpin the barn; and the whole was to be finished before "wheat harvest" in 1669. These buildings were situated in the extreme north-western

---

* See the agreement in Essex Registry of Deeds, at Salem, Vol. III., folio 45, Ipswich records.

corner of the present town of Georgetown. On searching, the old cellar might be identified. Regarding the lessee of this farm, little is known. From what we do know we should say that he resided here for several years, and in 1679 let himself to Rev. Francis Dane of Andover, where he died 14 Sept., 1682, in Dane's service. In 1680, Matthew Perry with his family, consisting of wife and six children, came from Ipswich, and took up their residence on this farm. Pickard made his will Sept. 6, 1683, and in it he bequeaths this farm, valued at two hundred pounds, to his wife, and after her decease to his son Samuel. Perry lived on the farm till about 1690, when he removed to Bradford, and Jonah Perry was appointed administrator of his estate, March 31, 1697. Nov. 29, 1686, he purchased sixty-seven acres of land of Samuel Stickney and Samuel Dresser, lying in Boxford, which he exchanged, a few years later, with John Pickard, for one hundred acres lying north of Pickard's farm in Bradford, now in Groveland. Matthew Perry m. 27 March, 1665, Elizabeth, dau of George Blake of Gloucester — afterwards an early settler of Boxford. Their children, born in Ipswich, were: 1. Matthew,[2] b. 16 July, 1666; d. young. 2. Samuel,[2] b. 15 April, 1668. 3. John,[2] b. 15 Aug, 1669. 4 Waitstill,[2] b. and d. about 1674. 5. Elizabeth,[2] b. 13 Dec., 1675. 6. Eliphalet,[2] b. — May, 1677. 7. Deborah,[2] b. 1 May, 1678. 8. William,[2] b. 2 Aug, 1679. The following were born in Boxford: 9 Matthew,[2] b. 1 May, 1681. 10 Ruth,[2] b. 15 Aug., 1682. 11. Masille[2] (dau), b 15 April, 1684. 12. Dorothy,[2] b 14 Feb., 1685.

In the earlier colonial days the governor, deputy-governor, &c., were chosen in London by all the freemen of the *Company* in the manner known as the "erection of hands." After transmitting the patent to New England, the governor and other high officers were chosen by the freemen of the *Colony*. The Village freemen, each year until 1670, made their annual tour to Boston to participate in the election, which was held upon the last Wednesday in every Easter term, which would vary from the 29th of April to the 2d of June. The General Court-Electory, as it was called, which consisted of the governor, deputy-governor, all the magistrates, and one or two deputies from each town, met at the place of meeting in Boston, on the day of election, to receive the votes of the freemen. The manner of voting was as follows. The voters entered the room at one door, and, in full sight of the Court-Electory, placed their votes (pieces of paper, after the style of the present day) upon a table, and then passed out at an opposite door. Those who could not be present sent their votes by proxies. The polls being closed, the governor counted the votes, and declared the result. The deputy-governor was chosen in the same way. The assistants were nominated, one at a time, by the governor; and at each nomination the freemen voted for or against the election of the nominee. The affirmative votes were pieces of paper with some marks made upon them: the negatives were blank. After 1670, because of the growth of the colony, and the inconveniences arising therefrom, the old rule was changed, and the election was held in each town, and the result sent to the Court-Electory at Boston, who declared the aggregate result, after the manner of the present day.* The Village

---

* In these elections, none but freemen could vote; and to become a freeman one must belong to some Congregational church, and be of good standing in society. But in 1664, and after, certificates from clergymen signifying them to be correct in doctrine and of good moral character were all that was necessary. This practice of making freemen was done away with before 1700.

The following is a true copy of a freeman's oath, as it was printed in the *Freeman's Oath*, the first paper published in New England, in 1634 : —

"I, ———, being by God's providence, an Inhabitant, and Freeman, within the jurisdiction of this Commonwealth, do freely acknowledge myself to be subject to the Government thereof: And therefore do here swear by the great and dreadful name of the Ever-living God, that *I* will be true and

freemen cast their votes at Rowley until the incorporation
of Boxford in 1685.

Every man of suitable age and proper qualifications, of
the early settlers of New England, was required to enter
the military ranks, and receive the instructions of the
officers Each town contained a company, who chose their
own officers. Massachusetts was divided into three sec-

faithfull to the same, and will accordingly yield assistance and support thereunto, with my person and estate, as in equity *I* am bound ; and will also truly
endeavor to maintain and preserve all the liberties and priviledges thereof,
submitting myself to the wholesome Lawes & Orders made and established
by the same. And further, that *I* will not plot or practise any evill against
it, or consent to any that shall do so , but will timely discover and reveal the
same to lawfull Authority now here established, for the speedy preventing
thereof.

"Moreover, *I* doe solemnly bind myself in the sight of God, that when I
shal be called to give my voyce touching any such matter of this State,
in which Freemen are to deal, *I* will give my vote and sufrage as I shall
judge in mine own conscience may best conduce and tend to publike weal of
the body. So help me God in the Lord Jesus Christ."

Those persons who were not allowed, or who declined to become freemen,
were styled *residents*, and not entitled to full civil privileges They, with
every other man above twenty years of age, having a residence of six months
and not enfranchised, were made to take the following oath before the governor, deputy-governor, or the two next assistants . —

"I do swear and call God to witness, that being now an inhabitant within
the limits of this jurisdiction of Massachusetts, I do acknowledge myself
lawfully subject to the authority and government here established , and do
accordingly submit my person, family, and estate to be protected, ordered,
and governed by the laws and constitution thereof , and do faithfully promise
to be from time to time obedient and conformable thereunto, and to the authority of the Governor and all other magistrates and their successors, and to all
such laws, orders, sentences, and decrees, as now are or hereafter shall be
lawfully made, decreed, and published by them or their successors, and I will
always endeavor (as in duty I am bound) to advance the peace and welfare
of this body politic, and I will to my best power and means seek to divert
and prevent whatsoever may tend to the ruin or damage thereof, or of the
Governor, Deputy Governor, or assistants, or any of their successors. And
I will give speedy notice to them, or some of them, of any seditions, violent
treachery, or other hurt or evil, which I shall know, hear, or vehemently
suspect to be plotted or intended against them, or any of them, or against
the said Commonwealth, or government established. So help me God "

tions, and the soldiers of each of these sections composed a regiment Essex and Norfolk counties, containing eleven companies, composed one of the regiments, which was commanded by Major Daniel Dennison of Ipswich The following order of the General Court was early passed : —

" Ordered, that all the souldiers belonging to the twenty-six bands in the Mattachusetts government shall be exercised and drilled eight daies in a yeare, and whosoever shall absent himself, except it were upon unavoidable occasions, shall pay 5s for every daie's neglect."

The eight days' training mentioned in the above order was to be all at one season. The Villagers trained in the Rowley company, which was commanded by Capt Sebastian Brigham, an original settler of that town But, Rowley totally disregarding the Villagers for several years, Major Dennison ordered them to train at Topsfield, which the Villagers gladly consented to, as Topsfield was much more convenient ; and many of the Villagers were chosen into military offices in the company.

The "iron-works," which were an important business enterprise in the early settlement of the town of Boxford, were established by Henry Leonard of Lynn in 1669. Henry, with his brother James Leonard, emigrated to New England about 1640, and set up the first forge for the manufacture of iron in Plymouth Colony.* Leonard carried on the "works" here till the latter part of the winter of 1673–74, when he removed to Taunton, Mass., and afterwards to the State of New Jersey, and established the manufacture of iron in that State.† His three eldest sons, Samuel, Nathaniel, and Thomas, tarried here, and on the

---

* These two brothers were engaged in making the first castings ever made in the United States. — *Great Industries of the United States.*

† Henry, son of Thomas Leonard, was born in 1618, and by his wife Mary had the following children, all born in Lynn, probably 1 Samuel; m. Sarah Brooks. 2. Nathaniel. 3. Thomas, m. in Virginia. 4 Henry, b. 14 June, 1656; died — Sept, 1657. 5 Sarah, b. 26 June, 1663; m. ——

6th of April, 1674, contracted with the owners of the iron-
works to carry them on.　After continuing a short time in
the business, they followed their father to New Jersey,
where numerous descendants are now living.

John Vinton was undoubtedly the successor of the
Leonards in the business　He was living here before 1677
and after 1680　He also came from Lynn, but whether
this was the emigrant or his son we cannot determine.
The family were of French descent; they having, as tradition says, about the beginning of the seventeenth century,
left the fair shores of France, for the sake of religion, and
settled on the eastern coast of England, and subsequently
removed to America, and settled in Lynn, Mass.*

Shortly after 1680, the business came to an end.　On
Fish Brook, near the sawmill of the late Mr Daniel
Andrews, indentations and upheavals on the surface of the
ground are said to mark the site of the iron-works.　This is
confirmed by the town records, which mention the "works"
as situated in that vicinity; and we have not the least
doubt but that is the original site　The capital stock of
the company was about a thousand pounds; and by the
Registry of Deeds we have ascertained the names of some
of the stockholders, viz : John Wildes of Topsfield confirms to Thomas Baker of Topsfield, $\frac{1}{32}$ of the iron-works,
15 March, 1670–71.　For forty-two pounds, Joseph Bixby
of Rowley Village sells Jonathan Wade of Ipswich, $\frac{1}{16}$ of
the iron-works, 29 Oct , 1673.　John Gould, sen., of Topsfield, owned $\frac{1}{16}$, and in 1679 purchased of John Safford
of Ipswich another $\frac{1}{16}$, which $\frac{1}{8}$ he deeded to his sons John
and Thomas in 1686.　John Baker of Topsfield sold $\frac{1}{32}$ in

Throgsmorton. 6 Mary, b. 13 Jan , 1666 , d. — Aug , 1667. 7. Mary　8 John ,
m. A Almy　The family is thought to have descended from the twelfth
Lord Dacre　The Leonard English ancestors were among the most noted
iron-manufacturers of the old country; and the American ancestors of
America's smelters.

　* See *N. E. Gen and Antiq Register*, Vol. VII , p. 164.

1674. Thomas Perley confirms to Mr. John Ruck of Salem, 30 : 10 m · 1671, for sixty pounds sterling, "one sixteenth part of the Bloomery or Iron workes, newly erected in the bounds of Rowly viladg, with the sixteenth pt of all ye houseing, buildings, water workes, dams, water cources, lands, woods, timber, tools, instruments, with all ye stock of cole & provissions of every kind that now belongs to it," &c.

A "minister's farm," so called, was laid out, probably, at about the same time as the Village lands were (1666 or 1667). This farm was near, and perhaps included, the Dollof Place in the East Parish, situated on the "Old Andover Road." The income of this tract of land, on which a barn was afterwards erected, — which barn the town purchased of William Smith for fifteen pounds, 12 May, 1727, — was to aid in supporting an orthodox minister when one was settled here: till then, the minister in Rowley was to receive the income. July 2, 1669, Rowley ordered the Village people to pay their proportional part of the taxes (town taxes probably); which part was to be applied, first, to defraying the necessary expenses of the Village, and the residue to the improvement of the "minister's farm." For many years after a church was formed here, we find that the town "raised" so much money in addition to the income of the "minister's farm" to pay the minister's salary. The farm was ultimately leased, May 7, 1754, for the term of nine hundred and ninety-nine years, for £456 8s 8d. The interest arising from this amount assisted in supporting the ministry in the First Parish,* and in 1824 was incorporated with the First Parish fund. The Second Parish attempted to obtain a portion of this money ; but, as we are informed, some necessary records not being found, nothing could be legally claimed.

May 20, 1667, the town of Rowley "voted that the Vil-

* The terms, East and First Parish, and West and Second Parish, are used synonymously.

lage people may pay one-half of their minister's rate where
they ordinarily hear (Topsfield), and the other half to the
town minister of Rowley, till they have a minister of their
own." Feb. 13, 1671–72, Rowley ordered " that the inhabitants of the Village may have liberty to retain three-fourths
of their minister's rate." If this fractional part was not
enough to pay their part of the minister's salary at Topsfield, the remainder was made up among themselves.
Thus, really, the Villagers were compelled to assist in
paying the ministers of both towns

Mr. Gilbert's pastorate in Topsfield was far from being
a smooth one.   He had difficulties with his people, who
sometimes arraigned him before the courts of law.   In
1666 he was brought before the court on a complaint of
sedition.*   In 1670 he was again arraigned on a charge of
intemperance.   This case was sadly disgraceful.   He went
into the pulpit in a disordered state, which he betrayed by
the confusion of his thoughts, and the clipping of his words,
and especially by forgetting the order of the exercises.
First he prayed, then he sang, then prayed again, and again
sang; and so might have gone on indefinitely, had not
Isaac Cummings risen, and begged him to stop †   This
twice-ejected minister died in Charlestown, in the year
1673.

* The testimony in this case shows that the language which he used, both
in prayer and sermon, was certainly rather strong. We find such expres-
sions as the following : "Christ Jesus should reign, in despite of all the
Devil's kings, do what they would." "God hath deceived us. Wee looked
for glorious days in England, Scotland, Ireland, for days of reform , but
behold a crooked Providence hath crost our expectation God hath befooled
us all." He, in prayer, begged of God either to forgive the king this per-
jury, or to give him repentance for it · "It is better to live here poore, and
to live in the wilderness, being covenant-keepers, than to sit on the throne,
and be covenant-breakers." He begged of God to convert the king and the
royal family from their superstition and idolatry. What was the decision of
the court in this case does not appear. He was probably let off easily. See
Cleaveland's *Address*, p. 33, and Appendix, note vii.

† Cleaveland's *Address*, Appendix, note vii

In 1672 Rev. Jeremiah Hobart, son of Rev. Peter Hobart, first minister of Hingham, and a noted personage in Massachusetts, was ordained over the Topsfield church.

5 March, 1671–72, Topsfield grants the Villagers liberty to build "a house to shelter there horſes in neere to ye meeting house where ye Selectmen and thay shall thinke fite or most Convinient and alſo a house to shelter themſelves in with a fier in it," as long as they attend the church there. In the fall of the next year (1673), a stone wall five or six feet high, and "three foote brod at the botom," was built around the meeting-house. On the south side the wall was twelve feet, and on the other three sides ten feet, from the meeting-house. Though an entrance is not mentioned in the record, it is supposable that there was one. Within this wall, at the south-east corner, a watch-house ten feet square was built, which was called in the beginning of the eighteenth century the "Old Meeting-House Fort." The Villagers were to lend aid in this work, and no doubt many weary days were spent in building the massive wall. The watch-house was also probably built with stone, — as we should judge from the dimensions, &c., given in the records, and not recorded here, — the wall forming a part of the south and west sides. Having in our minds the contemporary Indian hostilities, the watch-house tells its own use; and probably many anxious hours were spent in the limited space enclosed within its four walls.

For some reason, early in the year 1673, Abraham Redington and some others sent a petition to the General Court, asking for the dissolution of their connection with Topsfield, and praying to be annexed to Rowley. Others of the Village were strongly opposed to the movement, because of the convenience of the nearness of Topsfield; and, not discerning any reason why the change should be made, sent the following petition to the General Court:—

"To the Honorable General Court now sitting in Boston, this 7th of May, 1673. The Humble petition of divers well affected Inhabitants and House-holders of the Village commonly called Rowley Village.

"Humbly sheweth. That whereas yoͬ petitioners formerly purchased a tract of land of Joseph Jewett of Rowley, now deceased, on which we now dwell, wh. land was sold to us as village land, free from any engagement to the town of Rowley, ellse we had not purchased it;* as also it lyeing nigh to the now town of Topsfield, whose inhabitants about ten or twelve years since, called Mr. Gilbert to be their minister; he was unwilling to accept, unless we of the village would engage to pay our shares in and to publiqe charges at Topsfield. Upon this, Abraham Redington, Joseph Biggsby, John Cumins, and the rest of us, being free as we apprehended, agreed to pay our proportions as our honest neighbours of Topsfield did, only provided they would remove or sett the meetinghouse so as it might stand convenient for us; upon this a committy being appointed out of them and ourselves, agreed unanimously to set the meetinghouse toward the outside of Topsfield bounds to us ward, wh. was don, and now stands to our great conveniency, being allmost as near to us as to divers of Topsfield, viz. two or three miles, and our distance from Rowley is 7 or 8, if not nine miles, some of us. Farther, as to military matters, we were not regarded by Rowley for many years, but that service totally neglected, wh. the Major of the Regemͭ understanding, sent his warrant to us to traine in Topsfield; we obeyed, and that company and ourselves agreeing, some of us were chosen into office, mutually by both places, and were all as one town and company very loveingly agreeing. While such time as some of us, meditating other designs than we think were pretended thereby, as we conceive, broke the neck of Love and unity with our neighbors of Topsfield. Abraham Redington did put in some hands, we doe not say of boyes, and divers other persons, inconsiderable, to move this Honorble Court, to free us from Topsfield, and lay us to Rowley, to our great incumbrance and inconvenience every way, both to matters civile, ecclesiasticall, and military; our condition is hereby rendered extremely burdensome, divers of our people are already joined to the church at Topsfield, and more may soon be if God please to move yͬ hearts, it being the only nigh place where we can hear and enjoy the solemn and publiqe worship on the Lord's dayes; what division

---

* When these men bought this land, they supposed it was entirely free from any town authority, thinking that Jewett obtained it from the Colony.

this may in time produce, especially since the late law impowering none but persons in full communion to elect or have voice in electing church officers, &c., we cannot but, as our case stands, be afraide of. There being by this means a foundation layd for not only unpleasant variance, but future alienation with our Loveing brethen of that church.

"This is our distracted and wronged case and condition, by reason of our breaking with Topsfield, wh. we doe tender to your Honorble selfes, for redress and cure, Humbly beseeching your Honors herein, that our poor village, being but sixteen familyes, incapable of calling a minister or maintaining one, and so far from other towns, and so nigh to Topsfield, may be layd thither and united to that towne, which will be for the great behoofe of them and us both, in respect to township and militia, as well as church, and minister's encouragement, all of us being hardly able to maintayne one able minister honorably, wee beg wee may be declared a free village from Rowley, as our deeds of our lands, and lines, and bounds, demonstrate. These privileges, granted by your worships, will, we trust, tend to the honor of God, peace and comfort of our neighbours, and benefit of ourselves, your poor petitioners. We leave ourselves herein to the mature consideration of this Court; praying the only wise God to direct, council, and guide you in all things. Soe we remain your humble petitioners.

" ROBARD SMITH,
ROBARD STILES,
THOMAS ANDREWS,
EDMON BRIGGSS,
JOHN RAMDELL."

This petition was received by the Court, and the magistrates agreed to an order of notice; but the deputies did not consent. What further order was taken we are not informed. The Court probably came to the conclusion that the situation of the affairs here was best as they existed, and that it would be folly for them to interpose their authority.

Regarding the military drill of the Villagers, Oct. 7, 1674, it was ordered by the General Court, "that the trayned souldjers of the place called Rowley Village shall forthwith list themselves, & performed duty in ordjnary traynings, either at Rovly or Topsfield, as shall svite best with their incljnations & occasions, which being don shall so continue vntill such time as the sajd village is setled with a minister, and haue a sufficjent number to trayne among themselues & officers according to lawe appointed to excercise them." Taking advantage of the above liberty, the dissatisfied members of the Village trained with the Rowley company, and the others continued their practice with the company at Topsfield.

Boxford being a central town, surrounded on all sides by numerous settlements, and lying several miles from the frontier-line, the depredations of the savages were foreign to its inhabitants; but a period was now approaching, which threw the whole colony into greater excitement than had been experienced since the settlement of the country. The chapter of history that details the incidents of that season is filled with deeds of savage warfare and barbarity, which causes the reader to shudder as he dwells upon the melancholy doom of the helpless women and children who became the victims of the tomahawk and scalping-knife.

The Indian War of 1675–76 — or Philip's War, as it is more commonly called — was the first service into which our soldiers were ordered. Rowley was ordered to furnish twelve men, and fit them out with "warm, thick clothing, and arms." One of these men was Joseph Bixby of the Village. They were impressed into service in November, 1675, in the company of Capt. Samuel Brocklebank, whose melancholy fate, with most of his company, may be found in the history of the attack, near Sudbury, on the morning of April 21, 1676. Who were drafted from the Topsfield company has not come to our knowledge. Capt. Brocklebank's company probably entered service at Narragansett, first of January, 1676; returned home shortly after, and, at the end of a week's stay, was sent out again, and stationed at Marlborough; and when Capt. Brocklebank and most of his company went toward Sudbury to assist in making an attack upon the savages, Joseph Bixby and a few others remained behind to guard the garrison-house at Marlborough, and thus escaped the terrible fate of their comrades Eight out of the twelve who were drafted from the Rowley company, including Joseph Bixby, arrived home safe, and lived for many years to relate to their posterity the terrible incidents connected with the War of King Philip.*

In the spring of 1676 the Indians made some depredations at Andover and vicinity ; and it seemed, for a time, that the Village would be included in the dire list of assaulted settlements

Though the Village people attended church and trained at Topsfield, they had to attend town-meetings at Rowley. Tax-collectors were appointed by Rowley specially for the Village ; of which, in 1675, we had no less than three, — William Foster, Joseph Peabody, and John Kimball. In 1677 two were appointed, — Abraham Redington and John

---

* King Philip, who was at first friendly to the whites, soon proved to be their most deadly foe No doubt he had good reasons for becoming their enemy; for the English, in their dealings with the Indians, had not always treated them justly. Bancroft says that Philip was "hurried into his rebellion."

Before this, the whites had had no serious trouble with the Indians since the Pequot tribe were completely annihilated in 1638. We will not enter into detail, and therefore will only say that Philip, in 1674, got up a "national" conspiracy to destroy the English at one decisive blow The English were informed of the plot by an Indian preacher, for which he was murdered by some Indians, who were arrested, tried, condemned, and executed. This enraged Philip more than ever ; and he, with the assistance of some of the neighboring tribes, immediately commenced his work of burning, murdering, and other cruelties After the attacks on the towns of Swanzey and Mendon, the spirit of the English was fully aroused. The Indians were becoming bolder and more savage in their depredations, and every settlement was in danger of becoming the scene of a bloody battle, and a prey to the murderous hands of the savages.

The scenes during the fall of 1675 were mostly confined to the limits of Worcester County The people were harvesting their crops, and every hour of time and every sheaf of grain were needed for the long winter close at hand. This period is thus described by the historian "The laborer in the

Peabody. Tithing-men, or men to see that the sabbath was well kept, were also chosen by the town, agreeable to an Act of the General Court, passed May 23, 1677. In that year two tithing-men were appointed for the Village, — John Peabody and William Foster; in 1680, two, — Joseph Bixby and William Foster. In 1680 a list of the families in the Village was made out, viz.: "Goodman Black, Moses Tiler, Old Goodman Tiler, Robert Ames, Goodman Perry, John Kimball, Joseph Bigsbee, William Foster, John Peabody, Goodman Stiles, Goodman Bossell, Goodman Redington, Daniel Wood, Joseph Pebody, Josiah Bridges, Daniel Black, John Vinton, Samuel Simons, Widow Andrews, Thomas Andrews, Robert Smith, Zacheus Curtvout, sen., Zacheus Curtvout, jun., John Ramsdell, and After Carry." In this list the families number twenty-five; and by the petition sent to the General Court in 1673, signed by Robert Smith and others, we learn that there

---

field, the reapers as they went forth to harvest, men as they went to mill, the shepherd-boy among the sheep, were shot down by the skulking foes, whose approach was invisible. The mother, if left alone in the house, feared the tomahawk for herself and children. On the sudden attack, the father would fly with one child, the mother with another, and perhaps only one escape. The village cavalcade on its way to meeting on Sundays, in files on horseback, the farmer holding the bridle in one hand and a child in the other, his wife seated upon a pillion behind him — it may be, with a child in her lap, — as was the custom of those days, could not proceed safely — bullets would come whizzing by them. The Indians hung upon the skirts of the English villages like the lightning upon the edge of the clouds."

The depredations of the savages during the winter of 1675 and the spring of 1676 were almost innumerable. *Many* were the towns that had experienced more or less the effects of this disastrous period; and Drake says: "Few there were who were not in mourning for some near kindred."

After the battle at Sudbury, the spirits of the hostile Indians began to decline, and they were considered as nearly subdued; and the death of their famous chief, King Philip, who was shot at Mount Hope, in Bristol, R.I., Aug. 12, 1676, clearly decided their fate, doubts were no longer entertained of their appearing formidable. The war continued for a time in the province of Maine, but at length it ceased. The chiefs came and submitted themselves to the English, and a permanent treaty was established.

were sixteen families in the Village that year, which shows an increase of nine families in the seven intermediate years.

About this time several new settlers came, viz.: —

JOSEPH PEABODY, brother of Capt. John Peabody who had already settled here, was born in 1644, and settled on Fish Brook about 1671. His house stood near the residence of the late Mr. Daniel Andrews. The land on which he settled was his father's (Lieut. Francis Peabody), it being a part of the twelve hundred acres laid out to six of the early settlers. He was made a freeman October, 1690. After serving the town as selectman for several years, he died in 1721, at the age of seventy-seven years. His wife was Bethiah, daughter of Edmund Bridges, whom he married Oct. 26, 1668. Their children were: 1. Joseph,[2] b. 16 April, 1671. 2 Jonathan.[2] 3. Sarah,[2] b. 4 Sept., 1676; m. Benjamin Smith, 22 May, 1700. 4. Samuel,[2] b. 8 April, 1678; settled in Andover. 5. Bethiah,[2] b. 8 April, 1681. 6. Lydia,[2] b. 4 Feb., 1683; m. Jacob Perley, 9 May, 1709. 7. Alice,[2] b. 4 Jan., 1685; m. Thomas Holt of Andover. Joseph[2] m. Mary ——, was several years a selectman, and died in 1715, leaving eight children: three of his sons settled in Middleton, and one — Joseph — in Boxford. Jonathan[2] also lived in Boxford, where his posterity resided for several generations. Among the descendants of this settler we would especially mention Andrew Preston Peabody, who graduated at Harvard College, 1826; a noted minister in Portsmouth, N.H.; editor of *The North-American Review* from 1853 to 1863; Plummer Professor of Christian Morals, and Preacher to Harvard University, 1860; and LL. D. at Rochester University, 1863.

JOHN RAMSDELL was undoubtedly from Lynn. He married Elizabeth Perkins of Topsfield, 31 May, 1671, about which time he first appears in the Village. He was perhaps interested in the iron-works, and came from Lynn

with Henry Leonard, to assist him in carrying the works
on.   His daughter Mary was of Boxford, 1694; but of the
parents and the rest of the family nothing further is known
to the writer.   A John Ramsdell was taxed here in 1711,
and a Timothy Ramsdell from 1711 to 1723.   The children
of this settler were: 1. Elizabeth,[2] b. 4 Oct., 1672.   2.
Mary,[2] b. 27 Jan., 1674; m. Ephraim, son of Robert Smith
of Boxford, 6 Sept., 1694   3. Priscilla,[2] b. 20 Aug., 1677.
4 John,[2] b. 19 Jan , 1679.

EDMUND BRIDGES was living here in 1673.   Whether
this was the emigrant, or his son, we do not know.

JOSIAH BRIDGES, son of Edmund Bridges, the emigrant
from England, was born about 1650, and married, 1st,
Elizabeth Norton, 13 Nov., 1676; and, 2d, Ruth Greenslip,
19 Sept., 1677.   He lived first in Ipswich, and before 1680
removed to Boxford.   He was living here as late as 1704,
and a Josiah Bridges was taxed here in 1711.   He was a
surveyor in 1695, a juror of trials in 1699, and selectman
1700, 1704.   His children were: 1. Josiah,[2] b. 29 May,
1680.   2 Anne,[2] b 14 April, 1684   3. Edmund.[2]   4.
Mercy.[2]   5. Hepzibah.[2]   Edmund[2] m. Esther Wheeler of
Beverly, 28 Dec., 1710; resided in Boxford, and had three
children.   He was living here in 1716, and was the last
resident of the name

SAMUEL BUSWELL, from Salisbury, was born in 1628;
m. Sarah Keies, 8 July, 1656, and had the following children born in Salisbury: Isaac, b. 6 : 6 : 1657.   John, b. 7 :
8 : 1659.   Samuel, b. 25 : 3 : 1662; lived in Boxford.   William, b. 5 : 6 : 1664; d. 21 June, 1699.   Robert, b. 8 : 12 :
1666; m. Hannah Tyler, 9 Dec., 1697; lived in Andover.
James, b. 20 : 1 1668–69   Between the last-mentioned
date and 1674 he must have removed to the Village, as
he had a son Joseph born here 20 Aug , 1674.   A daughter
Mary was also born here 1 June, 1677.   After 1686, when
a highway was laid out from his house to the main-road

that led to Topsfield, his name is not found on the records.
His son John was a fence-viewer and surveyor in 1689.
He married Elizabeth, daughter of Robert Stiles of the
Village, and had three children born here. One of these
was a son John, who was born in 1703–04, married, lived,
and had two children born, in Boxford. This was the last
family of the name that resided here : the name has been
extinct for a century.

, DANIEL WOOD, probably son of Thomas Wood of Rowley, married and settled in the Village about 1675, his first
child being born here that year. At different times he
purchased several tracts of land situated on both sides of
the highway in the vicinity of the Stetson place. It is supposed that the house that occupied the site of the present
Stetson house was built by Mr. Wood, and by him and
his descendants occupied until 1815, when, in the terrific
gale in September of that year, it was blown down. The
place was sold to Seth Stetson from Hanover, Mass., who,
in 1818, erected the present dwelling. Mr. Wood was
made a freeman October, 1690. This settler stands at the
head of a long, worthy, and interesting line of descendants,
many of whom resided here, and some are with us even
now, still retaining the mental vigor, virtue, and position
of their fathers. Mr. Wood was a deacon of the First
Church, and was living as late as 1718, but the date of his
death is not recorded. He married, about 1674, Sarah
Andrews, — daughter of Robert Andrews of the Village,
then deceased, — who died 27 Sept., 1714, aged fifty-seven
years. Her remains, and his also probably, lie in the old
cemetery in the East Parish. Her gravestone is the oldest
remaining, one in the town. Their children were : 1. Dan-
iel,[2] b. {17 July, 15 Aug.,} 1675 ; d. 1 June, 1697. 2. David,[2] * b. 18

---

* The following is the line of descent of the present Wood residents of
Boxford from Daniel's son David . —

David[2] was a doctor and a justice of the peace. He m. Mary ——,

Feb., 1677   3 John,[2] b 25 March, 1680.   4. Abigail,[2] b.
3 Oct., 1684; d 25 July, 168–.   5 Huldah[2] (or Mary).
b 23 May, 1687   6. Mercy,[2] b. 21 Sept, 1689.   7. Jacob,[2]
b. 22 Aug., 1691.   8. Sarah,[2] b. 16 April, 1698.   John[2]
married Ruth, daughter of Capt. John Peabody of the
Village, and lived to be seventy-eight years old.   His
wife died at the age of seventy-four years.   Among their
children was Hon. Aaron Wood, a man of no little consequence in the history of the town.   David,[2] of whom we
shall speak hereafter, was a doctor, a cider-manufacturer,
and extensive farmer, and probably settled on the old place.
Jacob[2] had numerous descendants, most of whom were
citizens of Boxford

ARTHUR CARY was living here before 1677.   Nothing is
known of his previous history.   By his wife Sarah, who
was from Ipswich, he had several children, of whom the
following births are recorded on the town records, viz.: 1.
——nah (dau.),[2] b 8 Jan., 1702–03. 2. John,[2] b 5 Oct.,
1705   3. Keziah,[2] b. 7 April, 17—.   4 Stephen,[2] b. 6
Oct, 171–.   Elizabeth Cary, another child, probably, of
this settler, was baptized in the First Church, 19 July,
1703.   Elizabeth Cary, probably the same person of whom
we have just spoken, married Samuel Stiles of Boxford, 2
May, 170–.   "Goodwife Cary" was baptized in the First
Church, 31 March, 1706.   In 1691 the town voted not to
tax him.   In 1703 his wife asked alms of the selectmen,
who immediately warned her "to depart out of the town,

about 1701 ; and died 30 Aug., 1744. Ch : 1. Mary,[3] b 23 Sept., 1702; d. 11
May, 1712   2 *Daniel*,[3] b 22 Jan., 1705–06   3 Sarah,[3] b. 10 Oct, 1707   4
David,[3] b 19 Nov, 1709; d 5 March, 1785. 5. Hannah,[3] b 21 Nov, 1711 ;
m Joshua Andrews, 2 Dec, 1731. 6. *Jonathan*,[3] b 6 Dec, 1713   7. Samuel,[3] b 4 June, 1724; removed to Union, Conn, previous to 1750.

Daniel[3] m Sarah Peabody, 8 March, 1730–31, and d 31 March, 1746.
Ch   1. Sarah,[4] b. 29 Jan, 1731–32; d 19 April, 1788. 2 Joseph,[4] b. 29
March, 1734, d 7 May, 1801   3 Deborah,[4] b 12 Nov., 1736, d 1767   4
Daniel,[4] b. 13 July, 1739; d 27 June, 1819 5. *Lemuel*,[4] b 25 Oct, 1741.

. . . to the place of her former residence [Ipswich], the selectmen not allowing her to reside in our town." Moses Tyler, the constable at the time, 22 Oct., 1703, warned her to leave the town; but it seems she still remained here for some years after. Perhaps Ipswich assisted her where she was. In the warrants she is called "a poor body." Any thing further concerning this family is unknown to the writer.

GEORGE BLAKE — or *Black*, as it is frequently written on the old records — came from Gloucester to Boxford about 1675. He was born in 1611, made a freeman 1651, and died Feb. 17, 1698, aged eighty-seven years. His wife Dorothy survived him till Dec. 12, 1702, when she died. He was at first well-off; but became so poor that the town

6 Rebecca,[4] b. 26 Feb., 1743-44. 7. Frances,[4] b. 2 July, 1746; d. 27 March, 1790.

Jonathan[3] m Sarah Redington; and d. 19 June, 1781. She d. 11 Sept., 1775, aged 50 years. Ch.: 1. David,[4] b. 13 Nov, 1748. 2. *Jonathan*,[4] b. 14 Sept., 1751 3 Eliphalet,[4] b. 4 June, 1754. 4. Sarah,[4] b 27 Aug., 1757. 5. Enoch,[4] b. 21 Oct, 1759 6. Abner,[4] b 12 Dec., 1761. 7. Mary,[4] b. 29 Sept., 1764; d. 1 Feb., 1795. 8. Lucy,[4] b. 30 May, 1766.

Lemuel[4] m Frances Tyler, 21 March, 1782 ; and d. 1 July, 1819. Ch : 1. Lemuel,[5] b. 29 April, 1783. 2. Fanny Tyler,[5] b. 10 Dec, 1784. 3. Charlotte,[5] b. 25 Dec , 1786. 4. Mary Chadwick,[5] b. 22 July, 1789. 5. Aaron,[5] b. 2 Jan., 1791 , d. 24 Oct., 1794. 6. *Daniel*,[5] b. 10 Feb., 1793. 7. Aaron,[5] b. 27 Oct., 1797.

Deacon *Jonathan*[4] m. Abigail Hale of Brookfield, 1 Feb , 1787 ; and d. 3 Jan., 1797. Ch : 1. William Hale,[5] b. 27 Feb., 1789. 2. Abigail,[5] b. 20 June, 1790 ; m Samuel, father of Judge Samuel Peabody. 3. Sarah Redington,[5] b. 12 Sept., 1792; m Col. Charles Peabody. 4. David[5] and 5. Jonathan[5] (twins), b. 9 Aug., 1794; David[5] d. 3 Dec., 1873. 6. *Enoch*,[5] b. 20 Jan., 1797.

Daniel[5] m. 1st, Maria Barker, 12 Oct., 1820. He m. 2d, Abigail Tyler, who d. 27 April, 1879. Lives in the West Parish, at the age of eighty-six years. Ch.; 1. William Hale.[6]

Enoch[6] m Mehitable, dau. of John Tyler of Boxford, 25 Sept., 1828. A sea-captain from Salem port in early life. Lives in the West Parish, at the age of eighty-two years. Ch. . 1. Rebecca Tyler,[6] b. 26 Jan., 1830. 2. John Tyler,[6] b. 21 April, 1831 3 Enoch Franklin,[6] b. 17 Oct , 1832 ; a teacher in the Quincy City-School, Boston.

voted, in 1691, not to tax him. See Babson's *History of Gloucester*. Their children were: 1. Rebecca, b. in 1641 ; m. Robert Eames. 2. Deborah. 3. Prudence, b 1647 ; m. Moses Tyler 4. Elizabeth, b. 1650 ; m. Matthew Perry. 5. Mary, b. 1652 ; m. Zaccheus Curtis. 6. Thomas, b. 9 June, 1658 ; d. 25 June, 1658. 7. Ruth, b. 3 Sept., 1659. He had no descendants of his name.

THOMAS PERLEY, born in 1641, was son of Allan and Susanna (Bokeson) Perley, emigrants from England. He first appears in Boxford about 1684, having removed from Rowley. He probably settled where the late residence of Mr. Isaac Hale, deceased, now stands. Most of the land in that vicinity was in his possession, and a portion of it is still owned by lineal descendants. He was an influential man, filling most of the town offices with credit, and was chosen as one of the early representatives to the General Court. He was made a freeman 23 May, 1677. He married Lydia Peabody — sister of Capt. John Peabody of the Village — 8 July, 1667 ; and died Sept. 24, 1709. Their children were : 1. Thomas,[2] * b. 1668. 2.

* The following is the line of descent of the present Perley residents of Boxford from Thomas' son Thomas . —

Thomas[2] m. 1st, Sarah, dau of Capt. John Osgood of Andover, 1695, who d. 23 Sept , 1724. He m 2d, Elizabeth, mother of Gen. Israel Putnam, 15 May, 1727. Gen Putnam was at this time about eight years of age : he probably spent some of the years of his minority in his step-father's home at the Hale place Capt. Thomas Perley died in 1745. Ch. · 1. Lydia,[3] b. 21 June, 1696. 2 Mary,[3] b. 16 May, 1697 ; m John Baker, Esq , of Ipswich. 3. Hepzibah,[3] b. 14 Aug., 1699, m. Thomas Redington of Boxford 4. Moses,[3] b. 11 Dec., 1701 ; d. 9 Nov., 1702. 5. Sarah,[3] b. 2 Oct, 1703 , m. Dean Robinson of Andover. 6. *Thomas*,[3] b. 22 Feb., 1704-05. 7. Mehitable,[3] b. 26 June, 1708 ; d. 14 Oct., 1723. 8. Rebecca,[3] b. 28 Oct., 1710 ; m. David Putnam of Salem. 9. Allen,[3] b. 14 April, 1714. 10. *Asa*,[3] b. 10 Oct , 1716 11 Margaret,[3] b 23 Nov , 1719.

Thomas[3] m. Eunice Putnam — sister of Gen. Israel Putnam — 20 Sept , 1731, who d. 2 Feb., 1787, aged seventy-six years. He d. 28 Sept., 1795. Ch.: 1. Huldah,[4] b. 13 Feb , 1731-32 ; m. Joshua Cleaves of Beverly. 2. Rebecca,[4] b. 12 Jan , 1733-34 , d unm., 22 Aug., 1813. 3. Israel,[4] b. 2 July, 1738 , m. Elizabeth Moores ; settled on the St John River N.B 4 Mary,[4]

Jacob,[2]* b 1670. 3 Lydia,[2] b. 1672. 5. Mary.[2] 5. Hepzibah[2] This settler is the ancestor of the majority of the Perley family. His descendants have been prominently

b. 4 June, 1741 ; m. John Peabody of Boxford. 5. Oliver,[4] b 30 July, 1743; settled on the St. John River, N B. 6 Thomas,[4] b. 19 June, 1746; m. Sarah Wood of Boxford ; d. 20 April, 1831 ; no issue : he was a distinguished man in the town, and erected and resided in the house of the late William E. Killam 7. Enoch,[4] b 19 May, 1749; m. Anna Flint of Middleton, was one of the first settlers of Bridgton, Me. 8. *Aaron,*[4] b. 18 Sept, 1755

Major *Asa*[3] m. 1st, Susannah Low of Essex, 31 Jan., 1737–38, who d. 15 Jan., 1762 He m 2d, Apphia Porter of Danvers, 12 Aug., 1762, who d. 28 Dec, 1780. He m. 3d, Ruth Kimball, who d 24 April, 1806. Major Asa Perley was a member of the Provincial Congress. He d 10 April, 1806. Lived at the residence of the late Mr. Isaac Hale. Ch.: 1. Dudley,[4] b. 23 Nov, 1738, m. Hannah Hale of Boxford ; lived in Winchendon, Mass. 2. Asa,[4] b. 13 Dec, 1740; settled in N.B 3 Eliphalet,[4] b. 27 Aug., 1742; d. young. 4. Susannah,[4] b. 13 June, 1744; m Asa Peabody of Londonderry. 5. Allen,[4] b. 11 May, 1746, d. young. 6. Eliphalet,[4] b. 22 Nov., 1747, m. Anna Porter 7 Allen,[4] b. 9 June, 1750, m Judith Case. 8. Daniel,[4] b. 24 Sept, 1752; m Rebecca Porter of Boxford 9. *Henry,*[4] b. 17 Feb, 1755. 10. Samuel,[4] b. 15 Sept., 1757 ; m. Phebe Dresser of Rowley ; father of Hon Ira Perley 11. Solomon,[4] b. 25 Feb, 1760; settled in N B.

Aaron[4] m. Mehitable, dau. of Thomas and Margaret (Perkins) Wood of Boxford, 27 June, 1786, who d. 15 March, 1853, aged ninety-one years. He d. 10 Dec., 1831. Ch.: 1. Mary,[5] b. 10 Oct., 1786 ; m. Artemas Peabody of Boxford. 2. John,[5] b. 26 May, 1788; m. 1st, Sally Kimball ; 2d, widow of his brother Israel. 3. Israel,[5] b. 27 March, 1790; m. Asenath Gould of Boxford. 4 Enoch,[5] b. 1792; d 20 Feb, 1795. 5. Asa,[5] b. 27 June, 1793 ; d. unm., in insane-hospital, Charlestown, 12 Sept, 1845. 6. Enoch,[5] b 4 Feb, 1795; d. 24 May, 1814. 7. Thomas,[5] b 29 Feb, 1797, d unm, 18 Jan., 1856 8. Rebecca,[5] b. 21 April, 1799, lives in Boxford, unm. 9.

---

* The following is the line of descent of the present Perley residents of Boxford from Thomas' son Jacob : —

Jacob[2] m. 1st; Lydia, dau. of Capt. John Peabody of Boxford, 3 Dec., 1696. He m. 2d, Lydia, dau. of Joseph Peabody of Boxford, 9 May, 1709, who d. 30 April, 1732. He m 3d, widow Mehitable Brown of Rowley, (pub.) 24 June, 1733. Ch : 1 Lydia,[3] b. 5 Oct., 1697 ; m. Peter Ayers of Haverhill. 2 Jacob,[3] b. 19 Sept., 1700; m. Sarah Morse of Newbury. 3. Nathan,[3] b 17 Nov, 1703; m Lydia Hale of Boxford. 4 Francis,[3] b. 28 Jan, 1705–06, m. Huldah, sister of Gen Israel Putnam : father of Capt William Perley 5 *Moses,*[3] b 1709 6 Isaac,[3] b. 14 Feb., 1711–12 7 Hannah,[3] b. 28 Oct., 1716; m. Stephen Kimball of Bradford.

before the world, holding most offices of trust and honor; teachers of morals, religion, and science; practitioners of the law, &c. Among them we would mention Hon. Ira

Harriet,[5] b. 14 May, 1803; m. William N. Cleaveland, Esq ; d. 23 Jan., 1879. 10. Huldah,[5] b. 22 May, 1805; d. 1843.

Henry[4] m. 1st, Eunice, dau. of John and Mary (Kimball) Hood of Topsfield, 27 Oct., 1781, who d 11 Oct, 1790 He m. 2d, Mehitable Peabody, 30 Oct, 1799, who d. 28 Oct., 1844, aged eighty-one years. He d. 6 Feb., 1838. Ch.: 1. Eunice,[5] b. 14 April, 1782; m. Daniel Dresser of Bangor, Me. 2. *Henry*,[5] b. 14 Oct., 1784. 3. Susannah,[5] b. 16 March, 1788; d. 23 Nov., 1791. 4 *Samuel*,[5] b. 9 Oct., 1790. 5. Leonard,[5] b. 2 July, 1800; m. Mary Wells; lived in Boxford.

Henry[5] m. Hannah, dau. of Solomon and Phebe (Perley) Wood, — Nov, 1808, who d. — Jan., 1837, aged fifty-two years. He d. 13 Nov., 1841. Ch.: 1. *Albert*,[6] b. 11 Oct., 1809. 2. Charles,[6] b. 13 April, 1811; m. Lizzie Jane Herrick of Boxford. 3. Harriet A.,[6] b. 17 Jan., 1814; m. Dean Andrews of Boxford. 4. Phebe,[6] b. 25 Feb, 1817; m. Moses Dorman, Esq, of Boxford. 5. Henry E.,[6] b. 19 Feb, 1819, m. Lydia L. Gould 6. Catherine,[6] b. 26 March, 1821; m. Henry Long of Topsfield. 7. Osmore,[6] b. 25 Dec., 1825; m. Martha ——; d. 20 Feb., 1878. 8. Hannah E.,[6] b. 9 Feb., 1828.

Major *Samuel*[5] m. Nancy Peabody, 9 May, 1816, who d. 24 Aug., 1851, aged sixty years. He d. 1 June, 1874, aged eighty-three years. Ch. 1. *George*,[6] b. 5 June, 1817. 2. Sarah Peabody,[6] b. 13 Sept., 1819. 3. Lucy Ann,[6] b. 3 Jan., 1827.

Albert[6] m. Hannah Hayward, 23 Jan., 1840; and d. 21 Feb., 1876. Ch.: 1. Catherine,[7] b. 17 Nov., 1840; m. —— Buckley. 2. Mary E.,[7] b. 4 Sept., 1842; m. Asahel Todd. 3 Josephine,[7] b. 28 Dec., 1843; m. A. Austin Lake. 4. Albert E.,[7] b. 8 June, 1845; d. 21 April, 1877. 5. Jennie,[7] b. 1 Sept, 1849; m. George A. Wilkins. 6. Samuel,[7] b 22 Oct, 1851; m. Lucy Gurley. 7. Charles[7] and 8. Henry[7] (twins), b 16 Oct., 1854.

George[6] m. Mary P. Johnson, 4 March, 1845. Ch.: 1. Mary Ellen,[7] b. 24 Jan, 1846.

Moses[3] m. Hannah, dau. of Nathan and Sarah (Bridges) Frye of Andover, 7 Feb, 1740, who d 1 Nov., 1793, aged seventy years. He d. 23 Oct., 1793. Ch : 1. Lydia,[4] b. 18 May, 1741; m. John Perley of Rowley. 2. Moses,[4] b. 24 Jan., 1743; d. unm., in the Revolution. 3. Hannah,[4] b. 14 April, 1745, m Daniel Clark of Topsfield. 4 Stephen,[4] b 3 Dec, 1747; m Elizabeth Gould of Topsfield. 5. Jeremiah,[4] b. 14 Dec, 1749; m. Eunice Foster of Andover. 6. Nathan,[4] b. 9 March, 1752; m. Ruth Gould of Topsfield: Jeremiah Perley of Boxford is their son. 7. Peter,[4] b. 5 June, 1754; d. when "a young man." 8. Sarah,[4] b. 7 July, 1756; d. young. 9. Sarah,[4] b. 27 July, 1757; m. Roger Balch of Topsfield. 10. Betty,[4] b. 6 March, 1758, d.

Perley, Chief Justice of New Hampshire; Dr. Daniel Perley of Lynn; Gen. John Perley of the Massachusetts and Maine militia; John P. Perley of the Maine Legislature; Dr. Thomas F. Perley; Rev. Humphrey C. Perley; Jeremiah Perley, Esq.; Col. Charles S. Perley; Hon. William E. Perley, for more than twenty years a member of the Parliament of New Brunswick and of the Parliament of the Dominion of Canada; and Rev. William F. Perley, Methodist clergyman in Kingston, Canada.

JOHN PERLEY was living here as early as 1683. He was born in 1636, and was the first Perley born in America. He was brother to the preceding settler, and by trade a carpenter. He was a prominent man in the town, which he twice represented in the Legislature; many other positions of trust he also filled with fidelity. He was made a freeman October, 1690. About 1661 he married Mary, daughter of Thomas and Rebecca Howlett, who died 21 Oct., 1718, at the age of seventy-six years. He died 15 Dec., 1729, at the great age of ninety-three years. The bodies of himself and wife lie interred in the cemetery near the Third-District schoolhouse, their gravestones being well preserved. His lineal descendants have been residents of the town until within half a century. His children were: 1. Sarah,[2] b. about 1662; m. Joseph Andrews. 2. Samuel,[2] b. 1664; d. in Rowley, 24 Oct., 1746, aged eighty-two years. 3. John;[2] m (?) and resided here. 4.

unm., 16 Jan, 1822. 11. *Moody*,[4] b 16 March, 1760. 12. Phebe,[4] b. 14 Jan., 1763; m. Solomon Wood of Boxford. 13. Eliphalet,[4] b. 17 Nov., 1765; d. unm., 17 March, 1846.

Moody[4] m. Abigail, dau. of John and Elizabeth (Bradstreet) Gould of Topsfield, 10 Dec., 1793, who d. 23 Jan., 1851, aged eighty-one years He d. 23 Sept, 1833. Ch.: 1. Betsey Gould,[5] b. 24 March, 1796; m. Daniel W. Perkins of Topsfield; live in Georgetown. 2. Moody,[5] b. 15 April, 1798; d. 7 Nov, 1803. 3. Hiram,[5] b. 18 July, 1800; m. Ruth Ann Smith, d. 23 Feb, 1865 4 Abigail,[5] b. 19 March, 1803. 5. Fanny,[5] b. 4 April, 1806. 6. Moody,[5] b. 26 March, 1809. 7 Stephen,[5] b. 8 Feb, 1811; d. unm, 23 March, 1867. 8 Leander,[5] b. 14 Nov, 1815; d. 11 Oct., 1864, unm.

Thomas,[2] b. 1669, m. 1st, Abigail (Towne), widow of Jacob Peabody of Topsfield; m. 2d, Hannah Goodhue; lived first in Topsfield, and removed to Boxford about 1713. 5. Nathaniel.[2] 6. Isaac.[2] 7. Jeremiah,[2] b 1677; m. three times; no issue; was a prominent man, a captain in the militia, &c. 8. Mary.[2]

THOMAS HAZEN was born in Rowley, 29 : 11 mo. : 1657, and was son of Edward (the immigrant) and Hannah (Grant) Hazen. He probably resided near the "great meadows," in a pasture where an ancient cellar is still visible.* He came here immediately after his marriage with Mary, daughter of Thomas Howlett, 1 Jan., 1683–84. He was made a freeman 22 March, 1689–90 He was selectman for several years, and also regularly served in other town offices. In 1711, with most of his family, Mr. Hazen removed to Norwich, Conn., where he died 12 April, 1735, aged seventy-seven years. His wife died 24 Oct., 1727. His children were: 1 Hannah,[2] b. 10 Oct., 1684; m. John Symonds of Boxford, 13 Feb., 170-. 2 Alice,[2] b. 10 June, 1686; m. Jeremiah Perley of Boxford, 20 Dec, 1710 3. John,[2] b. 23 March, 1688; m. Mercy, dau. of John and Sarah (Perkins) Bradstreet of Topsfield; lived in Norwich, Conn. 4 Thomas,[2] b. 7 Feb., 1690; m. Sarah Ayer of Norwich, Conn., where he lived. 5. Jacob,[2] b. 5 Dec, 1691, m. Abigail ——; lived in Norwich 6. Mary,[2] b. 1 Sept, 1694, m. Increase Moseley, 4 July, 1711. 7. Lydia,[2] b. 1 Sept, 1694, twin with Mary; m Benjamin Abell of Norwich, 17 March, 1713–14. 8 Hephzibah,[2] b. 22 March, 1697; m Nathaniel Perkins, 15 Nov., 1716. 9. Ruth,[2] b 3 Oct., 1699; d. in Norwich, Conn., 18 Feb., 1739–40. 10. Jeremiah,[2] b 4 Jan., 1701–02. 11. Ednah,[2] b. 25 Dec, 1704, m. Joshua Smith of Norwich, 21 Oct.,

---

* Since the above was in type we have discovered documents indicating that Mr. Hazen's residence was near Reyner Pond; which is no doubt correct.

1724. Several years elapsed before Jacob Hazen settled here, about 1760. The old place spoken of above was last occupied about seventy-five years ago, by the above-named Jacob, the father of Hannah Hazen, who, it will be remembered by the older residents in that section of the town, created quite a sensation by doing works which were ascribed, at the time, to the power of Satan. The descendants of Thomas Hazen have been many, and of a distinguished character. Among them are Rev. Hervey Crosby Hazen, lately a missionary in India, and now a minister in Spencer, N. Y.; Hon. Abraham D. Hazen of Pennsylvania, now Third-Assistant Postmaster-General; Rev. Austin Hazen, pastor in Hartford and Berlin, Vt.; Rev. Allen Hazen, for many years a missionary in India; Rev. Jasper Hazen, one of the oldest and most honored ministers of the Christian denomination; Gen. William B. Hazen of the United States army, who distinguished himself under Sherman in the war of the Rebellion, and particularly by his brilliant capture of Fort McAllister, near Savannah, on the "March to the Sea;" Rev. Henry A. Hazen of Billerica; Rev. Timothy Allyn Hazen of Goshen, Conn.; Rev. James King Hazen, Secretary of the Board of Publication of the Presbyterian Church (South) at Richmond, Va.; and many others, mostly distinguished as divines.

In 1678-79, March, Topsfield made a rate for procuring powder and bullets. The total amount of the rate was £41 6s. 6d, of which the Villagers' share was £4 19s., to be paid in money, or Indian corn at two shillings a bushel. John Cummings was the gatherer for the Village.

The following order was passed by the General Court, Oct 15, 1684: "Ordered, that all persons liuing in Rowley Village, neere to Topsfield, who are liable to attend military service on fout, shall attend their duty vnder the comand of the cheift officer at Topsfeild, & be one company wth respect to military seruice." The following May, the General Court ordered that the above order should "be null & voyd, & that the villagers be excercised by such officers as the majo[r] generall shall appoint, till farther order." The reason why these orders were called into existence is unknown. Farther orders, intimated above, were not needed, as the Village was incorporated as a town three months later, and from that time the Villagers comprised a company of their own.

Mr Hobart's course in Topsfield was no smoother than that of his predecessor. The people accused him of immoralities, and withheld his pay. He, in his turn, sued the people, and obtained judgment. 7 May, 1680, Topsfield voted "that thay wars not Willing m[r] Hubbord should Continue in y[e] work of y[e] miniftry here at Topsfeild without m[r] Hubbord and y[e] Towne Can agree in a more Chriftan way then thay bee in at p[e]fent." Mr. Hobart was accordingly dismissed from the ministry before the season was out. Mr. Hobart was again settled at Hempstead, L. I., where he staid a number of years ; but after a while, finding that his congregation was fast leaving him, he concluded to go also. He was next settled at Haddam, Conn , and there he staid till his death, at the age of eighty-eight years. Although little sanctity seems connected with this early pastor of Topsfield, he is, however, closely related to several noted divines ; and Mr. Brainard, the celebrated missionary, was his grandson.

In this year (1680) considerable discussion was carried on about petitioning the General Court to have the Villagers and the Linebrook * people joined with the Topsfield people, "for y[e] Cariang one y[e] miniftry." Topsfield went so far as to appoint a committee to meet with the others to compose a petition. None was sent, probably.

* Linebrook was a small settlement in the west end of Ipswich, near to Topsfield It was incorporated as a parish in 1749.

In 1678 a gallery with seats in it was built in the meeting-house, one-third of which was sold in 1681 to the Villagers, for them to sit in.

No pulpit had, up to this time, adorned the church. In 1682 one was built by Samuel Symonds of the Village, ten feet long. The cost was ten pounds without the material, which the town furnished. The old meeting-house was used for the purpose of worship until a new edifice was erected in 1703. The old one was then sold for five pounds to John Gould, who moved it down to the turnpike, and used it for a barn. It was afterwards removed to the "river meadows," where some of its decayed timbers could be seen a few years since.

After several unsuccessful calls to the ministry there, one was accepted by Rev. Joseph Capen of Cambridge; and a committee (Thomas Perkins of Topsfield, and Joseph Bixby of the Village) was appointed "to goe to Cambrig to pilot m Capen to Topsfeild to Liu⁺ Pebodyes house." Another committee was chosen — among whom was Samuel Buswell, sen, of the Village — "to discorse with m⁺ Capen to ftay and preach here with us at Topsfeild a while." A salary of £65 — £20 payable in silver, and £45 in pork and beef per year — with the use of the parsonage-house, was voted to be given him. After preaching there one year, he was given an invitation to settle, which was accepted Sept. 18, 1682 : he was settled soon after.

Mr. Capen was a native of Dorchester, and a graduate of Harvard College. He continued in the ministry there for many years after the Villagers had withdrawn from the Church. He was a preacher of moderate abilities, as appears from one of his sermons which was published. His wife was Priscilla, daughter of Capt. John Appleton of Ipswich, a distinguished man in his day ; and through their daughter Elizabeth, Mr. Capen's blood flows in the veins of the writer.

CHAPTER IV.

INCORPORATION OF THE TOWN, &c.

INCORPORATION OF THE TOWN. — DIVIDING-LINE CONFIRMED. — NAMING THE TOWN. — THE TOWN RECORDS. — FIRST CEMETERY. — HOUSES, MANNERS, AND CUSTOMS OF THE EARLY SETTLERS. — SETTLERS, 1685–1700.

T is the highest ambition of every community to have a government of its own, and to be recognized by its own voice in the higher halls of legislation. Grand! must the inhabitants of our early New-England settlements have been, when they were recognized by the General Court as independent communities, and took their places with the neighboring towns, possessing like power in conducting the affairs of the body politic. And, indeed, it was no false pride; for they could look back upon the past, and observe that the acts of their lives, being for the good and for the advancement of the place, all culminated at last in their independent condition.

The Village having now increased to about forty families, the inhabitants turned their attention to procuring a town charter. While in their existing condition they had no power to settle a minister, or to raise money to support one if settled. Rowley had encouraged them to proceed in this direction; and it was on the 18th of May, 1685, that the inhabitants of the Village met together, in a lawful

and general meeting, and voted that they would petition
the General Court for a town charter, and that Abraham
Redington, sen., should be the bearer of it.   Nine days
later, the General Court convened, and this petition was
placed before them   The following is a literal transcript
from the original . —

" To the honoured General Court, held at Boston, the 27 : 3 mo.
1685. The humble petesion of the inhabitants of Rowley village to
the honoured General Court, wee being sensaball of the great need
of having the publick word of God preached amongst us, which wee
cannot have in the condesion that wee bee in at present, wee lying
so far remote from Rowley that wee cannot comfortably atend God's
public worship for the greatest part of the year, it is therefore the
general desire of the inhabitants of Rowley vilage to bee a preparing
to settle a minnester amongst ourselves as soon as convenantly wee
can, thearfore wee desiar, that the honoured General Court would
bee pleased to grant us township prevelig, that so wee might the more
comfortably cary on so needfull a woik, for the betor edication of our
children that cannot gooe fouer mieles to meting : severall of our
towne of Rowley have incoureged us to gooe about this work several
years agoen, teling of us that the vilag was laied out for that eand, and
it doth contaien a bought eaighteen thousand acores of land, which wee
think will comfortabully setuate one hundred families ; this vileg or
tract of land was obtained of the General Court by Rowley men to
bee an adesion to thear concern, which suen after they had mead it
suer to them saelves, they laied it ought to thear own townsmen, every
man according to his hoaes lote (saving a few mistakes), and also
laied ought a ministours farem in it, for a ministor to live on as suen
as the vileg should be capaball to maintaien a minnistor, and now wee
bee increased to the nuember of a bought forty famelies and more,
may bee a preparing satelment, ouer desiour is fierst to maek the minnister's farem to be fet and sutabull to entartain a minnister in, and
then to call a minister if wee can find on willing to come, and teall
then we shall bee willing to contrebut to those plases that wee doe
hear the word of God preached at, as formerly we have doaen,
severall of ouer ouen towen of Rowley have incoreged us to call a
minnester first, but wee havinge no power amonst our salves eather to
call a meeting, or to agree how much to give a minnester, or to com-
pel any persun to doe his dewty if he will not doe it of himself, there-

fore we dooe humbaly desair the honored Genaral Court woueld bee pleased to grant us ouer petesion herin.

> "ABRAHAM REDDINGTON, Sen.
> JOSEPH BIXBEE, Sen.
> SAMUEL BUSWEL, Sen.
> WILLIAM FOSTER,
> JOHN PEABODY.

"These in the name and with the consent of the reast of the vileg." *

In answer to this petition, the General Court order, that, "In ans⟨ʳ⟩ to the petition of Abraham Reddington, Joseph Bixbee, Samuel Buswell, W⟨ᵐ⟩ Foster, & John Peabody, in the behalf of the inhabitants of Rowley Village, the Court inclines to grant their request, prouided it may be with the consent of the selectmen of Rowley." † Rowley readily consented, and on the 7th of July their committee met with a committee appointed by the Village, and agreed upon a dividing-line. The session of the General Court held when the petition was acted upon had come to an end; and at the next Quarterly Court, which convened on the 12th of August following, Rowley sent in their consent, accompanied by a description of the parting line. Their consent is as follows:—

"The inhabitants of Rowley Village desiring to be a touneship, wee, whose names are vnderwritten, being a comitte chosen by yᵉ toune of Rowley, haue consented that they should be a touneship, prouided the honord Court see cause to grant their request. Wee, desiring also that the honnored Gennerall Court would be pleased to confirme the lyne wee haue agreed vpon betwixt the toune of Rowley & the village; and so your humble servants remajne, yoʳs, &c.

> " DANIEL WYCOM,
> JH⟨ᵒ⟩ TRUMBLE,
> STEPHEN MIGHILL,
> EZEKIEL JEWET,
> JH⟨ᵒ⟩ HOPKINSON,
> JOHN LIGHTON."

* This petition is copied from Gage's *History of Rowley*.

† Gage, in his *History of Rowley*, says that this order was passed June 5. Where he got his information we do not know.

These documents were accepted by the Court, and the
line, as agreed upon, was confirmed.   This line was nearly
the same as that which now divides the two towns.   A
few slight alterations have been made by the perambulators
in after-years ; and by an Act of the General Court in
1808 a small piece of land in Georgetown, on which was
situated the Samuel Spofford house, was set off from Rowley to Boxford, and afterward to Georgetown.   The "forked
oak" mentioned in the agreement stood across the street
from the cigar-manufactory of Mr. T. B. Masury, at which
place a split stone now stands, marked with the letters
"G" and "B."   The report of the committee that run the
dividing-line, as it was copied into the town records of
Boxford about fifteen years later, by Capt. John Peabody,
the town-clerk, is as follows : —

"Wee whoes names are vnder written being chosen by the Town
of Rowley on the one part and by the village of Rowley on the other
peart to a gree about a parting liene betwixt the Town of Rowly and
the Villiag being meet to gather the Seventh of July 1685 : do agree
as foloweth that the middel bound shall bee whear the foout Path
Esueth out of the Cart path not far ofe the bridg going ouer the great
medow and from the said middel bounds to a forked whit oack neear
the medow formerly layed out to Elder Rainer being a bound of that
peart of the said medoo that feall to Captin whippel one a devision :
and is also the corner bound of a persil of land layed out to Ezecal
northen being by Estemation a bout forty acors, and so going on the
same liene straight to Ipswich lien and from the a bove said tree of a
straight lien to the South weast corner of the three thowsand acors
which is a whit oake marked with · R · and · t · and so from the said
tree north ward on a lien betwixt the three thowsand acors and land
layed out to mistris Rogers and John pickard teall you come to a whit
oake marked with · S K · t · being the corner bound of John pick-
ards land standing in the lien betwixt bradforth and the vileg . we
forther agree that the inhabitance of the village shall bee free from all
Reats for time to come to the Town of Rowly Exsepting twenty
shillings in silver to bee payed by Josaph Bixbee sener John pebody
william foster Samuell Simonds and mosis tiler yearly to anney of the
Commety whiel thay have no orthodox minister setled in the village

and forther it is agreead that all the Coman land lying with in the
village undeuided shall Remaien to belong to the town of Rowly
Exsepting the fearm commenly called the minnistei s farme with in
the villeag : and anney thing that is dew to the Country for land lying
in the villiag is to bee paied by the in habitants of the villeage in Con-
formation of what is a bove written both pearties have seat tow thair
hands the day and year a bove spesified

"Ezecal Jueat   Josaph Bixbee
John hopkins   John Jonson
John layton   John Pebody
Robart Eames   Samuel plates Juenr
                         Samuel Simonds
                         Ezecall northen
"this is a trew Copey taken out of the Enstru-   William foster
ment of a greement between Rowly and the villiag   Daniell Wicom
in the day that Rowly seat the villaig thair bounds a   Mosis Tiler
cording as the general Court did order as attest John
pebody Town Clark for Boxford"   John Trumboll
                         Steephen myheall "

The twenty shillings mentioned in this agreement as an
annual acquittance of the Villagers was paid by them for
eighteen years, or until the first minister was settled here,
in 1702. The oldest record on the town-books is a copy
of the receipt for this sum for the first year.

Boxford, at the date of incorporation, probably contained
about two hundred inhabitants. These, in general, were
enterprising, industrious, and well-to-do people. At this
time agriculture was the principal business. Most of the
farms had large tracts of land under cultivation. Corn
was the main crop.

In selecting a name for the new town, recourse was
made to the Old Country. Perhaps some of the early
settlers who were natives of the towns of the same name in
England, "loving the old town at home, wished to preserve
its name in the new country." Rev. Mr. Phillips, the minister in Rowley at this time, was born in Boxford,* Berk-

* Boxford, Berkshire, England, is laid out in pleasant farms ; and characteristic of its American namesake, its quietude is peculiar. It is about

shire, in England ; and perhaps he persuaded the inhabitants of the Village to call it Boxford, or they did it out of
respect to him. However, it was from that time called
Boxford ; and with the *Village* we have no longer any
thing to do.

Several pages of the earliest records of the town have
become loose, and some of them have undoubtedly been
lost, as the records do not appear to be arranged in regular
order until several years are passed. The list of officers
chosen in 1686 are not to be found on the existing records
of the town, but from other contemporary records we have
obtained the names of the following, viz : constable, Robert
Stiles ; town-clerk, John Peabody.*

From 1690 the town-records have been well preserved.
The transactions of the town are given in as minute a man-

thirty miles out from London, on the Great Northern Railway. The chief
feature of the place is the large tunnel through which the above railroad
passes ; it is seven miles in length, and the largest tunnel in England —
Rev. Hilary Bygrave.

The following are descriptions of the two Boxfords in England, extracted
from *Moules' Counties* (Eng) : —

" In the county of Suffolk in Babergh Hundred is *Boxford*, on a branch of
the river Stour, five miles west from Hadleigh, sixteen miles west from
Ipswich, and ten miles north from Colchester in Essex , contains one hundred
and seventeen houses, and seven hundred and forty-three inhabitants The
village is pleasantly situated in a fertile valley, between two brooks, which
unite a little below it Here is a manufactory for dressing sheep and deer
skins ; and a considerable trade in malt is carried on. The annual fairs are on
Easter Monday and 21st December The church, dedicated to the Virgin
Mary, is a rectory, value twenty pounds, in the patronage of the crown : it
is a spacious edifice, with a spire Here is a free grammar-school, founded
by Queen Elizabeth. Coddenham Hall, an old seat of the Bennet family, is
now a farmhouse. Hadleigh is a hamlet of this parish."—Vol. I , p 254.

"In the county of Berkshire, in Faircross Hundred, is *Boxford*, four
miles from Newbury, and sixty from London ; contains one hundred and
eight houses, and five hundred and sixty-three inhabitants It is a rectory,
value twenty pounds, with Westbrook, in Kintbury Hundred."—Vol II.,
p 4

* For list of town-clerks and selectmen to the present time, see Appendix A and B.

ner as could be expected ; the style of recording remaining about the same to the present time The first volume of records of town-meetings is about half in the chirography of the first town-clerk, Capt. John Peabody ; the rest of the volume was written by various clerks who served only a few years at a time. This volume comes down to 1743. Five volumes are all there are of town-meeting records. There are several volumes of " tax-books " which contain the doings of the assessors back to the year 1711.* An old "commoner's book" is also in existence, dating from 1683 ; the land of which it contains the record is that now occupied by the East Parish village, and eight hundred acres of Zaccheus Gould's on the south side of Fish Brook. The earliest births, marriages, and deaths, to 1740, were recorded with the records of town-meetings ; since that time they have been recorded in separate volumes. The death record is very deficient, but that of births and marriages is very full.

The ancient cemetery near the residence of Mr. Walter French, in the East Parish, was undoubtedly the first place which the people used for the purpose of burying the dead. Prior to the date of which we are writing, and perhaps after, some of the settlers were interred in the cemeteries of the neighboring towns. The space used as a burial-ground was much larger than would be supposable from present appearance. This land was originally a part of the property of Abraham Redington, the first known white settler of the town. It was mentioned as "the burial-ground" as early as 1693. The oldest headstone now

---

* At the end of the first volume of tax-lists, which comes down to the year 1745, is inscribed the following (probably from the pen of Solomon Wood, and written about 1750) on its dilapidated state : —

> " All old things are not done away,
> But some old things do much decay;
> As you may see by this old book
> If you from end to end should look "

standing there, and which is also the oldest in the town, bears the following inscription : —

> HERE LYES BURIED
> THE BODY OF
> SARAH WOOD Y^e
> WIFE OF DEACON
> DANIEL WOOD WHO
> DIED SEPTEMBER 27
> 1714 & IN THE 57
> YEAR OF HER AGE.

This cemetery was used as one of " God's acres " until the beginning of the present century, when, the graves being so numerous that a new one could not be excavated without digging into another, it was abandoned. Mrs. Ruth Trask, who died in 1829, was the last person interred there. The cemetery was originally a corner of a mowing-field, we should judge, that had been set apart for that purpose ; in which the shrubbery has become so dense as to screen most of the dozen remaining monuments from the sight of the passer-by, and in which the stray cattle graze. It would seem as if Whittier had this old cemetery in view when he wrote : —

> " Our vales are sweet with fern and rose,
>   Our hills are maple-crowned ;
>   But not from them our fathers chose
>   The village burying-ground.

> " The dreariest spot in all the land
>   To Death they set apart ;
>   With scanty grace from Nature's hand,
>   And none from that of Art.

> " A winding wall of mossy stone,
>   Frost-flung and broken, lines
>   A lonesome acre thinly grown
>   With grass and wandering vines.

> " Without the wall a birch-tree shows
>   Its drooped and tasselled head ;
>   Within, a stag-horned sumach grows,
>   Fern-leafed, with spikes of red.

" There, sheep that graze the neighboring plain
   Like white ghosts come and go,
The farm-horse drags his fetlock chain,
   The cow-bell tinkles low.

" Unshaded smites the summer sun,
   Unchecked the winter blast ;
The school-girl learns the place to shun,
   With glances backward cast

" For thus our fathers testified —
   That he might read who ran —
The emptiness of human pride,
   The nothingness of man.

" Above the graves the blackberry hung
   In bloom and green its wreath,
And harebells swung as if they rung
   The chimes of peace beneath

" With flowers or snowflakes for its sod,
   Around the seasons ran,
And evermore the love of God
   Rebuked the fear of man."

The stones are fast yielding to the hands of time. Their once upright forms are now leaning; many are already gone, and leaving no trace by which the future historian can discover that this was once — a long while ago — a " city of the dead."

The imagination dwells with an ever-increasing interest upon the private history of the early settlers of New England. We would love to be able to follow them in their daily lives ; all through the new and interesting scenes which made up each day, each month, each year: in spring, while sowing their seeds ; in harvest, when gathering in their crops ; in winter, suffering from the cold, and in danger from the wild animals ; and minutely following them in their daily actions, studying their manners and customs, and learning from them self-denial, prudence, wisdom, godliness, industry, and simplicity. The annals of history that relate to that epoch which comprises the settlement of New England are so full of novelty, experience, and danger, that it is a subject upon which the descendants of the early settlers love to speak and contemplate. Truly may we quote the words of the Rev. Mr. Gammell : "All honor to the fathers and mothers of New England ! may their deeds never want appreciation ; and may God keep, in the hearts of their descendants, their memory forever green ! "

The earliest houses in town were probably with frames ; although, we doubt not, there were log cottages, the chinks of which were filled with clay, and thus made very comfortable. Down to 1700 the large, square style of architecture prevailed. The long, sloping-back roof next became popular, and that style continued for many years. The chimneys were built, in colonial days, of stone and lime, on the outside of the house. The furniture in the house was only sufficient for comfort, and the stoves of the present day have been substituted for the fireplaces of our ancestors.

As to the necessaries and comforts of life, they were pretty equally divided among the colonists. As the necessaries were of the cheapest and simplest kind, being mostly the fruit of the soil, they were very easily supplied by the industry of the inhabitants. New clothes were a luxury to the colonists ; and they believed, as one of their contemporaries sang, that

> " . . . patched clothes were warmer
> Than single whole clothing."

What foolishness the early colonists would deem the daily newspapers of the present day! Their medium of dispensing and gathering news was oral ; and probably a general circulation only occurred on Sunday, when they met together at the church. A newspaper was probably an unknown luxury here until years after the time of which we are writing.

In regard to other customs of the early settlers the interested reader can find full information in the written accounts and traditions which have come down to posterity, and which are embodied in many valuable volumes that are the product of years of labor and research.

After Boxford was incorporated several families came here almost immediately, and began long lines of descendants which have spread all over the world, and can be numbered by thousands. One of the first of these was

WILLIAM PEABODY. He was a brother of Capt. John Peabody of Boxford, and was born in 1646. He married Hannah Hale of Newbury, — sister to Joseph Hale, who shortly after resided here, — 14 Aug, 1684, and built a house where now is a small grove of gilead trees near the west corner of the late Samuel Peabody's house in the East Parish. Shortly after his settlement he erected a saw and grist mill, — one of which was supposed to stand near the summer residence of William A. Herrick, Esq., and the other farther down the stream at the foot of the meadow. He had lost the use of one of his arms, which somewhat disabled his working abilities. He had a servant, by name John Norman, letters of administration on whose estate were granted to his master, 5 Sept., 1698. Mr. Peabody was made a freeman 21 July, 1685. He served as selectman in the town in 1689, 1696, 1697, and 1699, and died at the age of 53 years, 6 March, 1699–1700. He died intestate, and letters of administration were granted to his widow 3 June, 1700. Amount of inventory of his estate, £913 8 s. 7 d., debts due from the estate, only £3 9 s. His widow died 23 Feb., 1733. Among their descendants is their son Oliver Peabody, a noted preacher at Natick, and *his* son Oliver, a minister at Roxbury; Dr. William Peabody of Corinth, Me.; Hon Oliver Peabody of Exeter, N H, President of Senate, Treasurer of State, &c.; Rev. Stephen Peabody of Atkinson, N. H., William Peabody of Milford, N. H., a magistrate and representative to State legislature for many years, Samuel Peabody, Esq.; Charles Augustus Peabody, judge of the Supreme Court of the State of New York; Rev. Ephraim Peabody, pastor of King's Chapel in 1846; and many other noted men William Peabody's children were: 1. Stephen,[2]* b. 5 Aug., 1685. 2. Mary,[2] b. 11 April, 1687; m. Joseph Symonds

* The following is the line of descent of the present Peabody residents of Boxford from William's son Stephen: —

Capt. *Stephen*[2] m. Hannah Swan, who d 17 April, 1764, a. 75 years He d. 7 June. 1759 Ch.: 1. Hannah,[3] b 1 Feb., 1709. 2. Richard,[3] b. 29 May, 1711; d 11 Oct., 1711. 3. Mary,[3] b. 29 Dec., 1713; d. 12 June, 1714. 4. William,[3] b. 29 June, 1715. 5 Hephzibah,[3] b 14 Feb., 1718; m. Ephraim Dorman. 6. Priscilla,[3] b. 22 Nov., 1719; m. John Hale. 7. Francis,[3] b. 12 Feb., 1721-22; one of the first English settlers of New Brunswick. 8. Stephen,[3] b. 1 Oct., 1724. 9. *Richard*,[3] b. 13 April, 1731.

Capt. *Richard*,[3] m. Jemima Spofford, who d. 19 Dec., 1811, aged 78, years. He d. 7 June, 1820. Lived on his father's homestead. Ch.: 1. Hannah,[4] b. 18 Feb., 1758; d. 17 Dec, 1832 2 Hephzibah,[4] b. 13 April, 1759. 3. *Stephen*,[4] b 27 Aug., 1760. 4. John,[4] b. 24 July, 1762. 5 Richard,[4] b. 16 April, 1764. 6. Oliver,[4] b. 6 March, 1766 7. William,[4] b. 10 Jan. 1768; a doctor in Corinth, Me.: see his biography. 8. Priscilla,[4] b. 1 Feb, 1770. 9. Francis,[4] b. 7 June, 1771. 10. Samuel,[4] b. 15 Sept., 1772; d. y. 11. Samuel,[4] b. 30 Jan., 1775. 12. *Joseph Spofford*,[4] b. 30 Jan., 1779.

Stephen,[4] Esq., m. Anna Killam of Boxford, 13 Dec., 1785, who d. 28 Dec., 1843 He d. 22 July, 1830 He was a J. P., and was somewhat noted in his day. On his marriage he purchased the house of Mr. Thomas Wood, that previously stood where the Third-District school-house now stands, and, after residing in it a few years, removing it to its present site (near the late residence of Mr C. C Stevens), he took away the large and low back-rooms, and, raising the building higher, made it as it now exists. Ch.: 1. Stephen,[5] b 17 Oct., 1787; d 19 July, 1806. 2. *Samuel*,[5] b. 6 Nov., 1788 3 Nancy,[5] b 28 Aug., 1796; d. 5 April, 1854, unm.

Joseph Spofford[4] m. Hannah Foster, 25 Dec, 1800, who d. 11 May, 1849. He d. 17 May, 1846. Ch : 1. Lavinia,[5] b. 20 Sept, 1801, m. Peter Johnson; d. 1 Sept., 1864. 2. Lucy,[5] b 27 Sept., 1802; m. Aaron Richardson; d. 27 Aug., 1825. 3. Dorothy,[5] b. 15 June, 1804; m Joseph Brown; d. 1 Jan., 1850. 4. *John*,[5] b. 19 Sept, 1806. 5. Eliza,[5] b. 2 July, 1808; d. unm. 12 April, 1826. 6 Salome,[5] b. 24 July, 1810, m. Stephen Small; d 12 June, 1845. 7. Clarissa,[5] b 20 June, 1812. 8. Joseph,[5] b. 4 Feb, 1815, m Lydia Hilton; d. 14 Feb., 1858.

Samuel[5] m 1st, Mary Bradstreet of Danvers, 30 April, 1818, who d. 1

of Boxford 3. Ephraim,[2] b. 23 April, 1689. 4 Richard,[2]
b. 17 Feb., 1691 ; m Ruth Kimball, in Bradford, 7 March,
1716. 5. Hannah,[2] b. — Aug., 1693 ; m. Jonathan Foster. 6. John,[2] b 1 Aug., 1695. 7 Abiah,[2] b. ——, 1697 ;
m Joseph Kimball, 19 Jan., 1724. 8 Oliver,[2] b 7 May,
1698 ; whose biography is given in this work. Stephen [2]
erected the old mansion which has for several years been
used by William Aug. Herrick, Esq, as a summer resi-

Jan., 1836, m. 2d, Mary Spofford of Boxford He d 1 Sept., 1862. He
resided on his father's place, and was a butcher. "He was prosperous in
business, and a man of remarkable integrity of character." Ch. 1. Stephen,[6] b ——, d y 2 *Samuel Porter*,[6] b 27 Nov, 1820 3 Stephen,[6] b. 25
Jan., 1822 ; m 1st, Maria F Cummings of B, 25 Dec, 1849, who d 15 Dec.,
1858 ; m. 2d, Tammy B. Smith of Newburyport, 26 Nov., 1863, where they
now reside He was educated at Phillips Academy, Andover, People's Gym-
nasium Academy, Pembroke, N H, and at Topsfield Academy, taught
school twenty-five years or more, chiefly in Newburyport 4 Mary Ann,[6]
b. 1 Sept, 1823, d. 22 Jan, 1865, unm. 5 Melissa,[6] b 2 Nov., 1824 ; m.
John Q. Batchelder. 6 Caroline Eliza,[6] b 21 April, 1826 ; d 1 April, 1869,
unm. "Mary Ann and Caroline E were sisters, . . and they both trusted
in Christ alone for eternal life." — *Monument.* 7 Albert Bradstreet,[6] b 1
Nov., 1828 ; minister in Stratham, N H see his biography.

Capt. *John* [5] m 1st, Henrietta S Baker of Georgetown, 27 Sept,
1831, who d 16 June, 1874 ; m 2d, Mrs. Elizabeth Clark Ch 1.
John Perley,[6] b. 18 June, 1832 ; m Sarah A True of Amesbury, 14 July,
1858. Lives in Salem, editor, publisher, and proprietor of the *Fireside
Favorite*, an extensively circulating monthly periodical ; dealer in fancy
goods, &c, in which business he has been very successful. 2. Hannah
Elizabeth,[6] b. 16 Feb, 1834 ; m Hosea W. Carr. 3 George Washington,[6]
b 26 Feb, 1836, m Cynthia G. Covert, painter in Chelsea 4. Richard,[6]
b 18 April, 1838, d 16 May, 1838. 5 Charles William,[6] b 20 (30 ?) March,
1840, m. Annie M. Allen of Salem ; d. 25 March, 1879 ; was a popular
fancy-goods dealer in Newburyport. 6 Eliza Ann,[6] b. 2 Feb., 1842 ; m.
James E Sheen of W. Peabody 7. Sarah Lavinia,[6] b. 10 Feb., 1844 ; m.
Asa Gentis of Haverhill. 8 Matilda H,[6] b 18 Dec, 1845 ; d 27 Sept, 1848.
9. Stephen,[6] b. 17 Nov., 1849.

Samuel Porter [6] m Mary Jane Bunker, 29 April, 1847, who d 17 Sept,
1860, aged 31 years. Ch 1. Mary Abbie,[7] b 9 May, 1848, m Henry
A. Long of N Andover, 6 Aug, 1872 2 Clara Jane,[7] b 18 July, 1849 ; m.
Oscar Fellows, 22 Nov, 1877 3. Samuel,[7] b 19 Sept, 1850 4 Porter
Bradstreet,[7] b 21 March, 1854, m. Harriet L. Fish of N. Andover. 5
Elisha Bunker,[7] b 7 March, 1858.

dence. This was built about 1707, and it has been occupied by his lineal posterity until about half a century ago. All the other sons married; and all but Oliver settled here, and helped to perpetuate the name for several generations

JAMES TANT (Taunt), in 1682, was living with Henry Lake in Topsfield Shortly after he was living in Boxford, where he was taxed in 1687 one shilling. He owned no property here, probably, and was one of the roving characters of the seventeenth century.

FRANCIS HEATH (or, LEATH), by his wife Mary, had a daughter Mary born in Boxford, Dec. 23, 1686, which is all we know of him

WILLIAM WATSON was in Boxford in 1687 and before. He was chosen selectman in that year, and also held other minor offices. He probably came from Ipswich. He married 1st, Sarah, daughter of Allan Perley, the immigrant, in 1670, by whom he had two daughters — Mary, born in 1671, and Sarah, 2 Nov, 1672 His wife dying, he married 2d, Mary, widow of Thomas Hale of Newbury (who, with her son Joseph Hale, had just taken up their residence in Boxford), 5 Feb, 1694–95. In 1692, April 26, Mr. Watson made a deposition, in which he agreed to give his daughter Mary half of his property if she would marry Joseph Hale, to which she consented, and they were joined in wedlock, Dec 15, 1693 Mr. Watson died June 27, 1710. His widow survived him till Dec 8, 1715, when she died at the age of 85 years. None of the name have since lived in the town.

JOHN CHADWICK was first chosen selectman in 1688, and he probably settled here shortly before After 1692 he is styled "Sergeant." He was a prominent man in the town, at different times holding various offices of trust. "Widow Chadwick" — probably widow of the above John — was taxed 1714, 1715. A John Chadwick, perhaps their son, married Mehitable ——, about 1705. She "suddenly" died

17 Jan., 1748-49, aged 62 years. Her husband survived her till 16 Feb., 1756, when he died at the age of 79 years. They resided in the West Parish. Their children were: Mehitable, Sarah, Ephraim, Thomas, Mary, David, and John. The four sons married and settled in Boxford, where their descendants have also resided almost to the present time. Thomas was deacon of the Second Church for many years. The present Chadwick families of Boxford are of Bradford origin, although perhaps their ancestors were of this family.

NATHANIEL BROWN is first mentioned on the town-records in 1687, — he then being chosen surveyor. He was made a freeman, October, 1690. He was also a select-man in 1690. This is all we know of him.

TIMOTHY DORMAN, born Dec. 12, 1663, in Topsfield, was son of Thomas and Judith (Wood) Dorman. He married Elizabeth, daughter of John Knowlton of Ipswich, Nov. 15, 1688, who was born March 1, 1659. He came here imme-diately after his marriage, and settled on undivided land of his father's. A large part of the original mansion which he erected for his dwelling is yet standing, and retained in the family, though it has been so altered its present out-ward appearance bears very little, if any, resemblance to the original. The westerly part, now standing, was built by Timothy's son John about 1729; a one-story extension on the east end was torn down in 1829, and a new addition was built in its place; and in 1850 the east end of the main part was torn down, and the house enlarged into its present form by its late owner. In this ancient edifice, from the date of its erection in 1688 or 1689, to the death of the late Thomas P. Dorman, Esq., five generations of his ances-tors have lived and died under its parental roof. Mr. Tim-othy Dorman was a selectman in 1703, and held other minor offices. He died about 1740, at the age of 76 years. Ch.: I. Timothy,[2] b. 18 Sept, 1689, d. 27 Feb, 1701-02.

DORMAN HOMESTEAD.

2. Elizabeth,[2] b. 7 Dec., 1691 ; m John Dagget. 3 Mary,[2] b. 26 Oct, 1693 ; m. Joseph Stanley of Topsfield. 4. John,[2]* b. 9 Feb., 1696 5. Hannah,[2] b 22 Dec, 1698 ; m. Israel Dagget. 6 Sarah,[2] b 7 Feb., 1701–02 , m. John Peabody. John[2] settled on the old homestead.

Ephraim and Jabez Dorman, cousin and brother of Timothy, also settled here. By his wife Martha, Ephraim had children : Ephraim, Mary, Elijah, Samuel, John, and Sarah. Jabez married Hepzibah Perley, and had Jabez, born 25

---

* The following is the line of descent of the present Dorman residents of Boxford from Timothy's son John · —

John[2] m Rebecca Smith, 28 Jan, 1729–30 ; and d 5 Feb, 1775. Ch. : 1. Timothy,[3] b 23 Dec., 1730 , m. Eunice Burnham of Lunenburg ; d 6 June, 1764 2. Rebecca,[3] b 26 Oct, 1732 , m Jonathan Foster. 3 John,[3] b. 12 July, 1735 , d. 22 Oct., 1737. 4. *John*,[3] b. 2 Oct., 1738. 5. Elizabeth,[3] b. 17 May, 1740 ; m Ezra Towne , d. 27 June, 1767

Deacon *John*[3] m. Hannah Jackson of Rowley, 8 May, 1762, who d 20 Nov., 1822, aged 87 years. He d 2 April, 1792. Ch : 1. John,[4] b. 18 June, 1763, married Hannah Andrews ; d. 25 Dec, 1857. 2. *Moses*,[4] b. 12 Oct., 1765. 3 Hannah,[4] b 23 Aug, 1767 ; d 9 Oct, 1828, unm. 4. Jesse,[4] b 23 March, 1769 , d 24 May, 1841. 5 Elizabeth,[4] b 30 July, 1773 , d. 3 Sept , 1843, unm. 6. Mehitable,[4] b. 5 March, 1775 ; d. 9 Jan., 1858, unm.

Moses,[4] Esq., m Huldah, daughter of Jacob and Elizabeth (Towne) Gould, 30 June, 1801, who d. 26 Oct, 1846. He d 13 Feb, 1850 He was one of the most prominent men that Boxford ever numbered among its inhabitants. Ch : 1 Huldah,[5] b 6 April, 1802 ; d. 28 Sept , 1804 2 *Moses*,[5] b. 25 Sept , 1803 3 Huldah,[5] b. 25 March, 1805 ; m. Benj Pike of Topsfield , d 24 June, 1867 4 Achsah,[5] b 2 May, 1808 ; m. Benj. French of Boxford ; d 31 Aug , 1851 5. Ancill,[5] b 1 April, 1819 ; m. Hannah, dau of John and Matilda Ann (Bailey) Hale of Boxford, 28 Oct , 1847 , justice of the peace ; resides in Boxford

Moses,[5] Esq , m. 1st, Huldah Gould, 1 April, 1828, who d. 3 Feb , 1839 ; m 2d, Phebe Perley of Boxford, 6 Nov., 1839, who died 30 Aug., 1848 , m. 3d, Mary N Foster, 27 Feb , 1851, who resides on the old place He d. 26 July, 1877. A justice of the peace, and a prominent man in the town. Ch.: 1. Huldah Elizabeth,[6] b 9 Aug., 1829 ; m. Joseph H Janes. 2. Moses Horace,[6] b. 10 March, 1841 , m. Sarah Cheever of Danvers ; merchant in New York City 3. Harriet Andrews,[6] b 20 March, 1843 , m John Everett Herrick of Peabody 4. Franklin Webster,[6] b. 28 Dec , 1844 ; m Isabelle W Taylor , merchant in New York City. 5. Thomas Perley,[6] b 4 Feb., 1847 ; d. 17 April, 1877, unm ; law-student.

January, 1715–16, who died 25 March, 1716. The mother died nine days after the child was born ; and he married secondly Abial Foster, and had another son of the same name. Dorman has always been a noted name in the town, especially in the last hundred years of its existence ; but the name will undoubtedly be extinguished with this generation.

ZERUBABEL ENDICOTT, born 14 Feb , 1664, was son of Dr. Zerubabel and Mary Endicott of Salem, and grandson of Gov. John and Elizabeth (Gibson) Endicott. He married Grace, daughter of Samuel Symonds of Boxford, July, 1690 He d 1706, aged forty-two years. Ch.: 1. Grace,[2] b. 10 April, 1691; m Samuel Killam of Wilmington, 21 Dec., 1715. 2 Zerubabel,[2] b. 10 Dec., 1692. 3. Elizabeth,[2] b. 8 May, 1695, in Topsfield; m. John Perkins of Ipswich. 4 John,[2] b. 22 Dec., 1697, in Topsfield; d. 2 Feb , 1697–98, in Topsfield 5. Mehitable,[2] b. 14 Aug , 1699, in Topsfield ; m. John Hart of Lynn. 6. Phebe ;[2] m. Ebenezer Jones of Wilmington. 7 Hannah ;[2] was never married. The son Zerubabel married Elizabeth (Phillips), widow of his cousin Robert Edwards Endicott, and died 16 May, 1737, childless His sisters inherited his property , and thus all the land left by the governor and his son, the doctor, in Topsfield and Boxford, went out of the name of Endicott His wife died before him. On the death of Zerubabel (the son), there were living in New England only his cousin Samuel and his family (by the name of Endicott), descendants of the governor.

JOSEPH HALE came with his widowed mother from Newbury about 1691. He was born in Newbury 20 Feb , 1670–71, and was son of Thomas Hale. His mother was Mary, daughter of Richard and Alice (Bosworth) Hutchinson, who was baptized at North Muskham, Nottshire, Eng , 28 Dec., 1630. The widow, in 1693, owned two hundred and eighty acres of land in Boxford, half of which she agreed to give her son Joseph, if he would marry Mary Watson, which he afterwards did (see WILLIAM WATSON, p. 95). The land where the Third-District schoolhouse now stands was early in his possession, and he probably settled near there. He owned considerable land here, and was a man quite prominent in the business of the town, serving as selectman, representative to the General Court, &c. He was successively ensign, lieutenant, and captain in the militia, and on the early records is termed " Clerk of the Band." He m 1st, Mary, dau. of William Watson of Boxford, 15 Dec., 1693, who d. 1 Feb, 1707–08. He m. 2d, widow Joanna Dodge of Ipswich, (pub) 19 Sept, 1708. He d. 13 Feb, 1761, lacking only seven days of completing his ninetieth year. He was the ancestor of all the Hales that ever resided in Boxford, and of thousands in this and other States. Their large family of fifteen children was as follows. 1. Joseph,[2]* b. 23 Aug., 1694 2. Jacob,[2] b. — Aug, 1695, m. 1st, Hannah Goodhue; 2d, Mary Harriman of Rowley; d 17 April, 1731. 3. Mary,[2] b 1 Oct, 1697; d. 28 Aug, 1722. 4. Ambrose,[2] b. 10 Feb,

* The following is the line of descent of the present Hale residents in Boxford from Joseph's son Joseph —

Joseph[2] m 1st, Mary Hovey, 5 Dec., 1723; who d 25 May, 1753, aged fifty-seven years He m. 2d, widow Sarah Hovey, 20 Sept., 1753 He m 3d, widow Lydia Brown, 1759. He m 4th, Susanna Fellows of Ipswich, 1771. He d 5 Oct, 1778; was deacon of the First Church. Ch.. 1 Mary,[3] b 14 Jan, 1724-25. 2 Jonathan,[3] b 5 Dec, 1729; d 24 June, 1731 3. Sarah,[3] b 6 Feb, 1731-32; m. Thomas Baker, jun, of Topsfield. 4. Jonathan,[3] b. 14 Feb, 1733-34, d. of smallpox, Feb, 1757 5 Joseph,[3] b 14 Sept, 1727. 6 Susanna[3] (by second wife), b. 2 Dec, 1756, m Joseph Symonds.

Joseph[3] m. Sarah Jackson of Topsfield, 7 Dec., 1749, who d 24 April, 1813, at the age of eighty-four years Ch : 1 Sarah,[4] b 13 Nov., 1751; m John Platts of Bradford 2 Mary,[4] b 22 May, 1754, m Levi Goodridge 3 Joseph,[4] b. 5 July, 1756, d 9 Nov, 1758. 4 Hannah, b 31 Oct, 1758, m Caleb Jackson of Rowley. 5 Joseph,[4] b 5 June, 1761. 6 Mehitable,[4] b 14 Nov, 1763; m John Merrill of Rowley.

Joseph[4] m Martha, dau. of John and Hannah (Wells) Friend of Wenham, 6 Oct, 1796; and d. 12 May, 1818. Ch.. 1 Sarah,[5] b. 18 April,

1698–99; m. Joanna·Dodge and Hannah Symonds. 5. Moses,[2] b. 25 Dec., 1701; first minister in Chester, N. H. (see his biography). 6. Sarah,[2] b 6 April, 1704; m. Jacob Kimball. 7. Abner,[2] b. 2 Aug., 1706; m. Ruth Perkins. 8. Hepzibah,[2] b. 29 Sept., 1709; m. John Curtis of Middleton. 9. Lydia,[2] b. 23 March, 1710–11; m. Nathan Perley. 10. Margaret,[2] b. 23 Feb, 1712–13; m. Amos Kimball. 11. Thomas,[2] b. 8 Jan., 1714–15; m. Mary Kimball : father of Dr. William Hale. 12. John,[2] b. 12 July, 1717; m. Priscilla Peabody : built the Lowe mansion. 13. Hannah,[2] b. 27 April, 1719; .m Benjamin Batchelder. 14. Benjamin,[2] b. 2 March, 1721–22; d. 4 Jan., 1722–23. 15. Mary,[2] b. 14 Jan., 1724–25. Most of the sons settled here, and had numerous descendants. Dr. Joseph Hale of Miller's Corners, Ontario County, N.Y.; Hon. Eùgene Hale (A.M. at Bowdoin, 1869), M. C. from Maine; Hon. Artemas Hale of Bridgewater, Mass., M. C. from Massachusetts,— are descendants.

EPHRAIM SHELDON (or *Shalton,* as it is spelled on the town-records) married Jane Peard in Lynn, 30 April, 1694. He immediately settled in Boxford, where the following

1798; lives in Boxford, unm. 2 Martha,[5] b. 14 Dec., 1799; d 12 March, 1808 3. *John,*[5] b. 9 Aug., 1801. 4. Hannah,[5] b. 13 Aug, 1803; d. 3 March, 1823 5 Joseph,[5] b. 26 Sept., 1805; m Martha W. Reed; d. 29 April, 1872. 6. Daniel,[5] b. 25 July, 1807; d. 17 Sept., 1831. 7. Martha,[5] b. 10 July, 1809; m Israel Dwinnell of Rowley. 8. Israel,[5] b. 18 Jan., 1812; m Fannie A. Holmes. 9. Isaac,[5] b. 5 May, 1814; m. Margaret Howe of Ipswich; d. 26 Oct., 1875.

John[5] m. Matilda Ann Bailey of Wenham, 24 Nov, 1825. Ch. 1 Hannah,[6] b. 3 Oct., 1826, m. Ancill Dorman, Esq. 2. *Matthew,*[6] b. 16 April, 1828. 3. Alfred,[6] b. 11 Nov., 1829. 4. John,[6] b. 22 Aug., 1831. 5 William,[6] b. 7 Oct, 1833, d. 4 Dec., 1862. 6. Matilda Ann,[6] b. 12 April, 1836; m Daniel W. Conant 7. Amanda,[6] b 19 June, 1838; m. Alfred Kimball , d. 27 May, 1860. 8 Harrison,[6] b. 8 Oct., 1840, d. unm, in the Rebellion, 6 Feb, 1863. 9 Isaac,[6] b. 6 Aug., 1844; m. Mrs. Martha A. Walker. 10. Daniel,[6] b. 12 June, 1846. 11. Mary Jane,[6] b. 24 May, 1850.

Matthew[6] m. Sarah S. Janes, 23 Nov., 1852; and d. in the Rebellion, 15 Aug, 1863. Ch : 1. Ellen Maria,[7] b. 21 Nov, 1855. 2. Lewis Dayton,[7] b 7 Feb., 1857.

children were born: 1 William, b. 13 Jan., 1694. 2. Rebecca, b. 20 May, 1697. 3. Ephraim, b. 13 June, 1699. 4. —— (son), b 5 Sept., 1701 5. —— (dau.), b. 1 Sept., 1703. 6. —— (son), b 13 Feb, 1706. Nothing more is known concerning this family; probably removed to Maine.

ROBERT WILLIS married Eunice Stiles, 15 Dec., 1——. Ch , born in Boxford : 1. Sarah, b. 13 Dec., 1——; "Sarah, daughter of Goodwife Willis," baptized in Topsfield church, 29 April, 1694 2. Robert, b. 27 March, 16—; baptized 23 May, 1697 The family became dependent upon the town for the necessaries of life. Among similar records we find that, 20 Jan., 1731–32, Stephen Peabody and Thomas Redington were chosen to supply Robert Willis and his wife with "necessaries for their comfortable subsistence."

SHERWIN —A Frances Sherwin was of Boxford, 1696, 23 Nov, when she married Isaac Cummings of Ipswich An Ebenezer Sherwin married about 1700, and had several children born here These two might have come to Boxford with their parents before 1696; however, it is conjectural. By his wife Susanna, Ebenezer had children born here : 1. Hannah, b. 6 Aug , 1701. 2. Jonathan, b. 8 Jan., 1703–04. 3. Ebenezer, b. 5 Jan , 1705–06. His widow died 29 Oct , 1762, aged eighty-three years. Both of the sons settled here, and the name was quite common till within a century. Most of them at last removed to Rindge, N.H. Thomas Sherwin, for forty years principal of the English High-School in Boston, was a descendant

PETER SHUMWAY was in Topsfield as early as 1677 In 1682, with James Waters, he was chosen by Topsfield to "ring swine." He was in Topsfield in 1686, and probably came to Boxford very soon after. He undoubtedly resided near Capt John Peabody, as he calls Peabody his "neighbor." Shumway made a will, which was proved in July, 1695 His will was, that his widow and sons should carry on the farm together. By his wife Frances he had children (all born in Topsfield): 1 Peter, b. 6 June, 1678. 2 John, b. 20 Jan., 1679. 3 Samuel, b. 2 Nov., 1681. 4. Dorcas, b. 16 Oct., 1683. 5. Joseph, b. 13 Oct., 1686. His son Peter married Maria Smith about 1700, and had six children born in Boxford. The family removed to Oxford, Mass., in 1714.

SPRAGUE — " Eaffae," son of James (?) and Sarah Sprague, died (born ?) 3 April, 169-. — *Town-Records.*

THOMAS WILKINS, son of Thomas Wilkins, one of the proprietors of the farms at Will's Hill, then in Salem (now in Middleton), married Elizabeth Towne of Topsfield, 19 Dec, 1694, and settled in that part of Boxford which was afterwards included in Middleton. Their children were as follows, viz : 1. Elizabeth, b. 10 Nov., 169-. 2. Hannah, b. 29 April, 169- 3. Mary, b. 23 March, 169-. 4 Thomas, b. 21 March, 1700 ; m Miriam Upton of Reading 5. Hezekiah, b. 15 April, 1702 ; m. Elizabeth Upton of Reading. 6. Miriam, b. 25 Aug., 1704 7 —— (dau), b. 12 Jan, 1705–06. 8. —— (son), b. 26 March, 1709.

Henry Wilkins was here as early as 1691 Bray Wilkins, probably brother of Thomas and Henry, also settled here subsequent to Thomas' marriage, and had several children. When Middleton was incorporated in 1728 these several Wilkins families were set off to said town ; and since that time the name has not been known here. The great-grandfather of these three Wilkinses was Lord John Wilkins of Wales.

LUKE HOVEY, born in Topsfield, 3 May, 1676, was son of John Hovey of that town. He married Susanna, dau. of Moses Pillsbury, 25 Oct, 1698, who was born 1 Feb., 1677 Mr. Hovey came to Boxford after the birth of his first child, and built the Hovey house, which was taken down by a descendant a few years since It was situated on the Bradford road, about a quarter of a mile north of the Second Church The site chosen for his residence was on the southerly slope of a hill at the base of which was a stretch of meadow and a pond He died 31 Oct, 1751, aged seventy-five years. His widow survived him until 22 Dec., 1767, when she died at the age of ninety years and ten months. Their sons resided here, and had many descendants, some of whom are the family of the late Thomas S Hovey. His son Luke settled near Mr. John Pearl's present residence. This settler's children were as follows, viz. · 1 Susanna,[2] b 25 July, 1699. 2 Dorcas,[2] b. 10 May, 1701 ; m. John Foster of Andover. 3. Hannah,[2] b 18 July, 1703. 4. Elizabeth,[2] b. 3 Oct., 1705 ; m. Benj. Kimball of Wenham. 5. Luke,[2] b. 18 May, 1708 ; m. Dorcas Kimball of Bradford, and widow Esther Runnells , had nine children. 6. Abigail,[2] b. 6 July, 1710. 7. Joseph,[2] [*] b. 17 July, 1712. 8. ——,[2] b. 3 Dec., 17— 9. ——[2]

For more early settlers, see Appendix F.

[*] The following is the line of descent of the present Hovey residents of Boxford from Luke's son Joseph : —

Joseph [2] m. Rebecca Stickney of Bradford, 21 March, 1743-44, who d. 19 Feb., 1788 He d. 23 Dec, 1785 Was deacon of the Second Church. Ch.: 1. Dolly,[3] b 30 Dec, 1744, m. Samuel Clark of Danvers. 2. *Joseph*,[3] b. 23 May, 1746. 3. Lucy,[3] b. 15 March, 1748, m. Thomas Cross of Bradford. 4 Ivory,[3] b 14 July, 1750, m. Lucy Peabody, d. Sept., 1832. 5. Lois,[3] b 24 Sept, 1752, d 5 Oct, 1758. 6. Rebecca,[3] b. 15 Dec, 1754, m. Amos Perley. 7. Amos,[3] b 31 May, 1757. 8. Lois,[3] b. 14 June, 1759, m. Amos Gage 9. Thomas,[3] b. 9 Feb, 1762

Joseph [3] m Mary Porter, 17 March, 1773, who d. 1 May, 1819 Ch · 1. Moses,[4] b. 7 April, 1773 2. Joseph,[4] b. 31 Oct., 1776, d. 6 May, 1816. 3. Aaron,[4] b 3 Feb, 1778, d 16 May, 1818. 4. Mary,[4] b. 1 Nov, 1781. 5. Hannah,[4] b. 16 Oct., 1783; d. 1 Jan, 1815. 6. Rebecca,[4] b. 17 April, 1788 ; d. 10 Sept., 1818. 7. Rufus Porter,[4] b. 5 Feb., 1790. 8. *Thomas Stickney*,[4] b. 18 Sept., 1792.

Thomas S.[4] m Sarah C. Parker, 4 Nov, 1822 Ch · 1. Orvilla Lawrison,[5] b 28 Feb, 1823. 2. Lucy Porter,[5] b. 6 Oct, 1826 3 Albert Parker,[5] b. 23 Nov, 1828 4 Joseph Henry,[5] b. 30 April, 1830. 5 Edward Beecher,[5] b 3 April, 1832

CHAPTER V.

Sir Edmund Andros. — King William's War. — Military Matters. — Trouble between Boxford and Topsfield; the
Dividing-Line settled — Other Bounds settled. — Roads
Laid out. — Our Ancient Tavern. — Taxes. — Town Meetings. — Sundry Town Offices. — Commons, and their Pasturage. — Witchcraft. — An Alarm from the Savages. —
First Meeting-House in Boxford

FOR several years after the incorporation of Boxford, the colony was in excitement, and in rebellion against the Government. In 1686 King
James II. took the control of the colony into his
own hands, and sent over Sir Edmund Andros, with a
number of assistants, to be the colonial governor. Andros
conducted his government in tyranny and oppression, and
thereby causing his subjects to "groan" under his injus-
tice and cruelty. Smith, in his *History of New York*
(p. 63), gives a just idea of his character in a very few
lines: "He knew no law but the will of his master; and
Kirk and Jefferies were not fitter instruments than he
to execute the despotic projects of James II." He was
checked in the midst of his oppressive measures by the
abdication of the king. This had been expected by the
colony, and eagerly desired. The Revolution was daring-
ly commenced in New England; and on the morning of
April 18, 1689, Andros and fifty of his supporters were
seized and confined, and the old government resumed

[*Holmes* I., 475]. Boxford was free in expressing its mind against Andros' government, and earnestly wished that Bradstreet would again take the gubernatorial chair. The following instructions were given, 6 May, 1689, to Capt. John Peabody,* the representative to the General Court, that had met to settle the affairs concerning the re-institution of the old government . —

"Wee the free houelders and in habetanc of the Towen of Boxford being vary fensabul of and thankfull to god for his great marcies to us in deliveiing vs from the Tiereny and opresion of thes ill men vndr whoes Jniustes & Cruelty we have fo long gioned with all Rendring our harty thanks to thoes so worthy & honerabul jentilmen who have been jngaged in foe good and nacesary a worck as the Confarvation of our peace finc that Revelution yet being also apprehancive of the many in Conveniencies and hazerds of the present vnsetelment of our affaiers doe declear that we doe expact that our honerad gouerner & dapety governer and asistanc Elactad & Swoin by the free men of this Colony in May 1686 to gather with the dapetyes then sent dauen by the Respactive Towens to the Cort the[n] haulden and which was never legally defolved shall Come and Reafuem and exarcies the gouerment as a general Cort a Cording to our Charter on the nienth day of may in Sewing nex & in So doing wee doe hear by promis and ingage to aied and asist them to the vtmost of oui power with our persons and estates praying god to gied them in the manigment of our ardeous affaiers and wee doe hope that all thoes that are Trew fiends to the peace and prosparety of this land will Radely and hartely Joyen with us hear in."

To the session of the General Court, which convened June 5, following, John Peabody, sen., and Thomas Perley, sen , were chosen representatives, — they to serve only one at a time. They were instructed "not to consent to set up any government contrary to our Charter privileges."

King James II., as we have before stated, fled to France, and stirred up the French to a revolution with England. The governor of Canada, as a good and loyal subject of the French king, began to assault the English colonies in New

* For list of Representatives, see Appendix C.

England. While yet in office, Gov. Andros and council
sent out invitations to the several towns for volunteers to
again enter the service. In response to this call, three men
entered the service from Boxford. These were Ephraim
Smith, who was out seventeen weeks; John Tyler, twenty
weeks ; and Jonathan Foster, four weeks. In regard to
their pay, the town agreed, 11 March, 1689–90, to give them
six shillings per week for all the time they were away from
home.

In King William's War, — as this conflict was called,
because that William, Prince of Orange, having succeeded
James II., was now reigning on the English throne, — the
French Canadians secured the services of the Eastern
Indians to assist in carrying on the war with the colonies.
The first blood was shed by the Indians at North Yar-
mouth, Me., in September, 1688 ; and thus commenced the
conflict which for five long years continued with greater
or less atrocity on the frontiers. Boxford was not wholly
free from apprehensions that the aborigines might try its
inhabitants next. On the 1st of July, 1691, three persons
were killed and some houses burnt at Amesbury, Mass.
Another, and still nearer, scene of the barbarity of the
savages was the murder of the Goodrich family in Byfield.
This last deed was committed by some Indian allies of the
Canadian French, who, tradition says, had been overcome
by a party of Englishmen in Andover; and, while returning to their homes, passing through the north-western part
of Boxford, which was then almost uninhabited, through
what is now Georgetown, into Byfield (Rowley), where they
wreaked their vengeance upon this quiet and inoffensive
family.

In 1689 the first stock of ammunition ever kept by the
town was procured. The selectmen met on the 8th of
January of that year, and made a rate of about eight pounds
for the purchase of said stock; and Moses Tyler, Thomas

Perley, Thomas Andrews, and John Andrews were ordered to gather it, and lay it out for "poudr & bullets and flents." Additions were made to the town-stock from time to time; and during the time of the Indian hostilities new additions were often made.* March, 1691, Boxford voted that the soldiers in the town should get themselves two pounds of powder apiece, and bullets and flints in proportion. On the 15th of the following December the town "chose some men to join with the committee of militia to advise with them concerning men who should go out to war from time to time and to engage with them in that affair; and their names are John Andrews and Daniel Wood, troopers; Sergeant Chadwick, Corporal Thomas Andrews, Corporal Joseph Peabody, William Foster, sen., and Samuel Symonds."

The regiment to which the Boxford company at this time belonged was made up of the Ipswich, Rowley, Gloucester, Wenham, Topsfield, and Boxford companies.

Oct. 6th, following the incorporation of Boxford, Topsfield chose a committee to treat with the Boxford people about their assisting in maintaining the ministry in Topsfield. A rate was made in Boxford expressly for the support of

* In 1690 three pounds was spent for powder and shot for the use of the town.

The following are records of various purchases of ammunition made by the town during a few of the subsequent years, to replenish their stock, viz : —

"28 June. 1694. delivered to Sargent Chadduck of the town money by order of the Selectmen for powdr and shot the Sumbe of — 09 — 03 — 02."

" 30th June 1694. Received of Sargent Chadduck one hundred and twelve pound of bullets [in] bages and three hundred flints which comes to two pound ten Shillings — 02 — 10 — 06 also a Small barrel of powder."

" 16 of Oct 1694, layed out in powder and shot and bullets and bringing £8 — 19 — 8."

" 14. August. 96 dilevared to quartermaster Tiler of the town stock of powder and bullets and flintes : ten pound of powder Sixty pound of bullets and 50 flintes and hee is to keep this part of the Town Stock teall the Select men See Caues to lodg it in Sum other place."

the ministry, annually, and was divided between the
churches of Topsfield, Bradford, and Andover, in proportion to the number of the inhabitants that attended divine
services at each place. Twelfth of December, 1689, the
town voted "that those men in Boxford that hear the Word
dispensed at Topsfield shall pay this year fifteen pounds,
five of it in silver, to the ministry, and the rest of the town
that go to Andover and Bradford to hear shall pay propor-
tionably where they do hear." Fifteen pounds was paid to
Topsfield for the support of the ministry, annually, until
1693, when it was increased to eighteen pounds.

A coldness was now creeping over the Topsfield church,
which was not entirely thrown off till years after the separation — in ecclesiastical concerns — took place between
the two towns. Fault was first found with the insufficient
number of pews, and the seating of the Boxford people.
In those times the people were seated, in respect to
the position of the pew, according to their respectability,
wealth, or age. Fault was often found because some had
more honorable seats than others. On the 14th of January, 1690, Topsfield chose a committee to "understand"
the grievances of the Boxford people, so that in some way
"peace and love" might be continued between the two
towns ; but the records do not inform us that any thing
was immediately further done. A spirit of alleviated
animosity seemed to prevail.

However, there were other difficulties between the two
towns at this time, principally in reference to a dividing-
line. After Boxford was incorporated, Topsfield obstinately refused to settle the line. In 1689, Dec. 12, Boxford
"chose Ensign John Perley, Quartermaster Thomas Perley, and Corporal Thomas Andrews to go to Rowley some
time this winter, and inquire of the town of Rowley if
there is any agreement between Rowley and Topsfield or
Ipswich concerning their line between Rowley and Tops-

field from Quartermaster Perley's to Ipswich River." At
the same time, John Peabody, sen., John Perley, Thomas
Andrews, Robert Ames, sen., Joseph Bixby, and Joseph
Andrews were chosen a committee to meet with the Topsfield people, and run the line the following April. The
line was not run the following April, and the next we·
hear about the matter is the appointment of John Perley,
Thomas Perley, Samuel Symonds, Thomas Andrews, and
John Peabody, in March, 1695, as a committee to perform
the same duty. The next March, Capt Wicom (of Rowley) was chosen to help the committee, if he would for
just compensation We will not take up more space in
pursuing the doings of the many committees which were
appointed by the town almost annually for the purpose of
settling the line between this town and Topsfield. When
the committees of the towns agreed to meet for this purpose, one of them would always be absent; and we are
sorry to say the Boxford committee were most often the
guilty party. Perhaps the greatest reason of their non-
agreement was the Gould and Endicott farms. These had
originally both been included in the limits of Rowley Village; and the Boxford people still wished to have them
annexed to their town, as the farms were large, and the
owners paid a considerable share of the town-rates. But
inasmuch as old Zaccheus Gould had years before "given"
his farm to Topsfield, the Topsfield people thought it was
rightly theirs. In 1699 Boxford petitioned the General
Court to have these farms lawfully annexed to their town.
Copies of the early grants, and so forth, were obtained, and
the petition received a hearing. A committee was sent
out by the General Court to view the farms; and it was
afterward ordered that Boxford should have the Endicott,
and Topsfield the Gould farm Before the town petitioned
the General Court they sent to Rowley to receive their
authority to settle the lines, for the authority vested in the

town at the time of its incorporation was not deemed explicit enough. The following is a copy of the communication and its answer : * —

" TO OUR LOVING NEIGHBORS OF ROWLEY, AND, IN SOME SENSE, OUR FATHERS.

" *Gentlemen,* — We give you many thanks for all the former kindnesses we have received from yourselves ; yet, notwithstanding, we would entreat you to add one more to all that we have received from you already, and that is, to grant our town the same power and privilege to settle our bounds with all the towns that do adjoin upon us, on every side, as you yourselves had, when we were both of us one town. We have had many meetings with Topsfield and Salem men, and they refuse to settle bounds with us, unless we can show a grant, either from the General Court, or from the town of Rowley, that we have power to transact in such settlements, as other towns have.

" So we remain your loving friends, to serve in what we may, hoping you will be pleased to grant us our desire herein.

" JOHN PEABODY,	
THOMAS PERLEY,	*Selectmen*
JOHN ANDREWS,	*of*
JOHN EAMES,	*Boxford.*

" Dated this 21st day of April, 1699."

(ANSWER.)

" We, whose names are underwritten, having been appointed by the town of Rowley May 11th, 1699, to empower the town of Boxford to settle bounds with the towns of Salem, Topsfield, Andover, and Bradford, or any other that the township of Rowley formerly granted was bordering upon , we do fully and absolutely grant and give to the town of Boxford as full power to settle any bounds, or run any line or lines, with any town or towns, farm or farms, that was formerly adjoining to the bounds of the town of Rowley before Boxford had the grant of a township, and what power we formerly had or still have. We resign up our sole power to Boxford town to transact any such business as if we, ourselves, were actually possessed of said township of Boxford, as formerly we were ; always reserving to ourselves

* The letter to Rowley is copied from Gage's *History of Rowley* . the answer is taken from our town-records.

the common land that lieth in the Village undivided, as may appear by an agreement bearing date the seventh of July, 1685, and the payment of the twenty shillings per annum in silver as expressed in said agreement, by Joseph Bixby, sen., John Peabody, William Foster, Samuel Symonds, and Moses Tyler, sen., and to be paid by them to the town of Rowley, or their orders, while Boxford have no Orthodox minister settled among them, — with the three pounds that will be due the seventh of July next, and already ordered to Captain Wicom.

"Dated May 12th, 1699, by Daniel Wicom, Joseph Boynton, and Samuel Platts of Rowley, and confirmed at a legal meeting of the town of Rowley, per an act of said town, May 16th, 1699.

"This is a true copy taken out of the town-book of Rowley, as attest, Joseph Boynton, clerk for Rowley.

"This is a true copy of that instrument, that the town of Rowley gave to us of Boxford, signed and attested to by Joseph Boynton, clerk of the town of Rowley, and copied out by John Peabody; as attest, John Peabody, clerk for Boxford."

At last, in 1731, after quarrelling for forty-six years, Topsfield and Boxford came to an agreement, of which the following is a copy : —

"We, whose names are underwritten, being a committee chosen and empowered by the towns of Topsfield and Boxford, respectively, to settle the bounds between Topsfield and Boxford according to the last resolve of the General Court, Anno 1707, have accordingly settled the line between said Topsfield and Boxford, from the apple-tree in Captain Perley's field to a stake and heap of stones at the south-easterly corner of Mr. Baker's farm, now in Boxford, and from thence to a dam, called Andrews' dam, near Mr. Thomas Gould's house, and from thence, it being the place where the water now runs under said dam, southerly to a stake and heap of stones by the Fishing Brook, on the easterly side of the rivulet running into said brook, and then as the said brook runs into the river called Ipswich River, then up said river to Middleton line.

"Dated at Topsfield, June 17th, 1731.

"JOHN HOVEY,	THOMAS PERLEY, JR.,
THOMAS PERLEY,	JOHN CURTIS,
THOMAS GOULD,	JOHN ANDREWS."

Not much trouble was experienced in settling the rest of the town's boundaries. In July, 1696, the bounds were

fixed between Boxford and the "Will's Hill men," * as follows, viz.: "From a tree, marked, by the river about forty
rods above the Indian Bridge; and from thence upon a
north-west course to a heap of stones a little beyond William Way's house; and from thence upon a north-west
course to· a heap of stones by Pout-Pond Brook; and
thence upon the same course to a forked white-oak tree,
which is now down, and a heap of stones in the room of it;
and from thence northerly to a rock in Beech Brook, where
the brooks meet; and thence upon a north-westerly course
to a white-oak tree, marked; and thence upon the same
course to a crooked white-oak tree marked with Bee."   The
Boxford committee that run this line were John Perley,
Thomas Andrews, and Samuel Symonds.

In 1700 the Ipswich bounds were perambulated and
settled anew by Abraham How and William Howlett of
Ipswich, and John Perley and Thomas Perley of Boxford.
Their report, containing a description of the bounds, is as
follows : —

"We, whose names are hereunto subscribed, being appointed by
Ipswich and Boxford respectively to perambulate the bounds between said towns, met this day, 8 April, 1700; and the following
bounds are them which are the standing bounds betwixt the said
towns : First beginning at the swamp called the Ash Swamp, where
there is a heap of stones by a path side upon the west side of said
swamp; thence running westwardly of said swamp to a little white-
oak bush with a heap of stones about it; thence running on the same
line to a heap of stones; thence running on the same line to two red-

* "Will's Hill men" were Thomas Fuller and his son Thomas, and
Thomas, son of old Bray Wilkins, who had, several years previously, purchased and settled on the grants of Major-Gen. Dennison and Richard
Bellingham, now situated in Middleton.   They were called "Will's Hill
men" because "Will's Hill"—so called from "old William," the last sur-
vivor of an Indian tribe that originally inhabited it—was a part of their
domain. Their possessions were annexed to Salem; and in 1728, quite a
village having sprung up, they formed a part of the newly incorporated
town of Middleton

oak trees with stones by them, and some stones placed betwixt them, thence running upon the same line to a heap of stones upon a ridge by the side of a meadow, called Perley's Meadow; thence running on the same line to a heap of stones in Lt Thomas Perley's field that has a walnut bush in the heap of stones; thence to a lopped white-oak that is dead, with stones about it, thence on the same line to a marked red-oak tree with a heap of stones about it, thence on a straight line to an apple-tree in Lt. Thomas Perley's field. As witness our hands, Abraham How, John Perley, William Howlett, Thomas Perley. This is a true copy of the return of the committee that did settle the bounds between Ipswich and Boxford, so far as said towns join together, and signed their doings therein, April 8th, 1700. As attest, John Peabody, clerk for Boxford."

As soon as the town was incorporated, an open road was laid out from Andover bounds to Topsfield along by Joseph Bixby's house. Also another, from "Zaccheus Curtis' house to the above-said highway, or roadway, along by the Works * through Abel Langley's farm; also, from the Works along by the south side of the Plain and so on to John Stiles', and so into the above-said way" Abraham Redington, sen, John Perley, Samuel Symonds, Moses Tyler, sen., and John Peabody, sen., were the committee to lay out " all needful roads," doing as little damage as possible to the owners of the land. Boxford voted that " this committee, or others for highways, shall accordingly give notice to all persons that they do lay any highway through their lands to be there; it is also further agreed that when the highways are to be laid through any man's, or men's, land, that always such man, or men, shall have as much power in ordering where the way shall go as any one of the committee till it is gone through his land."

Nov. 23, 1686, the committee laid out another open highway "from Maple Meadow by John Peabody's house, and so along to Topsfield's common-land in Bear-hill Plain, doing as little damage as may be: and it lies along in the

* The iron-works are meant

old path to John Andrews' slough, and so as near the hilly ground on the left hand as it can conveniently be laid to the next slough, and then still by the hills to Thomas Andrews' barn, and so to Crane Brook along the old pathway to Topsfield land." Another road was laid out "from Goodman Buswell's, through Goodman Redington's pasture to John Stiles' barn, and so along to the Works on the south side of the Plain, and so along to Zaccheus Curtis' barn." Also, " the committee agreed to lay out a way through Abel Langley's farm by the Works to the main roadway, as above."

These roads which we have just enumerated were all laid out in 1686, and, as may be recognized, were all situated south of the East Parish village. No more roads were laid out for several years.

It has been truly said of Boxford of late years, that it has no hotel. But it is with pleasure that we look back over the vista of time, and learn that our early settlers immediately turned their attention to the importance of having a public table kept in the town. William Foster, at a town-meeting held Aug. 19, 1687, was chosen their "*ordinary-keeper.*" For several years he kept a kind of public house, receiving his license from the town-clerk. On the 12th of the following month, after being chosen to keep an *ordinary*, it was voted that the town-meetings should be held at his house; and they probably continued to be held there till the meeting-house was finished in 1701, when they were held in that. The Foster house undoubtedly stood on the site of the late residence of Mr. Dean Andrews, deceased.

In the early settlement of Boxford, taxes were paid in corn or other produce, to the satisfaction of the constables, who were the collectors; and if the taxes were not paid by the time fixed by the selectmen, the delinquents had to pay one-third more. In 1780 the constables were paid three pence on the pound for collecting.   In 1684 the town rate of Rowley was £43 12 s. 11 d., of which the Villagers paid £8 7s. 7d.

The "country rate," because of the unsettled state of affairs, — the estates not having been valued as yet, — was neglected, and the town was reprimanded for not doing its duty. A committee of three (1687) was chosen to help the selectmen make the rate. Their share of this rate for 1688 was £11 7s. 10 d. It would be well to remark, that, during the first half-century of our history as a town, a separate rate was made for each charge that was brought against the town, — a rate to defray the regular annual charges, a minister's rate, a country rate, a rate to purchase ammunition, to build any building, or for any public improvement.

The annual election of town officers was usually held in the early part of March; but in 1798 it was voted that for the future it should be held on the first Monday of April. This custom continued till 1848, when it was changed to the first Monday of March. Thus it is at the present time. Until 1800 the town-meetings were always held in the East Parish; ever since, they have been held alternately in both parishes. The first town-meeting in the West Parish was held April 6, 1801. We cannot conceive why they were not held there sooner, as the West Parish was nearly as densely populated as the East Parish. The early custom of warning town-meetings was very curious, and bears quite a contrast to the present method. The constables walked from house to house throughout the town, telling every voter the date and place of meeting, and the articles of the warrant. If the day on which the meeting was to be held was stormy, it was postponed at the discretion of the selectmen. All those voters that were absent from the town-meeting were fined, in the earlier part of our history, one shilling; if they were only tardy, then the fine was sixpence. Neither could they leave until the meeting was dissolved, without permission, on the like penalty. The town would surely have a large revenue arising, if this law was prevalent at present. This appears to have been an unneeded and unnecessary practice; but perhaps it was very useful in getting a full meeting, and we do not think it would be a bad plan at the present day.

Surveyors of highways were first chosen in 1687. The first men chosen as such were Thomas Redington, Thomas Hazen, and Joseph Andrews. The number chosen from year to year was irregular, — sometimes only one, and other years two or three or more. The number was increased as the population augmented, and the conveniency of the town demanded that the roads should be kept in a condition better to facilitate travel. At present there are seventeen surveyors' districts, and as many surveyors chosen annually, one for each district.

The office of "fence-viewer" was an early acquisition, and those officers have been regularly chosen ever since Grand-jurymen and jurors of trials were regularly chosen.

"Sealers of leather" were first chosen in Boxford about 1700. The title indicates the duties of the office.

The first "sealer of weights and measures" was chosen March, 1691, and is recorded in the following words: "Corparel Thomas Andrus is Chozen Clark of the marcet to fee that all mesuers bee capt in good order a cording to the ftandard." Thomas Andrews held the office many years.

Some of our most prominent citizens were annually chosen to the office of "tithing-man." Their duties were, to see that the sabbath was well kept, and that all that could do so attended church. Various writers have pictured the duties of the old-fashioned tithing-man, which would be an anomaly to the duties of the present incumbent of that honorable office. During the last few years the office has become unpopular, and in most places it is left vacant. For an interesting account of the duties of the tithing-men of ye olden time, we would refer our readers to Mrs. Stowe's *Oldtown Folks*.

One constable only was chosen for the whole town till 1705, when two were chosen, one for the North, and one for the South district.* Thus it is at the present time; one constable is chosen for the West, and one for the East Parish. The duties have also changed since the early times.

"Commons" were laid out (see p. 40) for common pastures in different sections of the town, in which the cattle, horses, sheep, and swine were pastured. The animals were marked with the mark of the owner, which was generally a slit in the ear, or a hole of some peculiar shape; the same being recorded in the town's records. The following is one of these records —

"The Mark of Luke Hovey Junr for his Cattel and other Cretuis is as followeth (viz) a Croop of the Right Ear & a hole threw the same Ear

"Entred May the 14th 1739."

In 1687 the town ordered, "that all swine in the town above three months old shall be ringed from the middle of March to the first of November yearly, upon the penalty of —— a week for every swine that shall be found upon the Common without a ring in his nose; and half the money so forfeited shall be for the finder, and the other half

* The following are the earliest constables, i e, since the incorporation of the town: 1686, Robert Stiles; 1687, William Peabody; 1688, Thomas Perley, 1689, John Pe——, 1690, Ephraim Curtis; 1691, Joseph Bixby; 1692, Joseph Andrews; 1693, Abraham Redington; 1694, John Kimball; 1695, John Chadwick; 1696, Daniel Wood, 1697, Thomas Andrews, 1698, William Watson, 1699, Samuel Symonds, 1700, Joseph Hale; 1701, Zaccheus Curtis, 1702, Thomas Perley, jun., 1703, Moses Tyler; 1704, John Andrews, 1705, John Stiles and Jacob Perley; 1706, Timothy Dorman and Job Tyler, &c.

shall be for the use of the town.", At the same meeting it
was also ordered, "that all rams within the town shall be
kept up or sufficiently yoked from the first of August to
the first of November, upon the penalty of sixpence a time
that any ram shall be found doing damage, to be paid
to the owner of the sheep where he doth the damage." The
owners, on a penalty of two shillings per animal, were to
"yoke" the swine with a yoke two feet one way by twenty
inches the other, and place in their nose a suitable ring,
which was doubtless done to stop them from rooting. Pigs
over eight weeks old were ordered to be driven daily into
the woods, during the summer and fall seasons, for the
purpose of feeding upon the oak-acorns that must have
been abundant in the heavy growth of oaks that surrounded
the village in those colonial days. At night they were put
in some close place of shelter. This practice was continued
until 1774, when, the pride of the people being no doubt
touched by the custom, it gradually gave way, and was
entirely abolished in 1811.

In 1695, July 29, John Eames was ordered to make a
"pound," near Joseph Hale's house, and said Hale to be
pound-keeper. In March, 1697, the town voted that there
should be one built by Timothy Dorman's or Joseph Peabody's house, and to be erected at the town's cost. Sept.
21, 1700, John Eames was ordered to build another
"pound," in his end of the town, "by Moses Tyler's barn,
or near it in that road." John Peabody was also ordered
to build one "between Corporal Peabody's house and
Timothy Dorman's house, or in some other place in that
road, as may be convenient;" also, "Ensign Perley to see
that there is another pound made and set up by Joseph
Hale's house," where it had been before voted to be made.
April 20, 1703, the town voted to build another pound,
and to set it "between the meeting-house and Abraham
Redington's house." In connection with impounding cat-

tle is the office of "field-drivers," or "*Haywards*," as they were early called. We find scattered through the old records various notices of animals being taken up, and public notice of the same given. The following is one of these notices : —

"november the 9th 1719

"A Stray hors taken pr Dameg fesant by Jeremiah Perley of box-ford cryed and prezed as the Law Directs the hors being of a Dark Iron gray trimed and Shod before with fome white spots on his back."

A still older notice, which we find among the records at the Salem court-house, is the following : —

"Zacheus Curtice of Rowley Village hath a bay mare, with a star in the forehead, a slitt on the top of her neare eare & a little bit cut out of the same eare, & hare of her taile cut, no brand marke seene, taken vp for a stray the 21 of December, 1677, prized by John Vinton and After Cary at 20 *s.*"

While the Indians were busily perpetrating their hostili-ties along the frontier, the public mind, especially in Essex County, was most dreadfully distracted by what has been denominated the *Witchcraft Delusion.* The trouble began February, 1692, in a reverend gentleman's family in Salem Village A daughter aged nine, and a niece aged eleven years, were the first afflicted. Their physician said that "they were under an evil hand." These children accused a female Indian servant of pricking, pinching, and torment-ing them. Some other persons complained of suffering, and others were accused Complaints and accusations continued to be made through the spring and summer, throughout the county. A special commission of "oyer and terminer" having been issued out to Mr. Stoughton, the lieutenant-governor, Major Saltonstall, Major Richards, Major Gedney, Mr. Wait Winthrop, Capt. Sewall, and Mr. Sergeant, a quorum of them sat at Salem, June 2, 1692.

Aug. 19, 1692, Rev. George Burroughs was hung for witchcraft on Gallows Hill, in Salem Among the spectators was Rebecca, wife of Robert Eames of Boxford, who was about fifty-three years of age. She was in a house near the scene of execution ; and while there "the woman of the house" felt a pin stuck into her foot, as she said. Rebecca, not being as good as she might have been, was pointed out as the one who did it ; and the following warrants — two indictments — were immediately issued for her arrest : —

" Essex in The Province ⎫ *" Anno RR^s & Reginæ Gulielmi & Mariæ*
of the Massachusetts Bay ⎬ *Angliæ &c Quarto Annoq^e Domini : 1692.*
in New England ss. ⎭

"The Juriors for our Sov^{re} Lord and Lady the King and Queen doe present That Rebeckah Eames wife of Robert Eames of Boxford, in the County of Essex, aforesaid. In the year afores^d, and divers other dayes and times as well before [as] After Certaine detestable Arts Called witchcraft & Sorcerey Wickedly Mallishously and felloniously hath used practised and Exercifed at and in the towne of Andivor in the County of Efsex afores^d in upon and against one Timothy Swan by which said wicked acts the said Timothy Swan the day & yeare afores^d and divers other dayes and times both before and after was and Is Tortured aflicted Consumed Wasted Pined and Tormented and alfo for Sundry other Acts of Witchcraft to the said Rebeckah Eames Committed and done before and since that time againft the peace of our Sou^{re} Lord and Lady the King and Queen theire Crowne and dignity and the forme in the Statute In that case made and provided."

[The preceding is entitled : " Indictm^t ags^t Rebecka Eames For bewitching Tim^o Swan ;" the following : " Indicm^t ags^t Rebecka Eames for Covenanting with ye Devil."]

" Essex in the Province ⎫ *" An^o RR^s & Reginæ Gulielmi & Mariæ*
of the Massachusetts Bay ⎬ *Angliæ &c quarto Anoq^e Dom 1692.*
in New England ss. ⎭

"The Juriors for o^r Sov^r lord & lady the King & Queen doe present that Rebeckah Eames Wife of Robert Eames of Boxford in y^e

County aford About Twenty-Six years past in the Towne of Boxford in the County aforesaid Wickedly & fellonously A Covenant with The devill Speritt the Devill did make in & by which Wicked Covenant Shee the Said Rebeckah Eames her soule & body to the Devill did give & promifed to serve & obey him & keep his wayes, Contiary to the Stattute of the first yeare of yᵉ Reigne of King James the first in that Case made & provided And Against the peace of or Soveraigne lord & lady the King & Queen their Crowne & dignity." — *Witchcraft Records*, at Salem, Vol. II , pp. 25, 26.

These warrants were served, and her examination took place on the same day. The following is the testimony in the case : —

"Rebecca: Eames· Examined· before Salem Majestrates: Augˢᵗ 19 1692: She ownd She had bin in ye snare a month or 2: & had bin perswaded to it· 3 months · & that yᵉ devil apeared to her like a Colt very ugly; yᵉ first time: but she would not own yᵗ she had bin babtized by him she did not know but yᵗ yᵉ devil did perswade her to renounce god & christ & ffolow his wicked wayes & that she did take his counsell and that she did afflict Timo: Swan. she did not know but that yᵉ devil might ask her body & soul. & she knows not but yᵗ she did give him soul & body afterward she sᵈ she did do it & that she would forsake god & his works: & yᵉ devil promised her to give her powr. to avenge her selfe on them that offended her afterward she sᵈ yᵉ devil appeared to her 7 year agoe: & that he had tempted her to ly· and had made her to afflict persons but she could not tell their names that she first afflicted. Q who came wʰ yᵉ devil when he made you a witch. An: A ragged girl they came together and they perswaded me to afflict· & I afflicted Mary Warin & an other fayr face; it is about a quarter of a year agoe. I did it by sticking of pins but did you afflict Swan; yes but I am sorry for it. Q. Where had you your spear A. I had nothing but an all. but was it with yoʳ body or spirit you came to hurt these mayds A with my spirit. Q but can you ask their forgivnes A. I wil fall down on my knees. to ask it of them· She would not own that she signed yᵉ devils book when he asked her body & soul but he would have had her done it nor to a burch Rign; nor nothing· she sᵈ yᵉ devil was in yᵉ shape of a hors when he caried her to afflict. but would not own anybody went with her to afflict but yᵉ afilicted sᵈ her son Danˡˡ went with her to afflict Q. did you not say· yᵉ devil babtized yoʳ son Danˡˡ A. he told me so·

but: did you not touch the book nor lay yor hand on book nor paper A. I layd my hand on nothing without it was a peice of board: and did you lay yor hand on ye board when he bid you. A Yes: Mary Lascy: s^d she had given her son Dan^{ll} to ye devil: at 2 years old: & y^t her aperition told her so but. she could not remember it: she was bid to take warin & lascy by ye hand & beg forgivnes & did so: & they forgave her: she s^d if she had given her son Dan^{ll} to ye Devil it was in an Angry fitt she did not know but she might do it nor I do not know he is a wich but I am afrayd he is: mary lascy saw her son Dan^{ll} stand before her & s^d Dan^{ll} bid his mother not Confess he was a Wich: his mother: did not know she sd but. she might se him for she saw a burlling: thing: before her: Mary Lascy sd she had babtized her· son Dan^{ll} & y^t she had bin babtized in five mile Pond: she s^d ye reason she feard Dan^{ll} was a witch: was becaus he used dredfull bad words when he was angry: and bad wishes. being asked: the age of Dan^{ll}: sd he was 28 years old. she was told she had bin long a witch: then if she gave her son to ye devil at 2 years old· she owned she had bin discontented since she had bin in league. with ye devil: she knew not but ye devil might come once a day: like a mous· or ratt: she s^d she knew Sarah parker but did not know her to be a wich: but she heard she had bin crosd in love & ye devil had come to her & kisd her who was with you when you afflicted Swan A. no body but my son Dan^{ll} he was there when I came theether she would have Dan^{ll} perswaded to Confes· but was told she were: best to perswade him becaus she knew him to be a wich she was ask^t if she was at ye execution: she s^d she was at ye hous below: ye hill she saw a few folk: the woman of ye hous had a pin stuck into her foot: but she sd she did not doe it· but how do you afflick: A. I Consent to it but have you bin a wich 26 years. A. no plan (?) remember but 7: years & have afflicted about a quarter of a year: but: if you have bin a wich so long: why did you not afflict before seing you promisd to Serv ye devil: A. others: did not Afflict before: and the devil did not require it: but: doth not ye devil threaton you if you [do] not do what he sas· A. yes he thretens to tere me in peices but did you used· to goe to meeting on Sabath dayes: yes· but not so often as I should have done: what shape did the devil com in when you layd yor hand on ye board: A: I cannot tell excpt it was a mous "—*Ibid.*

Mrs. Eames was placed in jail, and received sentence of death Sept. 17. For some reason she was not immediately executed, and continued to lie in jail till the following March, when she was reprieved by Gov. Phipps. July 22, 1693, only about four months later, her husband died; she continued a widow till May 8, 1721, when she died at the age of eighty-two years. In 1710 she sent the following letter to the General Court, desiring them to restore her name to its former purity, and to allow certain bills of charge relative to her imprisonment, &c., which was fully complied with by that honorable body at their next sitting:—

"BOXFORD Septem 12—1710.

"to the honred Jentlmen of the Commitey greating It having pleased the grate and Jenaral cort to a piont your honars a commity to in quire who may be propr to [be] Justified in the bill refering to the taking of the attainder and what loss and damedg hes bene sustained by reasen of the tryalls whitch were for witchcraft In the yere 1692 Rebecka Emes releck of Roborth Ems late of boxford dececed being aprehended for witchcraft In the yere 1692 some time the begineng of ogust and sufered Imprisnment a bove Seven months and condemned and afterwards re preved by govrner feps: I Rebechar emes humbly pray and de sier that the attaintur may be tecken of and my neme may be re stored a gain with the cost and damedges [that] Is sustained thereby to my husbands Esteat: paid in moniy to the prision keeper and cort chardges four pounds eaighten shillings for the repreve to the goavners clark 1^{lb} — 10^s — 0^d for provisons and other nesecriy chardgs whils imprisened and upon my tryall expended by my husband for me whils under those doliful surcumstances I think I may safly say amounted to ten pounds more — 10 — 00 — 00 Yete If the Attaintur may be taken of and my neme re stored a gaine I am willing to take tene pounds all whitch I leve to your honers consideration

"I re maine you'r humbell Sarvant

"REBECKAH EMES"

—[*Witchcraft Records*, Vol. CXXXV., p. 151, Mass. Archives.]

Thomas Perley of Boxford was one of the jury during these exciting trials. These dreadful affairs are generally thought to be the result of the superstition of the times; but there are incidents connected with them which must be ascribed to some invisible power of the lower regions.

In 1695 an incident, although not occurring in our town, was rendered alarmingly interesting to a portion of our people. — On the 7th of October, in that year, five Indians attacked and plundered the house of John Brown, who lived on the westerly side of Turkey Hill, in West Newbury, and captured nine persons, only one of the family escaping to tell the tale. Search was instituted, and it was found that the savages were approaching the boundaries of Boxford. Night came on — and what a night that must have been to our north-eastern settlers! The next morning it was discovered that in the night the Indians had changed their course, and were now going to cross the Merrimac River. Troops were sent from Rowley and Ipswich, who cut off their retreat, secured all the captives but one, who was no doubt slain; and the Indians, after severely wounding several of the officers and soldiers, escaped. Such were the times, and the settlers had to conform to them.

Coming back to the ecclesiastical matters, we find the feeling of discord still prevalent in the Topsfield Church. Attempts to settle the boundaries between the two towns had not assisted in promoting the union or happiness of the church; and, as we near the close of the seventeenth century, the feeling seems to gain a stronger hold. As early as 1690 the Boxford people desired to loose their connection with the Topsfield church. Dec. 15, 1691, the town voted "that the Last Twesday in febewary next in fewing is a pointed a daye for to Choues a Commety for to Steat a pleac for to fet [a] meting houes in and other nafefary ocations if the Towen aprove of it." The town met on the 23d of February, 1691–92, and voted "to Choves a Commety on the ·8th· of march next insuing to fiend out a fit pleac to fett a meting hous." March 8th, "the town chose several men to measure from end to end and from side to side of our town to find out the centre;

and if that is not the most fit place to set a meeting-house in, then the committee that we choose are to consider of another place or places which they shall think most fit, and so make their report of what they shall do herein to the town of Boxford: and the names of the men chosen for the service above-said are Lt. John Gould, Lt. Thomas Baker, Sergeant John Hovey, Henry Wilkins,* Ensign John Perley, Lt. Thomas Perley, Quartermaster Moses Tyler, Samuel Symonds, sen, Robert Ames, sen, John Peabody, sen, and Zaccheus Curtis. This Committee are to meet on the first Tuesday of June next ensuing to do this service above mentioned." This committee met on the appointed day, and attended to their duty. The following is their report: "The Committee appointed by the town to find out a place to set the meeting house in met on the 7th of June, 1692, according to the town's order; and they have measured the town from end to end and from side to side: and from the fartherest houses by Will's Hill to George Bixby's field is seven miles; and from the farthermost corner of our land near Merrimac River to George Bixby's field is eight miles; and from the eight-mile tree to George's field is two miles and a quarter; and from Rowley line to the above-said field is about two miles and a half the nearest way, as some think."

For two years the subject appears to be dropped, as we find no record relating to it until the 24th of April, 1694, when the town voted that "they would build a meeting-house in convenient time thirty-four feet square and eighteen feet stud between joints; also to build and finish the meeting-house within the space of two years after the date hereof." On the 22d of the following January, it was voted to set the meeting-house "between William Peabody's house and George Bixby's house, as they can agree with

* The preceding members of this committee belonged to Topsfield; the following, to Boxford.

the owners of the land." Joseph Andrews and several
others dissented from the rest of the town about the place,
and nothing was further done at that meeting. A week
from that day the inhabitants met again, and chose Thomas
Andrews, Ensign John Perley, John Peabody, Quartermaster Tyler, and Thomas Hazen, to be a committee to
"carry on the work of building the meeting-house in the
town of Boxford according to their best discretion, improv-
ing men in our own town if they may be obtained reason-
ably ; also to agree with the owner of the land where the
meeting-house shall stand."

The Topsfield people, recognizing the intentions of the
Boxford brethren, and seeing that they were in danger of
losing their support, 1694–95, March 5, gave liberty to have
more seats made in the church for the further accommodation of their "neighbors of Boxford." It was also voted
that when the Boxford people removed they might sell
their pews to any one that contributed to the support of
the ministry, or to the town for what they paid for them.

June 18, 1697, it was voted " to carry the timber of the
meeting-house to the north side of the plain near to
John Buzwell's pasture, and there to frame it by the thorn
bushes, where the paths meet that come from William
Foster's and Abraham Redington's dwelling-houses." At
this meeting they chose a new committee, consisting of
Thomas Perley, Samuel Symonds, and John Peabody, to
. agree with workmen, or a workman, to build and finish it,
as cheap as possible, within one year and eight months
after the date of the meeting, if it could be done. The
proposed size of the building was also altered to thirty-four
feet long, and about thirty feet in breadth. This was probably the size it was erected. The roof was elevated from
the four sides of the building to a peak in the centre,
which was surmounted by a turret. This turret stood till
May, 1732, when the building was in such a bad condition

that the rain and snow beat in around it; and they took it down, and closed the aperture

At a town-meeting held Jan. 3, 1698–99, the town chose a new committee to carry on the work of building the meeting-house, consisting of John Perley, Thomas Andrews, Thomas Hazen, Daniel Wood, and Joseph Hale. It was also voted that every man in the town should have liberty to do as much work in building and finishing the meeting-house, as will come to his share, excepting the money part, the committee to set the price of each one's labor. The fee of the committee was three shillings a day from the 1st of March to the 1st of November, and half a crown a day during the rest of the year. John Perley, being a carpenter, and as we find his name on most of the committees, was probably the master workman.

At the above town-meeting, it was voted to have the meeting-house ready to be raised by the 10th of the following June, and to be finished by the 1st of January, 1700, or sooner if it could be conveniently done. Feb. 3 (1698–99), a new committee was chosen to finish the house, and "to make a gallery in it, and a pulpit as good as Topsfield's, and make seats both for the lower room and galleries sufficient for the whole house." This committee was Joseph Andrews, Joseph Bixby, Daniel Wood, John Eames, and Zaccheus Curtis. The committee at first agreed with the carpenters to build the pews, and set them as they were in the meeting-house in Andover; but Oct. 4, 1700, the inhabitants met in the new meeting-house, and chose John Perley and Samuel Symonds, with the carpenters, a committee to set the pews as they thought would be most to the town's advantage. The expense of building the meeting-house was to be paid at three payments, — the first, May 20, 1699; second, "next cresmus;" third, when the work was all done.

Then a season of eight months passes, and the building

was not begun, nor even its site decided upon. About eight years had elapsed since the first step was taken in the matter. On the 18th of September, 1699, with a view of finally fixing upon a proper site, the town chose a disinterested committee, consisting of the following distinguished men from the neighboring towns: Ensign Nehemiah Jewett, Capt. William Raymont, Dr. Philemon Dean, Deacon Nathaniel Knowlton, and Sergeant Ephraim Stevens. By the choosing of this committee it is inferred that the disputation of a proper site was the reason the meeting-house had not been erected. The committee met on the 3d and 4th of the following month, and selected "a small hill in the land of Abraham and Thomas Redington, where a stump stands with stones laid upon it upon the northerly side of the thorn bushes, and meeting of two ways."* Said Redingtons, the owners of the land, as soon as the decision was made, presented to the town, gratuitously, in a deed dated 23 Oct., 1699, the "small hill" decided upon. Where this hill is situated has been very clearly enunciated to have been the northern corner of the cemetery situated in the East Parish village, near the present church.

The meeting house was now commenced, and the work carried through with precision, without any interference whatever. Within the next twelve months it was entirely finished; and on the 9th of January, 1701, the committee presented it to the town. This must have been an exhilarating season; they had looked forward to this time for

---

* The bounds of this piece of land are thus defined : " First bound is a tree, which is Ensign Dorman's corner bound, and so northerly fifteen rods to a small white-oak, marked , from thence easterly ten rods to a great rock with stones laid upon it ; and from thence southerly thirteen rods and a half to a red-oak tree, marked ; and from thence eight rods westerly to the first bound. And this land lieth adjoining the twelve-rod-broad road which runneth from the thorn bushes to the other road which lieth from Andover to Topsfield."

many years, when their hopes would be realized. But, to sum it all up, we cannot think they had much to be proud of, as the building was *not* built in the best and most durable manner possible. We find it leaked very soon after its completion, and only about thirty years later it was found to be in such a poor condition that it could not be repaired.

CHAPTER VI.

1700–1730.

REV. THOMAS SYMMES — CHURCH ORGANIZED. — ROADS LAID
OUT. — STOCK OF AMMUNITION — SLACKNESS OF THE CONSTA-
BLES IN GATHERING RATES. — INDIAN DEEDS. — EDUCATION. —
PEABODY'S MILLS — EARLY PAUPERISM. — REV. MR. SYMMES'
PASTORATE AND DISMISSION. — REV. JOHN ROGERS SETTLED.
— DR. DAVID WOOD — DR. JOHN ANDREWS — THE TIMES. —
BATCHELDER'S SAW-MILL — HOWE'S SAW AND GRIST MILLS
— ANDREWS' MILLS. — INDIAN WAR OF 1722-25. — REPAIRING
ROADS. — THE BOOM PETITION — VARIOUS MINOR KINDS OF
BUSINESS CARRIED ON. — CEMETERIES. — NEGROES. — "MOTHER
DOWEN."

EV. WILLIAM SYMMES was ordained a minister in England, in 1588   His son, Zachariah
Symmes, was for more than forty years the
minister of Charlestown, Mass.   Zachariah had a
son of the same name, who was settled over the church
in Bradford, Mass   *He* had a son Thomas, who was born in
Bradford, Feb. 1, 1678, and entered Harvard College at
the age of sixteen, in 1694, from which he graduated with
honor in 1698.

Fourth of October, 1700, it was voted by the town "to
send Ensien John pearly and Clark Simons to inviet m^r
Simes [Rev Zachariah Symmes of Bradford] m^r persons
m Capen m^r barnit· to come to our towen and to afoerd
us thair halp in keeping a day of prayer to seek the Lord
for his blasing in our colling of a minnister to dispenc the
word of god amongst us in Boxford." Jan. 9, 1700–01, it

130

was voted " to give an Invitation to m^r Thomas Simes to
bee our minister if it pleas god to inclien him to take vp
with our invitation and what wee can give: also the Towne
have Choes Corperal daniel wood and Corperal Thomas
pearly to goe to Cambridg and Carey the Towns Vot and
declaer it to m^r Simes and bring the Town his answer
whether hee will Exsept of it or not or other wies." Why
Mr. Symmes was at Cambridge so late, we do not know.
He had completed his collegiate course in 1698, and he
might have been studying theology there with some divine.
The call was accepted; and on Sunday, April 27, of that
year, he preached his first sermon here. This was probably the first service ever held in Boxford. Mr. Symmes,
in speaking of his ministry, often affirmed that he began
too early, being at this time only twenty-three years of age.
At a meeting held April 4, 1701, the town voted to give
him sixty pounds in money, yearly, for his salary; also, to
build him a house forty-eight by twenty feet, and two
stories in height, and a back room of sixteen or eighteen
feet square; also, to finish the house by the next October,
come twelvemonth, and as much sooner as possible; also,
to find him thirty-five cords of wood yearly; also, to procure him ten acres of land, as convenient as they could,
not far from the meeting-house, which house and land they
agreed to give to him and his heirs forever, if he would accept of their invitation to settle with them in the ministry.
Immediately on his accepting their invitation the town set
themselves to work on the promised dwelling-house for
their pastor, which was completed much more readily than
the meeting-house, it being finished and taken possession
of by Mr. Symmes, July 22, 1702. It is supposed to have
stood in the cemetery, near the present First Church, on a
knoll, the site now being occupied by the monuments of
Messrs. Sayward and Dorman. No one living knows any
thing about the house, only that there was an old cellar

there, and that it was undoubtedly the site of the parsonage; the town records prove that it was situated near by. It has probably been razed to the ground more than a century. Benjamin Rogers, son of Rev. John Rogers, probably occupied and owned it last. It was no doubt a very substantial dwelling, and perhaps looked upon as a fine residence, as it cost quite a large sum of money. The ten acres of land were also obtained, and conveyed to Mr. Symmes. Instead of the thirty-five cords of wood which the town was to find him yearly, after the first year they paid him eight pounds in money in addition to his regular salary.

Until Sept. 25, 1702, the Boxford people continued to belong to the Topsfield church. On this day the church convened "to consider the application of sundry persons belonging to Boxford, who had asked their dismissal from that church, preparatory to being organized into a church in their own town." Upon this application, the church voted to dismiss the Boxford people when they shall have paid up all arrears. The result was that on the 4th of the following month the following members were dismissed, viz : John Peabody, John Perley, Thomas Hazen, Josiah Hale, Jonathan Bixby, Thomas Redington, Abraham Redington, John Stiles, Samuel Foster, Daniel Wood, and Luke Hovey. A short time after, Samuel Symonds, Zaccheus Curtis, Ephraim Curtis, and Joseph Peabody, jun., asked for dismission, but were refused, "by reason of the difference between the two towns as touching their limits." The first two obtained their dismission in 1709, but the others were probably not dismissed.

Rev. Mr. Symmes was ordained Dec. 30, 1702, at which time the church consisted only of those men who were dismissed from the church in Topsfield, Sept. 25, 1702. No record has been found descriptive of his ordination. After the church had been organized, and the pastor settled

over it, Jan. 17, 1703, Mary Watson, Mary B——, Sarah
Wood, widow Peabody, Elizabeth Stillman, Mary Hale,
Deliverance Stiles, widow Bixby, Sarah, wife of Jonathan,
Bixby, and Elizabeth Buswell, were added to it on dismis-
sion from the Topsfield church; also, Feb. 21, 1703, Joseph Bixby, Jonathan Foster, Timothy Foster, Thomas Perley, jun., Samuel Symonds, jun., John Symonds, Thomas
Perley's wife, Jonathan Foster's wife, Timothy Foster's
wife, Samuel Symonds' wife, and Goodwife Chub; and
also, on the 25th of the following April, twelve more, viz.:
Joseph Peabody, Jacob Perley, Timothy Dorman, John
Buswell, David Wood, Lydia, wife of Jacob, Perley, Timothy Dorman's wife, David Wood's wife, Abigail Bixby,
Hannah Kimball, and Ebenezer Stiles. By this time the
church must have contained nearly fifty members. No
more large additions were made, the increase being in
more regular order.

While Mr. Symmes is quietly pursuing his ministerial
relations we will return to 1696–97, March 2, when the
town laid out a new road "from the training-place to the
north-west end of the town, beginning at the training-field,
and so along the path by Abraham Redington's field to
the widow Stiles' new field, and so along the path to Cold-
Water-Meadow Swamp, and so over the swamp, and along
the path to Samuel Pickard's new field now in possession
of Jonathan and William Foster, from the east end of that
field to the east end of Meadow-pine Swamp, and from
thence on a north-west course on the south side of a great
valley and swamp straight to Andover road to Ipswich, not
very far from John Tyler's field, and so along Andover
road to the corner of Sergeant Chadwick's field, and from
thence to young Moses Tyler's barn, and so along the path
to Nathaniel Peabody's house, and so into a way the proprietors of Mr. Nelson's great farm have laid out for their
necessary use." About three years later, — July 17, 1700,

— it was agreed by the selectmen, "that the highway shall continue as it is used for that end, from the road by William Foster's field along to Rowley bounds near to a hill called Tobacco-pipe Hill" This above-said road is that which now leads from the residence of Mr. Humphrey Perley to Rowley line. On the same day a highway was laid out "from Francis Elliot's house to the mill-path as it is now improved, and as the trees are marked, and so on to Crooked-Pond Brook, and so on as the trees are marked to the edge of the long plain, from thence straight over said plain to the Fishing Brook, a little above the pout-hole, and so on to the road coming out of the field by Timothy Dorman's barn, — said road to lie one part upon said Dorman's land, and part on Corporal Joseph Peabody's land, — and so on to the meeting-house." On the 9th of the following September another highway was laid out "from the meeting-house, as straight as the ground will most conveniently allow of, to the upper end of the meadow that lieth a little ways below the widow Peabody's new mill, and so over the brook to the bounds of the land between the widow Peabody's land and Joseph Hale's land, and so along upon their bounds to Andover highway, part upon the widow Peabody's land and part upon Joseph Hale's land." This last highway is the Chapman road that is now obsolete.

In 1696, Aug. 14, the town's stock of ammunition was delivered into the hands of Quartermaster Tyler to remain in his possession till it was ordered otherwise. The stock consisted of ten pounds of powder, thirty pounds of bullets, and fifty flints.

Most of the early constables were slack in collecting the rates; some of them having collected not more than a half of any list which had been committed to their care. In 1697 a general reckoning took place between them and the town, to learn their financial condition. This showed sad neglect on the part of some of the constables. In

1699 a rate of £14 18 s 10 d. was given to William Watson to gather; but he, "pleading much infirmity," had neglected it "so that the whole rate was in danger of being lost;" and the selectmen placed it in the hands of Samuel Symonds to gather. In December, 1699, the constables were again called to an account.

Although John Winthrop had procured a deed, of the old sagamore Masconnomet, of the whole tract of land then included in the town of Ipswich (1638 — then including the town of Boxford), his three grandsons Samuel and Joseph English, and John Umpee, in 1700, laid claim to the territory of Boxford. A town-meeting was held Jan 15, 1700–01, at which their claim was not refuted, but a committee — John Perley, Thomas Perley, John Peabody, Thomas Hazen, and Josiah Bridges — was chosen to treat with the Indians about their demand. The committee and the Indians met at the house of Lieut. Thomas Perley — who furnished them with "vittels and drink" — and agreed, that, for eight pounds in money paid to Samuel English, and "two shillings and sixpenc in Silver and Rum and vittels enouf" to the other two, the Indians would give them a deed of the property. Jan. 16, Samuel English gave the town a quitclaim deed of the township. This deed is recorded on our town-records, but as it is similar in form, and of the same tenure as the deed which the other two Indians signed shortly afterward, we do not give it here. Samuel English signed the first deed with his mark: ∽; it was witnessed by Thomas Baker, Joseph Foster, and Moses Parker, and acknowledged before Dudley Bradstreet, Esq, of Topsfield, on the same day. The deed is here given that the other Indians signed. The heading shows that the deed was first written to receive the signatures of the Indian trio. This last deed is found recorded on the records of Topsfield; though why recorded there, and not on our own town-records, is a mystery. The deed is as follows : —

"Sam^{ll} English, Jos. English, John Vmpee, Indians, to ye Town of Boxford.

" Rec^d on record, Feb^r 24. 170¾

" **To all People** unto whom these Presents shall come, Samuel English, Joseph English, & John Vmpee, Indians, Grand Children & the next true, rightfull, and Lawfull heirs of Musquonomet, alias Muschonomet, Indian Chief, Sagamore, and native Proprietor of that whole Tract of Land Extending from the Southerly Side of the River Merrimack unto Naumkeeg, otherwise called Bass river, lying in the County of Essex, within his Maj^{tie} Province of the Massachusetts Bay, in New England, Send Greeting: Whereas, Divers Englishmen, many years since, in the Lifetime of the Said Musqunomet, al^s Muschonomet, with his Knowledge, Lycence, and good Liking, did Enter into, Subdue, Improve, Build, and Settle an English Plantation, Containing about Twelve Thousand acres of Land, more or less, now Called and Known by the Name of the Town of Boxford, within the afores^d Tract of Land, in the said County of Essex, which said Plantation or Township, and the Lands thereto Belonging are Butted and Bounded, Northerly by a marked Pine Tree on the Southerly Side of Merrimack River afores^d, which is the Corner Bounds, and then the Line Runs by Marked Trees that are between Andover and Boxford, and Southerly according as the Trees are marked betwixt said Andover and Boxford, as it hath been perambulated, till it Come to the Eight Mile Tree, so called, which is a Bound mark betwixt said Andover and Boxford, and Southerly to a White oak, which is the Bounds betwixt Wills Hill men and said Boxford, and then Southerly to a Wild Pear Tree, or Box Tree, standing by Ipswich River side, and then Easterly as the River Runs, till it meet with Ipswich Line, which said Line doth extend Six miles from said Ipswich meeting house, and then upon a Straight Line till it Come to an apple tree that is in Lieu^t Pearly's field, marked, and then it runs with Ipswich Line, until it meets with Rowley Line near Caleb Jackson's, and so till it come to a white oak in Bradford Line, as it is setled betwixt Boxford and Rowley, and then westerly till it meet with the Pine Tree first mentioned, parting Betwixt Boxford and Andover. Now, Know yee, that we, the said Samuel English, Joseph English, and John Vmpee, the true, Rightfull, and Lawfull heirs of the said Musquonomonet, al^s Muschonnomet, as afores^d, as well upon the consideracon afore^d, as for divers other good Causes and Consideracons us thereunto moving, more especially for, and in Consideracon of the sum of nine pounds, Current Silver money of New England, to us in hand, at and

before the Ensealing and delivery of these presents, well and truly
paid by John Pearly, Thomas Pearly, Thomas Hazen, John Peabody,
and Josiah Bridges, all of Boxford, afores^d, Yeomen, a Committee
and agents for the said Town of Boxford, The Receipt whereof we do
hereby acknowledge, and ourselves to be therewith well Satisfied,
Contented, and fully paid, Have Granted, aliened, Enfeoffed, Released,
Ratifyed, Confirmed, and forever Quit Claimed, and, by these presents, for our selves and our heirs, Do fully, freely, clearly, and absolutely grant, aliene, Enfeoffe, Release, Ratify, Confirm, and Quit
Claim, unto the said John Pearly, Thomas Pearly, Thomas Hazen,
John Peabody, and Josiah Bridges, and the Rest of the Freeholders
and Proprietors of the said Plantation or Township of Boxford in
their actuall possession, being all the afores^d quantity and Tract of
Twelve Thousand acres of Land, more or less, Scituate, Lying and
being in the s^d County of Essex, and butted, bounded, and described
as afores^d, or howsoever otherwise the same is bounded, or Reputed
to be Bounded; Together with all and singular the Trees, Timber,
Woods, Underwoods, Rivers, Brooks, Ponds, Streams, Waters,
Water Courses, Marshes, Meadows, Fields, Fishing, Fowling, Hunting, Edifices, Buildings, Rights, Members, Profits, Privileges, Commodities, Advantages, Hereditaments, Emoluments, and appur^ces,
whatsoever upon or Belonging to the said Tract of Land, Plantation,
or Township of Boxford afores^d, or to any part or parcell thereof, and
all the Estate, Right, Title, Interest, Inheritence, use, property,
Claime, and demand whatsoever, of us, the said Sam^ll English, Joseph English, and John Vmpee, and each of us, our and each of our
heirs, of, in, or to the same, and the Reversion and Reversions,
Remainder and Remainders thereof. To Have and to Hold all the
said herein before granted, Released, and Confirmed premises, unto
the said John Pearly, Thomas Pearly, Thomas Hazen, John Peabody,
and Josiah Bridges, and the Rest of the Freeholders and Proprietors
of the Town of Boxford afores^d, their heirs and assignes, to their
only proper use, Benefit, and behoofe, for Ever And we, the said
Samuel English, Joseph English, and John Vmpee, for ourselves and
our heirs, do hereby Covenant, grant, and agree, to and with the said
John Pearly, Thomas Pearly, Thomas Hazen, John Peabody, and
Josiah Bridges, and their heirs and assignes, on behalfe of themselves
and other the freeholders and Proprietors of said Town of Boxford,
their heirs and assignes, for ever, that we, the said Samuel English,
Joseph English, and John Vmpee, are the true, Rightfull, and Lawfull
heirs of the before named Musquonomonet, alias Muschonomet, and

that we shall and will warrant and defend all and singular the Lands and premises by us herein before granted, Released, and quit claimed, unto yᵉ sᵈ John Pearly, Thomas Pearly, Thomas Hazen, John Peabody, Josiah Bridges, and other the Freeholders and proprietors of the Town of Boxford aforesᵈ, their heirs and assignes for Ever, against ourselves and our heirs, and all and Every other person or persons Claiming any Right, title, or Interest therein from, by, or under our said Grandfather Musquonomonıt, alias Muschonnomet. In witness whereof, we have hereunto set our hands and seales, the — day of —— anno Dom : 1701 annoq; RRˢ Gulielmı Tertii Angliæ, &c., Decimo tertio.

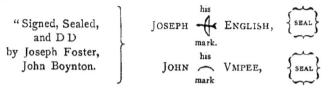

"Signed, Sealed, and D D by Joseph Foster, John Boynton.

JOSEPH ⊣⊣ᵏ ENGLISH, {SEAL}
his   mark.

JOHN ⌒ VMPEE, {SEAL}
his   mark

"Joseph English and John Vmpee appeared before me, the subscriber, one of his Maᵗˡⁱᶜˢ Justices of yᵉ Peace for the County of Essex, and acknowledged this Instrument to be their act and deed, this 22ᵈ of Octobʳ, 1701.

"DUDLEY BRADSTREET, J. Peace.

"Examᵈ p. Steph. Sewall, Recodʳ."

The first step toward the propagation of education in Boxford was taken by the town, Nov. 24, 1701, when they chose John Peabody to be their "scowel master." We do not find that a schoolmaster had taught here before this time; and perhaps they might not have hired one so early, had they not been reminded of their duty by an order from the General Court. Mr. Peabody taught the children here for several years. In 1712 Thomas Perley, jun., was chosen schoolmaster Aug. 25, 1713, the town agreed with Nathaniel Peabody to teach. Sept. 12, 1716, the town agreed with Thomas Jewett "to teach Scoul for writing reading & Arethemitick . . . to the 6 parts of yᵉ Town yᵉ Town is for give him forty shillings pur month for yᵉ six months & convenient diat & lodging." Covey Morgan taught in 1719 ; Ephraim Dorman, 1720. September, 1722, Thomas Redington was chosen " to learn persons to read,

write, and cypher." Dec. 21, 1725, it was voted "to give
Mr. John Rogers £25 to keep school the year ensuing,
provided he may be approbated as the law directs." He
accordingly entered upon his duties, and thus began the
first real advance in the cause of education in Boxford.
David Foster was chosen to this office in 1728. The
school was held for many years in private houses in different sections of the town, its sessions being held for a while
in each place alternately. These sessions were about a
month in length ; and, considering that this was all the
schooling which the children would receive during the
year, unless they attended the school of an adjoining
district, it is not surprising that education was so little
developed among the common people. The schoolmaster
of a century and a half ago rises before our view : browned
by the sun and heat while cultivating his arable acres ; his
hands like those of the sturdy yeoman, rather than a
schoolmaster's ; his gestures and walk betokening the com-
manding position which he holds, — are all brought to our
eyes while we hear him affirm that " g-e-s " spells " guess."
Down his back the long cue of those days dangles as he
steps among the scholars, who, if any one dared do it,
would pull it " just for fun."

Shortly before his death (1700) William Peabody erected
the first saw and grist mill that ever existed in the town
The grist-mill was situated on the stream that flows back
of the old Spiller house in the East Parish, where the
ruins are still visible ; the saw-mill was situated farther
down the stream. The original building of the grist-mill
stood until Sept. 23, 1815, when the terrific gale, which
our older inhabitants remember so well, blew it from its
foundation into the pond at its side. Richard Peabody
(grandson of the original proprietor), the owner at the time
of its fall, immediately re-erected it — the timber-trees with
which it was done having been blown down by the gale.

After Mr. Peabody's death in 1820, the place was sold to Mr. Nathaniel G. Spiller, who still resides in the town. About 1845 Mr. Spiller sold the mill to Messrs. William A. Gurley and Joseph Farley, who demolished it to give place to a saw-mill which they proposed to erect. Much of the lumber with which to do this was hauled there, and a massive stone wall built for the foundation of one side of their mill. But this was as far as they ever got. The wall — the cost of which ruined the company, it is said — still stands unchanged ; and, as a whole, the view of it is most picturesque. A visit to this romantic spot would well repay the trouble, especially to an artist. The place is now occupied during the summer by William A. Herrick, Esq., a prominent lawyer of Boston.

Every town that provides for its poor, and looks after them carefully, should contain in its History the history of pauperism as seen and provided for by them ; for this is a notable feature, and shows plainly the character and humaneness of its inhabitants in providing for the poor a home, and for the aged an asylum of rest. Boxford shows this feature as early as 1706, by voting to build a house for the poor, where they could be taken care of, and provided in a proper manner with food and raiment, and, what they would be sure of, a home. The voting part of the population held a meeting on the 5th of January in the above-named year, and voted to build a house for this purpose upon that "parcel of land devoted to the use of the town, where the meeting-house doth stand." The dimensions of this edifice were to be as follows: length, thirty-four feet, width, fourteen feet ; and six feet to the eaves, with "a convenient cellar" under one end of it. It was voted to be finished by the last of the following June ; but we do not think it, or any thing of the kind, was built, or purchased already-made, until the present town farm was bought, for two very conclusive reasons : viz., *First,* because we cannot find any record whatever that speaks of any building being built or bought for that purpose. *Second*, we find that the paupers were "boarded out" in different families in the town for years afterwards. Probably they came to the conclusion, that, as there were but very few paupers, it would be much cheaper to board them out.

A curious incident in connection with this subject occurred a few years previous to the time of which we have just been speaking. A family named Cary had lived here a number of years, and at last they became so poor that the wife asked for alms from the selectmen. She belonged in Ipswich, where she had been an inhabitant, and probably had not gained a residence here. In reply to her petition for help, she was warned out of town to Ipswich, to be provided for there. At this time she had a child only a little more than a month old. It seems, however, she did not go, as she had another child born to her here afterwards. This is the first and only instance of the kind we ever heard of. A very poor person ("poor body," as the warrants call her), having come from another town, and taken up her residence here, asks for help in her time of need, and, instead of giving her the needed assistance, and collecting the same of the town where she did belong, as is the custom at present, the selectmen warn her to depart. This seems a cruel as well as curious practice to follow, though perhaps no more so than many of the by-laws which our ancestors made from time to time. In connection with the above affair the husband is not mentioned, though he must have lived here at the same time. In 1725, when she was a widow, she was assisted by the town. We do not insert this as saying any thing against the character of the selectmen, who were all worthy and distinguished (in their own town) men, but to bring before our readers what curious acts our ancestors were capable of doing.

Rev. Mr. Symmes, in his pastorate here, met with uncommon difficulties; but the nature and reason of them are unknown. It appears, however, that they were such as he was unable to encounter; and, there being no reasonable prospect that they would cease during his continuance here, he was, in 1706, "thoughtful of removing from Boxford." He was not hasty in forming a decision, but was willing to wait the intimations of God's providence, to be directed by him, and principally to advance his glory. In his diary is found the following memorandum: " *Jan.* 29, 1707. — This day I had sweet communion with God, in secret prayer. The Lord helped me wonderfully to plead with his Majesty, for assurance, for a soft heart, and for his Holy Spirit to sanctify me, comfort me, guide and assist me; and for his presence to be with me, whether I remove from Boxford or not. I pleaded: Lord, if thy presence go not with me, carry me not hence. Lord, I cannot go, unless thou go with me. Lord, if thou wilt not go with me, stop me, disappoint me, hedge up my way with thorns; yea, let me die, rather than go one step without thee. Lord, if it be not for thy glory, and the good of souls, let me be here continued. I know that thou art all-sufficient, and canst provide for me here, and deliver me from my temptations here; and therefore I will wait upon thee, in the use of lawful means, to know what thy will is. Lord, help me so to do." In the following spring he sent in his resignation; and a town-meeting was held May 21, 1708, to consider of the same. They consented to Mr. Symmes' wish. The church met the same day, and, after "considerable agitation," concurred with the town. The elders of the neighboring churches, who met at Newbury on the 9th of the following month, advised the conclusion to which the town and church had arrived. The following is an extract from the town records: —

"21 May 1708. the Towen voted that this following information or declaration shoueld bee Recordad that so thaier may not bee anney mis vndrstanding of our Resons why our minister and wee doe peart on from the other if it should bee so.

"Thes may sertify whome it may Consearn that whear as our Reverand pastor mr Thomas Sims after a very Consedarabel tiem of trial and wee Conclued much Consedaration and advice doues as wee vnderstand yet Remaien vnder vncomfortabel surcomstances and vn-easy in his Contenewanc hear on that account Being apprehancive that hee might bee moer Comfortabel and searvesabel in sum other place then with vs and wee being sensabel after all that wee Can at Presant doe for him to a comedeat him . that wee Cannot doe what hee needes as sume other Places may doe : not that wee have anney dislick of his Person menistry or Conversation but should bee hartewly glad if wee might still in Joye his labores but unwilling to keep him allwaies in trubbel and uncomfortabel : wee have the moest of vs in Real love and good will towardes him : lovingly a greead that wee will no longer appoes his Removel but give way to it and say the will of the Lord bee dun in ceas the Revarant Ealdears met togather att newbery sum tiem in the begening of Juen next 1708 : or the major Peart of them doe advies us to dismis him from his pastoreal obligation to vs and in Ceas our Revarand paster mr Thomas Simes will Reles to the Towen of Boxford all that thay have dun for him by waye of setalment and also what hee hath layed out in finnishing of his houes and give what Instrewment they shall think proper to se-cuer it to them from him or anney others from by or vnder him laying Claiem theair to and if it bee so wee hartely wish him weeall and thank him for his labors amongest vs and pray god to bles him and his and mack them blassinges and doe hear by Recommend him to the Cristian felowship and Communion of what Ever Church and People hee may seatteal with."

The difficulties which Mr. Symmes met with here must have been exceedingly great; for in resigning his position he forfeited all right and title in the house and land, which, if he continued here in the ministry, would fall after his decease to his heirs. After he left Boxford, he soon received a call to settle in the ministry at Bradford, his father having died. He accepted the invitation, and was installed as pastor of the Bradford church in the same year of his departure from Boxford.

Rev. Mr. Symmes married first, Elizabeth Blowers (sister of Rev. Thomas, of Beverly) of Cambridge, by whom he had seven "very hopefull and desirable" children, six of whom — four sons and two daughters — lived to maturity. Four of them were born in Boxford, viz.: Thomas, b. Jan. 11, 1703; Andrew, b. May 20, 1704; John, b. Feb. 14, 1706; and William, b. Oct. 23, 1707. After her father's death the eldest daughter was received into the family of Rev. Benjamin Wadsworth, president of Harvard College. Mr. Symmes' wife dying April 6, 1714, he married, secondly, Hannah, daughter of Rev. John Pike of Dover, March 28, 1715. During his connection with her, they had two "very desirable" daughters, both of whom survived their father. On Feb 1, 1719, he was again called to mourn the loss of his wife. He was again married to Mrs. Eleanor, relict of Mr. Eleazer Moody of Dedham, and daughter of the well-known poet, Mr. Benjamin Thompson of Braintree, who survived him.

Although Mr. Symmes usually appeared to be in good health, yet for a number of years previous to his death, he was troubled with a poor appetite, indigestion, and pain in his head and breast. The first violent symptom of his disease was on the sabbath but one before his death, — bleeding considerably from the nose. This flow of blood increased until it destroyed his life on the morning of Oct. 6, 1725. He had appointed a fast, to be kept on his account, on Tuesday the 5th, in the afternoon of which day the assembly were interrupted by news of the apprehensions of his dissolution. A minister went to the house to pray with him, before he expired; and upon asking him if he was "freely willing to resign his soul to his Saviour," he lifted up his hand, and said, "Yes." He remained unable to express his feelings till the following morning, when he entered into the joy of his Lord, at the age of forty-seven years.

Mr. Symmes was a man of much learning, and very active with his pen, several of whose productions, both scriptural and secular, were published, and are to-day occasionally met with. Those by which he was best known are a sermon entitled "The Brave Lovewell Lamented," and "A Joco-Serious Dialogue Concerning Regular Singing." Prefixed to the first is an account of "The Fight at Pigwacket," which is the most authentic account of that sanguinary affair. Judging from the "Joco-Serious Dialogue," it is evident that wit and sarcasm were no strangers to its author.

Increase Mather, then in the sixty-second year of his ministry, says of Mr. Symmes: "I have known him from his youth. When he resided at the college where he was graduated by me, then presiding over that society, I observed real piety in him, and was then persuaded that the Lord would make him a blessing;" which has been done, as the church records of Boxford and Bradford plainly show. During his short stay of six years in Boxford, seventy-two persons were added to the church ; and many took dismissions from other churches, and united with this. The distinguished Rev. Mr. Colman says that Mr. Symmes "was out of the way of fame, or any worldly reward." His aim seemed to be good. It was the commendation of *Heaven*, which he esteemed and desired. To do his Master's work in the vineyard of the world was his highest ambition In the notice of his death in *The Boston Newsletter* of Oct. 9, 1725, is ingrafted this closing sentence of our sketch : "He was a correct and pertinent, pungent and undaunted preacher ; never feared the faces of men, nor shunned to declare the whole counsel of God."

It seems that for two months after Mr. Symmes' dismission no meetings were held in the meeting-house. June 21, 1708, the town voted that Rev. John Rogers of Salem should preach the four successive Sundays after that date. His services were again secured for a quarter of a year, at twenty shillings per week. He probably was successively engaged until he was permanently settled over the church in the latter part of the following year. No records remain whereby we can tell the particulars either of his or Mr. Symmes' ordination. Mr. Rogers was paid a salary of sixty pounds, which was increased in 1717 to eighty pounds. As a settlement, the house and land that had previously been in the possession of Mr. Symmes, and which he forfeited by his resignation, was conveyed to Mr. Rogers upon the same conditions as to Mr. Symmes. In this house he took up his residence on his marriage, two years later

When invited to assist in settling Rev. Mr. Rogers in the ministry here, the neighboring ministers refused; and with much trouble the ordination exercises were carried out, as we see by the following letter, which explains itself.

" The Church and Town of Boxford sendeth to the Town and Church
of Topsfield, greeting :

"*Brethren and Neighbors*, — We think it a little unchristianlike dealing, that there are so many scandalous reports in our neighbor towns, that our neighbor ministers make it a reason why they will not come to ordain our minister, when, if our town were indebted to you, and neglected or refused to pay, you might have made use of the civil law, and, if our church were indebted to you, then we think they should have been disciplined according to the order of churches. Now, brethren and neighbors, since it is our duty to follow peace with all men, and considering the gracious promise made to peacemakers, we make you the following proposals . —

" 1. That, if you assert that our town is indebted to you by a rule of righteousness, and yet not legally to be recovered, we therefore proffer you to leave the matter to a committee of unbiased men, two of them chosen by yourselves, and two of them chosen by us, they choosing a fifth ; all of them not belonging to Topsfield or Boxford.

" 2. That if you will choose a committee in your town, to join with a committee chosen in our town, to inform the abovesaid committee what has passed between us and you, relating to the ministry of Topsfield, both before and since we were a town.

"3 Also, said committee to be informed how Topsfield's representative made complaint to the General Court that our town lived at
loose ends, and had no minister, and came to their meeting, and troubled
them, and paid but what they pleased to pay. By that means our
town was doomed three pounds to a single country-rate, — two pounds
taken off Topsfield, and one pound off Andover, and laid upon our
town. That, being doubled several times, made us pay many pounds,
which we think, by a rule of righteousness, might be outset in this
matter of debt which you demand; if it appear to be a debt.

"4. That, if our church are indebted to your church in your esteem,
we desire that it might be left to said committee.

"5. That if you will bind yourselves, in a bond of fifty pounds, to
stand by the award of said committee, chosen as above, provided they
bring you in to our debt, that then we will bind ourselves in the like
bond, although we fall in your debt as a town or a church.

"BOXFORD, July 11, 1709.

"We have chosen our committee, and fully impowered them to act
in this affair; and their names are as follows: Lieut. John Peabody,
Lieut. Thomas Perley, Mr. Samuel Symonds, Ens. Thomas Hazen,
and Ser. Joseph Bixby."

Contentions between the two towns had been in existence for more than a quarter of a century, and continued as
long after this date The feeling was little more than the
result of a "family-quarrel."

Though we cannot boast of having a physician settled
among us at the present time, it is nevertheless true that
we could have done so a century and a half ago. And
down the many years almost to our present day, we had in
our midst one of those necessary practitioners. Our first
doctor filled the office of surgeon and dentist as well as that
of physician; and probably in some degree was among the
renowned of that profession. This was Dr. David Wood,
great-grandfather of Capt. Enoch Wood, now resident in
our town. He was son of Daniel and Sarah Wood, and
was born here Feb 18, 1677 He commenced the practice of physic at the age of thirty years, and remained the
doctor of the town and vicinity until his death, which

occurred Aug. 30, 1744. His account-books show a large and extensive practice, having continuous bills against the inhabitants of the neighboring towns. As a farmer, Dr. Wood was unexcelled in the extent of his operations. Ship-timber, which was sawed at his own saw-mill, — that stood in the rear of the residence of the late John Q. Batchelder, and of which we shall soon speak, — was a product of his extensive woodland. A large stock of cattle, as we judge from his accounts with Francis Perley the tanner, was his property. He had also a large cider-mill, in which he made a great quantity of cider for his own use and for sale, and hundreds of barrels annually for his neighbors. His residence was, no doubt, the house that previously occupied the site of the Stetson mansion, and which had been probably his father's before him. One now nearly a century old writes : " This house, by the side of the pond, I well remember, with its low-descending lean-to ; and its long ladder, reaching from the ground to the chimney, was ever in its place, that they might the more readily quench the sparks and cinders which often circled above the chimney-top in the cold winter evenings." Most of the real estate in that vicinity was in his possession ; and because of his wealth, and professional and social position, his voice was a power in the prosecution of the town affairs. Regarding his family and descendants, see page 71.

A "Doctor John Andrews" appears here in 1712, when he was chosen a selectman ; but we know nothing more about his appellation.

The season of which we are writing was a disastrous one to the people of New England The winters were very severe; and, the springs therefore being late, the planting was delayed. Many of the men were in the service of the colony, — the Indians having again begun their hostilities, — and, in consequence, the farming was in many places

neglected, and scarce enough was raised to supply the
family need. Provisions of all kinds were dear and scarce.
It was voted by the town, Dec. 5, 1710, to set Indian corn
at half a crown, merchantable wheat at four shillings, and
rye at three shillings, a bushel. The times, however, grew
better; and the high prices of provisions relaxed when
peace again settled over the colonies.

In March, 1710, the town gave liberty to Ensign Hazen,
Jacob Perley, and David Wood, to set up a saw-mill on
the "parsonage-farm," where they shall see fit, and to
have convenient yard-room, with a road to the mill, for
thirty years, the above men paying all damage to the land
to the town. A part of the old mill is still in existence,
though greatly tumbled down. Its situation is on the
stream which leads from Wood's, or Stetson's, Pond, to
Four-Mile Pond, just below where the old Dresser road
crosses the brook, and in the rear of the residence of the
family of the late John Q. Batchelder.

At a meeting of the proprietors of the common lands in
Boxford, Sept 18, 1710, it was voted: "whear as Richard
Kimbol Eapharam dorman and Sammeueal fisk doe appear
to Seat vp a Sawmill vpon the fishing broock with ouer
Consent and incorigment wee the . . . . propriatoer[s] doe
freely consent that thes thre men shall seat vp a sawmil
vp on the foels by Josaph Bixbes houes also wee doe freely
give them the veas of as much of our land as thay need for
flowing and a yeard to lay thair louges and bordes and timber vpon for the ves above s^d so long as thay or thair
heaiers or Sucksesaers shal keep vp a going mill and for
the trew performenc of what is promised on our sied wee
doe biend our sealves heaiers and sucksesaers to the above
mensioned Kimbol dorman and fisck and thair lawful sucksesaers that thay shal peassabelly in Joye the ves of the
land a bove said with out anney molistation from vs or
anney from by or vnder us." This mill was accordingly

erected, and has continued to be a "going mill" to the present time. About the year 1800, or before, the business was carried on by Asa Foster (father of Richard K. Foster), who owned the mill, together with a grist-mill that had been previously erected. Mr. Foster died in 1831; and the heirs, in 1849, sold the mills to the late Augustus Hayward, who purchased the grist-mill stones that had been taken out of the grist-mill that stood where the match-factory now stands, and sold to a Mr. Bailey, and carried to Amesbury. Mr. Hayward hauled them back again, and put them in his mill in place of the old stones. Mr. Hayward did a thriving business, especially in the furnishing of ship-timber to the vessel-builders in Essex and vicinity. After his death, in 1872, the mills were sold to Mr. Solomon W. Howe, who has kept them almost constantly at work ever since.

Probably about the time of which we are now writing, the Andrews saw-mills were erected, though we have never arrived at any definite conclusion regarding their origin. Parts of the mill-buildings are very ancient, but not so much so as an elderly man would have them, when they were recently repaired. Some one remarking that the mill was very old, he said he once saw a deed of it dated ——, mentioning a date several years anterior to the arrival of the Pilgrims in New England. But, from a lack of knowledge of history, he mentioned a date which could not be credited; and so his account fell into disrepute. As far back as any one now remembers, they were in the possession of the Symonds family, Capt. Joseph Symonds being the last owner of that name. Upon his death, the late Dean Andrews purchased the mills, and by them sawed the large quantities of lumber in which he dealt. After his death they were owned by the late Daniel Andrews.

After enjoying the fruits of peace for nine years, in 1722 another Indian war broke out, though no great violence was done during the three years that it continued. In the autumn of 1724, the inhabitants of the frontier towns on Merrimac River seem to have been dissatisfied with the manner of carrying on the war with the Indians, and wished to adopt offensive measures Accordingly a company was organized at Dunstable, of which John Lovewell was captain, Josiah Farwell lieutenant, and Jonathan Robbins ensign These officers offered a petition to the Legislature, in which they say, "that if said company may be allowed five shillings per day in case they kill any Indians, and possess their scalps, they will employ in Indian-hunting one whole year; and, if they do not within that time kill any, they are content to be allowed nothing for their wages, time, and trouble." * This petition was granted, changing the terms into a bounty of one hundred pounds for every scalp taken during one year. Capt. Lovewell was a bold and adventurous officer, and, stimulated by this offer, he immediately led his company against the hostile savages. A part of his company was composed of Boxford men, — Phineas Foster, Jacob Ames, Jeremiah Perley, Jethro Ames, Jacob Perley, and perhaps others.

In February, 1725, the last year of the war, the company, numbering sixty-two persons, began their march on snowshoes, carrying their provisions on their backs Toward Winnipiseogee Lake (N. H) they came on the Indian trail. During their march they discovered a bear in his den in a hollow tree, which, by help of their dogs, they killed. He could not be got out where he went in, having become so fat during his winter's residence. They soon had a fire, and roasted, and feasted on, his flesh, — a very timely supply, as their provisions were nearly exhausted Continuing their march, they soon came to the above-named lake, where they lost the trail, there being no snow on the ice There appeared to follow the Indians a large flock

* *History of Dunstable*, p. 111

of ravens, lighting on and hovering over the trees on an island of the lake, indicating their situation, which was also considered ominous of the destruction of their enemies.

The party, soon after following these ravens, found themselves within hearing of the Indians, who were hunting beaver and other game; and, having had a "great hunt" that day, Capt. Lovewell thought best to halt, and wait till the Indians, from eating heartily at supper, should sleep soundly. They built no fires, and took the precaution to tie up the mouths of the dogs, and keep them close, so as to surprise the enemy at midnight. They attacked them in camp while asleep, about one o'clock, killing eight and wounding one; another, in attempting to run away, was overtaken by the dogs, and despatched, so that all were destroyed, nine men and a boy. The boy was armed with a lancet on a pole, as was supposed, to drive and torment prisoners. It was thought these Indians were going to Cocheco (now Dover), to destroy the few families settled there. The Indians were scalped, and their bodies left as food for the ravens.* Lovewell and his men then marched to Dover, N. H., thence to Andover, Mass., where they were entertained at Joseph Parker's, from which place the men probably separated to their respective homes, without the loss of a single man.

In 1733, as payment for their services, the Legislature granted the soldiers in this expedition wild land in Suncook, N. H., and Petersham, Mass.

After the roads were laid out, the minds of our early settlers were troubled about keeping them repaired for summer travel. This was at first accomplished by hiring men to do the work, paying them out of the regular town-tax; but Oct. 22, 1717, the town voted to repair the highways, by a separate rate assessed for that purpose, to equal a certain sum annually; also, the right was given to each

* See *The Book of the Indians*, Book III., Chap. IX.

highway-tax-payer to work out his part of the tax if he desired to do so. The town was divided into wards, and in each ward was appointed a surveyor to superintend operations, and to collect the highway-tax. The following rates or prices of labor were adopted by the town two years later : "Those that labored from the beginning of May till the first of September shall have two shillings and six pence per day ; and from the first of September to the end of the year, two shillings per day ; and one shilling a day for a pair of oxen, and six pence a day for a *tumberell* or cart."

In 1751 sixteen pounds were raised to repair the highways that year; also, "voted to allow one shilling and eight pence per day for such as shall work at mending roads ; and eight pence per day for a yoke of oxen, and four pence for a cart." In 1761 each one had to work out his highway-tax in the months of May and June.

In 1780 £3,600 (which, by the depreciation of the currency at that time, would only be, in gold or silver, £96)* were raised by the town to repair the highways that year. The following year, £3,000 (about £75 in gold) were raised for that purpose.

Before the year 1788 the roads were not cleared of snow in winter. They were left as the heavy storms of years ago left them, filled several feet deep with the snow, and level with the tops of the walls, — the snow-storms of those days being much worse than those of the present time. Those

---

* This item shows how almost valueless was the paper currency which was issued by the Government at the close of the Revolution. A week's board then in paper money was $105; but, in silver or gold, only about $2 or $2.50 People were greatly involved in debt, there was but little coin in circulation, and paper money and public securities had become nearly worthless ; and many men, by taking this emission-money in payment for their sales, were ruined. In 1780 one gold dollar was worth $4,000 in paper money. The *new* emission-money, which was soon after issued, was worth considerably more than the old.

were the days of snow-shoes, and horseback-riding, which was the prevailing custom of the inhabitants of New England from the time of the first settlement up to the period of which we are writing. But about this time wheel-vehicles began to be more common ; and sleighs were introduced, which bore off a large degree of popularity among the inhabitants. These improvements necessitated the removal of the snow from the roads so as to make them passable.

In 1799 the town voted to allow a man seventy-five, a yoke of oxen forty, a cart twenty, and a plough forty cents per day, for working in repairing the highway. This rate has grown to a larger and larger sum, until now the price per hour for a man is fifteen or twenty cents. The law in regard to a highway-tax-payer's right to work out his tax on the road has been also changed to a law that gives the surveyor the sole right to work out the entire ward's tax himself if he chooses to do so.

A petition signed by Samuel Symonds, John Howe, Francis Elliot, Daniel Kenney, Edward Nichols, and nine or ten others, praying that they may be set off to join with others belonging to the neighboring towns, to be made a separate town, was presented to the town at their annual meeting in March, 1727   It was put to vote, and passed in the negative. At the next annual meeting it was again presented, put to vote, and passed in the affirmative. These, together with other families belonging to the towns of Topsfield, Salem, and Andover, after obtaining leave from their respective towns to be incorporated into a new town, petitioned the General Court to grant them a township charter. Their request was complied with; and they were incorporated, under an act of that honorable body, June 20, 1728, as a town, bearing the name of Middleton. Hitherto Boxford and Salem adjoined ; now Middleton was located between them. The line was consequently changed to that which now divides Middleton and Boxford. Some six hundred acres were taken from Boxford, and the population was reduced about a hundred, by this subtraction.

It had been the custom for many years to have timber cut in New Hampshire on the banks of the Merrimac River, and floated down the stream to the coast, where it was transformed into vessels. Most, and perhaps all, of this timber was used at Newburyport and Salisbury. There being nothing but the exertions of the ship-builders to stop the logs from being carried out at sea when a storm was sweeping along the coast, thousands of tons of valuable ship-timber were thus often lost. The people of northern Essexshire at length, deeming it too great a loss to the colony, petitioned the General Court to have a boom placed across the river between Gage's and Griffin's ferries, just above Haverhill. The Boxford petition was sent in February, 1727, and was signed by Stephen Peabody and Jonathan Tyler, in behalf of the town. These petitions were granted by the Court at their next sitting. The boom was to stop the logs, from which they were conveyed to the ship-builders, probably by being made into rafts.*

A tannery was erected here about 1725 by Francis Perley. It was in operation in 1751, and later. He resided on the farm, now in the possession of Mr. DeWitt C. Mighill, the old house in which he lived having been removed and the present dwelling erected, some sixty years ago. Mr. Perley hired some workmen, and, from some accounts that we have seen, we should judge that he did considerable business. This was the first tannery erected in the town; and, until near the close of the eighteenth century, in it were probably tanned all the hides produced by the farmers of Boxford.

Jacob Smith and Ebenezer Sherwin were the coopers at the time of which we are writing. Zebediah and Jeremiah

* See the original petition in the Mass. Archives, Vol. CV., p. 124.

Foster were wheelwrights. Josiah Bridges was a black-smith about 1700. John Stewart was a blacksmith about 1730; and Solomon Stewart kept a kind of store, we presume, as we find him selling stationery and legal blanks. Ephraim Smith was the only cabinet-maker in the town at this time, of which we have learned. John Woster was a basket-maker, and made most of his neighbors' baskets.

Nathan Dresser moved from Rowley to Boxford in 1728, and immediately erected a blacksmith-shop near his residence on the old Dresser road, in the East Parish. Here he did an extensive business. His son, John Dresser, born here in 1735, worked at that trade with his father when he became old enough, and, after his father's death, carried on the business alone. John had a son Nathan born to him in 1790, who became his successor in the business. Nathan Dresser died Sept. 13, 1829; and his widow Susanna, the following year, married Elijah Wilson of Salem, N.H., who resided on the old place, and demolished the shop about 1835. In shoeing horses in early days, it was customary for the customer to furnish the stock, — if he did not he would be charged so much extra for finding it. The shoes were manufactured only as fast as they were needed. Such items as this render the early accounts interesting: "June 22, 1735, cr. by shoeing horse, all round; I found iron for one shoe." The coal used by the smith was the charcoal of our ancestors, which was manufactured by himself or some of his neighbors. It was not uncommon among the wealthier families to have kilns, in which they burned their charcoal. Some families in ye olden time did little else than burn charcoal; one of these being undoubtedly Richard Tyler's, as he appears to sell considerable coal, and buy a great deal of "swamp-wood," out of which it was manufactured.

The old cemetery in the West Parish was the first one used there. The most ancient gravestone now standing

there bears the following inscription, which proves its
antiquity : —

> HERE LYES BURIED
> THE BODY OF
> HEPHZIBAH Yᵉ WIFE
> OF JABEZ DORMAN
> WHO DIED FEBRUARY
> Yᵉ 4 1716 IN Yᵉ
> 35 YEAR OF HER
> AGE.

In May, 1785, the parish bought of Mr. Tyler Porter, for
thirty shillings, a piece of land, which they annexed to the
original area, and " fenced the front side with a handsome
stone wall, four feet high, and the other three sides with a
common stone wall, three and a half feet high." This is
probably the same wall which now surrounds the premises,
except on the south side. A few years ago another strip
of ground was annexed to the south side.

The Harmony Cemetery near the residence of B. S.
Barnes, Esq., is nearly, if not quite, as old as the preceding. The oldest headstone there bears the following inscription : —

> HERE LYES BURIED
> THE BODY, OF FAITH
> BOOTMAN, Yᵉ WIFE OF
> MATHEW BOOTMAN
> WHO DIED MARCH, Yᵉ
> 4, 1717 & IN THE
> 23 YEAR OF HER
> AGE.
>
> UNDER THIS TURF YOU MAY BEHOLD
> A LAMB OF GOD FET FOR Yᵉ FOLD.

The original plot was only about half the size of the
present. It extended toward the road as far as the tomb
of Thomas Perley. June 3, 1766, it was enlarged by the

purchase of the new part, for four pounds and three shillings, of Thomas Wood (who lived across the road), by twenty-three * of the families in the vicinity.

The first mention made of colored people in Boxford is about 1730. From that time to 1780 the names of some twenty-five appear upon the records   On the adoption of the State Constitution, in 1780, they all became free; after that time but few, perhaps not more than three or four, resided in the town.   At present there are three residents of color.

The following are some of the names of the early slaves, viz.: *Tamsin, Notur, Flora, Candace, Rose, Cæsar, Primus, Hagar, Titus, Phillis, Dinah, Scipio,* and *Pompey.*   Tamsin belonged to Benjamin Porter; was born about 1720, and had several children.   She was noted for the foul use of strong liquor.   Mark Snelling was a mulatto, born about 1720, and lived most of the time with Dr. Wood.   He took to himself a wife, and became the father of Asa Snelling (who died at Phineas Perley's, in 1823, aged eighty-six years), whom our older residents remember.   Dinah, born about 1759, was a slave of Deacon Thomas Chadwick from four years of age.   About 1800 she went to live with her sister in North Andover.   In 1826 she was still living there, having been almost blind for some time.   The families of Chadwick and Porter probably owned most of the slaves, though several families held them as servants. The Rev. John Cushing had a small negro-boy named Timon.   Most of the slaves appear to have been owned in the West Parish.

A queer character, who was at the height of her career a

---

* Their names were as follows, viz · Thomas Perley, Moses Perley, Paul Prichard, Jonathan Wood, Aaron Wood, William Perley, Daniel Nurse, Asa Perley, Joseph Hale, jun , Moses Hale, Francis Perley, Solomon Wood, Huldah Perley, Nathan Wood, Joseph Hale, Richard Peabody, Nathaniel Perley, Nathaniel Perkins, John Butman, Jacob Hazen, Ezekiel Jewett, Benjamin Perley, and John Hale, all of Boxford

century and a half ago, was an old woman known for miles around as "Mother Dowen" She lived in a cave, which was an excavation made on the southern declivity of a hill, not far from the residence of Mr. Gardner S. Morse. The sides of the cave were stoned up, and the top covered with boards or similar material Her maiden name was Mary Snelling. She had several children, and her husband (Robert Dowen, whom she married in Haverhill, Nov. 13, 1719) was dead. For a living, she stole sheep, and, to hide her thefts, threw the refuse of the animals into Mare Pond. One of her children, Mary, was admitted to the Second Church in 1744, and in 1751 married Amos Foster of Upper Ashuelot. Another, John, born about 1727, was bound out by the selectmen, June 21, 1739, to Ebenezer Webster, a farmer of Haverhill, for nine years and six months.

CHAPTER VII.

INCORPORATION OF THE PARISHES, &c.

NOTHING occurred out of the regular routine of a pastor's duties during the first thirty years of Rev. Mr. Rogers' pastorate. In that time, however, great changes had been going on in the society. As we have before inferred, the meeting-house had been rather shabbily built, and before it had been in existence thirty years was regarded as almost unfit for use. In a warrant calling a town-meeting in December, 1730, an article was inserted to see if the town would build a *new* meeting-house. It was put to vote, and passed in the negative. It was again voted on in January, 1734, with the same result. The reason of this was, that the north-western part of the town had increased in population to such an extent that they were able to maintain a minister among themselves. Most of them attended and belonged to the churches in Bradford and Andover. In 1730, or about that time, they conceived the idea of erecting a church of their own. In view of this, they had repeatedly resisted the older part of the town in their endeavors to obtain a vote of the town to build a new meeting-house.

Before the north-western inhabitants endeavored to be separated from the south part of the town, and made into a lawful precinct by themselves, they had got their timber prepared for the frame, and all the materials ready to prosecute the erection of a meeting-house, so that it was raised on the thirteenth day of June, 1734, and finished so that they had preaching in it that summer. This edifice was situated in the "meeting-house lot," a little way south of the new cemetery. In the following winter they prepared a petition, which they sent to the General Court, praying that they might be set off, and be incorporated into a separate precinct. The following is a copy of the petition : —

"A petition of Samuel Tyler & other inhabitants of the northerly part of the Town of Boxford shewing that they live at a great distance from the place of public worship in said town, so that many of their familys are detained at home on the Lord's day by reason of that difficulty, that they have erected a meeting house in that part of the Town, And at their own Charge supported the Preaching of the Gospel among them, and therefore praying that they and their families and estates may be freed from the charge (which they till now have borne) of supporting the minister in the other part of the town and be erected into a separate precinct by the following Bounds, Viz. From a pine tree standing in Andover line northerly to the lower end of long pond, then upon the pond to the upper end thereof, then between land of Dr Wood and Worster's farm and land of Jonathan Kymball and Samuel Spafford to Rogers tree, and so bounded on Rowley, Bradford and Andover."

The petition was read in the House of Representatives on Thursday, April 10, 1735 ; and the petitioners were ordered to serve the town of Boxford with a copy of the petition, that the town might show cause, if they had any, why the prayer of the petitioners should not be granted

Three families there were against their being organized

into a separate parish, but were desirous of being annexed to Bradford. These families (John Peabody's, John Hovey's, and George Carleton's) prepared and sent to the General Court a petition embodying their views of the matter, to counteract that of Samuel Tyler and others. In the Council it was read, and referred to the next May session.

The subject came up before the Court the second time, Wednesday, June 4, 1735, when the petition (Samuel Tyler and others') was again read, together with the answer of the town of Boxford ; and the parties being heard at the "board," and the matter fully considered, it was ordered that (in answer to the petition of Samuel Tyler and others) Samuel Thaxter, Joseph Dwight, and John Cushing, jun., Esqs., should be a committee to view the situation, and consider the circumstances of the petitioners, as well as the petition of John Peabody, John Hovey, and George Carleton, with their situation and circumstances, seasonably notifying the town of Boxford of their committee, and that they report to the Court at their next sitting what they judge proper to be done thereon ; and that the petition aforesaid be referred to the next sitting of the Court for further consideration. On the same day the petition of John Peabody and others was brought up, but was referred to the next sitting of the Court. The committee of the Legislature came to Boxford, and after examining all parties interested, and the situation of the premises, reported that the prayer of the petition of Samuel Tyler and others ought to be granted. Accordingly, June 28, 1735, the Legislature ordered that the report of the committee should be accepted, and that the petitioners, together with John Peabody and others above mentioned, and their families and estates, should be set off " a distinct precinct," and that the charge of the committee, which amounted to thirteen pounds and three pence, be paid by the petitioners   The Council con-

curred with the House in the order, July 1. The East
Parish also came into existence at the same time.

In the House of Representatives, Wednesday, July 2,
1735, it was ordered "that Mr. Luke Hovey, one of the
principal inhabitants of the new precinct, be authorized and
empowered to assemble the freeholders and other qualified
voters, as soon as may be, in some convenient place, to
make choice of principal officers to stand till the anniversary meeting in March next." Accordingly a parish-meeting
was called, and held on the twenty-second day of the same
month, this being their first parish-meeting. The following officers were chosen: For assessors, Cornelius Brown,
John Kimball, and John Woster; collector of taxes, John
Chadwick; treasurer, Capt. John Tyler; and parish-clerk,
Zebadiah Foster. Mr. Foster held the office of clerk until
1747, when Joseph Hovey was chosen; Mr. Hovey was
superseded by Stephen Runnels in 1763, and Mr. Runnels
by William Foster in 1771. John Cushing, son of the
first minister in the West Parish, was chosen clerk the
next year, and held the office for a long period.

At a meeting Aug. 12, the parish "voted to appropriate
fifty pounds for preaching, as far as it will go from the time
they were made a parish." At this meeting it was voted to
have the pews of the church in two bodies. They had not
built any of the pews as yet, nor laid any of the floor in the
galleries, which was voted to be done. Aug. 28, they chose
Daniel Wood, Job Tyler, and John Woster, a committee to
oversee and manage the work of finishing the meeting-
house so far as it was voted. At this meeting Ensign
.Luke Hovey was ordered to provide "a Law Book, a Clerk
book & an assessors Book," the two last being well preserved at the present time. It was also voted that the first
Tuesday in March should be the day of their annual meeting Dec. 1, 1735, it was voted "to Build the Gallerys
Stears and Build the fronts of all the Gallery, — and three

Seats In Each Gallery." Feb. 12, 1735–36, voted "to Lath and plaister the meeting house and to putt In Joyce In the Beames to plaister on and to Case the Winddows." March 2, voted to "Ceaill the meeting house With Boards from the Bottom to the Bottom of the Windows Round." Also, voted to "plaister yᵉ meetting house overhead and under the gallieryes With the Walls, only what is Excepted In the above Sd voat."

Before the parish was incorporated as a legal district, the inhabitants had preaching among them for some time ; but, as no record was commenced until after its incorporation, we have no means of knowing the particulars. Their records say that Mr. John Rogers preached until Dec. 1, 1735, for which service he was paid two pounds per Sunday. Feb. 12, 1735–36, it was voted to hire Mr. John Cushing to preach the next quarter, which he did. When this quarter was out, April 22, 1736, the parish voted to set Thursday, May 13, apart as "a day of fasting in order to call a minister and take advice of other ministers." Revs. John Rogers of Boxford, Barnard of Andover, Parsons of Bradford, and Chandler of Rowley, were invited "as yᵉ ministers to give advice & assist in yᵉ Sd day of fasting." Rev. John Cushing, who was then supplying the pulpit, was evidently proposed; as a committee was chosen, May 25, "to discourse with Mr Cushing, and know the terms he will settle on, or whether he inclines to settle."

Dec. 9, 1736, was kept as a day of fasting and prayer by the people of the West Parish, previous to the ordination, and in order to the gathering of the church, at which several of the neighboring ministers were invited to be present. The exercises were as follows : Rev. Mr. Barnard of Andover began with prayer ; Rev. Mr. Parsons of Bradford preached from Eph. ii. 20 ; and Rev. Mr. Barnard (?) "incorporated the church." As soon as it was incorporated, the church gave a unanimous call to Rev. Mr. Cushing, who was present, "to settle in the work of ye Gospel ministry among them ;" to which invitation he assented, as he had done before the church .was fully empowered to call a minister. The 29th of the same month, Thursday, was appointed as the day of ordination. The neighboring churches were invited to be present by their elders and delegates, to assist in the ordination. On the day appointed the Rev. Mr. Cushing was ordained to the gospel ministry there by the following exercises : Rev Mr. Balch of Bradford began with prayer ; Rev. Mr Phillips of Andover preached from Matt. xxviii. 18–20 ; Rev. Mr. Cushing of Salisbury gave the charge ; Rev. Mr. Barnard of Andover gave the right hand of fellowship ; Rev. Mr. Parsons of Bradford concluded with prayer ; and the four last-mentioned gentlemen imposed hands.

The church when at first incorporated consisted of members dismissed from the First Church in Boxford, and the First Church in Bradford. The following, who signed the covenant when the church was embodied, were dismissed from the First Church in Bradford, viz. : Cornelius Brown, Nathan Eames, Daniel Wood, Stephen Runnells, Luke Hovey, jun , Joseph Hovey, Jonathan Sherwin, Ebenezer Sherwin, Caleb Brown, Jonathan Cole, John Crooke, Mary Eames, Sarah Eames, Sarah Wood, Dorcas Hovey, Mary Sherwin, Hephzibah Sherwin, and Judith Cole ; and the following were dismissed from the First Church in Boxford, viz. : Luke Hovey, John Hovey, Zebadiah Foster, John Kimball, Nathan Kimball, John Woster, James Scales, Mehitable Chadwick, Margaret Foster, Sarah Porter, Elizabeth Tyler, Sarah Spofford, Elizabeth Tyler, Elizabeth Kimball, Sarah Kimball, Ruth Tyler, Mary Woster, and Mary Scales

Jan. 23, 1736–37, John Chadwick, Samuel Spofford, Richard Tyler, and Samuel Tyler were admitted as members of the church upon their dismission from the First Church in Boxford. The same day Jeremiah Eames was admitted a member of the church upon his dismission from the First Church in Bradford,

The original covenant of the church was as follows: —

"We whose Names are hereunto Subfcribed apprehending ourselves called of God to join together in *Church-State*, and to Embody ourselves In Order to become *a particular Church* or Flock of yᵉ Lord Jesus; (acknowledging our unworthiness of Such an honor & Priviledge) We do piofess & declare our serious Belief of yᵉ Christian religion, as Contained in yᵉ Sacred Sciiptures, and as expressed in yᵉ Confession of Faith, Commonly received by yᵉ Churches in this Land, heartily resolving to Conform our Lives to yᵉ Rules of that holy religion as Long as we Live. And therefore

" We do now in yᵉ presence of God himself, his holy Angels & all his Servants here present, give up ourselves unto yᵉ Lord Jehovah, who is yᵉ Father, yᵉ Son & yᵉ holy Ghost, and avouch *Him* this day to be our God.

"We give up ourselve to yᵉ Lord Jesus Christ, relying on him as our Priest, Prophet & King, promising by yᵉ help of his Grace to glorify God in all the Duties of a Godly Sober & righteous Life; and very particularly to uphold Family & Closet worship, and to attend yᵉ Publick worship of God, the Sacraments of yᵉ New Testament the Discipline of Christ's Kingdom, and all his holy Institutions in Communion with one another, & Caiefully avoiding all Sinfull Contentions.

" We do give ourselves one to another in yᵉ Lord, Covenanting to walk together *as a Church of Christ* according to yᵉ Rules of God's holy Word, promising faithfully to watch over one another in Brotherly Love and to Submit ourselves to yᵉ Discipline & power of Christ in his Church, and Duly to attend yᵉ Seals and Censures, or whatever ordinances Christ has commanded to be observed by his people, So far as yᵉ Lord by his word and Spirit has or shall reveal unto us to be our Duty.

" We also present, this Day, our offspring with us unto the Lord promising to give them a Christian Education, and avouching yᵉ Lord to be not only our God but also yᵉ God of our children, Esteeming it a very high favour that yᵉ most high will accept of us, and our children with us to be his People.

" And now, that we may keep this our Covenant with God & with one another, we desire to Deny ourselves and to depend wholly on yᵉ free mercy of God, and yᵉ merritts & Grace of Christ Jesus . and wherein we shall fail to wait on God for Pardon thro' yᵉ name of Chⁱist, beseeching yᵉ Lord Jehovah to own us as *a Church of Christ* that He would take delight ⁴to Dwell among, and that his blessing may be upon us & on our families, and his glorious Kingdom be advanced by us. Amen."

Mr. Cushing was paid, in the early years of his minis-try, one hundred and forty pounds in money, and twenty-five cords of wood, annually. His settlement fund was three hundred pounds. In 1748 his salary was increased to three hundred pounds. In December of that year the parish voted "to give yᵉ Revᵈ Mʳ Cuſhing 400 & Twenty pounds old Tenʳ for his Salery for ye year Ensuing."

It was voted, Feb. 4, 1736–37, to purchase for the observ-ance of the Lord's Supper "proper and sufficient uten-sils," consisting of two flagons, four tankards, and two dishes, together with suitable table-linen ; also, a baptism-basin. The church was presented shortly after with four tankards by the wife of Ephraim Foster, two dishes by the wife of John Foster, a baptism-basin by the wife of Nathan Eames, and another tankard by the wife of John Woster.

The deacons were chosen Feb. 28, 1736–37. The first deacon was John Woster, and the second, Caleb Brown. The sacrament was to be administered on the first Sunday of each odd month (January, March, May, &c.). Ebenezer Sherwin was voted to "tune the Psalm ;" in 1748 Luke Hovey, jun , was chosen to that office.

The General Court, June 13, 1740, ordered the families of David, Ephraim, John, and Moses Foster, Joseph Rob-inson, Joseph Robinson, jun., and Samuel and Timothy Sessions of Andover, with their lands, to be annexed to the Second Parish. During the following five years several more Andover families were annexed to the parish : some of them who were subsequently annexed to the parish were

the Barkers, Merrills, and Lacys. These families have
continued to belong to that parish, the present parish-clerk
being an Andover man

After this date (1735) the town ceased to have any voice
in church matters. Each parish afterward separately conducted its ecclesiastical affairs.

The first meeting held by the East Parish was on
Monday, Nov. 17, 1735, at which Thomas Redington was
chosen parish-clerk He held the office until 1742, with
one exception, in the year 1737, when Joseph Hale filled
the position For a number of years, commencing 1743,
Amos Perley was the clerk.

In 1736 Josiah Batchelder, on recompense of three
pounds and ten shillings, surveyed the parish for the purpose
of finding the centre, in which they proposed to set their
new meeting-house, to the building of which none were
now opposed. Oct 5, 1736, it was voted that, when the
parish erected their meeting-house, it should be set on
the hill behind Mr. Rogers' residence, — where the old one
stood. It was also voted that it should be built thirty-eight
feet wide, forty-eight feet long, and twenty-four feet stud ;
"the meeting-house shall be studded and boarded, and
clapboarded on the stud on the outside, and lathed and
plastered on the inside, both on the ends and sides
and also overhead under the beams ; and that there shall
be a fashionable roof, well finished, the boards pointed with
lime, and good decent windows, agreeable to the quality of
the house" Toward defraying the expense of erecting
the meeting-house the parish granted six hundred pounds.

Nov. 10, 1740, the parish voted that their meeting-house
should stand on "the northwardly corner of the pasture
that was purchased of John Buswell, deceased, a little to
the south, or south-west, of the place where Mr. Batchelder
declared the centre of the parish was." It was ultimately
placed in front of the present meeting-house. Whether

this is the spot designated by the above vote, or not, we do not know. At the same meeting it was voted to "repair the old meeting-house, so that it would be tight and warm till the new one should be ready, in the following manner, viz. : to shingle the foreside of the roof, clapboard both ends and the foreside, make new doors, new window-frames and casements, reset the glass, and, where the glass is broken and gone, to put in new panes."

June 12, 1744, it was voted to "plaster the meeting-house under the beams and down to the sills, and under the galleries." It was also voted "to have an alley made, leading from the fore door to the pulpit, the width of the door; and a row of seats each side of the alley, and a convenient alley elsewhere." The whole was to be "underpinned well and pointed with lime." Feb. 13, 1745, it was voted that there should be twenty-one windows in the meeting-house, to be arranged in two tiers, one above the other. Those in the lower tier were to contain twenty-eight, and those in the second tier twenty-four, panes each, each pane to be seven by nine inches. The pulpit was lighted by a window; one was also placed in each gable. A large "sounding-board" was placed directly above the pulpit. Its dimensions were so great that it seemed as if the slender rod which held it in its position in the air would give way, and it would come dashing down on the parson's head.

The meeting-house was so far finished * that the sale of the pews took place Sept. 17, 1745, at an average of about twenty-seven pounds apiece. They were bid off by the following persons : 1. Robert Andrews; 2. John Symonds; 3. John Peabody, jun.; 4. Francis Perley; 5. Nathaniel Symonds; 6. Joseph Hale, jun.; 7. Thomas Perley, jun.; 8. Thomas Andrews, jun.; 9 widow Martha Dorman; 10. (was not sold); 11. Amos Perley; 12. Asa Perley; 13.

---

* On a timber in the frame of the old edifice were engraved the figures "1742." This was probably the year in which it was raised.

Oliver Andrews, 14 John Wood; 15 Jonathan Bixby; 16. John Hale, 17 Jeremiah Perley and Thomas Redington; 18. Aaron Kimball.

The meeting-house was accepted by the parish Dec. 10, 1745. Its entire cost was about fifteen hundred pounds. The old church continued to be used until the first Sunday in January, 1747, when religious services were first held in the new meeting-house Probably the reason of this was that no regular services were held in the parish, in consequence of the dissolution of Mr. Rogers' ministerial relation with them in 1743 ; after which for many years the church was kept in a complete hubbub.

What the cause of Mr Rogers' dissolution of his relation with the church was we have not been able to determine. Perhaps the sketch of the life of his son, Rev John Rogers, jun, may throw some light upon it, although it might have been from secular causes, or he might have wished to retire from the ministry altogether, which he did The house and land that had been first owned by Rev. Mr. Symmes had been conferred upon Mr. Rogers, under the same conditions. After his dismission, according to the agreement, he should have given up the house and land to the town ; but he refused to do it, and therefore the parish were very wroth against him. They tried all possible persuasions to have him do as they wished; but he remained stubborn, and would not give in. Charges were also instituted against him, but he would not quail to them. What these charges were has not come to our notice.

Mr. Rogers removed to his son's in Leominster just before 1750. After his removal several letters passed between him and the society, regarding the charges, &c, laid to him. One, dated Jan. 8, 1751, is all that we have found entire. It contains some very spicy clauses, and is withal very interesting We insert it in full : —

"Beloved brethren : In yours of Dec 21, 1750, you say 'we should be glad to be informed what council you esteem to be regular,' &c.   I will make you glad   Such a council is one chosen, the one half by you, the other by me, according to the platform of the Word of God, and, as in such a case as this, there must be a concurrence of each party ; so the business of a council in general is to judge of the Christian conduct of the members or officers of a church : to receive and forgive the penitent, to eject obstinate offenders or heretics after the second admonition, they to be esteemed as heathens or publicans. Ecclesiastical council is not as a civil court about seculars, but spirituals, of a church.   Not coercive by mulcts corporal or pecuniary but suasory and directive, to the unholy and profane, &c.   See 1 Tim. i, 9, 10 verses, &c   I desire you may have the preeminence to choose first for you are many.   I will take your leavings to fill up the council, to be held in Boxford when and where you please.   But send me a letter to inform me in the affairs : what you have done.   As to the charges,* I don't think it hard for you who are rich to bear them, but it would not be prudence for me, who have little, or nothing, to promise to pay till you pay me, &c.   Nor do I see any reason for the poor accused to oblige himself to help the potent accusers to defray the charges of their prowess against him.   Some, it may be, will say 'if you will not join with us in bearing the charges as well as the result of the council, we will have none.'   But, I say, where then is your zeal for purging out the OLD LEAVEN, for the reclaiming or punishing the scandalous brother.   But, if you had used the previous steps which our supreme Lord has prescribed to gain a brother, you should have seen upon due conviction his confession, free and public, enough.   But seeing you love to skip or stride over to the council I am willing they should hear all those things my visible accusers lay to my charge, and if the accusations be proved by authentic, impartial, unbiased witnesses, I will bear the reproof due to me, for 'if the righteous smite me it shall be a kindness,' &c.   They may show me my transgressions and the error of my ways more clearly and fully than I have yet known, to my further humiliation and repentance.   I believe in the future judgment, about which I have more concern than any human, and know I must ere long appear before a far more awful and strict tribunal to give an account of all the thoughts, words, and actions of my whole life, my principles, motives, ends, and manner of my conduct in the sight of God and man; 'for God will bring every work into judgment with every secret thing, whether good or

* Charges or expenses of the council

evil.' The Lord enable us to live in the exercise of repentance toward
God, against whom we have sinned, —oh, how many ways, how griev-
ously!—and that we may live in the exercise of faith on our L. J. C ,*
by whom we receive the atonement and consequently love and new obedience and patience that we may be followers of those who through
this faith and patience are now inheriting the promises, always looking
to Jesus Christ, the author and finisher of our faith, &c. In a word my
constant prayer is, that we may be found in him, not having on *our
own* righteousness, but that which is through the faith of Christ, the
righteousness which is of God by faith.   Amen and amen.

"JAN. 8, 1751.

" P. S. Though I would pay due deference to your letter of the 21
of Dec., 1750, yet I must be excused if I say such is my dulness of
apprehension that I see not the least shadow of reason to alter my
opinion expressed in my letter to you of Dec. 1, 1750, concerning
yours of July 10, containing your articles of charge."

We cannot find that any council was held, and do not
think there was.   Their disagreement was continued year
in and year out, neither party coming to terms.   Mr.
Rogers would not give up his title to the house and land
until the parish paid him the balance of his salary, and the
parish was as contrary the other way.   The parish-clerk
says, "our long perplexed and distressed circumstances"
were settled in March, 1752; but the acknowledgment of
settlement is dated Sept. 7, 1761.   Mr. Rogers died in
1755, leaving the matter unsettled, which was continued
by his widow, the executrix of his will ; and after her death,
which happened two years later, it was carried on by her
executors, her sons John and Nathaniel Rogers of Leominster, who settled for the sum of £210, and gave a
paper to the parish, of which the following is a copy, for
the acknowledgment of the receipt of the money, which
ended the trouble.

"This may certify that we, the subscribers, John Rogers of Leominster, in the County of Worcester, in the Province of the Massa-

* Lord Jesus Christ.

chusetts Bay, in New England, clerk, and Nathaniel Rogers, of the same town, county, and province, gentleman, have, as executors of the last will and testament of Susanna Rogers, late of said Leominster, deceased. received of Thomas Perley, Thomas Andrews, and Solomon Wood, a committee and agents for the First Parish in Boxford, the sum of two hundred and ten pounds, lawful money, which we acknowledge is in full for all the demands we have upon the First Parish in Boxford as executors of the will of said Susanna Rogers, or as heirs to the Rev. John Rogers, late of Leominster, deceased, formerly the pastor of the said First Parish in Boxford, respecting any contracts between the town of Boxford and the said John Rogers, originally their pastor, respecting his salary, or on account of any votes passed by the said First Parish in Boxford, touching salary, or maintenance, and the arrears of salary, or on account of any demand, real or personal, either upon the said town or First Parish in Boxford, from *the beginning of the world* until this day, either upon account of heirship, or executorship, to the late said John and Susanna; for which consideration we do by these presents finally acquit and discharge and covenant to indemnify the town and First Parish in Boxford of and from all demands, as well real as personal of the said John, his heirs, executors, or administrators of what name or nature soever. Sealed with our seals, and dated at Leominster, September the seventh, one thousand seven hundred and sixty-one, and in the first year of his Majesty's reign.

"Signed, sealed, and delivered   "JOHN ROGERS   [SEAL]
    "In presence of

"JONATHAN WHITE,   "NATHLL ROGERS.   [SEAL]
"THOMAS WILDER."

Rev. Mr. Rogers was son of Jeremiah Rogers of Salem, who belonged to a family which claims the distinction of descent from "the martyr," "the first of that blessed company who suffered in the reign of Mary," and which is really entitled to the renown of having furnished to the New-England churches, through five generations, some of their most able, faithful, and godly ministers. One of our John's descendants has a Bible which is claimed to be the one which his ancestor bore to the stake at his execution. It is partly burnt

Felt says that Mr. Rogers' parents seem to have been

in humble life and indigent condition. (Felt's *Annals*, p. 380.) He graduated at Harvard College in 1705, and four years afterwards was settled over the Boxford church, which was probably the only place where he was ever settled as a pastor. He married Susanna Marston of Salem, March 24, 1710 (?), who survived him two years, he dying in 1755, and she in 1757, in Leominster. Nine children were born to them, viz.: Susanna, b. June 28, 1711; John, b Sept. 24, 1712 (see his biography); Benjamin, bapt. Oct 24, 1714; Mehitable, bapt Aug., 1716; Nathaniel, bapt. July 8, 1718; Lydia, bapt. Aug 7, 1720; Eunice, bapt Aug., 1724; Lucia, bapt. Feb. 5, 1727; Samuel, bapt. July 5, 1730. The eldest child, Susanna, married, Feb. 18, 1735, Dr. Jacob Peabody, a physician in Leominster for many years; Benjamin married Alice (Perley) Foster, and lived in Boxford; Lydia married Abijah Smith; and Nathaniel married Rebecca Symonds, and lived in Boxford and Leominster.

During the thirty-four years of Mr. Rogers' ministry here two hundred and two persons were admitted to the church. More persons were admitted, on a yearly average, than during the ministry of any other clergyman that was ever settled in Boxford. Mr. Rogers was very forcible in his speech, and earnest in its application to the desired end. The cause of his falling out with the church was probably his bluntness or frankness in preaching, which characteristic will always produce enemies even in the pulpit. We know of nothing against his moral or Christian character, but rather the reverse

CHAPTER VIII.

1730-1770.

OVERSEERS OF THE POOR — DEER-REEVES — SCHOOLS AND
SCHOOLMASTERS — PEARL'S MILL. — THE "WOOD-SPELL." —
TROUBLE IN THE SECOND CHURCH — MILITARY MATTERS —
FRENCH WAR. — CAPT. ISRAEL HERRICK. — FRENCH NEU-
TRALS. — FRENCH AND INDIAN WAR. — CAMPAIGNS OF 1759
AND 1760. — REV. ELIZUR HOLYOKE SETTLED OVER THE FIRST
CHURCH. — COVENANT OF FIRST CHURCH OF 1759 — NEW
SINGING-BOOKS INTRODUCED INTO THE CHURCHES. — EMIGRA-
TION — DEATH OF REV. MR CUSHING — HIS MINISTRY AND
LIFE — ATTEMPT TO SETTLE ANOTHER MINISTER. — HERRICK'S
SAW-MILL. — TAILORS. — A POEM OF SOLOMON WOOD'S —
FISH TROUBLES. — SUNDRY BUSINESSES — POTASH MANUFAC-
TURED — PROPERTY IN BOXFORD IN 1768.

NTIL the year 1732 the selectmen were what
we now term overseers of the poor. They took
entire charge of the paupers, furnishing them
with every thing needed for their comfort. May
22 of that year the town chose a man to officiate in
that duty separately, to take the whole care upon himself.
This man was Deacon Timothy Foster, who thus became
the first overseer of the poor in Boxford The practice of
"boarding-out" town paupers was still continued.

At the period of which we are writing the wild animals
of the larger varieties were not at all scarce. Game, as
the population increased, began to decrease, and the town
found it expedient to do something for its protection. The
General Court, in May, 1739, passed an Act to that effect;

and the town chose John Wood and Thomas Peabody to
see that the law was enforced. Deer being the principal
variety of game, these officers were called "deer-reeves."

Up to this time bears were frequently found in the woods;
but they very soon became scarce, and the last one known
to have been seen within the limits of the town inhabited
the swamp in the rear of the residence of Mr. Charles A.
Spofford. Discovering her retreat, some hunters took away
her cubs: on returning to her den the old bear pursued
the hunters to the highway, where, with her fore-paws
placed upon the top-rail of a pair of bars, she gave utterance to a prolonged and disconsolate howl, after which she
immediately made her way to the Merrimac River, which
she crossed, and, entering the wilds of New Hampshire,
was never seen again in her old retreat.

Some discussion was carried on, in 1738, about building
some schoolhouses, the want of which was very much felt.
At a town-meeting held in the following spring, May 14,
1739, it was accordingly voted that the town would divide
into five parts, each part to provide its own schoolhouse.
Whether this vote was carried into effect, and the schoolhouses built, or not, we do not know, but a clause in the
school-report for 1764 has led us to think they were not,
although previous to 1765 a schoolhouse stood in the new
part of the cemetery, near the present Third-District schoolhouse; and in 1774 another stood near the house of the late
Moses Kimball. In 1779 four hundred pounds was raised
for the support of schools that year. A Mr. Page was
hired to teach school in 1740; Mr. Persons taught in 1742;
John Tucker subsequently taught here for several years;
Mr. Lesslie for several years, about 1748; Mr. Varney
in 1750; Hon. Aaron Wood during 1752 and spring of
1753; Mr. Butler in spring of 1754, and Mr. Brown the
rest of the year; and in 1776 Moses Putnam was schoolmaster.

Richard Pearl * removed from Andover to Boxford, and built the house owned and occupied by the late George Pearl, Esq (Richard's great-grandson), in 1738. Near his residence, on the stream that connects Mitchell's Pond with Parker River, he shortly erected a grist-mill, which was the first ever built in the West Parish. This ancient mill was gone before 1824; and on the same site John Pearl and James Carleton founded a saw and box mill about 1848. Mr. Carleton sold out his share in the mill about four years later, to Deacon J. T. Day, who sold it about 1865 to Daniel Pingree, who now owns it, Pearl having sold to him the share which he possessed.

The "wood-spell" was recognized as one of the few holiday seasons of our ancestors. This was the time of getting together the minister's supply of wood, which then formed part of his salary. With shouts of the youngsters, and the hoarse voice of the drivers, the farmers came into the yard, bringing their share of the supply; and, after unloading, entered with their neighbors the back-room of the parsonage, where, in the fireplace which the present generation knows so little about, a huge fire, supplied by a veritable yule-log, was kept burning. The season of the year was winter when this grand turn-out took place, and the parson would have "something to take" all smoking hot; for such was the custom of those days, and the "good old New-England rum" was a reputable drink. Chatting and sipping the liquor, they would sit there all through the long forenoon, — the people of those days arose early, —

---

* Richard Pearl was born in Bradford (in the portion of that ancient town that is now included in Groveland) 20 May, 1702, and died in Boxford 20 Dec., 1793. His father was John Pearl, a native of Skidby, Yorkshire, Eng., who was a miller by trade. His mother was Elizabeth, daughter of Richard Holmes of Rowley. Richard Pearl, in company with another man, built the original mill that occupied the site of Hale's factory in South Groveland. Richard Pearl was also grandfather of Peter Pearl, whose long life was passed and filled with public offices in the town.

and then, wishing him prosperity, the parson was left alone. Mrs. Stowe has beautifully pictured this scene in her *Oldtown Folks.* Modern custom has long since laid aside the romance which clung around the lives of our ancestors, and has left civilization in a cheerless and unlovely form.

Early in the eighteenth century, a wonderful attention to religion had been excited in various sections of New England, terminating in a genuine revival. Soon after this the celebrated Whitefield, whose sincere and honest piety Cowper has immortalized in the most glowing colors, and whose eloquence vanquished on one occasion even Franklin's philosophical caution, came to New England from his fruitful labors at the South. He preached considerably in our neighborhood, mostly in the open air, and wherever the people could be got together to be addressed. Mr. Whitefield urged a more earnest devotion to the work of God, and the leading of a higher life, — closer communion with the Father. In consequence of his teaching, many lay-preachers sprang up, who boldly proclaimed the truth, and their right, under the immediate command and influence of the Holy Spirit, to preach. These " New Lights," as they were called, rose up in many of the towns in this vicinity and throughout New England generally. In Boxford, the Second Church was disaffected by the " new doctrines," and some of their members, one of whom was John Woster, one of the deacons of the church, being persuaded of the correctness of the doctrines, embraced them ; and lay-preaching was carried on in some of the houses, Deacon Woster's being one of them. The church-records mention two of these itinerant preachers, — Joseph Adams and Francis Woster, — one, if not both, being residents of Boxford. This was in the summer of 1744. The church expounded upon the matter, and, believing the doctrines taught to be contrary and dangerous to the platform of the church which was then common throughout New England, they came to the conclusion that these members had committed a sin worthy of excommunication; and because they would not recant their opinions in regard to itinerant preaching, and refuse the said preachers the use of their houses, they were suspended from communion. One of them said that his wife was sick on her bed, therefore not being able to attend services at the meeting-house, and he thought it no more than right that he should have preaching in his house, where his wife could hear. The church was kept in an uproarious state for about four years, when the members were restored to the fellowship of the church. Deacon Woster had removed to Leicester in 1745. Nov 28, 1744, the parish voted that "Benjamin Porter Should Keep the Keyes of the meeting house Carefully that the meeting house doors bee not opened to any Preachers Conterary to the mind of our Revnd Pastor, the Church and parish or the major part of them."

From 1725 to the beginning of the French War of 1755-59, the Indian depredations were few. The colonists heard but little of their disturbances, and the times were getting to be more peaceful and prosperous. Through this intervening period the town kept a full supply of ammunition on hand. Dec. 8, 1741, the town allowed Nathan Peabody £2 for procuring and bringing a barrel of gunpowder from Newbury, £60 having been voted for its purchase the preceding May. The next September (1742) Capt Jeremiah Perley was ordered to keep one-half of the town stock, and John Symonds the other half. March 24, 1747, it was voted by the East Parish that their ammunition should be kept in the meeting-house.

Only one short period of a few months' duration disturbed the equanimity of the lives of the colonists during this long period of peace. We have reference to the capture of Louisburg, on the island of Cape Breton. Soon

after the treaty of 1713, in which the French gave up
Nova Scotia and Newfoundland to Great Britain, the
French built a large and formidable fort at Louisburg.
They had been twenty years at work upon it, and had
made it so strong that it was regarded as a sort of
Gibraltar.

Troubles had commenced in 1744 between Great Britain
and France. The colonies were considered by the Canadian French as a part of Great Britain, and as such they
greatly annoyed the colonial commerce. As this fortress
was the retreat of the depredators, the colonies were very
eager to capture it. To accomplish this a naval fleet was
first got ready for sea. Next, 4,366 men were raised from
the various towns in the province. How many and who
went from Boxford we have not ascertained. The fortress
was built in two divisions, — the town and the batteries, —
and cut off from the main land by a wide marsh. They
surprised the French, and easily captured the batteries
and the outposts. But the town was not to be so easily
taken. The colonists, having taken two months' provision
with them, were determined upon a siege. The men easily
crossed the morass that surrounded the town, but it was
so soft the horses could not pass over. Fourteen days and
nights were spent in dragging their cannon across. At
last fire was opened upon the town. The siege lasted
forty-nine days; and on the 17th of June, 1745, the town
and island surrendered.

When the capture of this important post was made
known, France quickly prepared a large fleet of forty ships
of war, and fifty-six transports, with forty thousand stand
of arms, to re-capture the fortress, and punish the colonies
for their insolence. But by the interposition of Divine
Providence a violent storm arose after they were at sea, and
only two or three of the ships ever reached Halifax. Soon
after, their admiral and vice-admiral died ; and, when the

remnant of the fleet attempted to do something, another storm arose which prevented the ships from acting in concert, so that nothing was done by the French of any importance, except upon the Canadian frontiers. A treaty of peace between England and France was at last made, and signed at Aix-la-Chapelle, in October, 1748.

During this conflict we find the names of some of the Boxford men who were in the service. They were in the company of Capt. Joseph Frye of Andover, doing service at Scarborough. We give their names and time of service, viz. : —

Ebenezer Ayer (Sergeant)	. from Dec. 1, 1748, to Dec. 16, 1748.
John Bradstreet . . .	" " " " " "
Moses Spofford . . .	" " " " " "
George Carleton . . .	" " " " May 1, 1749.
Samuel Fisk	" April 27, 1748," " "

Hast Williams of Boxford was in the company of Capt. Daniel Hills of Newbury, at Gorham Town and New Marblehead. Time of service, from Dec. 5, 1749, to Jan. 5, 1750–51.

Again, when the Eastern frontiers were being troubled, in 1754, the following men went out from Boxford, in the company of Capt. Humphrey Hobbs of Souhegan, for their defence : —

NAMES.	TIME OF SERVICE.
Israel Herrick * (First Lieut.) .	April 23, 1754, to Sept. 19, 1754.
Daniel Perkins (Clerk of the Co.)	May 31, 1754, " Sept. 22, 1754.
Perley Rogers	" " " " "
Nathaniel Bixby	" " " " "
John Bradstreet	" " " " "
Thomas Wood	" " " Sept. 15, 1754
William Spofford	" " " " "

* Israel Herrick was soon afterward commissioned captain, and commanded a company in the French War. He also fought at the battle of Bunker Hill. Mr. Herrick was a son of Joseph Herrick, sometime of Topsfield, and a lineal descendant of Sir William Herrick. He married,

Also, in the company commanded by Capt. Abiel Frye
(probably an Andover company), in service from May 1 to
Sept. 20, 1755, were James Andrews (Sergt.), Asa Andrews
(Corp.), Abner Curtis, and Robert Willis.

Joseph Stickney was in Col. Winslow's expedition to
Nova Scotia as a private from Boxford. His brother Jedediah Stickney is also found on Col Winslow's manuscript
journal as one of the soldiers who assisted him in removing
the Acadians. These two brothers were also in Major
Preble's company May 28, 1755 (Jedediah as a private from
Boxford), on board *The Sea Flower*, Samuel Harris, master.

In 1755 the French of Nova Scotia took the oath of
allegiance to the British crown. But they were soon after
accused of furnishing support and intelligence to the
French and Indians, and annoying the colonies. Some
of them being found in arms, it was determined to remove
them (they being in all about two thousand souls) to New
England, and distribute them among the various towns.
About March, 1755, the General Court ordered to Boxford
thirteen of these people, to which were soon after added
two more, making in all fifteen. These were Ommer
Landry, his wife, and four children ; Renar Landry, his
wife, and one child ; Paul Landry and his wife; a young lad ,
and three others. The semi-annual bills for their support
presented by the town to the General Court are kept on
file in the Massachusetts archives, and form our medium
of information concerning these French "neutrals." These
accounts commence June 1, 1756. Some of the French

June 22, 1749, Abigail, daughter of John and Abigail (Symonds) Killam of
Boxford, who was born Nov. 30, 1725 He resided in Topsfield till 1753,
when he removed to Boxford, and built the residence of our present towns-
man Mr. Israel Herrick, his descendant, in which he resided till after 1762,
when he removed to Lewiston, Me., where he died, having attained to the
rank of major. He entered the army in 1745, and was out in nineteen campaigns. Gen. Jedediah Herrick of Maine, deceased, was Capt. Herrick's
grandson

resided in a house belonging to Jonathan Foster, for which he charged four shillings per month as rent. They were supplied with fuel, provisions, &c., by the selectmen at the town's charge. Others were let out to the highest or lowest bidder, according to their ability to work. Capt. Francis Perley kept " Old Landry" and two others who were wholly supported by the town. Five of the number were young children, and several of the remaining ones were sickly and hardly able to work a large part of the time. In the winter of 1756–57 one of the men received a bad wound in the leg, which prevented him from working for several months. In the winter of 1757–58, after an illness of about five months, the " old woman " died. Her funeral charges were 9s. 4d. The " old man " probably survived but a few months. The same winter the town, thinking they were doing more than their share in maintaining the " neutrals," — though why, we do not know, as the Colony paid the bills, — sent the following petition to the General Court, praying for an alleviation of their burden. —

" MASACHUSETTS-BAY

" *To his Excellency the Governer the Honble his Majestyes Council and the House of Representatives In General Court assembd*

" The petition of the Town of Boxford humbly sheweth that Whereas there was by order of this Goverment sometime about the month of March anno 1755 thirteen of the Inhabitants of Nova-Scotia sent to sd Town to which number there was Two more soon added & still likely to Increase. an old man with his wife & one Chield has wholly relied on the Town for their support ever since they came to sd Town, Two others heads of families have been for six or eight months past Disabled for labour by reason of sickness & Lameness so that there families have been In great measure supported by the Town Whereby sd Town is very much burthend with the Charge & trouble Therefore there Circumstances being so Indigent, Your humble Petitioners pray, that if it may be Confistant with this Honble Court, that some of the sd French Inhabitants may be remov'd to some adjacent Town where their is none of sd French, or any other way agreable to the wifdom of s^d Court, whereby your humble Petitioners shall be greatly relive^d

"As in Duty shall ever pray &c.

		"Thos Perley	
		Aaron Kimball	*Selectmen*
P us	{	Jos. Hovey	*of*
		Jacob Cummings	*Boxford.*
		Mos Porter"	

IN THE HOUSE OF REP^R Jany: 6, 1758.

"Read and Ordered That the Prayer of this Petition be so far granted as that the select men of the said Town of Boxford, have liberty, if they see Cause, to remove six of the french people mentioned that have been fent to them to the Town of Middleton, Viz^t Ommer Landerie, his wife and family; and the Select men of the Said Town of Middleton are hereby directed to receive the said Ommer Landerie and his family Accordingly

"Sent up for Concurrence

"T. Hubbard *Spk^r*

"In Council Jany 6 1758

"Read & Concurred

"Thos Clarke *Dpty Secry*

"Consented to

"T Pownall."

So six of their number, to quote the words of the selectmen, "a family most able to provide for themselves," were sent to Middleton. After 1758 the town took little care of them. July 3, 1760, Paul Prichard, a constable of Boxford, was ordered by the selectmen to remove Joseph Landry, John Baptist Landry, and Roseale Landry to Danvers; and Margaret White, *alias* De Blank, to Manchester. Joseph Landry was in Chelsea, and so Prichard did not warn him; the others were supporting themselves, so he only warned and did not remove them. On the 17th of the same month the General Court's committee ordered these French to be removed from Boxford. Some of them went to Canada, but the number of the survivors was small. When the French were ordered away, Renar and Paul Landry were being supported by the town. The following is one of the items of the bills of their support: "To a pair of Lether Briches for Renar Landry, 8 *s.* 8 *d.*"

A writer of those days says of these neutral French, that "they were remarkable for the simplicity of their manners, the ardor of their piety, and the purity of their morals; that the cloud of their sorrows was never dispelled; and in a land of strangers many of them pined away and died."

In May, 1756, eight years of peace having passed, Great Britain declared war against France. This declaration began the tedious conflict known in the annals of American history as "The French and Indian War." The Canadian French struck the first blow in America by Gen. Montcalm's attacking and taking Oswego, the American key to Lake Ontario, including sixteen hundred of the provincial troops, and a large quantity of cannon and military stores. This great disaster came upon the colonists very suddenly; but they immediately prepared for action, and quickly sent troops into the service.

An expedition was planned against the fort at Crown Point, in which at least one of our young men entered, in the company of Capt. Israel Davis. This was Nathaniel Bixby, aged twenty years, son of Jonathan Bixby. He was taken sick at Fort Edward, and brought to, and placed in, the hospital at Albany. His uncle Elias Bixby was living at Sheffield, Mass., and, hearing of Nathaniel's condition, went to see him, and found him almost beyond hope of recovery. His uncle took him to his home in Sheffield, where, by careful nursing and good doctoring, after a stay of five weeks, he was able to come home (in October, 1756), his uncle attending him the one hundred and sixty miles of the journey.*

The placing of William Pitt (Lord Chatham) at the head

---

* See Mass. Archives, Vol. LXXVIII, p. 55.

of the British Ministry in 1758 infused a new spirit into all the affairs of the government. He sent letters to all the American governors, requiring them to raise as many troops as they could. They quickly complied with his request; and Massachusetts, New Hampshire, and Connecticut alone raised fifteen thousand men. Boxford raised a "company of foot" for a "general invasion of Canada," which was placed under the command of Capt. Israel Herrick, in Col. Jedediah Preble's regiment. John Pearl enlisted in this company, 30 March, 1758. Under the attack of these troops, Louisburg, which had again fallen into the hands of the French, and the whole country from the Gulf of St. Lawrence to Nova Scotia, surrendered.

The campaign of 1759 was an important one to the English. Niagara, Ticonderoga, Crown Point, and, most important of all, Quebec, surrendered to the American troops. In this campaign Capt. Herrick again commanded a company of provincials from Boxford and vicinity. He was also out the next year (1760).

Samuel Stickney of Boxford was in the company of foot commanded by Capt. Israel Davis (a Topsfield (?) company), Col. Jonathan Bagley's regiment (1759): entered service April 2, and served until Nov. 1. He was in the same company and regiment at Louisburg, and served from Jan. 1, 1760, until April 14, 1761, but entered service Nov. 2, 1759.

In the campaigns of 1759 and 1760, Capt. Francis Peabody of Boxford had a company under his command. Lemuel Wood (father of our present resident, Mr. Daniel Wood) was a private in Capt. Peabody's company; and from a diary kept by young Wood during these two campaigns, we have gleaned abundance of information relative to the history of the company. The company met and started on their march, Thursday, May 24, 1759. They reached Springfield a week later, and lodged just by Connecticut-River ferry, after making a stop of two days they again started on their march toward Albany,'which they reached on Tuesday, June 12, having been ten days on the road, and much hindered by heavy rains. They left Albany on the 15th, went to Stillwater, then to Fort Miller, and then to Fort Edward, where they arrived on the 20th. The whole army was stationed there; but on the arrival of our company they marched for the lake, under the command of Gen. Amherst. July 4, three of the company were placed in the train of artillery, a party consisting of fifty-five men. July 21, they marched to Ticonderoga, and assisted in making breastworks and intrenchments in front of the fort, while all the time the French kept their cannons and mortars in constant use, trying to drive the provincials from their work. Every thing was ready to open fire upon the fort at break of day on the morning of July 27 ; but on the preceding evening the French took what they could carry with them, and went aboard their boats, and sailed off, leaving a lighted slow-match attached to the fort's magazine, which blew up about eleven o'clock, making a terrific noise. The fort was immediately repaired, and taken possession of by our troops. On the next day (July 28) our Boxford company helped to transport provisions, whale-boats, and bateaux, over the land from Lake George to Lake Champlain, in order to advance toward Crown Point. The labor being tedious and hard, many of them having to take their place in the ranks of the sentries, and their only provisions being pork and bread, they felt their duty to be very hard. The French having deserted Crown Point, Capt. Peabody's company remained at Ticonderoga, spending their time in fishing and hunting, sometimes having some narrow escapes from the savages, till the end of the season, when they returned to their homes.

On Thursday, April 24, 1760, the company again left home to participate in the Canada expedition. Following

nearly the same line of march as the year before, they
reached Albany, May 16. Till the 24th they were engaged
in transporting flour and provisions from Albany to the
"Three-Mile House." Tuesday, May 27, there was a draft
on Capt. Peabody's company for twelve privates and one
corporal Monday, June 2, they left Albany, and went by
water to Stillwater ; and after being employed more or less
of the time in conveying provisions, &c , from one place to
another, they reached the Lake the 10th inst. After waiting two days for the boats to be got ready, they set sail for
Crown Point, where they arrived June 16. Major Rogers,
with some provincials, — one of whom, at least, belonged
to Capt Peabody's company, — on Monday, June 23, returned from a scout, bringing with them "twenty-six prisoners and two scalps" On the following Friday morning,
several companies, under command of Col Ingersoll, among
whom was Capt. Herrick's (of Boxford), went up the lake
to Putnam's Point to cut timber with which to build
bateaux. Monday, Aug 11, the whole army embarked for
St. John's (Canada), and the next Saturday came in full
view of the fort. Here they built breastworks, placed
their cannon, and after firing for ten days upon the fort
the French evacuated it on the night of Aug. 28 ; the next
morning it was taken possession of by our troops Aug.
30, they pursued the French in their bateaux to Fort
Chambly. Here they built some breastworks, and three
times sent a flag of truce to demand the surrender of
the fort, which was acceded to at the third time. Hundreds of the French surrendered to the King's colors and
authority, and many lent wagons or carts to our troops to
convey their baggage in They left Chambly, Sept. 8, proceeded to the St. Lawrence River, each place surrendering
to them as they advanced, and returned to Crown Point by
way of their outward trip. The season was getting late,
and the weather cold and stormy, in consequence of which

hundreds of the men were taken sick, and many of them
died. Many had been previously sent to their homes,
which they never reached. Ten of Capt. Peabody's company died while stationed at Crown Point, some of whose
names are given by our journalist, viz.: John Pemberton,
died Sept. 11; Israel Dwinnels, Sept. 26; Samuel Rowell,
Oct. 9, and Mrs. Samuel Fisk, Oct. 6. Mrs. Fisk had
probably gone to the fort to help take care of the sick,
and fell a victim to the disorder. The winter was close
upon them; and, considerable snow having already fallen,
the soldiers proceeded to Ticonderoga, where they encamped
over night, and hurried on their homeward way next morning. They marched in as direct a line as possible, through
Vermont and New Hampshire, and reached home just
before the first of December.				.

Timothy Barker was a private in Capt. Edmund Wooer's
(of Haverhill) company, in Col. Bagley's regiment, serving
from Nov. 2, 1759, till Jan. 12, 1761.

The following served as privates in a company commanded by Capt. Gideon Parker of Ipswich:—

David Jewett	.	.	.	from May 31, 1761, to Dec. 13, 1761
Benjamin Williams	.	.	.	" June 9, 1761, to Jan. 6, 1762.
John Smith	.	.	.	" June 10, 1761, to May 27, 1762.
Daniel Wood	.	.	.	" June 12, 1761, to Jan. 10, 1762.
John Riddell	.	.	.	" June 20, 1761, to Dec. 13, 1761.

Ebenezer Staples served in the army from Nov. 2, 1762,
till June 10, 1763. Philip Bunker also served from Nov.
2, 1762, till July 18, 1763.

The officers of the Boxford militia companies in 1762
were: First Company, Asa Perley, captain; John Hale,
lieutenant; and Thomas Andrews, ensign. Second Company, Isaac Adams, captain; Nathan Barker, lieutenant;
and John Chadwick, ensign.

The wages paid per month at this period were: captain,

£9; first lieutenant, £5; second lieutenant, £3; sergeant, £2; corporal, £1 18s.; and a private, £1 16s.

In 1763 peace was made between the contending nations,
by which all the possessions of the French, north-west of
the United British Colonies, came into the hands of Great
Britain, to whom they still belong.   Except the Revolution
the French War was the most important conflict in which
the Americans had to deal.   "Nearly one-third of the
effective men," says Minot, "were in military service in
some mode or other; and all this zeal was manifested after
the most depressing disappointment, and a burden of taxes
which is said to have been so great in the capital as to
equal two-thirds of the income of the real estate."

Let us go back to the year 1743, when Rev. Mr. Rogers
suspended his ministry   The church was again destitute
of a settled pastor.   Meetings were irregular, and therefore very annoying.   The parish hired miscellaneous ministers to preach for a few Sundays only, though some
of them continued here a number of months.   Prominent
among them were Rev. Jacob Bacon, Rev. Aaron Putnam,
Rev. William Symmes, Rev. Josiah Stearns, Rev. Moses
Hale of Byfield, Rev. Mr. Thayer, Rev. Mr. Foster, Rev.
Mr. Upham, Rev. Stephen Minot, Rev. Mr. Robart, Rev.
Mr. Bass, Rev. Mr. Fisk, Rev. Joseph Swain, Rev. Mr.
Gardner, Rev. Moses Hale of Haverhill, Rev. Mr. Verney,
and Rev. Mr. Ainger.

Tiring of this irregular worship, the parish met together
Aug. 8, 1752, and voted that Thursday, the 22d inst.,
should be set apart for a day of fasting and prayer, to
take the advice of the neighboring ministers as to whom
they should settle in the ministry.   The council consisted
of the following reverend gentlemen: Messrs. Clark,
Wigglesworth, Phillips, Emerson, Chandler, and Cushing.
The result of this meeting was not adequate to the ideas of
the people, and so nothing was done

Six years more passed before they did any thing further.
Nov. 3, 1758, the parish invited Rev. Elizur Holyoke of
Cambridge to become their pastor, agreeing to give him
£160 on settlement, and £66 13 s. 4 d. with twenty cords
of wood as salary, annually. About a month later, he
accepted their call by the following letter : —

"To the First Church and Parish in Boxford, honoured and beloved: Inasmuch as you have called to the sacred office of a Gospel
minister among you, and have voted me such a maintenance as, according to the situation, may be sufficient, together with such an agreeable
harmony among yourselves in desiring a re-settlement of the ordinances
of Christ, and your unexpected unanimity, both in church and parish,
and having taken those previous steps necessary to determine myself
in such important affairs, I take the present opportunity to express
my gratitude to you for having such an esteem for me, which I trust
has moved you to act as you have, and hereby testify my acceptance
of your invitation with an humble dependence upon Divine grace that
I may be enabled to act in the station of a minister of Christ among
you, agreeable to those sacred rules delivered to us from Heaven ; at
the same time entreating your earnest prayers for me that, in the
course of my ministrations among you, we may be preserved in that
unity and charity, with all other Christian graces, necessary to be exercised between those who stand in so near and sacred a relation to
each other. And it is my earnest desire and prayer to God that we
all may be perfect and of one mind, living in peace, that the God of
Love and Peace may be with us.

"ELIZUR HOLYOKE.

"CAMBRIDGE, Dec. 29, 1758."

Jan. 8, 1759, the church met, and sent letters to the First
Church in Boston, Third Church in Dedham, church in
Wilmington, First Church in Danvers, Second Church in
Boxford, First Church in Bradford, church in Topsfield,
Second Church in Rowley (now Georgetown), and church
in Byfield, desiring their assistance, by their elders and
messengers, in the ordination of Mr. Holyoke. Jan. 31,
every thing being ready, the ordination duties were performed. The exercises began with prayer by Rev. Mr

Morrill ; Rev. Mr. Cushing then preached from 1 Thess. v. 12, 13 ; Rev. Mr Clark prayed, and gave the charge ; Rev. Mr. Emerson prayed after the charge was given ; and Rev. Mr. Parsons of Bradford gave the "right hand of fellowship." To the record of the exercises, which was made by his own hand, Mr. Holyoke adds, "And thus to one who is less than the least of all saints is this grace given, that he should preach the unsearchable riches of Christ."

A church-meeting was held April 2, 1759, at which Aaron Kimball and Joseph Hale, jun., were chosen deacons. A church-covenant was also adopted, which we here give verbatim : —

"We, whose names are hereunto subscribed being members of the first church in Boxford, in consideration of the unsettled state we have been in for some years past, but now through the goodness of God *whose tender mercies are over all His works*, are blest in the resettlement of the gospel ministry and ordinances ; hoping that in some degree we have *learned obedience by what we have suffered;* would now give thanks for what we enjoy.' And first of all we confess ourselves utterly unworthy of such distinguishing favors, admiring that free grace which triumphs over so great unworthiness ; with an humble reliance on which, sensible we hope of our own inability to perform that which is good, do wait on God while we thankfully lay hold of his Covenant & choose the things that please Him. — We declare our serious belief of the Christian Religion as contained in the Sacred scriptures, which we own, and acknowledge, to be the only rule of Faith and Practise, heartily resolving to conform ourselves unto the precepts of that Holy Religion as long as we live. We give up ourselves to God the Father as our Father and receive him as our Portion forever. We give up ourselves to God the Son as our Redeemer, the Great-Head of His people in the covenant of grace as our Priest, Prophet, and King, to bring us to eternal blessedness. We give up ourselves to God the Holy Ghost as our Sanctifier, Guide & Comforter to Eternal Glory. — We acknowledge our everlasting & indispensable obligations to glorify God by a Sober, Righteous, & Godly Life, & very particularly in the Duties of a Chh State depending upon his gracious assistance for the faithful Discharge of the Duties incumbent on Us. We desire & intend (by ye help of Christ's Powerful Grace) to walk togeather as a Chh of the Lord

Jesus Christ in the Faith & Order of the Gospel so far as the same shall be revealed unto us. — Conscientiously attending the Public Worship of God, the Sacraments of the New Testament & the Discipline of His Kingdom, & all his holy Institutions in Communion One with another ; Watchfully avoiding all sinful Stumbling-Blocks as becomes those whom God hath called into so near & holy Relation to himself. And with the same Seriousness & Solemnity we do also present our Ofspring unto the Lord, purposing & promising by the Assistance of his Spirit to do our Duty to them in the methods of a religious Education — that they also may be the Lord's. — And all this We do repairing to the Blood of the Everlast."

With the spirit of this covenant, under the ministerial charge of Mr. Holyoke, and rejoicing in the again settled state of affairs, the church began to revive. During the first year of Mr. Holyoke's ministry a small· legacy was bequeathed to the parish by the will of Capt. Jeremiah Perley, which was applied to paying a portion of Rev. Mr. Holyoke's settlement. The church was also newly painted of an olive color.

In October, 1782, Mr. Holyoke asked for an addition to the amount of his salary (about £66), and was granted six pounds extra.

During the years of 1766 and 1767 much of the First Church records was taken up by records of meetings held to see whether "Tate and Brady's New Version of the Psalms" should be introduced and sung by the choir instead of the "Old Version." It was proposed in December, 1765, by Mr. Holyoke, who said he had compared the two Versions with the Scriptures, and found the New Version to be much better than the Old, giving a more clear and instructive sense of the Psalms ; and that the "Hymns" (which formed an appendix to the New Version) were suited to Christian worship. After the New Version had been sung for six weeks, a lecture was appointed for Wednesday evening, Feb. 12, 1766, when a discourse was delivered from Col. iii. 16. As the vote was not unanimous the New Version was not immediately introduced. Several meetings were held on account of this matter, which were of little consequence. Nov. 5, 1767, Mr. Holyoke received a petition, signed by six members of the church and eighteen of the congregation, signifying their desire that "Dr. Watts' Psalms" be sung six sabbaths upon trial, and after that time to take a vote whether they should be introduced or not. After they were sung six weeks it was put to vote, but no vote could be obtained either for or against their introduction.

"Tate and Brady's Version" continued to be used until they were superseded by "Dr. Watts' Psalms" in 1801. "Dr. Watts' Hymns" were jointly introduced two years later. March 30, 1772, the Second Church voted "to sing Dr. Watts' version of Psalms in the congregation instead of the Old Version." Many of the elder members thought, no doubt, they would be ungodly if they changed the old-time customs. They had become habitually attached to the Old Version of the Psalms, from which they had sung year after year; and to change for the new-fangled tunes would be like putting out the light of the gospel from the service of the sabbath.

The State of Maine was now fast being settled. Many settlements were newly instituted, and in a short time were thriving villages. Several of these settlers were from Boxford, and most of them from this vicinity. In 1766 several men in this section of Essex County obtained a grant of the present town of Bridgton, Me., among whom was Richard Peabody of Boxford. Solomon Wood of Boxford was employed by the proprietors to lay out all that part of the township lying west of Long Pond, into lots of half a mile in length, and one hundred rods in width, containing one hundred acres each. Mr. Wood, with five assistants, — Stevens, Stacy, Adams, Parker, and Field, — commenced this work on the 8th of September, and completed it on the 16th of October, 1766. He was accompanied by, and acted under the direction of, a committee of the proprietors, consisting of Moody Bridges (from whom the town received its name), Richard Peabody, and Col. Thomas Poor. The families of Amos Gould, Daniel Perley, Reuben Burnham, and David Hale were among the earliest settlers. Enoch Perley went there in 1776, married two years later, and built the oldest house now standing there, and which is in possession of his grandson Hon. John P. Perley, who resides upon the old farm

The settlement of Harvard, Mass., was partly composed of Boxford families. Caleb Brown went there in 1743; Jonathan Cole, 1746; Ambrose Hale, 1765 (?); and other families removed there early.

Amherst, N. H., was also partly composed, originally, of Boxford families. Among these were Andrew Bixby, who removed thither, 1745, and John Cole about 1764.

Thomas (son of Joseph) Bixby, with his two nephews, Joseph and Abner, sons of Joseph Bixby, removed to, and settled in, Hopkinton, Mass., in 1727. Their families were prominent in advancing the new settlement.

Lunenburg, Mass., was settled by Essex-County people. Several sons of Samuel Gould of Boxford married and settled there about 1730. Abijah Hovey removed thither in 1765.

Brookfield, Mass., was increased in population, about 1750, by several Boxford families, — the Goulds, Hales, and others

Rindge, N. H., was first settled about 1752. About 1776 several of the sons of Capt Isaac Adams of Boxford settled there. Richard Kimball settled there at the same time; and also Jonathan Sherwin, who became the progenitor of a worthy posterity. Thomas Ames removed to Rindge about 1778

Oliver, Israel, and Asa Perley, Francis Peabody, John

Hale, and others of Boxford, were among the first English inhabitants of the Province of New Brunswick. They settled on the St. John River about 1765, and began, with others of Essex County, the settlement of that now populous province.

From that time to the present, families have continually removed from Boxford, and joined the first settlers, and helped lay the foundation, of many prosperous towns and cities. When the West began to be settled, Ohio received the first instalment of our emigrants who have gone to reside in the new States ; and from that time forward a few have settled each decade upon that fertile prairie-land, and reaped the first cultivated crop. And as civilization has pushed on, farther and farther, until it has reached the Pacific Coast, our emigrants have gone farther west, so that we can now literally affirm that our representatives can be found from Maine to California.

Let us return to Rev. Mr. Cushing's ministry in the West Parish. Mr. Cushing's health failing him, he was not able to preach regularly after the summer of 1763. The next winter's services were very much broken, — so much so that the parish voted, Sept 17, 1764, to hire some one to preach four sabbaths The next month a committee was chosen to discourse with Mr. Cushing about the pulpit's being supplied, to see what measures he proposed to adopt as to how the pulpit should be supplied, if he remained "weak and unable to carry on the ministry." No conclusive discussion was held with him until about a year afterwards, when he agreed to pay "Tow Thirds of the Cost Exclusive of the Horses Keeping," if the parish hired a minister. The parish did not desire to enter into this compound way of obtaining their preaching, as Mr. Cushing was not likely to recover from his illness; and therefore, May 19, 1766, chose a committee to call on him, and learn his mind, if possible, about resigning his pastoral charge

After due consideration, he offered to accept of £30 per annum and his firewood, "togather with other Things mentiond in a former mefsage," as terms for resigning his pastoral office; which was accepted by the parish.

Mr. Cushing continued to linger until Jan 25, 1772, when he died, being in the sixty-third year of his age, and in the thirty-sixth of his ministry. He was son of Rev. Caleb Cushing of Salisbury, where he was born April 10, 1709. His mother was Elizabeth, daughter of Rev. John Cotton. He graduated at Harvard College, 1729. He had two brothers, Caleb, State Counsellor, and Rev. James (H. C., 1725) of Plaistow. His grandfather was Hon. John Cushing, one of the governor's assistants in 1688.

Mr. Cushing married Elizabeth Martin of Boston, April 8, 1740. The result of this union was but one child, John, born May 1, 1741, who married Dorothy Bagley, and had a number of children. This son was known as Esquire Cushing, was a graduate of Harvard College in 1761, and a very learned man, being employed on all kinds of committees, &c, and filling many offices of trust with honor and fidelity. We should judge he was the very counterpart of his father, who appears to be a man of extensive learning, and a very popular preacher.

Rev. Mr. Cushing resided across the street from the residence of Mr. Wyatt. His son resided on the place after his father's death, till he removed to Waterford, Me., where he died in 1815.

July 1, 1767, was appointed as a day on which to hold a "fast," previous to calling a minister, which the neighboring ministers were invited to attend. But no one was invited to preach until Sept 28, when the parish concurred with the church in extending a call to Mr. Edward Perkins Sparhawk, who had been occupying the pulpit for about two years. Mr. Sparhawk declined the invitation, and probably left the pulpit at the same time. Another "fast" was called Oct 1, 1770, at which the neighboring ministers were invited as before. But this also resulted in nothing.

Mr. John Hale built the late ancient Low mansion about 1750, and a few years later erected the saw-mill, which has been constantly in use ever since. When the "Janes Road" was laid out in 1772, we find the mill mentioned as "Hale's new mill." About the same time it came into the possession of Nathan Low (father of Gen. Solomon Low), and was kept in the family until the death of Major William Low (son of Gen. Low) in 1870, when it was sold to Mr. Israel Herrick, who is engaged in getting out ship-timber, as well as various kinds of other lumber, in addition to his extensive farming operations.

Boxford was also supplied with tailors during the period of which we are writing One of these was Joseph Stickney. Nathan Perley, as we find by some ancient account-books, was hired to "cut wescutts."

When Solomon Wood, who was a man of much learning for that time, and a surveyor of note, was elected clerk of the East Parish, a new blank-book for records was placed in his hands : on one of the fly-leaves we find the following "caution" to his successors in that office : —

"A CAUTION TO CLERKS.

BY SOLOMON WOOD.

A Clerk Should be an Honest man
Not one that is Self willd
Nither an Ignoramous
But one that is well Skilld

Not only for to write a line
With Letters fair and Clean
But to indite that Readers may
Know what his Records mean.

ye[a] He Should be a Carefull man
and Not trust his own brain
that those that trust him Never may
have Reason to Complain.

Ah one that Never bribed Can be
by gold nor what men tell
For Such as will its plain to me
Expose them Selves to Hell

For my Successors this I Leve
be faithfull to your trust
you Shall be Blest if wholly Right
if E—ie So often Curst. —

The Curs thats Causleff Shall not Come
No Shuning whats your Due —
But merit none and then Ill Say
a happy man are you.

By What I Here Exhibit Do
Successors good I Seek
That when Im Dead and gone I may
by this too you yet Speak. — Amen.

" BOXFORD, March ye 20th AD 1765.   S. W."

A century ago trouble about the various dams across
the streams was in continual foment. This was because
the fish could not go up the streams on account of the
obstructions " July 26, 1763, the town voted to choose a
man to join with other men, chosen by the towns of Topsfield, Danvers, Middleton, Wenham, and Reading, to agree
with the proprietors of the mill-dams in the town of Ipswich that prevents the fish going up the rivers or brooks
into said towns, — which they otherwise would do if there
were no dams across Ipswich river, — to open waste-ways
sufficient for the fish to go up the brooks or rivers." This
was the beginning of a new office known as the " Fish
Committee."

About this time we find a new blacksmith here, — Solomon Wood. His shop stood near the residence of the late
Mr. Albert Perley, which house was built and occupied by
Mr. Wood. Paul Prichard was a house-wright at this time;
and he erected and resided in the house now owned and
occupied by B. S. Barnes, Esq. Prichard's wife was an

able doctress, more by nature and experience than by the study of medical works, and her skilful treatment was much sought.   The family removed to New Ipswich, N. H., just previous to 1777.   A new innholder also presents himself. This last is Solomon Dodge, who denominates himself "innholder" in 1754.

A century ago, or more, a potash-manufactory, or leach-ery, was located near the residence of Mr. Cornelius Pier-sons in the East Parish.   The brook that runs south of his house was flowed, and by the pond thus formed the ashes were leached.   Quite a business was carried on.

In an old memorandum-book, found among some pri-vate papers belonging to the Hon. Aaron Wood, the wor-thy servant of the town in the last century, is contained a list of the taxable property in the town.   It is interesting in showing to what extent the farmers of the present gene-ration in Boxford have decreased in the raising and keep-ing of cattle, as well as in other particulars.   The list is as follows : —

"What the town of Boxford is set at in the list of valua-tion in the several articles, in the year 1768 : Heads ratable, 209; heads not ratable, 13; houses, 134; shops, 1; tan-houses, 1; mills, 6¾; trading stock, £30; money at inter-est, £843 13 s. 4 d.; horses, 132; oxen, 270; cows, 609; sheep, 1,200; swine, 113; acres of pasturage, 2,836 — will pasture 960½ cows; tillage, 646 acres — produce, 9,692 bush-els; cider, 1,392 barrels; acres of mowing-land, 1,880; acres of upland, 448; acres of meadow-land, 1,076¾; and salt-hay brought into town, 298 tons."

CHAPTER IX.

THE REVOLUTION.

THE STAMP ACT. — REPRESENTATIVE'S INSTRUCTIONS. — RE-
SOLVES. — CARDING, SPINNING, AND WEAVING, INTRODUCED
INTO ALL CIRCLES. — FURTHER ACTS OF GREAT BRITAIN;
RECEPTION BY THE COLONISTS. — ENGLISH SOLDIERS IN
BOSTON — DUTIES, EXCEPT ON TEA, REPEALED — "BOSTON
MASSACRE." — MORE RESOLVES — "BOSTON PORT BILL" —
COMPANY OF MINUTE-MEN FORMED.

E are about to enter upon a series of scenes which have not had their parallel in modern history, and which have been acknowledged by the whole world to have been, in the result, an achievement to be wondered at. The British colonies in America united in one strong band, fought the British crown, and proclaimed themselves independent of Great Britain. That mighty nation was forced to accede to their requests, and thus the United States was ushered into existence. This struggle, — for liberty which had been denied them, — between a few feeble colonies, much debilitated by the French and Indian war, and the powerful nation of England, demands our closest attention, as the part that Boxford took in it was almost unparalleled throughout the land. Though the Yankees, being encouraged by the aspect of liberty before them, fought with earnest zeal and unbounded patriotism, yet we must ascribe the result to Him who rules all nations, and setteth the bounds of men's habitations.

201

When the Sugar Act was passed by Great Britain, Boxford made no dissent to it, as far as we can learn from the
town-records; but when the Stamp Act was passed, Jan.
10, 1765, without the Colonies being represented, as was
their legal right, the town met, Oct. 8 (1765), to instruct
their representative (Hon. Aaron Wood) to join in no
measure countenancing the Act.   His instructions were as
follows: —

" We, the free holders and inhabitants of the town of Boxford,
being met this eighth day of October, 1765, to give you our advice and
directions respecting the state of the Province at this difficult and
dangerous conjuncture.   We acknowledge it to be our duty to make
supplications, prayers, and intercessions for the King, and for all men
that are in authority, that we may lead quiet and peaceable lives, and
that we should submit ourselves to every ordinance of man for the
Lord's sake, so far as they are consistent with natural Constitutional
reason, and religion; and would be always careful to render unto the
King the things that are his.   When there was occasion to make our
yoke heavy we did cheerfully submit to it, but when there is no
greater occasion, to add to our yoke, and to make 'a little finger
thicker than a man's loins,' is a just reason for a non-compliance.   It
fills us with great concern to find that measures have been adopted by
the British Ministry, and Acts of Parliament made, which we apprehend press hard upon our natural rights and liberties, and tend
greatly to distress the trade of the Province, by which we have heretofore been able to contribute something towards enriching the land of
our forefathers.   But we are more particularly aroused at the last
Act, called the Stamp Act, by which a very grievous and, we think,
unconstitutional tax is to be laid upon the colonies.   By the Royal
Charter, granted to our ancestors, the power of making laws for our
internal government, and of levying taxes, is vested in the General
Assembly.   And, by the same charter, the inhabitants of this Province are entitled to all the rights and privileges of natural, free-born
subjects of Great Britain.   The most essential rights of British subjects are those of being represented in the same body which exercise
the power of levying taxes upon them, and of having their property
tried by juries.   These we apprehend are the very pillars of the
British Constitution, founded on the common rights of mankind.   It
cannot be said that we were in any sense represented in the Court of
Great Britain when this Act of taxation was made; and, as we under-

stand the Act, it admits of our properties being tried in certain contro-
versies, arising from some internal concerns, by Courts of Admiralty,
without a jury; a thing which, we think, we may fully abhor. But, we
admit, though we had no complaints of this sort, yet we should have
reason to except against the inequality of these taxes. It cannot be
denied that the people of this Province have not only settled here
at the greatest hazard, but have enlarged and defended the British
Dominion in America at a large expense of blood and treasure. They
have also exerted themselves in a very distinguishing manner in
services for their King, by which means they have often been reduced
to the greatest distress; and in the late war, more specially, by their
ready and surprising exertions, they have loaded themselves with a
debt almost insupportable; and we are well assured that if these
expensive services (for which very little, if any, advantage hath ever
accrued to themselves) together with the necessary charges of supporting and defending his Majesty's Government here, had been
estimated, the moneys designed to be drawn from us by this Act
would have appeared greatly beyond our proportion. We look upon
it as a peculiar hardship that, when the representative body of this
Province had prepared and sent forward a direct remonstrance against
those proceedings, while they were depending in the House of Commons, it failed of admittance there; and this we esteem the more
extraordinary inasmuch as being unrepresented. It was the only
method whereby they could make known their objection to measures
in the event of which their constituents were to be so deeply interested. This Act, if it is carried into execution, we fear will afford a
precedent for the Parliament to tax us in all future time, and in all
such ways and measures as they shall judge meet, without our consent. In short, the duties imposed on us by this Act are so heavy that,
if complied with, they would bring us and our posterity into slavery
and bondage as long as the Stamp Act continues and is enforced upon
us. We, therefore, think it is our indispensable duty, in justice to
ourselves and posterity, as it is our undoubted privilege, in the most
open and unreserved, but decent and respectful terms, to declare our
greatest dissatisfaction with this law. And we think it incumbent
upon you to, by no means, join in any public measures for countenancing and assisting in the execution of the same; but to use the best
endeavors in the General Assembly to have the inherent, unalienable
rights of the people of this Province asserted and vindicated, and left
upon the public records, that our posterity may never have reason to
charge the present times with the guilt of tamely giving them away.
And we further instruct you to take particular care that the best econ-

omy may be used in expending the public moneys; and that no present grants may be made to those who serve the government. And we, in general, recommend to your care that the moneys of the Province, drawn from the individuals of the people at a time when almost every avenue of our trade is obstructed, may not be applied to any other purpose, under any pretence of necessary contingent charges, or of making up private losses, but what were evidently intended in the Act for supplying the Treasury. And, in the managing all other things that may come before you in the General Assembly, we wish you that wisdom which may be profitable to direct you therein."

Though the Stamp Act was repealed the following year, the mother country voted that she had a right to tax America whenever she found it expedient, which vote was, in principle, the same as the Stamp Act. On the 29th of June, 1767, the King, George III., signed another Act, which was even worse than the Stamp Act had been.

These acts of aggression worked on the minds of the colonists so that almost unanimously they agreed not to purchase clothing, &c., of the English; but to use, as much as possible, their own manufactures. This was the time when nearly every household introduced the old-fashioned spinning-wheel and loom, and set about making their own cloth. The inhabitants of Boxford, on the 22d of March, 1768, "taking into consideration the deplorable circumstances this country is under respecting the great decay of trade, the scarcity of money, and many other things, and that it is highly necessary that they should take all prudent and legal measures to encourage their own produce and manufactures, and discourage the unnecessary use of all foreign superfluities, and discountenance all vice, and promote and encourage industry, economy, and good morals," it was therefore voted that Mr. Thomas Perley, Aaron Wood, Esq., and Mr. Luke Hovey, be a committee to prepare some proper resolves to lay before the town at their meeting the next May; at which time the following resolves were accepted by the town : —

" Whereas, this Province labor under a heavy debt incurred in the late war ; and the inhabitants by these means must be for some time subject to very burdensome taxes : and as trade has for some years been on the decline and is now particularly under great embarrassment and burthened with heavy imposition; our medium trade thereby greatly become very scarce and the balance of trade turned against the country, and this town, in their proportion with other towns, feel the sad effects thereof. As it is the duty of every individual to aim at the public good of the society whereof he is a member, so it is the duty of every incorporated body to aim at the general good of that country of which they are a part And although this town is but small, among the many towns in the country, yet it would do every thing in its power towards promoting every public good, and discountenancing all vice. Because of the poverty of the town, and its situation, the inhabitants have never been able to go into the use of many articles mentioned in the votes of the freeholders and other inhabitants of the town of Boston, at their meeting at Faneuil-Hall, on Wednesday, October 28, 1767; yet they cannot wholly excuse themselves from the use of some of the superfluities mentioned in said votes Therefore, the town would strongly recommend to every house-holder and head of a family to endeavor, as much as they possibly can, to lessen in their families the use of all foreign superfluities, and to use such things in the room thereof as shall be of their own manufacture, and to do every thing they can to promote industry, economy, and frugality, and to discountenance all sorts of vice and immorality."

This resolution was so generally adhered to, that the consumption of British merchandise was greatly reduced in the Colonies, especially in the large and populous towns. In Boston alone, having then about fifteen thousand inhabitants, it was lessened in the year 1764 more than ten thousand pounds sterling in value; that is, about fifty thousand dollars. But this, instead of inducing the English to relax the severity of their measures, only caused them to persevere in their oppression. As matters grew worse, societies were formed; of which, probably, the most notable were the "Sons of Liberty." They consisted of those men who were determined to unite (which they did by a kind of national compact) in resisting parliamentary oppression. Other societies were formed, of quite a different kind. These embraced persons of all ages, and of both sexes, who were more willing to do without luxuries, and live by their own industry, than to depend on Great Britain.

Instead of wearing imported cloth, the wealthy people were soon seen in dresses of their own manufacture; and, for fear there might not be wool enough for this purpose, the use of sheep for food was discouraged. The most fashionable people could now card, spin, and weave their own cloth, and deny themselves the use of all foreign luxuries. Close economy became the order of the day.

In 1767 a law was passed by Great Britain, which obliged the several American legislatures to provide quarters for a part of the British troops, and furnish them with necessaries. Still more than this: an Act passed Parliament, establishing a custom-house and board of commissioners in America. The duties were to commence Nov. 20; and early in that month three of the commissioners arrived at Boston. This inflamed the Colonists more than ever. The consequences were resolves, petitions, and remonstrances, from all parts of the country. A general petition of the Colonies on the subject was sent to the king, which greatly offended the British Administration, who, in their turn, sent a circular to the Colonies, demanding that they should retrace the steps they had taken, and crush in the bud the rising propensity among them to act in concert; but all to no purpose.

The Colonies generally agreed, as we have before affirmed, that they would not allow any kind of goods or merchandise to be imported from Great Britain for one year, except a few articles which they specified; nor to purchase British articles of the same kind from other colonies or nations who had procured them from England.

As time passed, and the indignation of the people increased, the board of commissioners found it harder and
harder to perform their duties.   As it was asserted by
England, to help the commissioners prosecute their affairs,
two regiments of British troops were sent across the Atlantic, and stationed in Boston.   This act created a more
general and inflamed indignation throughout the Colonies
than any previous vote of the Crown.

In the early part of 1770, an Act was passed by the
British Parliament for repealing all the duties which caused
so much complaint, except the duty on tea.

Though the British soldiers and the people of Boston
were continually insulting each other, there was no open
quarrel until the 5th of March, 1770, when a mob gathered,
and, proceeding to the custom-house, attacked the sentinel.
He called to his aid the remainder of the guard, who
marched out with guns loaded ; and, after being bullied by
the mob, and stumped to fire, fired upon them, killing three
persons, and wounding several more   The governor at last
persuaded the mob to disperse, and go quietly to their
homes   The next morning the troops were ordered off to
Castle William, one of the city fortifications.

In the following May, Boxford expressed its mind, regarding the train of events through which we have just been
leading our readers, in the following terms.   It is very
expressive of the patriotism that the town sustained all
through the Revolution

"At a meeting of the freeholders and other inhabitants of the town
of Boxford, legally assembled, on Thursday, 24th of May, A.D. 1770:
the town taking into their most serious consideration the distressing
circumstances this people are reduced to by means of the hard and
oppressive acts imposing duties on sundry articles usually imported
here from Great Britain, which, till of late, was unknown to us , and
the sending of troops here to force us to comply with the same, under
pretence of aiding the civil magistrates, and their most inhuman and
barbarous actions since their being quartered in the town of Boston in

abusing, wounding, and killing some of the inhabitants thereof, contrary to the laws of God and man ; and the unparalleled patience and prudence of the inhabitants of the said town of Boston, being very desirous of doing all in their power to try and preserve their liberty ; and sensible that the virtuous resolutions of the merchants and traders, not to import goods and merchandise from Great Britain, ought to be applauded by all,

"Therefore, *Voted*, That the quartering of troops in this Province in a time of profound peace, under pretence of aiding the civil magistrate, when justice, until they were quartered here, was so impartially administered, is a great grievance , and that their so barbarously shedding innocent blood, with their other cruelties committed on the first of March last, in the town of Boston, is alarming and shocking to the last degree , and that the patience and prudence of the inhabitants of the town of Boston, in consequence of that horrid and bloody scene, ought always to be remembered and spoken of to their praise.

"Secondly, *Voted*, That they will, to their utmost, encourage the produce and manufacture of all such articles as have formerly been imported from Great Britain and used among them.

" Thirdly, *Voted*, That they will not use any foreign tea, nor suffer it to be used in their families (cases of sickness excepted), until the duty upon it shall be wholly taken off, — the duty on which has so largely contributed towards the support of such a . . * set of men.

"Fourthly, *Voted*, That they will not by any means whatever, knowingly, have any sort of trade or dealings with those detestable persons who have preferred their own little interest to the good of the country in contriving to import goods contrary to the non-importation agreement of the merchants and traders on the Continent , and that whosoever shall be found to trade with them, knowingly, shall be *deemed unworthy to hold any office, or place of trust, in the town forever hereafter.*"

We have never seen, in plainness of speech, a set of resolves so becoming a " Son of Liberty," as were these passed by Boxford. They expressed their total abhorrence of those persons who claimed to be friends of the British municipality, and who upheld the doings of the British

* Hon. Aaron Wood, who was town-clerk when these resolves were passed, being a moral man, left this word out and inserted a blank in its stead.

troops, in a manner perhaps too forcible. As time passed the feeling against Great Britain increased, especially in Boston and the immediate vicinity, and the people could not restrain themselves from giving expression to their feelings as the repulsive acts of the mother country were constantly bearing down upon them harder and harder.

The people of Boston met on the 20th of November, 1772, prepared a set of resolves, stating the rights of the Province, and setting forth the infringements thereon, had them printed in a pamphlet, and sent them to each town in the Province, desiring the people to express their opinion in the matter, and to pass such votes and resolves thereon as they should judge proper. A committee was chosen to conduct the correspondence. In due time Boxford received one of the pamphlets, accompanied by a letter; whereupon a town-meeting was appointed Jan. 21, 1773, but was adjourned until the 4th of the following month, when the inhabitants assembled, and, after the letter and pamphlet were "publicly read and duly considered," it was voted "that the thanks of the town be offered to that respectable community; not only for their own unalterable firmness and heroic exertions in the cause of liberty, but also for the care and vigilance they have exercised in rousing up their brethren through the Province to consider of some proper methods which may be taken to avert the many unconstitutional innovations that have been and still are imposing upon us. We judge it unnecessary to particularize the many grievances we labor under, or to enumerate the many bold and glaring attempts offered by the British Parliament and Ministry to deprive us of our natural rights and charter privileges; but concur with the results of a meeting of the town of Boston, held on the 20th of November last, both in stating the rights of the Province, and in setting forth the infringements thereon, they being agreeable to our sentiments, which we think not only our indispensable duty to show at this critical time, but also that it is the duty of every incorporated town throughout this Province, although ever so small. On these principles we have acted, knowing ourselves to be enrolled in the lower class of these bodies ; yet *are desirous to exert our utmost abilities in all legal and Constitutional methods to break, if possible, the iron band of oppression, and prevent the welding of the last link in our chain of impending slavery.*" It was voted to transmit a copy of these resolutions to Boston.

Again, on the 27th of December following, eleven days after the tea was thrown overboard in Boston Harbor, the town assembled to consider a letter and other papers which they had received from Boston, relating to the infringements and violation of their rights, by the East India Company's endeavoring to force upon the Colonies large quantities of tea, subject to a duty from them, which they had but recently been privileged to do by an express Act of Parliament. After " having taken under our deliberate consideration the many and grievous acts of the British Parliament to deprive us of our Charter rights and privileges, but more alarmed at the *late* Act of the British Parliament, passed in the last sessions of Parliament, whereby the East India Company in London are empowered to export their teas on their own account to the British Plantation in America, and to expose the same for sale, subject to a duty payable in America, to be collected by a *set of men worse than Egyptian taskmasters,* which, if submitted to, we fear will prove fatal to the Colonies. Therefore, *it is the resolution of this town to do all that is in their power, in a lawful way, to heave off this yoke of slavery, and to unite with their brethren of the town of Boston, and the other towns in the Province, to defend our rights and Charter privileges, not only with our estates but with our lives ;* considering how dear those rights and privileges were purchased for us by our forefathers at the expense of their own blood and treasure. Whereas some of the merchants of Boston, to their shame, and contrary to their agreement, have imported teas subject to a duty payable here: although it is but a small quantity yet we look upon all such persons who import teas upon any pretence whatsoever, subject to the payment of a duty in America, as, in an eminent degree, enemies to their country, and ought to be treated with contempt; and the town return their hearty thanks to the committee of correspondence of the town of Boston, and to the inhabitants of said town, for the heroic exertions of themselves in the defence of all our rights and privileges against such persons as have sought to enslave us." It was voted to send a copy of these resolves to Boston.

The next act of aggression of Great Britain was the " Boston Port Bill," which would not allow any goods to be landed in Boston, thus placing it in a blockade. But the Americans were bound to be at the head , for no sooner had this Act been passed than a *League and Covenant,* as it was called, — an agreement not to trade any more with England, — was signed by multitudes.

In the progress of the year 1774, the governor of Massachusetts, who was a favorite of the King, began to fortify Boston Neck; this being done, he sent out troops, and seized upon the powder-magazine at Charlestown. In Portsmouth, N. H., the Colonists seized upon the fort, though garrisoned with British troops, and carried off every gun and every pound of powder. The people of Newport, R I, also took possession of forty pieces of cannon in the same way. Many will remember the stratagem the Colonists used to remove their stores of munitions of war from Boston, where they were deposited, into the country. Thus matters went on. The British took all the cannon and stores of ammunition that they heard of in the vicinity,

while the Colonists were gathering every thing that would
help them in the tempest which they foresaw must soon
break upon their monotonous lives. The Provincial Congress had given out orders to have the whole Province
armed, and that twenty thousand soldiers should keep
themselves in readiness to march at a moment's warning.
And, as soon as Boxford received the order, nearly every
man and boy that was old enough and able to carry a gun,
who was not obliged by law to train, and others, separated
themselves from their companies, making the number of
fifty-two in all, and enlisted as minute-men. There were,
therefore, now three companies, — two of the regular militia, and one of the minute-men, — all of which contained
one hundred and forty-two soldiers. *One hundred and
forty-two men* out of a population of only about nine hundred! Think of the spirit which animated the breasts of
our inhabitants at this early period in the history of the
Revolution, when the first gun had not been fired, and, as
yet, almost nothing had been done. But they had been
cautiously watching the movements of the British in Boston ; and as they watched they grew more confident that
an open affray would soon take place ; and their watching
was not in vain.

No orator has so eloquently described the interest that
was manifested when the British began their attacks, as
these simple figures. When we consider that the soldiers
were not called out by any special order of authority ; that
their patriotic spirit had not been stirred by the appeals of
the press, or by the eloquence of orators whose hearts were
burning with the love of liberty and the hatred of oppression ; that they only knew from the signal-guns, and the
fires on the neighboring hills, that the British were in
motion ; and that nearly, if not quite, every able-bodied
man in town, must, of his own accord, have left the work
upon which he was engaged, and shouldered his musket,

and marched, at a moment's warning, to meet the foe,—
we cannot help giving them a large place in our history.
With this spirit they entered the conflict of seven years'
duration ; and may the gallantry and honest-heartedness
that they ever manifested in the service of their country
be recorded to their praise !

As a proof of the belief that the minute-men would soon
be needed, we find that the town voted, March 14 (1775),
"that the minute-men shall train one half day in a week,
for four weeks after this week is ended." The town also
voted, on the 5th of the preceding January, to give something to those soldiers that would arm, equip, and hold
themselves in readiness to march in any emergency in
defence of the Province. How many did this, we have
already seen ; their *names* may be found in the following
chapter.

CHAPTER X.

THE REVOLUTION — Concluded.

BATTLE OF LEXINGTON. — MUSTER-ROLLS. — CAPTAINS CUSHING, GOULD, AND PERLEY. — BATTLE OF BUNKER-HILL. — ASSISTANCE SENT TO GLOUCESTER. — WASHINGTON CHOSEN COMMANDER-IN-CHIEF. — MANUFACTURE OF GUNPOWDER. — CONCURRENCE OF THE TOWN IN DECLARING INDEPENDENCE. — ROLLS. — EVACUATION OF THE BRITISH FROM BOSTON. — INTRENCHING TOOLS. — THE HESSIANS. — EXPEDITION AGAINST THE SIX NATIONS. — EVENTS OF 1777. — SOLDIERS HIRED. — ANTI-TORY SENTIMENT. — EVENTS OF 1778–1781. — SOLDIERS. — HENRY PERLEY. — THE ARMY DISBANDED.

E cannot longer procrastinate in coming to the opening conflicts of the Revolution. The British troops were already committing depredations in the surrounding country; and the militia everywhere were constantly engaged in training themselves for real service. Excitement, such as has been known in few periods of the history of our country, prevailed wherever the people were congregated, and the condition of affairs was the theme of the hour.

Late in the evening of April 18, 1775, Gov. Gage sent out eight hundred of the British troops to destroy some military stores at Lexington and Concord, — about fourteen miles north-west of Boston. But, in spite of the lateness of the hour and the secrecy of their movements, they were discovered, and messengers, like Paul Revere, quickly carried the news to the neighboring towns. Many of the farmers in Boxford had already begun their daily labor on this beautiful spring morning, when they heard the alarm-gun fired at Andover , and, unhitching the oxen, they left their plough in the furrow.   Hurrying to their rendezvous, the three companies began their march to Lexington, where, they were informed, the fighting was going on.   Hardly daylight when they started, the sun arose in all the glory of a sunrise in spring;

> " And, as they neared Lexington town,
>   The hands pointing six on the clock,
>   They heard the bleating of the flock,
>   And the twitter of birds among the trees,
>   And felt the breath of the morning breeze
> Blowing over the meadows brown."

But they arrived as the dead were being laid out, — too late to participate in the fight at either Lexington or Concord.   But their long march was not to be for nothing, and they fell in with the provincials, before whom the British were retreating back to Boston;

> " . . . And gave them ball for ball,
>   From behind each fence and barnyard wall,
>   Chasing the red-coats down the lane,
>   Then crossing the field to emerge again
>   Under the trees at the turn of the road,
>   And only pausing to fire and load."

They pursued the British back to Boston, which was reached about sunset, and took up their position with the rest of the militia in Cambridge, as we find by the rolls that they went from forty to sixty-five miles, and were in the service from four days to a week   Probably some of them could not conveniently be away for so long a time when there were so few men remaining at home.   We give below verbatim copies of the rolls of the two companies of militia and the company of minute-men, each of which marched on the alarm of April 19, 1775.

These rolls have been carefully transcribed from the originals in the State archives of Massachusetts.

"A muster roll of the Comp^y under the Command of Capt John Cushing, in Col^o Saml Johnson's Reg^t of Militia which march'd on the Alarm Apr^l 19th 1775." [Mass. Archives, "Lexington Alarm," Vol. XI., p. 259.]

Names.	Quality.	no. miles out & home	Amo^t @ 1^d p. mile	no. days ea. man was in service.	Wages due to ea man	Total of travel & Wages
John Cushing . . .	Capt	62	5/2	6	£1 .. 5 .. 8/2	£1 . 10 . 10/2
Jon^a Foster . . .	L^t	63	5/3	6	0 .. 17 .. 1/2	1 .. 2 .. 4/2
Amos Spafford . .	Ens^n	24	2/.	1	0 .. 2 . 6	0 .. 4 .. 6
Abr^a Tyler . . .	Serj^t	64	5/4	5	0 .. 8 .. 6/2	0 .. 13 .. 10/2
Moses Tyler . . .	d^o	24	2/	1	0 . 1 .. 8/2	0 . 3 . 8/2
Lemuel Wood . .	d^o	60	5/.	4	0 .. 6 .. 10	0 . 11 .. 10
Sammuel Runnels .	Drum^r	62	5/2	3	0 . 4 .. 8/2	0 .. 9 .. 10/2
Thos Adams . . .	Priv^a	64	5/4	5	0 . 7 . 1/2	0 . 12 . 5/2
Daniel Adams . .	d^o	64	5/4	4	0 . 5 . 8/2	0 . 11 . 0/2
John Chadwick .	d^o	61	5/1	4	0 .. 8 .. 6	0 .. 13 . 7
Gilbert Chadwick .	d^o	61	5/1	5	0 .. 7 .. 1/2	0 .. 12 . 2/2
Thos Chadwick . .	d^o	60	5/.	5	0 .. 7 .. 1/2	0 .. 12 .. 1/2
Isaac Chadwick .	d^o	60	5/	5	0 . 7 . 1/2	0 . 12 . 1/2
Enos Carlton . . .	d^o	63	5/3	5	0 .. 7 .. 1/2	0 . 12 . 4/2
Joseph Carlton . .	d^o	24	2/.	1	0 . 1 . 5	0 . 3 . 5
Eph^m Foster . . .	d^o	64	5/4	4	0 .. 5 . 8/2	0 .. 11 .. 0/2
John Hovey . . .	d^o	54	4/6	4	0 . 5 . 8/2	0 . 10 .. 2/2
Luke Hovey . . .	d^o	63	5/3	5	0 . 7 . 1/2	0 .. 12 . 4/2
David Kimball . .	d^o	63	5/3	4	0 .. 5 .. 8/2	0 . 10 .. 11/2
Pelatiah Lakeman .	d^o	64	5/4	6	0 . 8 . 6	0 .. 13 .. 10
Wm Porter . . .	d^o	60	5/	4	0 .. 5 .. 8/2	0 .. 10 .. 8/2
Saml Porter . . .	d^o	62	5/2	5	0 .. 7 .. 1/2	0 . 12 . 3/2
Benj^a Porter . . .	d^o	62	5/2	5	0 . 7 . 1/2	0 . 12 . 3/2
Tyler Porter . . .	d^o	62	5/2	5	0 . 7 . 1/2	0 .. 12 . 3/2
Nathl Peabody . .	d^o	62	5/2	3	0 .. 4 . 3	0 .. 9 .. 5
John Pearl . . .	d^o	60	5/.	4	0 .. 5 .. 8/2	0 .. 10 .. 8/2
Steph^n Spafford . .	d^o	64	5/4	5	0 . 7 . 1/2	0 .. 12 . 5/2
Parker Spafford . .	d^o	64	5/4	5	0 . 7 .. 1/2	0 .. 12 . 5/2
Parker Tyler . . .	d^o	59	4/11	4	0 .. 5 .. 8/2	0 .. 10 . 7/2
Jon^a Tyler	d^o	62	5/2	5	0 . 7 .. 1/2	0 . 12 .. 3/2
John Tyler	d^o	62	5/2	5	0 . 7 .. 1/2	0 . 12 . 3/2
Reuben Gragg . . .	d^o	24	2/.	1	0 .. 1 . 5	0 .. 3 . 5
Wm Foster	d^o	61	5/1	2	0 . 2 .. 10	0 .. 7 .. 11
						£19 .. 4 . 1/3*

* This roll was made up Jan 26, 1776.

"A Muster roll of the Company under the Command of Capt Jacob Gould in Col^o Samuel Johnson's Regiment of Militia which marched on the alarm April 19, 1775."
[Mass. Archives, "Lexington Alarm," Vol. XII., p. 101.]

NAMES.	Quality	no. miles out & home.	Amo⁴ @ 1ᵈ p. mile	no. days ea man was in service.	Wages due to ea· man.	Total of travel & Wages
			s. d.			
Jacob Gould . . .	Cap.	65	5 . 5	6	£1 . 6 . 6	£1 . 11 . 11
John Dorman . . .	lieu.	65	5 . 5	6	17 . 1	1 . 2 . 6
Jed. Stickne . . .	Ens.	57	4 . 9	4	10 . 3	15 . 0
Asa Peabody . . .	Serj.	65	5 . 5	6	10 .	15 . 5
John Curtis	d⁰	65	5 . 5	6	10 .	15 . 5
Israel Perley . . .	d⁰	57	4 . 9	4	6 . 8	11 . 5
Amos Perley . . .	Cop	65	5 . 5	6	9 . 4	14 . 9
Sam Kimball . . .	d⁰	65	5 . 5	6	9 . 4	14 . 9
Jacob Perley . . .	d⁰	65	5 . 5	6	9 . 4	14 . 9
—— Killam . . .	Priv.	65	5 . 5	6	9 . 4	14 . 9
Abner Curtis . . .	d⁰	65	5 . 5	6	8 . 6	13 . 11
Jacob Eyles . . .	d⁰	65	5 . 5	6	8 . 6	13 . 11
David Foster . .	d⁰	65	5 . 5	6	8 . 6	13 . 11
Jacob Andrews . .	d⁰	65	5 . 5	6	8 . 6	13 . 11
Sol⁰ Gould	d⁰	65	5 . 5	6	8 . 6	13 11
Asa Kimball . . .	d⁰	65	5 . 5	6	8 . 6	13 . 11
Dan Kimball . . .	d⁰	65	5 . 5	6	8 . 6	13 . 11
Ephᵐ Mathews .	d⁰	65	5 . 5	6	8 . 6	13 . 11
Moses Perley, jr. . .	d⁰	65	5 . 5	6	8 . 6	13 . 11
Enoch Perley . . .	d⁰	65	5 . 5	6	8 . 6	13 . 11
Aaron Perley . . .	d⁰	65	5 . 5	6	8 . 6	13 . 11
Daniel Perley . . .	d⁰	65	5 . 5	6	8 . 6	13 . 11
Thomas Perley, jr. .	d⁰	65	5 . 5	6	8 . 6	13 . 11
Simeon Stiles . . .	d⁰	65	5 . 5	6	8 . 6	13 . 11
James Andrews . .	d⁰	65	5 . 5	6	8 . 6	13 . 11
Wᵐ Hale	d⁰	65	5 . 5	6	8 . 6	13 . 11
Wᵐ Eyles . . .	d⁰	65	5 . 5	6	8 . 6	13 . 11
Joseph Hobbs . . .	d⁰	65	5 . 5	6	8 . 6	13 . 11
Thoˢ Dwinnel, jr. .	d⁰	65	5 . 5	6	8 . 6	13 11
Richᵈ Foster . . .	d⁰	65	5 . 5	6	8 . 6	13 . 11
Steph Simons . . .	d⁰	65	5 . 5	6	8 . 6	13 . 11
Jos. Mathews . . .	d⁰	65	5 . 5	5	7 . 1	12 . 6
Jos Peabody, jr. . .	d⁰	65	5 . 5	6	7 . 1	12 . 6
John Killam . . .	d⁰	65	5 . 5	6	7 . 1	12 . 6
Benj. Dwinnel . .	d⁰	65	5 . 5	6	7 . 1	12 . 6
Jonᵃ Peabody . . .	d⁰	65	5 . 5	6	7 . 1	12 . 6
Jacob Cumings . .	d⁰	65	5 . 5	6	7 . 1	12 . 6
Nat Smith	d⁰	65	5 . 5	6	7 . 1	12 . 6
Jacob Smith . . .	d⁰	65	5 . 5	6	7 . 1	12 . 6
Anᵈ Gould	d⁰	65	5 . 5	6	7 . 1	12 . 6

NAMES.	Quality.	no. miles out & home.	Amo¹ @ 1ᵈ p mile	no days ea man was in service	Wages due to ea man	Total of travel & Wages
Joshua Rea . . .	Priv.	57	4 . 9	4	5 . 8	10 . 5
Elijah Dwinnel . .	do	57	4 . 9	4	5 . 8	10 . 5
John Willett . .	do	57	4 . 9	4	5 . 8	10 . 5
Nathan Low . . .	do	57	4 . 9	4	5 . 8	10 . 5
Moses Putnam . .	do	57	4 . 9	4	5 . 8	10 . 5
David Hale . . .	do	57	4 . 9	5	7 . 1	11 . 10
Broadstreet Tyler .	do	57	4 . 9	4	5 . 8	10 . 5
Richᵈ peabody . .	do	57	4 . 9	4	5 . 8	10 . 5
Moses Perley .	do	57	4 . 9	4	5 . 8	10 . 5
Eben Curtis . . .	do	57	4 . 9	4	5 . 8	10 . 5
Nat. Hale . . .	do	57	4 . 9	4	5 . 8	10 . 5
John Stiles	do	57	4 . 9	4	5 . 8	10 . 5
Tho perley . . .	do	57	4 . 9	3	4 . 3	9 . 0
John Herrick . .	do	57	4 . 9	3	4 . 3	9 . 0
Andᵂ Peabody .	do	57	4 . 9	3	4 . 3	9 . 0
Jere. Foster, jr . .	do	57	4 . 9	3	4 . 3	9 . 0
Wᵐ Cummings . .	do	57	4 . 9	3	4 . 3	9 . 0
						£37 . 9 1/2*

"*Muster Roll of the Minitte Men under the command of Cap William Pearley in Colᵒ James Frye's Regiment from the 19th April 1775 to the 25th of said April.*"
[Mass. Archives, "Lexington Alarm," Vol. XIII., p. 44.]

NAMES.	time in Service	Whole Amᵗ	dis traveled	per m	total.
Wᵐ Perley, Capt . . .	7 dys	£1 . 10 . 0	40	3 . 4	£1 13 . 4
John Robinson, Lt. . .	7 dys	1 10 . 0	40	3 . 4	1 . 13 . 4
Benj Perley " . .	7 dys	17 . 6	40	3 . 4	1 . 0 . 10
Jacob Hazen, Serj . .	7 dys	12 . 0	40	3 . 4	15 . 4
Eben Peabody " . .	7 dys	12 . 0	40	3 . 4	15 . 4
Asa Smith " . .	7 dys	12 . 0	40	3 . 4	15 . 4
John Towns " . .	7 dys	12 . 0	40	3 . 4	15 . 4
Moses Kimball, Corp . .	7 dys	11 . 0	40	3 . 4	14 . 4
Ivory Hovey " . .	7 dys	11 . 0	40	3 . 4	14 . 4
Andᵂ Peabody " . .	7 dys	11 . 0	40	3 . 4	14 . 4
Allen Perley " . .	7 dys	11 . 0	40	3 . 4	14 . 4
Benj Foster, Drum . .	7 dys	11 . 0	40	3 . 4	14 . 4
David Sessions, fifer . .	7 dys	11 . 0	40	3 . 4	14 . 4

* This roll was made up Dec. 12, 1775; pay allowed Feb. 10, 1776.

NAMES.	time in Service	Whole Am^t	drs. traveled	per m	total
Robert Andrews, Private .	7 dys	10 . 0	40	3 . 4	13 . 4
Joshua Andrews " .	7 dys	10 . 0	40	3 . 4	13 . 4
Daniel Nurss " .	7 dys	10 . 0	40	3 . 4	13 . 4
Sam. Brown " .	7 dys	10 . 0	40	3 . 4	13 . 4
Rufus Burnham " .	7 dys	10 . 0	40	3 . 4	13 . 4
Elijah Cole " .	7 dys	10 . 0	40	3 . 4	13 . 4
Sam. Cole " .	7 dys	10 . 0	40	3 . 4	13 . 4
Dan Cole " .	7 dys	10 . 0	40	3 . 4	13 . 4
Moses Carlton " .	7 dys	10 . 0	40	3 . 4	13 . 4
Thos Dwinnel " .	7 dys	10 . 0	40	3 . 4	13 . 4
Job Davis * " .	7 dys	10 . 0	40	3 . 4	13 . 4
Steph Emery " .	7 dys	10 . 0	40	3 . 4	13 . 4
Dudley Foster . " .	7 dys	10 . 0	40	3 . 4	13 . 4
Elijah Gould " .	7 dys	10 . 0	40	3 . 4	13 . 4
Steph. Gould " .	7 dys	10 . 0	40	3 . 4	13 . 4
Asahel Goodridge " .	7 dys	10 . 0	40	3 . 4	13 . 4
Allen Goodridge " .	7 dys	10 . 0	40	3 . 4	13 . 4
Thos Goodridge " .	7 dys	10 . 0	40	3 . 4	13 . 4
Edm. Herrick " .	7 dys	10 . 0	40	3 . 4	13 . 4
Nat Hale (?) " .	7 dys	10 . 0	40	3 . 4	13 . 4
Enoch Kimball " .	7 dys	10 . 0	40	3 . 4	13 . 4
Steph Merrill " .	7 dys	10 . 0	40	3 . 4	13 . 4
Stephen Perley " .	7 dys	10 . 0	40	3 . 4	13 . 4
Moses Porter " .	7 dys	10 . 0	40	3 . 4	13 . 4
Dan Peabody " .	7 dys	10 . 0	40	3 . 4	13 . 4
Robert Perkins " .	7 dys	10 . 0	40	3 . 4	13 . 4
Jed. Peabody " .	7 dys	10 . 0	40	3 . 4	13 . 4
Jos Peabody " .	7 dys	10 . 0	40	3 . 4	13 . 4
Jerem Robinson " .	7 dys	10 . 0	40	3 . 4	13 . 4
Joshua Rea " .	7 dys	10 . 0	40	3 . 4	13 . 4
Ezra Stiles " .	7 dys	10 . 0	40	3 . 4	13 . 4
Joseph Simons " .	7 dys	10 . 0	40	3 . 4	13 . 4
John Town, jr " .	7 dys	10 . 0	40	3 . 4	13 . 4
Jon^a Wood . " .	7 dys	10 . 0	40	3 . 4	13 . 4
Moses Wood " .	7 dys	10 . 0	40	3 . 4	13 . 4
Eliph Wood " .	7 dys	10 . 0	40	3 . 4	13 . 4
John Wilet (?) " .	7 dys	10 . 0	40	3 . 4	13 . 4
Aaron Woodbury " .	7 dys	10 . 0	40	3 . 4	13 . 4
James Boynton " .	7 dys	10 . 0	40	3 . 4	13 . 4
					£37 . 3 . 10†

The first of the three rolls above given is that of the
company of the regular militia of the West Parish, under
the command of John Cushing, and containing thirty-three

* He was allowed by the town Aug. 20, 1782, for services in 1775, £33 s.
† This roll was made up Jan. 1, 1776; pay allowed Feb. 23, 1776.

men. The second roll is that of the regular militia company in the East Parish, under command of Jacob Gould, and numbering fifty-seven men. The two companies which comprised the Boxford militia were in Col. Samuel Johnson's regiment. The third roll which we have given is that of the Boxford minute-men, numbering fifty-two in all, which had formed themselves into a company Feb. 16, 1775, in obedience to the command of the Province.

Of these three captains it is desirable that more should be said : —

CAPT. JOHN CUSHING was son of Rev. John Cushing of Boxford, and was born here May 1, 1741. He graduated at Harvard College in 1761 ; and the positions held by Mr. Cushing show that his knowledge was not meagre, and that he was able and faithful in the prosecution of all business that was confided to his trust. He was known as "Esquire" Cushing. He married Dorothy Bagley, by whom he had Elizabeth, born 1767, Dorothy, John, Jonathan, and Edward. In 1779 (?) he removed to Waterford, Me., where he died in 1815.

CAPT. JACOB GOULD was born in Topsfield, 6 Feb., 1728–29, and was son of John and Phebe (Towne) Gould. He married Elizabeth Towne of his native place, 27 Oct, 1751, and settled on the farm in Boxford now owned by Mr. McLaughlin. Manifesting considerable interest in public affairs, a few years before the Revolution he was chosen captain of the East Parish company of militia, and marched with them under his command to the battle of Lexington. After having reared a large family, and living to a good old age, he bid farewell to the scenes of time in 1809, at the age of eighty years. Jeremiah Perley, Ancill Dorman, Esq., and the late Nathaniel Smith, natives and residents of Boxford, are grandsons of the old captain.

CAPT. WILLIAM PERLEY was born in Boxford, 11 Feb., 1735, and was son of Capt. Francis Perley. His mother was Huldah, sister of Gen. Israel Putnam, from whom William probably received his patriotic impulses. March 26, 1761, he married Sarah Clark of Topsfield, erected the present almshouse, and settled down to a yeoman's life. Ten children — Rev. Humphrey C. being the eldest, and thirteen years of age — had already shared their parents' care, when the father was chosen by the minute-men to be their captain. He led them to the battle of Lexington, and in the battle of Bunker-Hill several of his command were left dead upon the field. Pursuing the cause of freedom with an earnest, interested zeal, he lived for many years to enjoy its worth, and died March 29, 1812, at the age of seventy-seven years. He was the ancestor of an interesting and worthy posterity, who have now become scattered all over the Union, and some of whom have become distinguished as physicians, merchants, and public officers.

The minute-men were encamped in the neighborhood of Boston, with the army of twenty thousand minute-men who were stationed there. They encamped around Boston in a semicircle, as if to shut up the town on every side but the water.

May 18, 1775, an order was given to Nathan Andrews, of £10 14 s. 7 d., for finding twenty-one blankets for the "solgers" May 23, 1775, the town gave an order to Capt. William Perley of £16, to find blankets for his company.

Some time in May, Howe, Clinton, and Burgoyne, three British generals, arrived in Boston with a re-enforcement of British troops. Gov. Gage now offered a pardon to all the rebels, as he still called them, except John Hancock and Samuel Adams, — who had been very active in rousing the people to resistance, — if they would lay down their arms, and be peaceable subjects. But, as no listening ear could be found among the patriots, he actively prepared for war.

There now began to be skirmishing between the two

armies almost every day. The Americans concluded at
length to fortify Dorchester Neck (now South Boston) and
also Bunker Hill in Charlestown. In order to effect the
latter purpose, about one thousand men (including our Boxford company of minute-men, under the command of Capt.
William Perley), under the command of Col. Prescott, about
nine o'clock in the evening of June 16, 1775, following the
glimmer of dark-lanterns, crossed the Neck. Here they
overtook several wagons loaded with intrenching-tools, the
sight of which first apprised the inferior officers and
privates of the design of their darksome march. A controversy arose as to the proper hill to be fortified. Bunker
Hill — the only one on the peninsula then designated by
a name — was explicitly mentioned in the order; but the
remoteness of that elevation from Boston induced them, in
the face of their instructions, to move farther on to the
eminence afterwards known as Breed's Hill, though not so
high as Bunker Hill by fifty feet. Owing to the dispute,
the sward was not broken till near midnight. The spades
were struck, and the men toiled unceasingly till the first
rays of the sun shone over the sparkling water, revealing
to the astonished Britons the ominous defences reared,
while the familiar cry, " All's well!" had lulled them to
sleep. None but the farmers from the hillsides of the
rock-bound coast of New England could have plied the
spade with such unceasing activity. But it was something
more than their well-developed muscles : it was — what?
They could glance down from the walls of the redoubt into
the town of Boston, and see the hated enemy, and, out in
the harbor, their frigates. *This sight* was what stimulated them to action, and strengthened every nerve in their
body. In those few hours, from midnight to dawn, the
work had been so vigorously pushed that a strong redoubt
had been thrown up, flanked on the left by a breastwork
extending down the hill in a northerly direction, and terminating south of an impassable slough.

They kept at work enlarging their walls till near noon, while all the time the British were incessantly pouring in cannon-balls and bomb-shells from their ships and the battery which they had established on Copp's Hill; and, strange to relate, had lost all this while but a single man. Lord Howe, finding he could not dislodge them in this manner, planned an attack. The Americans, in the mean time, had been re-enforced by about five hundred soldiers, and Generals Warren, Pomeroy, and Putnam.

The British, having collected about three thousand men, marched on towards the narrow neck of land, which is the only entrance to the peninsula, and which was defended by Col. Thomas Knowlton's (see his biography) and Col. Stark's companies, who were stationed behind a breast-work which they had formed of fence-rails and new-mown hay. About three o'clock in the afternoon, the right British wing, under command of Lord Howe, began to ascend the hill in front of the breastwork Lord Howe looked with contempt upon the breastwork of hay, and the back-woodsmen behind it. He fully expected that its defenders would fly in dismay at the first shot, leaving him free to attack the main body in flank, while Gen. Pigot carried the works in front. But he sadly mistook the reception which awaited him. The column came marching on as if to certain victory. Reserving their fire until the enemy came within six or eight rods, the provincials poured upon them incessant volleys. The enemy fell by scores at every volley, till hundreds lay in heaps upon the earth. Yet, as huge gaps were opened, others stepped bravely forward to fill the vacant places, and share the same fate.

The Boxford company was in the redoubt, firing at Gen. Pigot's troops, who were storming the breastwork in front. A new plan was adopted by the British : they determined to take it in flank, in the open space between the redoubt and the breastwork of hay. Several cannon were brought,

and placed in position to enfilade the breastworks in the
rear. But let one of the participants of that battle give
his own account of this new and final movement : *

"Behold the proud Briton, dressed out in all the pride
and pomp of military show, advancing with firm step and
square front on to gory conquest; with their thousands of
bristling bayonets glittering in the clear shining of a bright
sun. Now turn, and view the other side of the picture:
the Americans principally covered from the sight of the
enemy, still having them in full view ; observing every evo-
lution and manœuvre until the awful word *Fire!* was given,
when all was a steady rattle of small arms, mixed with roar-
ing cannon from their floating batteries, and shipping, and
hills in Boston, with their field artillery, together with our
own pieces. The sound for some minutes was almost deaf-
ening ; then a calm succeeded, the air cleared, and the line

---

* From a letter addressed to Hon. Richard Frothingham, historian of
Charlestown, written by Enos Reynolds of Boxford, in 1839, — Mr. Reynolds
being eighty-two years old. The letter was never sent. It is full of the
enthusiasm of the old soldier, and breathes of the spirit of the Revolutionary
patriots.

Mr. Reynolds was in Stark's regiment, and had marched to the battle from
Medford, where the regiment had been stationed. He was, unlike some of
the actors in that scene, exceedingly chary of his words in speaking of that
terrible day. "There was much confusion in the battle," he was wont to
say. "Did you see Putnam that day?" it was asked of him. "Yes, if I
saw anybody." "Where did you see him?" "At the breastwork." "Are you
sure he was in the battle?" "Yes, if *I* was there." "Did you see him
again?" "Yes, when we were going off the field." "Did you see his hands
full of spades and pickaxes?"[1] "No," replied the veteran firmly (these
were nearly his words), — "no ; but I remember seeing his sword as he was
waving it far in the rear of the retreating Americans."

Mr. Reynolds' next service was as a volunteer in the expedition of Arnold to Quebec. It was his eventful lot to encounter more than the common
hardships of that perilous enterprise. He represented his keenest sufferings
to have been in the night, when, with a hundred others, he reached an island,
and the river rose so rapidly around it that they could not get off until the
next day. It was bitter cold, and wood was scarce. Game, too, was by no

---

[1] "Gen. Putnam rode off with a number of spades and pickaxes in his hands." — *Dear-
born's Account of Bunker-Hill Battle.*

retreated, and formed for their second attack, which soon commenced with reanimated fury, and as soon subsided. They formed the third time, and being re-enforced with fresh troops from Boston (ammunition failing the Americans), they carried the fort at the point of the bayonet. The left of the Americans was for a short time longer engaged with the right of the British, but was soon obliged to join the retreat, and leave the field."

In this battle the British had two hundred and twenty-six killed, and eight hundred and twenty-eight wounded. Of the Americans, one hundred and thirty-nine were killed, and three hundred and fourteen wounded and missing. Out of the Boxford company eight were killed ; their names have not been ascertained, except Isaac Adams, Joseph Simmons, —— Carleton, and James Boynton.

means abundant. They could do nothing but wait and suffer. Anguish had stamped that night's events indelibly upon his memory. "I thought I should have died," he said in relating them. For thirty-three days in this march he did not sleep in dry clothes. In December (1775) he was taken prisoner, and remained in the hands of the British until the succeeding October. He spoke of Gen. Carleton with touching gratitude for his humanity towards himself and fellow-prisoners.

Subsequently, and at the time of Arnold's treachery, he was stationed at West Point. He performed guard-duty in the same room with Major André on the last night of his life. The frankness, manly bearing, and fine personal address of the prisoner, won the sympathy of the whole army. Mr. Reynolds represented this sympathy, both in intensity and duration. He was charmed chiefly with André's manners ; for that night he said but little during the time Mr. Reynolds was with him. "André," the veteran would say with emphasis, "was the handsomest man I ever laid my eyes on." He paraded with the troops ordered out to the execution. not an eye but was bathed in tears , and, as the veteran recalled the scene, the solemn funeral procession and the events of the gallows came so vividly before him, that his emotion almost choked his utterance.

After the close of the war he devoted himself to the labors of peace. He was the vice-president of the first Whig State Convention, held at Faneuil Hall in September, 1842. He died Aug. 11, 1845, aged eighty-nine years. His son Stephen, it will be remembered by the older residents, was the Mr. Reynolds who was so prominent among the Sandwich-Islanders , and by whose influence several of the natives came to Boxford, where they settled.

In addition to those members of the three companies in Boxford, we find on the 1st of August, 1775, that Stephen Merrill and John Towne were in the company of Capt. Samuel Gridley, in Col. Richard Gridley's regiment.

Twenty-five men went out to the assistance of Gloucester (Cape Ann) this year. The following enlisted for fourteen days, viz.: James Andrews, Asa Peabody, James Andrews, Asa Kimball, Daniel Perley, Nathan Andrews, jr., Joseph Peabody, Nathaniel Smith, Jacob Eils, Daniel Chapman, Ephraim Matthews, and John Killam.

After their term of enlistment was through, the following also enlisted in the .same service, and for the same length of time, viz.: David Stickney, Abner Curtis, William Cummings, David Foster, Darius Adams, Edmund Chadwick, Samuel Chadwick, Ephraim Peabody, Benjamin Spofford, Thomas Adams, Thomas Chadwick, Jonathan Tyler, and William Lacy.

Washington was appointed commander-in-chief of the American troops by the Provincial Congress, May 10, 1775. As soon as he had taken a survey of the whole ground, he called a council of war. The council, without a dissenting voice, gave it as their opinion, that the posts around Boston, though numerous, must be occupied and sustained; and that, for this purpose, a force of at least twenty-two thousand men was necessary. They also recommended to the colonies of New England to make up the deficiency.

One great difficulty which stared them in the face was the want of ammunition. Washington had found, to his surprise, that there was not powder enough in the whole American army to furnish nine cartridges to each man. This was a most alarming fact, and perplexed even the commander himself. When it became known, many of the inhabitants went into the business of manufacturing powder and running up bullets. The towns also caused it to be done ; at any rate, to manufacture what they needed for their own troops. To corroborate this statement, we find on the town-records of Boxford the following: "Sept. 25, 1775. Gave an order to John Stiles of one shilling for the use of his shop and one bushel of coal in running bullets."

March 19, 1776, the East Parish "gave leave to Deacon Symonds to take out the dirt under the meeting-house for the use of the saltpetre ; he leaving the same as good as he finds it." Linebrook Parish (Ipswich) also " voted, that Daniel Chapman of Boxford, should have the dirt under their meeting-house, to make saltpetre." * Thus we see that the business was carried on to some extent in this town, and perhaps more instances could be found on further research.

It was voted, March 23, 1776, " that one-third of the town's ammunition be kept in the Second (West) Parish in the future."

In the summer and fall of 1775 Boxford was the repository of the ammunition belonging to Salem and Beverly. It was a custom that year, when the British troops were so near, to carry the ammunition away from the coast, and keep it in some private place.

Jonathan Foster was another captain of the Revolution. An orderly-book of his is preserved in the family.

Agreeable to a resolve of the House of Representatives, June 7, 1776, on the subject of declaring the independence of the colonies, the town of Boxford met on the 17th, and "*voted unanimously that if the Honorable Continental Congress should for the safety of the Colonies declare them independent of the Kingdom of Great Britain, they, the said inhabitants of Boxford, will solemnly engage with their lives and fortunes to support them in the measure.*" The Declaration of Independence was adopted only seventeen

* Felt's *History of Ipswich.*

days later, namely, on the 4th of July, 1776; and, after being read in the churches, was engrossed on the town-records.

The following lists, or rolls, contain the names of those men that were in the service at various places, and for different periods of time, during the year 1776, which we have not mentioned on the preceding pages. We give them as given on the rolls. The first list is that of those men who enlisted for eight months in the Cambridge campaign: Jacob Hazen, Asa Smith, John Towne, Andrew Peabody, Allen Perley, Robert Andrews, Joshua Andrews, Samuel Brown, Rufus Burnham, Thomas Dwinnell, Job Davis, Stephen Emery, Edmund Herrick, John Hale, Stephen Perley, Daniel Peabody, Joshua Rea, Jonathan Wood, Moses Wood, Eliphalet Wood, John Wild (or Willet), Seth Burnham, Nathaniel Fuller, Jacob Perkins, Ivory Hovey, Samuel Cole, Eliphalet Cole, Moses Carleton, Nathan Kimball, jr., Enoch Kimball, Benjamin Foster, Asahel Goodridge, John Stiles, John Towne, jr., Elijah Gould, Joseph Simmons, Robert Perkins, Joseph Peabody, Stephen Gould, jr, Daniel Cole, Dudley Foster, Moses Kimball, Ebenezer Peabody, Stephen Merrill, Moses Porter, jr, Jeremiah Robinson, David Sessions, Elijah Clark, and Jonathan Gilman. Whole number of men, forty-nine.

The following were in the Cambridge campaign, but we do not know for what time : Gideon Bixby, David Kimball, and Levi Goodridge.

The following were stationed at Roxbury and Winter Hill (the time is not known) · John Curtis, Ephraim Kimball, David Hall (or Hull), Aaron Perley, David Foster, Daniel Kimball, Abner Curtis, Ephraim Matthews, Jonathan Dwinnell, Abraham Tyler, Joseph Hovey, jr., Parker Spofford, Thomas Adams, Edmund Chadwick, Samuel Chadwick, Enos Carleton, Jesse Hardy, Asa Hardy, Ephraim Peabody, John Tyler, Luke Hovey, jr, Thomas

Chadwick, jr, Amos Hovey, Seth Peabody, and Tyler Porter. Whole number of men, twenty-five.

The following enlisted in the Continental and Northern Army. These men probably served in Capt. Peabody's company (in Col. Wigglesworth's regiment), stationed at Ticonderoga in August, 1776, where they probably remained during the next winter. John Pearl, a private in the company, in a letter to his wife dated Oct. 12, 1776, says: "It has been very sickly in camp with the camp-disorder, but the sick ones are now getting better. We don't expect any fighting here this fall, for we are very strong, both by land and by water; have twenty-three sail off the line." Their time of service is not known. The list follows: John Stiles, Isaac Perkins, David Emery, Moses Porter, jr., Eliphalet Cole, Hannaniah Barker, Seth Peabody, Jonathan Gilman, Robert Andrews, Eliphalet Wood, Allen Perley, Joshua Rea, Seth Burnham, Timothy Stiles, Thomas Killam, David Foster, William Cummings, Ephraim Matthews, Daniel Kimball, Thomas Adams, John Chadwick, jr., Edmund Chadwick, Enos Carleton, John Pearl, Benjamin Spofford, and Parker Tyler. Whole number of men, twenty-six.

The following men were stationed at Dorchester for an unknown period: Stephen Gould, John Herrick, Samuel Stiles, Jesse Burbank, Pelatiah Lakeman, and Joseph Reynolds.

The following were stationed at New York for two months: John Curtis, Nathan Low, Solomon Perley, Ezra Wildes, Joshua Andrews, Abraham Tyler, Samuel Carleton, John Tyler, David Wood, jr, and Benjamin Foster.

The following were also stationed at the same place for the same length of, but at a different, time : John Dorman, Elijah Averill, Nathan Wood, Abner Curtis, Joseph Hovey, Benjamin Dwinnell, Daniel Chapman, Enoch Wood, and Samuel Chadwick.

The following were stationed for two months at Winter Hill: John Dorman, Jedediah Stickney, Jacob Smith, Daniel Chapman, Daniel Nurse, Francis Perley, William Rea, Nathan Low, David Stickney, and Jeremiah Foster, jr.

The following enlisted into the Continental and Northern Army, at a different time from those on the preceding page (their length of service is not known): Stephen Symonds, Jacob Perley, Elijah Dwinnell, Jacob Gould, Solomon Gould, Amos Perley, Moses Peabody, Amos Perley, John Butman, Francis Perley, Nathan Andrews, Thomas Perley, jr., John Curtis, Asa Peabody, John Andrews, Nathaniel Smith, Aaron Perley, Nathan Andrews, Samuel Kimball, Richard Foster, Joseph Hale, jr., Isaac Perley, Nathan Perley, Benjamin Porter, 3d, Jeremiah Perley, John· Hovey, jr., John Foster, Moody Perley, Thomas Chadwick, Ephraim Foster, Richard Hovey, Ephraim Peabody, Simeon Stiles, and Daniel Peabody. Whole number of men, thirty-four. ·

The following were in "the remainder of the Continental Army:" Stephen Spofford, Jonathan Tyler, Samuel Carleton, Oliver Foster, Joseph Hovey, Gideon Tyler, William Porter, Moses Tyler, Isaac Adams, Thomas Chadwick, Ephraim Chadwick, John Chadwick, Joseph Sessions, and Isaac Chadwick.

The whole number of men contained in these rolls is two hundred and eleven.

Among the notable events which occurred during the year 1776 was the evacuation from Boston of the British, who sailed to Halifax, and shortly afterwards returned, and took up their position at the New-York end of Long Island. This caused Washington also to take up his position at New York; and in that vicinity several battles were enacted between the contending armies. Among them we would mention the battle of Sullivan's Island, battle of Long Island, and battle of White Plains. As we do not know in which of these battles the Boxford men took part, we shall pass on without a more extended account of them.

The following order is found recorded on the selectmen's records : —

"Boxford Novr 16th 1776 Then Committed to Treasurer Nathan Wood the sum of nine pounds four shillings and ten pence, being what the Genl Court have allowed for providing the town with intrenching tools agreeable to an Act of the Genl Court.

> "ISAAC ADAMS   ⎞ *Selectmen*
> NATHAN WOOD   ⎬   *of*
> JOHN CUSHING   ⎠ *Boxford.*"

Nov. 28, 1776, the town voted "to pay the expenses of such men as shall be called upon by authority to go into the public service for the future."

Dec. 5, 1776, Capt. Jacob Gould, Mr. Nathaniel Perley, and Ens. Gideon Tyler, were appointed a committee to hire soldiers for "future public service."

Dec. 23, 1776, the town voted "to raise £1,000 to defray expenses arising from the war."

In the spring of 1776 England hired seventeen thousand soldiers from the little state of Hesse, in Germany, called *Hessians*, and transported them to America to assist the British in prosecuting the war. As was the custom in ancient times, the soldiers' families followed the army, and were taken prisoners with them. More than a dozen of these *Hessian* prisoners were kept here in Boxford. Several of them lived with Capt. William Perley, others with Rufus Burnham, and one entire family resided in the Emerson house that stood near the residence of Mr. Francis Marden. One of these was Capt. Leach of the Queen's Light Dragoons. Kate Dunn and Sergeant Donaldson, and an old man, by name Dunckleogleby, were some of the others.

The Six Nations, as they were called, of Indians, had promised to be neutral in the war; but all except the

Oneidas became at length quite troublesome, — plundering, murdering, and burning, — being, no doubt, instigated by the British agents. Gen. Sullivan, with a part of the American army, was at length sent out against them. Nov. 15, 1776, orders were issued to Daniel Lane of Buxton, Me., to appoint his inferior officers, and enlist a company of eighty-six men ; said company to be under his command, and which ultimately was prominent in being connected with Sullivan's army. A bounty of twenty dollars was given to those who enlisted for three years, or during the war. Capt Lane appointed Ebenezer Peabody of Boxford for lieutenant, and James Laury of Berwick, Me., for ensign. Shortly afterwards the rest of the officers were appointed, — among whom were Stephen Merrill as sergeant, and Enos Reynolds and Jonathan Gilman as corporals, from Boxford. Three Boxford men also enlisted in the company as privates ; viz., Seth Peabody and John Stiles, April 14, 1777, and David Kimball, April 21, 1777. The rest of the company was made up from various towns. It contained sixty-three men, including the officers, and was under the command of Col. Ichabod Alden of the Sixth Massachusetts Regiment.

In the spring of 1777 the company took up their station with the American army. One of the privates from Buxton died May 5, and on the 22d Seth Peabody died. July 1 they were at Cambridge, and also on the 20th. On the succeeding day the captain, a sergeant, and two privates were taken prisoners ; nothing further is known as to what became of them. Aug. 31 they were on Vansheit's Island ; and Sept. 8 they removed to Stillwater, and encamped with the American army. They were probably in the engagement at that place on the 19th, when a severe battle was fought for four hours, which was only checked by the darkness of night. Both armies, however, had suffered so much that they did not choose to renew the battle next morning. They were in sight of each other till Oct. 7, when a second battle was fought near Saratoga, in which Burgoyne was defeated. In this second conflict Capt. Lane's company lost one of its privates, and Lieut. Peabody was wounded by a ball which passed through his belt, hit his thigh-bone, and, glancing upwards, came out near his shoulder. The belt which he wore at the time, showing the bullet-hole, is still treasured by the family of his son, the late venerable Benjamin Peabody. The regiment probably spent the winter at Albany. By triplets, pairs, and single men, the company gradually grew less in numbers. John Stiles died Feb. 3, 1778, and at the same time two more privates were sick in the general hospital. Oct 18, another private died.

At the destruction of Schoharie, about fifteen miles from Albany, by the English and Indians, May 30, 1778, this company was engaged, and three of its privates killed. June 16, another private died The company was then reduced to forty-two men. June 22, they were still at Albany. Shortly after, they were stationed at Cherry Valley, one of the frontier settlements of New York. Col. Alden's command, then numbering between two hundred and three hundred men, took up their station in the fort there Early in the following November Col. Alden was apprised of the march of *Brant*, an *Onondaga* chief of the *Mohawk* tribe ; and, when urged to receive the inhabitants into the fort, observed that there was no danger, as he would keep out scouts who would apprise them of the approach of the enemy in season to remove. Scouts were accordingly sent out (two of whom at least were of Capt. Lane's company), and one of them built a large fire, and lay down to sleep. *Brant's* warriors were not misled by so luminous a beacon, and the scouts were made prisoners. This was on the night of Nov. 9, 1778. On the morning of the 11th, favored by a thick and hazy atmosphere, the savages approached the fort. A Mr. Hamble was fired upon as he was coming from his house to the fort by a scout, which gave the first notice of the enemy. He escaped, and gave the alarm to Col. Alden, who, strange as it may appear, was still incredulous, and said it was nothing more than some straggling Indians. The last space of time was thus lost!—and, in less than half an hour, all parts of the place were invested by the enemy. As few arrangements had been made for such an assault the inhabitants fell an easy prey. Col. Alden was one of the first victims. The fort, containing about two hundred soldiers, was not taken, although several attacks were made upon it.

In a letter to his brother-in-law, John Pearl of Boxford, dated at Fort Alden, Cherry Valley, Dec. 13, 1778, Lieut. Peabody says: "I am almost naked for want of shirts, stockings, &c. . . . When the enemy were here they killed, scalped, and burnt thirty-two men, women, and children, and carried thirty-two prisoners to Niagara; killed, of the Continentals, Col. Ichabod Alden and twelve privates, and scalped those that could not get to the fort. I was at my quarters, and tried to get to the fort; they liked to have got me, but I made my escape. . . . The enemy have burnt one hundred and forty-odd buildings, and made the place desolate of inhabitants. . . . Do not expect to leave the place this winter; should like to; hope to get home in the spring." In another letter to Mr. Pearl, dated at Cherry Valley, Jan. 3, 1779, Lieut. Peabody says. "We live on Salt Beef & bread; can get no Syder nor Apples, nor no kind of Sarce. . . . Its very healthy at present. . . . Hope to get home in the Spring."

The soldiers staid at Cherry Valley till June 18, when they marched into the *Seneca* country. They joined Sullivan's army at Tuego, about the 25th of August, and participated in a fight with *Brant* and *Butler* (another

chief) Aug. 29, at Newtown, now Elmira, N.Y., when the
Indians were thrown into confusion. The Americans destroyed all traces of vegetation, such as fruit-trees, corn, and
so forth, that lay in their path. It has been said that a
hundred and sixty thousand bushels of corn were destroyed
that summer (1779). In the fall the company disbanded.

The spring of 1777 opened. The British commander in
New York amused himself by sending out detachments of
troops to ravage the country; the towns of Peekskill, N.Y.,
Danbury, Conn., and others, suffering from their many
depredations. The towns constantly sent out troops
to re-enforce the American army, which was intrenched
among the hills of New Jersey.

Boxford held their annual town-meeting on the 18th of
March, but assembled again only three days later, and
"voted to allow £20 to every man that shall enlist into
the service of the Continent for three years, or during the
present war."

The committee appointed to hire soldiers hired the
following, viz. : " thirteen Boxford men, — John Stiles, David
Emery, Joseph Peabody, James Andrews, Moses Carleton,
Enos Kimball, Stephen Merrill, Seth Peabody, David Kim-
ball, Jonathan Gilman, Napline (a negro), and Hannaniah
Barker, at £30 each, and Jesse Emery at £20; sixteen
Boston men, — John Jackson (?), Seth Webber, Moses Porter, John McAnally, Charles Rider, Charles Grand, John
Targs, Antony Mannuel, John Delley Howard, Moses
Grant, William Taylor, Edward Blake, Joseph Derby, John
Gills, and Thomas Etheridge, all at £20 each; two Scar-
borough men, — John Croxford and —— Derlin, at £20
and £18 respectively ; one Wenham man, — Asa Porter,
at £20; and one Bridgton man, — Jeremiah Burnham, at
£20   Total amount paid out, £778."

The spring and summer of 1777 passed, and Washington had not stirred. Purposing an attack upon Philadel-

phia, Sept. 3, the British army rapidly approached the city. Washington, who had kept an eye on their movements, was on the road to meet them. The two armies met at a place called Chad's Ford, on the river Brandywine, about twenty-five miles south-west from Philadelphia; and on the 11th inst. a severe battle took place, which continued nearly all day, and ended in the defeat of the Americans with great loss. They then made the best of their way to Chester, where they arrived that night, and the next day proceeded to Philadelphia.

Washington concluded to quit the city, and repair to a strong position on the Schuylkill, twenty miles northward. After their departure from the city, the British entered and took possession

The British also gained some other advantages about that time; among which may be mentioned the surprise and defeat of Gen. Wayne.

The battle of Germantown was fought on the morning of the 4th of October; in this the British were repulsed at several points, and about one hundred and twenty taken prisoners. After the battle, Washington resumed his former position, but in a few days removed to White Marsh, eleven miles north-west of Philadelphia. The British, on their part, left Germantown, and retired to the city, where they spent the winter. As winter came on, Washington and his army retired for winter-quarters to Valley Forge, a deep and rugged hollow twenty miles north-west from Philadelphia. On the 18th of December they began to build huts. These were sixteen by fourteen feet, and were made to accommodate twelve men each. They were so numerous, that, when the encampment was completed, it had the appearance of a town, with streets and avenues. Troops from each particular State had their quarters together, in this temporary village of log-huts, and here they suffered together, for it was a winter of the utmost severity ; thousands had no blankets, and were obliged to spend the nights in trying to get warm, rather than in sleeping. They also suffered greatly, at times, from want of food.

Leaving them suffering with hunger, cold, and nakedness, some of our Boxford patriots among them, we will just glance back at the capture of Ticonderoga, by the British, where Capt. Richard Peabody * was stationed with a company of volunteers. Ticonderoga was defended by three thousand men under the command of Gen. St. Clair Discerning that the British had more than thrice their number of soldiers, besides a large body of artillery, the Americans concluded to leave the fort , but as they were doing so were forced to fight, and a very disastrous battle ensued.

A story connected with Capt Peabody in this battle is thus stated · When the long roll of the drum, the call to muster, was sounded, as the British came in sight, the troops were at dinner. All the soldiers immediately left off eating, excepting Capt. Peabody's company, who were inclined to do so, but he advised them to finish their meal. After they had finished, he called his men together, and with the words, "Thank the Lord, now we are ready for them," he marched toward the foe. One of his sons, who was but thirteen years of age, was in the battle with him.

On the 17th of October, Gen. Burgoyne surrendered his entire command, numbering some six thousand men, to Gen. Gates of the American army. At the surrender, Lieut. Ebenezer Peabody was present with Col Brooks. The prisoners, numbering 5,752 men, were kept at Winter Hill, where they were guarded by troops raised for that purpose. Nov. 10, Stephen Gould, jr., Asa Kimball, Jacob Smith, Nathan Stickney, Enoch Wood, John Herrick, and Jesse Burbank volunteered in the above service, to be under the direction of Gen. Heath. Seth Burnham, Jonathan Peabody, Robert Andrews, Eliphalet Wood, Nathan

* He also commanded a company at Lake George.

Stickney, Andrew Peabody, Ezra Gould, and Nathaniel Hale also served during the following winter, in the same service, in the company of Capt. Nathaniel Gage, Col. Gerrish's regiment, in which company John Dorman of Boxford was lieutenant.

The disgust of the Tory sentiment by the inhabitants of Boxford had grown to such an extent that on the 2d of June, 1777, they "voted to choose some suitable person to procure all the evidence that may be had respecting any one that is suspected of being unfriendly to the rights and liberties of . America, agreeable to the direction of the General Court. Voted that Lieut. Benjamin Perley be the person." We have no knowledge of any Tory being brought before a tribunal in town because of his sentiments, although we doubt not that more than one was made to know what the Yankees thought of them.

Sept. 23, 1777, the town hired two more soldiers, — Caleb Goodwin of Penobscot, who enlisted into Capt. David Allen's company, in Col. Crain's regiment; and Nathaniel Cook of Boston, who enlisted into Capt. Scott's company, in Col. Handly's regiment, — at £67 each. The town paid out to the soldiers in 1777, £324 2 s They also paid Capt. William Perley £2 8 s. 6 d., Nathaniel Perley £1 9 s. 6 d., and Lieut. Benjamin Perley £2 4 s. 2 d., for services as committee-men to hire soldiers for the "Continental service."

Very little was further done by either army until the latter part of June, 1778. On the 18th the British evacuated Philadelphia, and began their march toward New York. When they had got as far as Monmouth (sixty-four miles out), they found themselves attacked by the American army. On account of the misconduct of Lee, the Americans were thrown into confusion; but order was again somewhat regained by Washington, and the battle vigorously sustained till dark, when it was postponed until morning. The troops camped where they were, during the night, but when the sun arose next morning the British were among the missing. In this battle both parties suffered severely ; and many of the soldiers died from the effects of the heat, the day being so excessively hot.

Among the greater events of that year was the battle at Newport, R. I. ; but the South witnessed most of the scenes of the conflicting armies during the year.

The northern department of the American army chiefly passed the winter of 1778–79 near the Hudson — some on the New Jersey side, and some on the other. Two brigades were as far up as West Point. Three brigades were also quartered near Danbury, in Connecticut.

Ancill Stickney served in Capt. Dodge's company, — stationed at Winter Hill, from July 2 to Dec. 17, 1778.

Benjamin Foster enlisted as a sergeant July 1, and Joshua Rea as a private, July 3, 1778, in Capt. Jonathan Foster's company, in Col. Nathaniel Wade's regiment, — stationed at Middleton, R I , — for the term of six months.

We now come to the opening of the year 1779, which was less distinguished for splendid or brilliant achievements by either of the two contending armies, than any year since the commencement of the war. Amid the general paucity of events, there were two brilliant and somewhat decisive actions in the vicinity of New York during this year. We refer to the capture of Stony Point and Paulus Hook, two strong military posts guarded by the British.

During the winter of 1779–80, the greater part of the American army camped in Morristown, N. J. There were, however, strong detachments at West Point and other posts along the Hudson, and a body of cavalry in Connecticut. The winter proved to be a very severe one, and the suffering of the army was very great.

Ancill Stickney served at Winter Hill, under the command of Capt. Dodge, from July — to Oct. 9, 1779, when he was detached as re-enforcement to the Northern army, in Capt. Addison Richardson's company, Col. Jacob Gerrish's regiment

Joseph Sessions and William Robinson died in the army in 1779.

John Dorman was allowed, April 20, 1779, £13 6 s., for services at Winter Hill. Jesse Emery was also in the army this year.

Simeon Cole, a private in the Revolution, was granted a pension of £96 per year, April 3, 1819, in conformity to the Pension Law of March 18, 1818.

The events of the war during 1780 were mostly in the South. The first part of the year was a season of continual defeats to the Americans ; but at the latter end of summer several conflicts resulted greatly in their favor

In the year 1780, Nathan Andrews let his horse go into the army, for which the town afterwards paid him.

Jedediah Stickney enlisted as second lieutenant, June 27, 1780, in Capt. Jonathan Ayer's company, Col. Nathaniel Wade's regiment, to re-enforce the Continental army, and served till Oct. 10, 1780.   -

The following "6 month's men" were raised in Boxford, in 1780, viz. : —

	entered service		discharged	
Amos Gage	entered service	July 10, 1780,	discharged,	Jan. 10, 1781.
David Kimball	"	"	"	"
Joseph Kimball	"	"	"	"
Caleb Foot	"	"	"	"
James Mosley	"	"	"	"
Enos Reynolds	"	"	"	Dec 7, 1780.
Asa Hardy	"	"	"	Jan. 4, 1781.
Amos Hovey	"	July 27, 1780;	"	Dec. 16, 1780.
Robert Andrews	"	"	"	"
Eliphalet Wood	"	"	"	"

Oct. 12, 1780, the town voted to raise £16,000 * to buy beef for the soldiers with , shortly afterward £44,625 *

* See foot-note, p. 153.

more. "October the 29: 1784 gaue an order to Ruth Curtice of one pound ten Shillings She being alowed Sd Sum for Seruics don in the town in purcheshing Beef."

In the winter of 1780–81, the American troops quartered at the same places as they did the year before.

Jan. 4, 1781, the town voted to pay soldiers, who would enlist for the ensuing three years, one hundred and twenty silver dollars per year.

The three following orders were given to Capt. William Perley with which to purchase corn for the soldiers, viz.: Jan. 11, 1781, £5,000 *; Jan. 23, 1781, £5,000 *; and Feb. 21, 1778, £3,000.*

The Southern part of the army gained a brilliant victory, Jan. 17, 1781, at a place called Cowpens, in South Carolina, over a detachment of British troops under the command of Col. Tarleton. The Americans were immediately pursued by Lord Cornwallis, who was, at the time of the defeat of Tarleton, on the point of invading North Carolina; and on the 15th of March an engagement took place between them, the British coming off at last victorious, though to them it was little less injurious than a defeat. Another battle was fought on the 25th of April, near Camden, in which the Americans were obliged to retreat. These victories of the British were dearly bought, and were fast reducing their strength. Lord Cornwallis had taken most of his troops from South Carolina, and marched to York-town in Virginia. The Northern and Southern sections of the American army now came together, and laid siege to Yorktown on the 6th of October. The siege was carried on with so much vigor, that on the 19th Lord Cornwallis found himself obliged to surrender, with his whole army of more than seven thousand men.

Soon after the surrender of Cornwallis, the Northern division of the American army returned to their old position on the Hudson.

* See foot-note, p 153.

After waiting a number of months, in which only a few slight skirmishes occurred, a treaty of peace was signed, Nov. 20, 1782, and America's independence acknowledged by Great Britain in the following year.

Another Revolutionary patriot from Boxford was Henry Perley, father of the late Major Samuel Perley. Being, in the spring of 1775, twenty years of age, he let himself to a farmer in Stoughton, Mass. At the battle of Lexington he was in Capt. William Bent's company; and, after the battle, enlisted as a private in Bent's company, in Col. John Greaton's regiment, where he remained till the end of the year, when his engagement was out. He immediately re-enlisted in the same company, at Fort No. 2, in Cambridge, for one year. About the 18th of March they were ordered to New York, *via* Connecticut. They took shipping at Norwich, sailed to New London, crossed Long-Island Sound, and marched by land to New York, where they sojourned about three weeks. They were ordered to Canada by the way of Albany, and were under the command of Gen. Thompson, who died at Chambly, of small-pox. The troops were ordered over most of Lower Canada. A great part of the army being sick with the small-pox, they were obliged to retreat before the enemy, leaving their sick and languishing upon the ground. They retreated to the island of Au Noix, and from there marched to Crown Point, and then to Ticonderoga. When the regiment was ordered to Mount Independence, Mr. Perley was taken sick, and was discharged Nov. 1, 1776, by Gen Gates, commander of the Northern army. Henry's brother Eliphalet was in the army with him in 1776. In 1778, July 31, he was detached from Capt. Jacob Gould's company, to march to Rhode Island. He was placed in Capt. Simeon Brown's company, of Salem, in Col. Wade's regiment, in Gen Sullivan's expedition to Rhode Island, and belonged to Marquis de Lafayette's division. After the retreat they were disbanded. 'In 1779 he was a soldier in Capt. Jeremiah Putnam's company (of Danvers), Col. Tyler's regiment, and was stationed at Providence till the enemy left Newport. The regiment was stationed at Newport until their engagements were out, which was Jan. 5, 1780.

During the year 1781, Peter Chadwick and William Runnells died in the army.

Ancill Stickney enlisted in Capt. James Malloon's company, Col. Putnam's regiment, to re-enforce the Continental army, serving from Aug. 21 to Dec. 4, 1781.

In 1781 orders to the amount of £1,413 3 s. 2 d. were issued by the town for the payment of soldiers.

The American army was kept together till the third day of November, 1783, when, after suitable preparation had been made, it was disbanded in due form. At New York, Washington, in an affectionate address, first bade farewell to his soldiers, and subsequently to his officers. These last, at parting, he took by the hand separately.

Thus ended the Revolutionary War, of eight years' duration, in which a hundred thousand lives were lost, and hundreds of millions of dollars were expended, and which left the United States in a debt of forty millions of dollars. But a new nation had been brought forth, — a nation founded on liberty; a nation which has for its principles only those that are proper for a perfect republican government; one that is cherished by every native, whether at home or abroad, and one that is most highly conducive to all right, education, and those things that make a prosperous and model nation.

CHAPTER XI.

1770–1800.

THE Second Religious Society had now been without preaching — excepting what they occasionally
hired — for several years Among the ministers
hired to preach to them were Rev. Samuel Webster, Rev. Mr. Woodman, Rev. Lemuel Le Baron, Rev.
Mr. Cutler, Rev. Daniel Osgood of Andover, Rev. Isaac
Mansfield, Rev. John Marrett of Newton, and Rev. Isaac
Bigelow of Weston.

The old meeting-house in the West Parish was getting
to be in such poor condition that it was thought by the
society to be beyond repair. With a view to building a
new house of worship, and first wishing to find the centre

of the parish, in which spot it was desired to be built, a parish-meeting was held Jan. 3, 1774, at which it was voted to find the centre of the parish by measuring the roads ; which was accordingly done, and the centre found to be "four and a half rods to the north of Moses Porter's house." At a meeting held Jan. 10, they voted to set the meeting-house at the spot above named. It was put to vote, to see whether they would build a new meeting-house, or take down and move the old one ; when it was voted to build a new one. Capt. Isaac Adams, Nathaniel Peabody, and Lieut. Jonathan Foster were chosen to draw a plan of the new meeting-house. At a meeting held Monday, Jan. 24, Capt. Isaac Adams, Ensign John Barker, and Lieut. Samuel Runnells were chosen a committee to provide materials for building the meeting-house, and to see the work effected. At a meeting held Jan. 31, it was voted to build the meeting-house "according to the same plan by which the meeting-house in New Rowley was built, excepting a steeple, instead of which we are to have a porch built as at the other end of the meeting-house." March 21 they voted to find the centre of the parish by measuring the land, which was done by Benjamin Stevens of Andover, for which service the parish paid him £2 9s. ; and the centre proved to be " six or seven rods to the eastward of Benjamin Foster's house." After considering the centres found by measuring the roads and the land, it was thought best to set the meeting-house "in the corner of Deacon Chadwick's land, near to Rocky Point, so called, being between the centre found by taking a plan, and the centre found by measuring the roads " When spring opened, the work on the meeting-house commenced The contract for building it was granted to Mr. Stephen Barker. It was probably finished by the middle of the next November. Regarding the ultimate disposal of the old meeting-house, the parish voted in March, 1775, " to sell it for what it will fetch."

Aug. 19, 1774, Rev. Moses Hale, who had been preaching there for about four months, was invited to fill the pastoral office. He accepted their invitation Oct. 16; on the receipt of which the necessary letters of invitation were sent to the neighboring churches to assist in the ordaining exercises. The elders and messengers sent from the various churches in the vicinity met at the house of Ensign Gideon Tyler on the day of the ordination, Nov. 16, 1774, previous to repairing to the meeting-house, formed into a council, and voted that (at the ordination) Rev. Mr. Noyes begin with prayer; Rev. Mr. Chandler pray, and give the charge ; Rev. Mr. Symmes make the last prayer ; and Rev. Mr. Holyoke give the right hand of fellowship. The Rev. Mr. Hale of Newbury preached the sermon, from 2 Cor. v. 20.

Mr. Hale's regular salary was £80 per annum. By the depreciation of the currency during the Revolution, the value of paper money was reduced almost to nothing. Because of this the parish granted Mr. Hale in 1779 £1,500 more than his stated salary (£80). In 1781 they granted him £6,000; but he refused it as insufficient, and asked for more, when it was voted to pay him his regular salary in specie.

Mr. Hale was stricken down in the twelfth year of his ministry ; and he died in the thirty-eighth year of his age, May 25, 1786. He was son of the Rev. Moses Hale of Newbury, and was born Feb. 19, 1749, in Rowley. He married Elizabeth ——, by whom he had the following children, viz. : Elizabeth, bapt. Nov. 10, 1776 ; Moses, bapt. Sept. 27, 1778; Stephen, bapt. Dec. 6, 1780; Sarah, bapt. Dec. 8, 1782 ; and Mary Emery, bapt. May 8, 1785. His wife died April 24, 1785; and he followed her, as we have said above, about a year afterwards. Mr. Hale graduated at Harvard College, 1771, and soon after preached in the pulpit in which his labors were so soon ended.

His epitaph is as follows : —

> "In the dark caverns of the silent Tomb,
> The old, the young, the gay, all ages come.
> Here lies interr'd the Priest in sable Urn ;
> Here meet his flock & each to dust return.
> These iron gates no more shall e'er be burst,
> Till heav'ns command shall wake the sleeping dust,
> And then Creations vast, immense shall rise,
> And men with Angels throng th' ethereal skies.
> The God of Nature thus from heav'n hath spoke,
> Nor Men nor Angels can his word revoke.
> It must be so ! then let my soul resign,
> And be prepared for his will divine."

Little is known concerning the character or ability of Mr. Hale ; the church records, as well as those of the parish, being silent in the matter. He resided in the house that once stood across the street from the present residence of Mr. Daniel Wood. After Mr. Hale's death the place was owned and occupied by Lemuel Wood.

After Mr. Hale's decease the pulpit was occupied by Rev. Mr. True, Rev. Solomon Aiken of Hardwick, and Rev. Gilbert Williams.

May 12, 1789, the parish concurred with the church in inviting Rev. Peter Eaton of Haverhill to the pastoral office, agreeing to give him £80 and twelve cords of fire-wood annually as salary, and a settlement of £160. His letter of acceptance was read before the congregation Aug. 2, when letters inviting their assistance at Mr. Eaton's ordination were sent to the neighboring churches. The ordination took place on Wednesday, Oct. 7, 1789. Previous to the ordination on said day, they repaired to the house of Major John Robinson, and made out a programme of the exercises, which contained the following items : The first prayer by Rev. Mr. Smith ; the ordaining prayer by Rev. Mr. Merrill ; charge to the pastor by Rev Mr. Holyoke of the First Church ; the right hand of fellowship by Rev. Mr. Symmes; the last prayer by Rev. Mr. Peabody; and the sermon delivered by Rev. Mr. Adams. The text was Phil. ii. 29. Thus was Mr. Eaton ordained to the ministry, in the twenty-third year of his age.

Rev. Mr. Eaton erected the residence of Mr. Henry Barker at the time of his settlement, in which he lived during the many years of his ministry here.

In the spring of 1788 the desire to have a parsonage built was prevalent, but not enough so to have it erected.

In the summer of 1777, "by general desire," the First Church commenced to begin the public worship of the sabbath with singing. A few of the leaders of the choir that successively held the office were Nathaniel Perley, Moses Peabody, and David and Samuel Kimball. March 19, 1782, it was voted "that the singers should have the east half of the front gallery, exclusive of the back pew." During the intermission of the services on the sabbath, the "Scriptures and other books of piety" were read as early as 1774. The persons chosen for that purpose were members of the church, and they held their office about three months at a time.

In 1777 Jonathan Foster owned a mill in the West Parish.

It seems that as late as 1770 wildcats were yet found here. A few years previous to that date, a bounty had been offered by the town for the capture of dangerous wild animals, agreeable to an order from the General Court. "24 May, 1770, the town voted, that Samuel Dorman should have pay for a wild-cat's head if it shall appear that he has not had his pay therefor before."

Thomas Perley was chosen to represent the town in a convention to be held at Cambridge, Sept. 1, 1779, for the sole purpose of forming a State Constitution agreeable to a resolve of the General Court; and the town instructed him to use his influence that the form of Constitution that

might be agreed upon be printed, and a copy sent to each
town in the State for their approbation or disapprobation,
agreeable to a resolve of the General Court, June 15, 1779.
The Constitution was formed, and a copy sent to each
town, agreeable to the wishes of our townsmen. Accordingly a committee * was chosen to examine it, and report to
the town, which they shortly did in the following words : —

"BOXFORD, May 30, 1780.

" The committee appointed to inspect the Constitution beg leave
to inform the town that as far as we are able, according to the time we
have had, we have endeavored to investigate the Constitution, and
point out the errors, and shall lay before the town our objections and
remarks thereon

" First objection As the third article in the ' Declaration of
Rights ' is rather obscure and ambiguous, we therefore want some
further explanation on said article before we can accept it

" Second objection · We object against the freemen of any town or
plantation being excluded from giving their votes for the choice of a
representative while they are subjected to pay their proportion of
State taxes

" Third objection · The House of Representatives being intended
as the representative of the people, we object against any free inhabitant twenty-one years of age being excluded from giving his vote in
the choice of a representative

" Fourth objection: We object that the quorum of the House of
Representatives is too small where the House consists of three or
four hundred members, and where they are invested with power to
levy duties and excises on all wares, merchandise, and commodities
whatsoever.

" Fifth objection   We object the Governor's simply acknowledging
himself of the Christian religion is not sufficient, — that he ought to
declare himself a Protestant

" Sixth objection : We object against the Legislature's being invested with power to alter the qualifications of any officer in the State
whatever until this Constitution shall be revised

" Seventh objection · Fifteen years we think too long for this Constitution to stand · we think eight years is long enough.

* This committee were Capt Jonathan Foster, Capt. Isaac Adams, Capt.
John Robinson, Dr William Hale, and Thomas Perley, jun

"First remark, or addition : That settled ministers of the Gospel shall not have a right to a seat in the Council, Senate, or House of Representatives.

"Second remark · That the House of Representatives shall at least once a month lay before their constituents the several votes that may be determined by yeas and nays in said House, that the people may be able to judge who are friends to their country and who are not.

"Third remark : That the towns may have authority to recall their representatives at any time when they shall act any thing inimical to the liberties of this Commonwealth, and to choose others to succeed them.

"Fourth remark. That the House of Representatives be subjected to a trial by jury for any failure of their promises to the people of this Commonwealth."

On Wednesday, Jan. 9, 1788, the convention of the Commonwealth of Massachusetts, to ratify the Constitution of the United States, convened in Boston. The representative from Boxford was Hon. Aaron Wood, who negatived its adoption. The result was that the Constitution was adopted by a vote of 187 to 168. The convention continued till the 7th of the following month, when they arrived at the above conclusion. Those who composed the minority acquiesced in the result of the convention, and said they would support the Constitution as much as if they had voted for it, on the ground that a majority had more judgment and wisdom than a minority. The oath of allegiance as prescribed by the Constitution was subscribed to by numbers of the leading men in Boxford. The following names are recorded on the town-records : Capt. William Perley, Broadstreet Tyler, Asa Peabody, Thomas Perley, jun., John Dorman, John Robinson, Capt. Francis Perley, Ivory Hovey, Aaron Perley, and Asa Merrill.

The first "fall-election" under the State Constitution was held Sept. 4, 1780, with the following results, viz.: For governor, Hon. John Hancock, 32 votes; for lieutenant-governor, Hon. James Bowdoin, 22; for counsellors and senators, George Williams 16, Samuel Johnson 15, Samuel Holton 20, Aaron Wood 14, Azor Orne 14, Stephen Choate 8, Elbridge Gerry 8, Richmond Derby 5, Jonathan Webster 14, Samuel Osgood 8, and Moses Little 8. The choice of governor continued to be unanimous for several years.

The first grave-digger in town — John Boswell — was chosen in 1716. March 19, 1776, the East Parish chose Timothy Patch and Joseph Matthews (one for each cemetery), to dig graves and attend funerals

The following is a list of prices agreed upon by a committee appointed by the town to fix prices upon the different kinds of merchandise, labor, and so forth, in consequence of a recommendation of a convention held at Concord, July 14, 1779 : —

Beef, of the best quality, 6 *d*. per pound, till Sept. 1, and after that 5 *d*. per pound.
Butter, 12 *d*. per pound.
Cheese, 6 *d*. per pound.
Indian Corn, 4 *s*. 10 *d*. per bushel.
Veal, 4 *d*. per pound.
West-India Rum, 6 *s*. 6 *d*. per gallon.
New-England Rum, 4 *s*. 16 *d*. per gallon.

Breakfast at Taverns, 15 *d*.
Dinners at Taverns, of boiled and roast meat, 18 *d*.
Flip, or *Toddy*, made of West-India Rum, 16 *d*. per mug.
Oats at Taverns, 3 *d*. per quart.
Lodging at Taverns, 4 *d*. per night.
Horse-keeping at Taverns, at grass, 9 *d*. per night.
Ox-keeping at Taverns, at grass, 12 *d*. per night, per pair.

Barrels, made of sap-staves, 3 *s*. 6 *d*. per barrel.
Bark, good oak, delivered at the tanner's, 15 *s*. 6 *d*. per cord.
Hides, raw, 3 *d*. 8 *far*. per pound.
    Tanned sole-leather, 22 *d*. per pound, and all other tanned leather in proportion.
Blacksmith's Work. — Horse-shoeing (plain shod), all round, 4 *s*. ; and work of all other kinds in the same proportion.
Cloth, tow (good), 21 *d*. 4 *far*. per square yard.
    Linen, the same.

Cloth, woollen, fulled, colored, and made of the best wool, three-quarters yard wide, 5 *s*. per yard.

Charcoal, delivered at the door of the buyer, 6 *d*. per bushel.

Flax, good and well-dressed, 12 *s*. per pound.

Hay, English, 30 *d* per cwt.

Horse-hire, horse and saddle, 2 *d*. 6 *far*. per mile.

Carpenter, house, 53 *d*. per day.

Farm Laborer, 32 *d*. per day.

Oats, 25 *d*. per bushel.

Staves, white-oak barrel-staves, 55 *s*. per thousand.

Tallow, tried, 12 *d* per pound.

Shoes, men's best, 6 *s*. per pair.

Tailor's Work, 40 *d*. per day.

Wood, good oak, delivered, 9 *s*. per cord.

Wool, sheep's, of the best quality, 29 *d*. per pound.

Teaming Work, at 10 *d*. per mile, for every ton's weight.

Weaving, common shirting, at 4 *d*. per yard.

Cider, good, 5 *s* 10 *d*. per barrel (exclusive of the barrel).

After the close of the Revolutionary War, the people being loaded with a heavy burden of taxation arising from the great expense of carrying on the fearful struggle, many who were willing to go to war with Great Britain, rather than submit to taxation without representation, were now willing to go to war with the government rather than pay their share of the expenses which the war had occasioned. In different parts of the State tumultuous crowds assembled, and obstructed the proceedings of courts and other legal bodies. Daniel Shays, who had been a captain in the Revolutionary War, was considered as the head of the insurgents: hence the movement took the name of "Shays' Insurrection." Troops were raised which quickly quelled the insurgents; and conditional pardon was offered by the Legislature to all the rebels, of which most availed themselves. Fourteen were tried, and received sentence of death; but were, one after another, finally pardoned. To suppress this rebellion, it is not known that any troops went from Boxford; and the following extracts from the instructions that the town gave to Mr. Nathan Andrews, the representative for that year, bearing date May 24, 1787, is all that the public records of Boxford give concerning it : "We, your constituents, being chosen by the town of Boxford to instruct you, our representative, think it is our duty to declare our sentiments on the present alarming situation of public affairs. The transactions of the General Court this year may possibly determine the fate of this State for many generations ; for now there is such a concurrence of alarming circumstances as our fathers never saw, each singly portending and all jointly conspiring the ruin of this State." "That you do your utmost to have the General Court removed out of Boston, to some convenient place in the country." "That you endeavor that all those that are termed insurgents have a free pardon, except those condemned, on supposition that they return to their several places of abode, and become peaceable subjects." "That all officers and soldiers raised in the winter past be dismissed, and put out of pay directly, as an armed force is dangerous to the liberties of a people in time of peace."

After the death of Dr. Wood in 1744, the town appears to have been without a physician for a few years. As early as 1753, Dr. Benjamin Foster was practising the healing art here. He was born in Ipswich, Nov. 25, 1700, and was son of Benjamin and Ann Foster. He came to Boxford with his father about 1720, and married Lydia Burbank, Oct. 2, 1730, by whom he had several children. Jan. 17, 1760, his wife died of the small-pox ; and he married, the following year, widow Sarah Low of Ipswich. He died of asthma, Dec 19, 1775, at the age of seventy-five years. Felt, in his *History of Ipswich*, says of him . " He had been in the practice of his profession over fifty years, was a distinguished botanist, and a successful and skilful physician." Dr Foster's residence was in the West Parish.

Dr. Foster was followed, as the physician of the town, by Dr. William Hale, about 1770. Dr. Hale was born in Boxford, Nov. 9, 1741, and was son of Thomas and Mary (Kimball) Hale. He married, (pub. Oct. 13, 1770), Anna, daughter of Elijah and Dorothy Porter of Topsfield. He erected the Sayward house, in which he took up his residence at the time of his marriage. He died about 1785, leaving two young daughters, Elizabeth and Dorothy. His wife, who survived him, was again married, Capt. William Perley being her second husband.

The next physician seems to have been Dr. George Whitefield Sawyer, who was born in Ipswich in 1770; married Polly Killam of Middleton, 1800, and subsequently settled in Boxford as a physician, on the farm now occupied by his son, Mr. Thomas Sawyer. He was acknowledged to be a good physician for the times; and his natural bluntness of speech ofttimes amused his patients. After honoring his profession for many years by a life of integrity and trust, he died March 23, 1855, at the age of eighty-five years.

The last settled physician in Boxford, and contemporary with Dr. Sawyer, was Dr. Josiah Bacon, son of William and Mary Bacon, who was doubtless a native of Bradford. He came here with his parents when quite young. He commenced the practice of his profession about 1820, and continued it about a score of years.

Dr. Bacon, it is claimed, was a descendant of Lord Bacon, the distinguished philosopher and scholar of the sixteenth and seventeenth centuries; and, by the hereditamental law of Nature, the doctor received a large share of his ancestor's character and qualities. Lord Bacon was the most learned man of his day: so was the doctor skilled in many languages, and the practice of physic, besides being cultured in most branches of education, and he was acknowledged to be an excellent physician. But both their careers teach the moral lesson that the tree of knowl-edge is not the tree of life. Lord Bacon held the office of high chancellor, but showed himself morally unfit for it · the doctor, with a good practice, and winning an excellent reputation, was addicted to the use of strong drink, so that he could not attend to his duty, and therefore lost his practice, his reputation, and his character. The family to which he belonged is said to have been very aristocratic and wealthy. He built and resided in the house afterwards owned and occupied by the late Mr. Elbridge Perley. He died March 23, 1855, at the age of seventy years; it is an uncommon coincidence, that Dr. Sawyer also passed away on the same day. His wife was for many years a housekeeper for Gen. Lowe, and after the marriage of the general with Mrs. Merriam, Mrs. Bacon built, and till her death lived in, the cottage at the East Parish village, where her daughter Abbie recently died. A son — Edward — of the doctor still survives. John Bacon, so prominent in town-affairs half a century ago, was a brother of the doctor. John Bacon was the author of *Bacon's Town-Officer*, one of the earliest works of the kind.

Dr. Sawyer getting to be aged, a young and unmarried physician, Charles P French, came to Boxford, and secured board with the late Major William Lowe, and commenced practice in 1848. Dr. French was born in Lyndsborough, N. H., in 1824, and was son of Isaac P. and Clarissa B. French. Continuing here nearly two years, in 1849 he removed to Topsfield, and continued his professional prac-tice there. The following year he married Miss Mary S, daughter of Oliver T. and Sarah A. Peabody of Boxford, who died a few years since. Dr. French is still in practice, though not in this vicinity. He was much liked for his humorous disposition; and his medical knowledge was deemed sufficient for good practice.

To return to our schools. In 1791, Nov. 10, the town

voted to divide itself into six districts, and to have a school-house built in each district, for which purpose six hundred pounds were raised. The Third and Sixth District school-houses were immediately erected; that of the Fifth District, in 1797; and the remaining districts were supplied with the schoolhouses that were then in use

The names of the heads of families contained in these six districts in 1791 are found on the town-records, which we transcribe, viz.: —

FIRST DISTRICT. — Nathan Andrews, sen., Nathan Andrews, jun., Jacob Andrews, widow Ruth Curtis, John Dorman, Timothy Dorman, Solomon Gould, Stephen Gould, Capt. Jacob Gould, Jacob Gould, jun, Jacob Gould, 3d, Samuel Gould, Cornelius Gould, John Killam, Asa Peabody, Samuel Peabody, Bimsley Peabody, Benjamin Perley, James Russell, Nathaniel Smith, Isaac Smith, John Stiles, Stephen Symonds, and widow Anna Williams.

SECOND DISTRICT. — James Andrews, Gideon Bixby, David Butman, Isaac Preston Durant, Jacob Dwinnell, Richard Foster, John Giddings, Benjamin Gould, Elisha Gould, widow Anna Hale, Edmund Herrick, Nathaniel Herrick, Rev. Elizur Holyoke, John Kimball, Samuel Kimball, David Kimball, Joshua Rea, William Rea, Asa Riggs, Moses Peabody, Simeon Stiles, Timothy Stiles, Joseph Symonds, and John Towne.

THIRD DISTRICT. — Daniel Chapman, John Dresser, Benjamin Emerson, Daniel Gould, John Herrick, Richard Peabody, Moses Perley, Nathan Perley, Capt. William Perley, Capt. Francis Perley, Moody Perley, Stephen Spofford, Jedediah Stickney, Jonas Warren, Nathan Wood, Moses Wood, Jonathan Wood, Solomon Wood, widow Mehitable Wood, widow Lydia Wood, and widow Margaret Wood

FOURTH DISTRICT. — John Blaisdell, Samuel Brown, Thomas Butman, John Butman, James Chute, Joseph Hale, Joseph Holden, Nathan Hood, Benjamin Hood,

Joshua Jackson, Nathan Low, Stephen Peabody, Jesse Perley, Major Asa Perley, Mr. Thomas Perley, Nathaniel Perley, Amos Perley, Henry Perley, Jacob Smith, John Smith, and Benjamin Spofford.

FIFTH DISTRICT. — Capt. Isaac Adams, Enos Carleton, Lieut. Moses Carleton, Joseph Carleton, Samuel Chadwick, Moses Chadwick, Isaac Chadwick, Deacon John Chadwick, Capt. Jonathan Foster, Oliver Foster, Ephraim Foster, Reuben Gragg, Jeremiah Harriman, Amos Kimball, Enoch Kimball, Nathan Kimball, Moses Kimball, widow Sarah Kimball, John Palmer, Tyler Porter, widow Mary Porter, Mr. Moses Porter, Samuel Spofford, Parker Spofford, Amos Spofford, Daniel Swan, Ensign Gideon Tyler, John Tyler, Abraham Tyler, Broadstreet Tyler, and David Wood.

SIXTH DISTRICT. — John Buckmaster, Samuel Carleton, sen, Samuel Carleton, jun., Obadiah Carleton, Thomas Chadwick, David Coburn, Samuel Cole, Simeon Cole, Lieut. Richard Head, Joseph Hovey, Capt. Ivory Hovey, widow Mehitable Hovey, Luke Hovey, Richard Hovey, John Hovey, David Kimball, widow Elizabeth Kimball, Stephen Merrill, William Parker, Richard Pearl, John Pearl, Lieut. Ebenezer Peabody, Daniel Peabody, William Porter, John Robinson, Esq., Lieut. Samuel Runnells, widow Hannah Runnells, Ensign Enos Runnells, Josiah Sessions, heirs of David Wood, Lemuel Wood, and Joseph Wood.

The situation of the several schoolhouses at that time may not be uninteresting to our readers. The First-District schoolhouse stood a little west of the present building, on the same side of the street; the Second, in the western corner of the late Deacon Palmer's house-lot; the Third, near the house of the late Edward Batchelder; the Fourth stood a few rods nearer the junction of the two roads from where the schoolhouse of that district was lately removed, near the residence of Mr. William P. Cleaveland; the Fifth stood near the junction of the two roads near the residence of the late Moses Kimball, on the northerly side of the way ; the Sixth stood a few rods west of the residence of the late venerable Benjamin Peabody, between the two roads. The after-history of these school-edifices is as follows · The First-District schoolhouse was supplanted by the present one in 1854 ; the Second, ditto, in 1845 ; the Third was sold when that and the Fourth Districts were united, in 1869 ; and the Fourth was used as a schoolhouse until 1851, when it was sold to Mr. John Hale, who still uses it as an out-building, and a new one was erected a few rods in the rear of the old one. This occupied its site until 1869, when, as we have stated above, the Third and Fourth Districts were united, and this building was moved to its present position near Harmony Cemetery, which was a central place between the two districts. The Fifth stood on its original site until the district was discontinued, in 1869, when the schoolhouse was sold to Capt. Samuel Kimball. The Sixth was removed to the site of the present schoolhouse. About 1840 a new district, called the Seventh District, was created, and a schoolhouse built, which is the one situated near the Second Church.

During, and previous to, the period of which we are writing, but one session or term was held annually, probably during the winter season. No regular system of study was followed, and the text-books used by the scholars were of various authorities. Previous to the year 1795 the selectmen hired the teachers, inspected the schools, and filled the office of school-committee generally. The extent of the branches taught is well represented in that well-known sentence, "to read, to write, and to cipher." English grammar was introduced into our schools about 1795, but was only used to a slight extent.

In 1792, £60 was raised to support the schools for that year.

When the will of Hon. Aaron Wood was opened after his death in 1791, it was found that he had bequeathed to the town, for the support of a grammar-school, all the income of his house and other buildings, his real estate, &c. (it being the farm lately owned by C. C. Stevens), in the following words, viz.: "I give the improvement and income of my dwelling-house and all other buildings, and the improvement and income of all my lands in Boxford, to be used and improved for and towards the support of a grammar-school forever in the said town of Boxford. The manner of leasing out said premises I order to be under the care and direction of three deliberate persons chosen by the inhabitants of the said town of Boxford at a legal meeting for that purpose, and said committee to be chosen for so long time at each choice as the town shall think proper; and, in case of the death or removal of any or either of said committee, then another or others, as the case may be, to be chosen at the next annual town-meeting. I give the use of my pew in the meeting-house to the same purpose as my real estate."

In April, 1793, the town chose a committee, according to the provisions of the will, to take the care of and lease out the estate. The committee * consisted of Thomas Perley, jun., John Robinson, Esq., and Capt. Francis Perley, " three discreet persons," who immediately sold the leases (which ran for a thousand years) at auction, realizing from the sale $2,061.33. This sum yields an annual interest of $123.68,

---

* The thanks of the town were voted to the committee May 8, 1826, in the following words, viz.:

" *Voted*, That the thanks of the town be given to the committee appointed by the town to take the care and management of the donation devised to said town in the last will and testament of the Hon. Aaron Wood, for the use of a grammar-school in said town forever, that they have so wisely, faithfully, and carefully managed the proceeds of said donation, that the town has not experienced a cent's loss during thirty-four years, the time of their service in that capacity."

which is applied to the support of the schools in the town.

In consideration of the benevolence and usefulness of Mr. Wood, the town caused to be erected to his memory, at a cost of $78.53, a monument bearing the following inscription : —

Sacred
to the memory of
the Hon. Aaron Wood, Esq., who suddenly expired on the twentieth of January, MDCCXCI.,
Etatis LXXI
He commenced a member of the
General Court in MDCCLXII, and during
the remainder of his life
he enjoyed the confidence of his country,
being employed in the
House of Representatives, Senate, Council, &
Conventions of the
Commonwealth of Massachusetts.
By a Devise in his last Will & Testament
he left a valuable Estate
toward supporting a Grammar School, forever,
in the town of Boxford his native place.
The inhabitants of Boxford in town meeting
assembled, on the nineteenth of
September, MDCCXCIII, to perpetuate this
act of his benevolence have erected this
MONUMENT

Sept. 22, 1795, the first school-committee, whose duties were "to hire schoolmasters and dames, and to inspect the schools if thought proper," were chosen. This consisted of John Robinson, David Kimball, Jonathan Wood, Thomas Perley, Jonathan Foster, Enos Runnells, and Timothy Dorman. Heretofore the selectmen had performed these duties.

At the end of the school-report which follows will be found the names of the school-committee for the succeeding year, 1796 : —

"The committee appointed by the town of Boxford for attending to the business of the schools in the several districts beg leave to report that, since the rising generation have a just claim upon us to afford them all the opportunities and advantages which may be in our power, after deliberating impartially upon the subject, they are of opinion that it is a duty incumbent on us to provide for the instruction of our youth in those ways which will most directly lead to the desired end (viz.), the diffusion of knowledge and the promotion of virtue, and therefore have submitted the following articles for the consideration of the town.

"1st, That it is the duty of school-committees when employing masters or mistresses for instructing the youth in the several districts in this town to require satisfactory evidence of their being qualified for that purpose agreeable with law; also, that the selectmen be directed to give no orders for the payment of any instructors who shall not produce the evidence aforesaid.

"2d, That some regular system of instruction ought to be adopted in the schools, and that the scholars attending the same school ought to be furnished with the same kind of books, that the instructor may be enabled to divide his pupils into suitable classes

"3d, When masters are engaged they should be required to open and close the exercises of their schools with prayer, which will assist in preserving order and good government in them, and also that they be desired to observe any particular mode of instruction which the committee and they shall judge will become most beneficial

"4th, That the committee shall visit the masters' schools twice annually (viz.), when they are opened, and previously to their being closed; on their first visit specimens of the writing, &c, of the scholars shall be lodged in the hands of the committee, and they shall take, so far as may be, an exact state of the schools, which will enable them to form a better judgment of the proficiency of the scholars at the closing visitation.

"5th, That it be recommended to the several instructors in those instances where scholars are tolerably forward, and can read with proficiency, to instruct them in English grammar, that they may be led into the principles of the English language.

"6th, That it might have a beneficial tendency, should the town see it proper to advance a trifling sum (say one dollar for each district) to be laid out for books, and those to be given by the committee to the scholars who, in the judgment of the master, shall have made the greatest proficiency in several branches.

"7th, That it is the duty of every committee to report annually to the town the particular state of each school.

> "PETER EATON,
> JOHN ROBINSON,
> SAMUEL HOLYOKE,
> THOMAS PERLEY,
> FRANCIS PERLEY,
> JOSEPH SYMONDS.

"BOXFORD, Oct. 31st, 1796."

The town debt in 1793 was £452. This continued at about the same amount for many years. In 1858 $500 of the debt was paid; in 1859, $700; in 1860, $500; and so on to the present time. The debt, now amounting to $5,095.44, is covered by notes and bonds and other securities.

July 19, 1799, the West Parish "voted that Instrumental Musick be Introduced into the meeting on Sundays." The people of color were also appointed a separate seat, in the gallery, where they could be clear (?) from the whiter population.

July 17, 1792, a committee were appointed to make a report of the First Parish's funds. Their report states that the funds consisted of a State note of £148 18 s 5 d., dated Dec. 5, 1781, having three years and nine months interest paid, and miscellaneous bonds and notes amounting to £99 18 s. 11 d. 2 far., besides sums due on petty accounts to the amount of £30 19 s. 11 d., and £10 11 s. 10 d. in cash; amounting in the aggregate to £290 9 s 1 d. 2 far. These funds were combined with the First-Parish fund when it was originated in 1824.

During these few years of which we have just been writing, various repairs on the meeting-house in the East Parish had been made from time to time. These repairs were generally to stop leaks, and fill up cracks where snow blew in in the winter, mend broken glass, patch the plastering, and to paint the meeting-house on the outside,

which was at the beginning of this century of a stone-color.
The walls on the inside, from time to time, the parish
voted to whitewash. There is only one instance of its
being re-shingled, which was in 1785, at which time the foreside and two ends were newly clapboarded, and the whole
painted.

In 1802 the West Parish presented Rev. Mr. Eaton the
sum of one hundred and twenty-five dollars gratuitously.
In 1804 they built a shed and woodhouse for him.

In 1799 the Second Parish thought of putting in a stove
to warm the meeting-house ; but nothing was done about it
until 1824, when two stoves were purchased and set up.
When this was done the people were very uneasy, fearing
that the meeting-house would catch fire.

Nov. 11, 1824, the East Parish voted to have a stove put
into their meeting-house, for the " convenience and comfort" of the inhabitants. The *comfort* which this afforded
to the church-goers is too well known to need definition,
but the *convenience* would perhaps not be so clear in the
minds of the uninitiated. To make the language of this
record clear, we would state that previous to this time, and
even later, the people carried to meeting the old-fashioned
foot-stoves. These were square tin boxes enclosed in an
ornamental wooden frame, large enough to place both feet
upon, in which the people placed hot glowing coals fresh
from the hearth, when they started to meeting. When
noon came their coals would emit no heat, and to obtain a
fresh supply they would be compelled to borrow some
more *live* coals from those people that lived near the
church. When the stove was placed in the meeting-house,
the people found it much more convenient to fill their foot-
stoves in the meeting-house.

When the vote regarding the stove became known, the
parish were surprised with the gift of an "elegant cast-
iron stove and funnel." The donors were Solomon Towne,

Jeremiah Peabody, Jacob Peabody, Charles Scudder, Gilman Prichard, Timothy Dorman, William G. Lambert, Elizur Holyoke, and Samuel Peabody, all of whom were of Boston. The stove was received, and placed in the aisle in the centre of the meeting-house.

In early times most of the congregation stopped at the meeting-house all day. This gave rise to the " Sabba'-Day houses," which some of the wealthy families built for their convenience. They were sheds with another story above finished off into a tidy room where they could spend the noons. The shed beneath was used as a shelter for their horses. Whether any of these buildings were ever erected in Boxford, or not, we have never learned ; but they were in use at the Topsfield meeting-house when the Boxford people attended church there.

The *Essex Musical Association* was an extensive organization in its day; and, as implied by the title, was composed of Essex-County vocal musicians. Several members belonged to Boxford, some of whose names, and perhaps all, follow : Deacon Parker Spofford, Ensign Joseph Symonds, jun., and Mr. Stephen Kimball. Samuel Holyoke, the distinguished composer, was prominent in this association ; and it was probably through his influence that their annual festival was several times held here. Sept. 3, 1798, the First Parish voted that they " may have the liberty of the galleries in the meeting house as may be convenient for them at their annual public exhibition." In the falls of 1806 and 1807, we believe, the festivals were again held here. Shortly after this, the association died out. In their exhibitions, which continued through the day, the singers, numbering upwards of fifty, were arranged in the three galleries of the meeting-house, and the audience occupied the auditorium below. This was a gala-day to the people of Old Essex. Refreshment-booths were erected, wagons at whose tail-end refreshments of all kinds were sold were drawn up in order, and other things incident to such times were created; and the people came in teams, on horseback, and on foot, from all sections of the county. Those who remember these festivals declare that the musical talent here congregated has rendered to Boxford a name and a fame that will enliven the annals of those dull old times.

As we write, a copy of the *Salem Gazette*, of Jan. 3, 1800, lies before us. A deep black border is placed upon the four pages, and the reading-matter is entirely devoted to the death of George Washington. An assured belief in Washington's greatness and goodness, and praise and honor to his illustrious name, is the spirit of its columns. The actions taken by the highest legislative bodies of our National Government, letters from the leading men of the country, and miscellaneous articles of prose and verse, are congenial in their reverence of the departed President. Washington died at his home at Mount Vernon, in Virginia, between eleven and twelve o'clock Saturday night, Dec. 14, 1799, at the age of sixty-seven years. On the anniversary of his next birthday, Feb. 22, 1800, Rev. Mr. Eaton delivered "a well adapted oration in commemoration of the sublime virtues of General George Washington." At the next annual town-meeting, a vote of thanks was tendered to him for the same by the town

In 1788 a tavern was in vogue in the West Parish, it being carried on by Lieut. Asa Merrill. In that year the militia company of that parish met at the tavern, and were reviewed. About the year 1800 two taverns were flourishing in the town, one in each parish. The one in the West Parish was kept by Mr. Phineas Cole, at the Clement place. Mr. Cole soon afterward removed to Pelham, N. H., and instituted another tavern in that place. The tavern in the East Parish was kept at the late residence of Mr. Charles C. Stevens, near the "old camp-ground." As we have observed a few pages back, after Hon. Aaron Wood's

death, the place was sold by lease to Deacon Parker Spofford. He refitted the old mansion, as far as need be,
into a fine country tavern. This flourished until his death
in 1836, and received during that time the commendation
of the entertained. The first post-office ever in town was
kept in this tavern until 1826, the mail being conveyed
by the old stage-coaches. This was one of the stopping-
places of the famous stage-driver Pinkham, whose route
was over the old Andover road The people living so far
away from the post-office, a general distribution of the mail
took place only on Sundays, when Mr Spofford would
carry the mail-matter to church, and deliver it to the various
owners. A slow procedure, to be sure ; but the people
of those days were not in so much haste as at the present

Mr. Elisha Bunker also kept a tavern, during the year
1836, at the mansion now occupied by Mr John I. Ladd,
near the Second Church. He was succeeded, on his removal to the East Parish in 1837, by a Mr. Brown, who,
however, retained the business there but a short time

CHAPTER XII.

1800 – 1830.

Rev. Mr Holyoke's Death. — His Ministry and Life. —
Rev Isaac Briggs settled — Powder-House — Black-
smiths in East Parish — Cemetery near the First
Church — Private Cemetery — Chadwick Bequest —
Grocery-Stores — Match-Factory. — Militia. — War of
1812. — Mind of the Town in regard to the War —
Events of the War — Soldiers drafted. — First-Parish
Fund founded. — Trouble in the First Religious Soci-
ety — Hearses, &c. — Day's Grist-Mill — Porter's Mill.
— Blacksmiths in West Parish in " Old Times."

N February, 1793, Rev. Mr Holyoke, pastor of the
First Church, was prostrated by a paralytic shock,
which unfitted him for constant duty in the pulpit
during the rest of his life. During the following
summer he preached but seldom. He grew more ill as the
year advanced, so much so that he did not preach after
the end of the year. Mr Holyoke's salary was continued
the same, and the same ·relations were regarded by both
pastor and people, — in a pecuniary view, — though the
parish hired other ministers to discourse to them on the
sabbath. Sept. 1, 1793, Rev. Francis Quarles .was hired
to preach a few months. During the ensuing four years,
various clergymen officiated in the pulpit; some for a
shorter, and some for a longer, time.

On the 13th of October, 1797, a committee appointed by
the parish went to Mr. Holyoke's house, and conversed

with him on the subject of his resigning the ministry, and having a new minister settled among them. Mr. Holyoke fully acquiesced with the desire of the parish, and also in their choice of the Rev. Nathaniel H. Fletcher as their pastor. During these four years of Mr. Holyoke's illness, his regular salary continued to be paid to him. In 1798 a committee was appointed to offer to Mr. Holyoke an annual sum for his support during the remainder of his life, on condition that he resigned his office of pastor. The committee repaired to his house on the 6th of June, and made known to him the proposals of the parish, and proposed a conference on the subject at any time that would be most agreeable to him. Thursday, the 4th of July, being assigned by Mr Holyoke, the committee waited upon him on that day ; but, Mr. Holyoke's infirmities being so much increased, he excused himself from taking a part in the conversation, which, thereby devolving upon his family, was chiefly conducted by his sons, who informed the committee that, in various conversations with their father, they had become acquainted with his views and sentiments concerning the matter. The sons observed that their father was fully satisfied with the existing establishment, and did not on his account wish for any change of measures , but that, if he agreed to any other arrangement, it would be to accommodate himself in some measure to the wishes of the parish ; and, conformable therewith, they had made calculations for finding the amount of the sum suitable to be received as an acquittance and discharge of his stated salary, and proposed fifteen hundred dollars as an acceptable sum. The committee observed that that sum was considerably beyond what any person in the parish had contemplated, and in their apprehension could not be agreed to. The family, in reply, said if the sum proposed was improper, the parish might mention what they *would* give. They described the debilitated state of Mr.

Holyoke as requiring much attention, care, and labor from
the family, and consequent need of a support from the
parish, of whom they spoke in terms of respect, and did
not discover any aversion to attempting a settlement in the
manner proposed, if the parish chose some person to conduct the business on their part. They also said that Mr.
Holyoke was desirous of retaining his ministerial relation
to his people, but, in case the parish could settle a minister only by his resignation, he would relinquish his ministerial relation, provided a council should advise thereto.
The idea of making some deduction from the stated salary,
while things continued on the present establishment, was
proposed by the committee. In reply, the family said that,
by the change of times since Mr Holyoke's settlement
over the parish, the salary was reduced almost one-half,
and they did not see how they could do with less than
the usual salary After this conference with Mr. Holyoke's
family, no further advances were made toward effecting
the proposed settlement; and the idea of having another
minister settled among them while Mr. Holyoke was alive
soon ceased to exist But, contrary to appearances, Mr.
Holyoke agreed, the following winter (1798–99), to take
two hundred dollars, and ten cords of wood hauled to his
door, as an annual sum of acquittance and discharge of
his salary during the remainder of his life During the
remaining time that Rev Mr. Holyoke lived he was out of
doors but seldom, his paralytic complaint compelling him
to undergo less exercise.

After enduring his illness for thirteen years, Mr. Holyoke quietly died on Monday, March 31, 1806, at the age
of seventy-four years and ten months. His wife, who had
tenderly cared for her beloved husband, survived him little
more than two years, dying Tuesday, Dec. 20, 1808, at the
age of seventy-two years. Their remains he interred in
the cemetery near the church, and the monument erected

to his memory by the parish bears the following inscription : —

> "This Monument erected
> by the 1st Parish in
> Boxford as a Testimony
> of Respect to the memory of
> the REV. ELIZUR HOLYOKE,
> 3d Pastor of the 1st Church in
> this Town who died on
> the 31 of March 1806,
> Ætatis 75 & 47 of
> his Ministry.

> Lost to the world adieu! our friend adieu!
> Unblemished spirit, seek those realms of light,
> Where boundless Mercy only meets the view,
> Faith lost in wonder, Hope in full delight

> Come ye, whose throbbing bosoms know to feel;
> Come, let me point you to the loosen'd sod;
> Behold the tomb, in humblest reverence kneel,
> Here learn humility, yourselves and God."

Rev. Mr. Holyoke was born in Boston, May 11, 1731. His father, Samuel Holyoke, born 1693, through Elizur[3] and Elizur[2] was a great-grandson of Edward Holyoke[1] of Tanworth in Warwickshire, Eng., who married, 18 June, 1612, Prudence, daughter of Rev. John Stockton, rector of Kinkolt, in Leicestershire. Edward Holyoke, brother of Samuel, and uncle of our minister, was the president of Harvard College for many years. Rev. Mr. Holyoke's mother was Elizabeth, daughter of Joseph Brigham of Boston

Mr. Holyoke married Hannah, daughter of Rev. Oliver Peabody of Natick, Nov 13, 1760, the result of which union was eight children, — six sons and two daughters, viz. : Samuel, b. Aug. 5, 1761 ; d. Aug. 8, 1761. Samuel, b. Oct. 15, 1762 (see his biography) Elizur, b. Nov 17, 1764; d. about 1829 Elizabeth, b. May 28, 1767, d Aug. 2, 1767. Oliver Peabody, b April 14, 1769. Edward, b Jan. 15, 1772; d. July 1, 1846. Hannah, b. Oct. 16, 1774; d unm., Dec. 5, 1865, at the old homestead. Charles, b Nov. 11, 1781.

Mr. Holyoke first resided in the old house that formerly stood where the present Holyoke house now stands. After living in it two or three years, Mr. Holyoke's father, a rich merchant of Boston, razed it to the ground, and erected the present house at a great cost. The old mansion is known far and wide as the " Old Holyoke Homestead." It is now owned and occupied by Mr. Elvin French, the well-known musical director. Decay is fast creeping upon it, and soon it will be numbered with the things of the past. To strangers the old place is a peculiar curiosity. They desire to frequent the old house, and examine its passages, halls, and numerous rooms, each containing some curious work of antiquity. Gazing at the relic, underneath whose shadows so many happy as well as sorrowful scenes have been enacted, whose clapboards and trimmings have been worn rough and thin by the beating of storms for more than a century, and looking upward at the gabled roof overgrown with moss, and hanging over it the distended and drooping boughs of the gigantic elms which stand around, surely it does not need a Hawthorne to place before the thoughtful man its unwritten history. It was owned and part of it occupied by Hannah, Rev. Mr. Holyoke's daughter, until her death, which occurred in 1865, Dec. 5. The rest of the house was tenanted by many different families, one of whom was that of Mr. Benjamin French, father of Elvin French, the present owner and occupier, who was born in the ancient dwelling.

Regarding the old mansion, Mrs. M. L. Emerson, lately a resident of the town, who has written some excellent poetry, contributed the following lines to the *Salem Gazette :* —

"'Neath sheltering elms the ancient dwelling stands,
  Where several highways socially clasp hands;
  Its general air speaks of the 'auld lang syne,'
  And years have left their marks in many a line.

" The moss-grown shingles, broken and decayed ;
  The loosened clapboards, where the winds have played ;
  The shattered window-panes, the door-stone low, —
  All tell the story of the long ago.

" Within, what tales those mouldering walls could tell,
  If they could break their silence' mighty spell, —
  Of childhood, age, of happiness and tears,
  Of life and death, through all these hundred years !

" Old sunken floors, by many footsteps worn ;
  Paper once gay, but mildewed now and torn ,
  The embellished doorways, and the panelled hall, —
  The generations of the past recall

" Two antique portraits, older than we know, —
  Perchance were old a century ago, —
  Hang in the upper hall ; faint shadows they
  Of faces long since passed from earth away.

" Up narrow winding attic-stairs we climb,
  To see the only gleam a bygone time
  Has left, of horror, in this lonely place,
  Which soon will crumble, and will leave no trace.

" From a high beam there still suspends a rope,
  Where, years ago, some one bereft of hope
  Essayed to end her life ; but all in vain ·
  Life's rugged pathway she must walk again.

" A few brief years, and the old house no more
  Will stand a way-mark on Time's stormy shore ;
  And few will mourn, as few will ever prize
  These relics of the past, with all their teachings wise."

When Mr. Holyoke was settled over the society here, he
was but twenty-seven years of age, and unmarried He
had graduated at Harvard College in 1750, while yet in his

teens. Where he had spent the intervening years, has not come to our notice.

Few ministers or men have lived in a place so long, so quietly, and so happily, as Mr. Holyoke. The cords of harmony between him and his people were ever perfect, even to reverence and love. His ministry,* extending as it did through the period of forty-seven years, was very uncommon and unprecedented in the ecclesiastical history of New England. In 1765, to show their love and respect, the parish presented to him a small tract of land near to his residence.

The cold "orthodox" air seems not to have found its way even among those where it would have been expected by others of a different denomination, who have always defined that class of ministers as haughty in their speech and manner, and restrained in showing the cords of love and affection. He seems to have departed from this rule, and sought and found shelter in a more friendly and unrestrained manner.

During Mr. Holyoke's illness, miscellaneous clergymen were hired for a few sabbaths at a time. Principal among these were Revs. David Smith, Samuel Dana, Joseph Brown, and Henry Bigelow.

In January, 1808, Rev. Ebenezer Hubbard of Ipswich was invited to settle over the First Church; but he refused because of so small a salary, which he said "would be insufficient to enable him to live as he ought to." On the 8th of the following August, the parish concurred with the church in inviting Rev. Isaac Briggs of York, Me., to settle here; agreeing to give him four hundred dollars salary annually, and two hundred and fifty dollars as a settlement, to be paid in three months after his installation; also, six cords of "good oak wood" annually, delivered at his door †

---

* Sixty-four persons were admitted to the church during his ministry.

† He was to relinquish all claims to the income of the "Parsonage Lands," and money which might arise from leasing the same.

Rev. **Mr.** Briggs consented to settle with them by the following letter : —

"To the First Church and Religious Society in Boxford ·

"*My Christian Friends,* — Whereas, He in whose hands are the hearts of all men, and who can turn them as the rivers of water are turned, hath in His all-wise providence inclined you unanimously to invite me, who am most unworthy, to the pastoral charge over you in the Lord, I do now return you my most grateful acknowledgment for the honor conferred on me in your election.

" And with respect to the important affair proposed to my consideration · after serious inquiry as to what was my duty, and having consulted my friends and some of my fathers in the ministry, I do now with a trembling heart but a willing mind hereby manifest my acceptance of your invitation, and offer to settle with you in the work of the Gospel ministry And although I have thought it my duty to obtain such a maintenance as might free me from the necessity of encumbering myself too much with the things of this world, yet I humbly trust I can truly say, that I *principally* seek, not *yours,* but *you.* May the Great Shepherd of Israel, who dwelleth between the cherubims, shine forth upon us all, uniting us with His light and love. I would likewise, with the greatest importunity, ask an interest in your prayers at the throne of Divine Grace, that you would strive with me in your prayers to God for me, that I may be enabled to discharge with fidelity every duty incumbent upon me ; that I may both save myself and those that hear me.

" May we all have abundant reason to rejoice together in peace and unity in this world, and be crowned with eternal glory in the world to come

" Isaac Briggs."

The installation took place on Wednesday, Sept. 28, 1808, with the following exercises : Introductory prayer by Rev. Mr. Briggs of Kittery, Me. ; preaching by Rev. Mr. French of North Hampton, N H., from 2 Cor. vi. 4 ; charge to the pastor, by Rev. Mr. Stone of Reading ; prayer of consecration, by Rev Asahel Huntingdon of Topsfield , Rev. Mr. Eaton of the West Parish gave the right hand of fellowship ; and Rev. Mr. Chandler of Kittery, Me., made the concluding prayer. Samuel Holyoke, the noted composer, took charge of the music during the occasion.

. In 1801, May 4, the town "voted to build a house to keep a stock of ammunition and military stores in." The "powder-house," as it was called, was situated on a piece of land, bought of Capt. Francis Perley, which is situated north of the late Third-District schoolhouse. It was built eight feet square, and seven feet and nine inches in height. The sides were of brick, and the roof of wood, with a double door to close the entrance. The cost of it was $132.41. The powder-house stood until 1856, when it was sold at auction in town-meeting, being bid off by Mr. Joseph H. Janes at $10.75.

Thomas Dresser,* brother of Nathan, having learned the trade in his father's shop, purchased, in 1795, some land, a part of which is now included in the Savage place, on which he erected the Savage house, and across the road built a blacksmith's shop,† which business he continued to carry on until about 1800, when he removed to Andover, Me It was then owned successively by Thomas Butman of Marblehead, and John Dorman of Boxford. In 1813 Dorman sold out to Phineas Barnes. Thomas W. Durant hired the shop of Butman, Dorman, and Barnes, successively, until about 1815, John Poor of Newbury, hiring it in May, 1816 Poor stopped but a short time, being followed by James Patterson in August, 1817. May 24, 1819, Barnes let the shop to Fitch Weston and Amos Cowdrey. They continued in the business there until 1822, when, with the help of Amos Perley and others, Weston erected a shop, and commenced the business, near the residence of Mr William P. Cleaveland The old shop was demolished by Mr. Barnes in 1825. Weston continued to work at his

---

* Thomas Dresser married Hannah Hazen, the celebrated witch of the neighborhood She was daughter of Jacob and Abigail (Perley) Hazen, and was born in Boxford, July 3, 1764

† So we are told But, from the town-records, we should judge that this was the shop in which John Stiles worked in 1774 and after.

trade in his new location for a few years. After he left town, Jacob Lofty, John Woodman, and others, carried on the business until about 1850, when the building was removed to a meadow of the late William N. Cleaveland, Esq., where it is yet standing, it being used as a storehouse for peat.

At this time (1800) Samuel Peabody was the blacksmith at the East Parish village. His shop was located near the residence of Ancill Dorman, Esq. Mr. Peabody is remembered as a man of great strength and endurance. He died June 7, 1824, aged fifty-six years. About 1800, Capt. Joseph Symonds, who lived in Mr. C. Piersons' house, left off blacksmithing. His shop stood near by.

In 1807, Asa Peabody presented to the public a lot of land near the First Church, to be used as a cemetery; it being that which has ever since been used for that purpose. Mr. Peabody was the first person interred in it, as we are informed by his epitaph : —

In memory of
Mr. Asa Peabody,
Obt. Oct. 19, 1807,
Aet. 67

Lived respected & died lamented.
First interred & giver of this ground

In 1875 it was enlarged by the addition of a piece of adjoining land given by Mr. John Sayward, who, by a strange coincidence, was the first one buried in the addition.

There is a private cemetery situated on the banks of Ipswich River, near the residence of Mr. Thomas Sawyer. It has been used by the Curtises and Killams for more than half a century.

In 1809 widow Sarah Chadwick, in her will, bequeathed two thousand dollars to the West Parish for the promotion of education.

John Dorman, who was living at the Savage place, — probably having purchased it of Thomas Dresser, on his removal to Andover, Me., about 1800, — worked at shoe-making across the road near the barn belonging to the late Amos Stevens, in a building of considerable dimensions. About 1814 Samuel Stiles opened a store in one half of the buildings, and continued to make shoes with Dorman in the other part. About 1817 Stiles removed the build-ing to the Holyoke place at the village, and continued the business in that locality. In 1825 James Whittemore succeeded Stiles in the business. In 1826 Col. Charles Peabody bought and moved the building to the Sayward place (which had been previously owned by Capt. Tobijah Davis), and, having obtained the commission of postmaster, incorporated the post-office within its walls. On Col. Pea-body's removal to Barre, Ill., in 1836, he sold out to Mr. Elisha G. Bunker, from Barnstead, N.H., who continued in the business, and also in the office of postmaster, until he removed from the town. Gamaliel Harris then owned it until it was burnt; Osgood Dale having hired the store after Mr. Bunker had left.

About 1790 iron-smelting was begun at the match-fac-tory; Samuel (father of Capt. Samuel) and David Kimball, brothers, being a part of the proprietors. Ore was brought from the neighboring towns, as well as from our own lands, to be smelted, and no doubt quite a business was done. After 1805 we hear no more about it.

The mill-site was next owned by Solomon Towne, who altered it into a grist-mill, his brothers Asa and John being millers successively. At the same time, two brothers by the name of Redington carried on, in another part of the mill-building, the manufacture of wooden trays, bowls, &c., and did various kinds of turning, such as hubs for wheels. Having entered into cotton-manufacturing, in the spring of 1832, Mr. Towne sold out to George Blackburn, who let

the place to John Bentley, a cotton-manufacturer of Yorkshire, England, who removed the grist-mill, and began
more extensively the manufacture of cotton yarn, wicking,
and batting. Mr. Bentley lived in the house now occupied
by Mr. Parkhurst. He employed some fifteen or twenty
hands in the mill, a number of them being Englishmen,
and, as we have been told, hired some of the neighbors to
wind the yarn and wicking by some simple appliance at
their homes. The business was carried on until a few
years before Mr. Bentley's death, which occurred Feb. 13,
1864, at the age of sixty-seven years. He was a native
of Yorkshire, England, and was son of John and Mary
Bentley.

The building and machinery remained as they were until
Messrs. Byam & Carlton purchased the property. in the
summer of 1867, of Mr. Blackburn, who still possessed it.
The machinery was taken out, and the old building removed
to give place to the spacious factory-building within whose
walls so many matches are daily turned out. The company
immediately set up their match-machinery, and did their
first day's work Sept. 2, 1867. Their first foreman was
N. E. Harris He was followed in the fall of 1868 by
—— Whittemore ; and Mr. Whittemore, May 1, 1869, by
Mr. John Parkhurst, who still retains the position.

The number of hands requisite to run the machinery,
&c., is twenty. Their method of match-manufacturing is
as follows : The logs are taken into the mill, and the clear
timber between the knots carefully cut out, which process
is termed " *bolting*." The knots and other refuse are used
in feeding the large thirty-horse-power steam-engine. These
junks, thus cut out, are then sawn into two-inch, round-
edged plank. This is called "*planking*." These plank are
passed to the " *trimmer*," whose business it is to square-
edge them The plank are then carried to the steam-house,
when, after being thoroughly "*steamed*," they are taken

out and "*slashed*," that is, cut up into thin boards two inches wide, and of the thickness of a match. They are then conveyed to the dry-house to be "*dried*," after which they are carried to the "*gang-machines*," three in number, at which two employees work, — one to saw the matches with the gang-saws, and the other to pack them in boxes as fast as they are sawn. These boxes contain ten or fifteen gross each, and are conveyed by rail to Boston to be "*dipped*," preparatory to offering them for sale. About 350 gross, or about 5,000,000 single matches, are turned out per day, and some 1,800 tons of timber consumed annually. The company have some $30,000 invested in the business, and turn out about $40,000 worth of goods annually. A saw-mill is also in connection with it, and also box-machinery to manufacture boxes for their own use, and for sale.

In the beginning of the nineteenth century the militia-companies drilled twice a year; viz., April and October. During the October training, the regiment met together for regimental inspection, and were reviewed by the general. Oct. 17, 1810, and Oct. 7 and 9, 1811, they were reviewed by Gen. Peabody of Newburyport.

The equipment of the militia was as follows, viz. · one musket, one bayonet, one iron rod, one scabbard and belt, three flints, one wire and brush, one knapsack, and twenty-four rounds of cartridges and balls. For being deficient of a cartridge-box and cartridges, the fine was thirty cents ; for not training, two dollars.

The Boxford companies formed a part of the Third Regiment, Second Brigade, Second Division (of which Benjamin Jenkins was lieutenant-colonel commandant), of the State militia.

From the beginning of the decade of time of which we are writing, England began to be hostile with the United States. American ships abroad suffered considerably by the British men-of-war that were sent out for that purpose. At last events terminated in an open declaration of war in June, 1812.

The West Parish company of foot, in 1812, consisted of the following men., viz : *Captain,* John Tyler ; *Fifers,* Charles Kimball, William Runnells ; *Drummers,* Jacob Parker, John Merrill ; *Sergeants,* Samuel Clement, Frederic Carleton, Gardner Ames, Isaac Hovey ; *Privates,* Daniel Adams, Billy Bradstreet, John Bacon, John B. Buckmaster, Edmund Barker, Richard Carleton, Leonard Carleton, James Coburn, William M. Coburn, Samuel Cree, Daniel Currier, Henry Clement, John Day, Nathan Dresser, Jeremiah Harriman, Daniel Harriman, Thomas Hovey, Benjamin Herrick, Micaiah Kimball, Benjamin Kimball, Moody Kimball, John Kimball, jun., Peter Pearl, Jonathan Porter, Stephen Porter, James Pettingill, Rufus Porter, Abraham Peabody, jun, Jonas Runnells, Eliphalet Runnells, Samuel S. Runnells, William Ross, John Ross, John Runnells, Thomas Spofford, Francis Swan, William Tyler, Joseph S. Tyler, Joseph Wood, Daniel Wood * (49).

Before war had been declared, pursuant to an Act of Congress of April 10, 1812, men were drafted to guard the seaports all along the coast, as it was expected that England would again commit her depredations upon our Atlantic ports.

Pursuant to an order from the lieutenant-colonel commandant, the company met at the West Parish meeting-house on Monday, May 25, and the following soldiers were drafted, viz : Frederic Carleton, sergeant ; and Billy Bradstreet, Leonard Carleton, Henry Clement, Benjamin Pearl, Rufus Porter, Moses Ross, and Joseph S. Tyler, privates.

As soon as war was declared with Great Britain, the inhabitants of Boxford came together at a town-meeting

---

* Daniel Wood is the only one now living of this company. He resides in the West Parish, and enjoys good health.

appointed for that purpose, and chose a committee, which consisted of Thomas Perley, Parker Spofford, Jacob Gould, Ebenezer Peabody, and Jonathan Foster, jun., to take into consideration the condition of affairs with Great Britain. The committee accordingly retired, and made out their report (which is inserted below), which was accepted by the town. It will be seen, on perusing the report, that the town greatly blamed the United States for doing as they did.

REPORT

"The committee appointed to take into consideration the present alarming situation of our country in consequence of the late Declaration of War by our Government with Great Britain, to express their minds on the subject, and to adopt such measures as will be thought fit and proper to avert so dreadful a calamity, viewing with inexpressible anxiety the awful situation of our country by the measures and declarations of the Government now involved in the calamities of war, and exposed to all the numerous train of evils inevitably resulting therefrom;

"In this situation it highly becomes good men and lovers of their country to consider and perform their duty to the Government. Under these apprehensions the following resolves are submitted, viz : —

"Resolved, that as citizens of a free Government we consider it to be our duty, and that we will support all constitutional laws and authorities of the United States and this Commonwealth, and being orderly assembled according to the provision of the Constitution, to consult on the common good of our country, are constrained to say, that when the United States were in a state of neutrality and at peace with all nations, for a series of years under the late and present administrations, under fearful apprehensions we have seen the Government of the United States proceeding in a course of measures of aversion and irritation with one powerful nation, and of complaisance and submission to another powerful nation. In the prosecution of such measures we consider the Government to have lost sight of, or to have disregarded, the best interests of the people, who by the late acts of the Government are now become exposed to all the horrors of war, and a numerous train of evils which will follow from a continued war with the power of Great Britain, and must result in the greatest of all evils, an alliance with, and subjugation to, the Emperor of France.

"Resolved, that we cannot see any just cause of this war · it will be destructive to the prosperity, the happiness, and the morals of the people; and if proceeded in we have reason to fear the loss of much blood and treasure, together with our national rights and independence.

"Resolved, that we admire the late speech of his excellency, Caleb Strong, to the Legislature, replete with wisdom and with moderation.

"Resolved, that we highly approve of the address of the House of Representatives to the people of Massachusetts, clearly pointing out to them their danger, the causes of their sufferings, and their remedy.

"Resolved, that in this deplorable situation of our public concerns, we will endeavor to cultivate a spirit of amity among ourselves; and, being of opinion that a unity of sentiment expressed by towns and counties is become necessary, this town will, on their part, appoint a delegate to meet, deliberate, and advise with the delegates that are or may be chosen for that purpose by the other towns in the county of Essex."

Not much was accomplished during the campaign of 1812, by the army of thirteen thousand men which had been raised by the Government, although the British could scarcely muster three thousand men on their whole line from west to east.

The next spring opened with the capture of York, in Canada, now called by its original Indian name, *Toronto ;* and again, on the 27th of May, Fort George was taken by the Americans. These, with several other victories on the water, among which may be mentioned Perry's victory on Lake Erie, made the season quite successful to the United States.

In 1814 Congress made provision for raising more men for the army. In the month of July orders were received by the West Boxford military company to detach a sergeant and a private from their company: accordingly Dean Chadwick and Eliphalet Runnells were drafted, — Dean Chadwick being appointed sergeant. The East Boxford company also received orders to draft two men to serve in

the army · Oliver Wood and Jacob Dresser were accordingly drafted. They were to serve for three months, and were
ordered to march on Monday, the first day of August
following. In the following September eight more were
drafted for the service of the State. Their names are as
follows, viz Francis Swan, Daniel Mitchel, Moody Kimball, and Stephen Pike, from the West Boxford company ;
and Joseph S. Peabody, Francis Peabody, John Perley, and
Abraham How, from the East Boxford company. They
were ordered to march to Beverly as soon as possible.
The late Capt. Aaron Spofford was also a soldier in this
war. He was at work, farming, in Andover, when he was
drafted. In 1878 the government granted him a pension.

The following were a part of the East Boxford "company
of foot" in 1814, viz.: Abraham Perley, captain ; Charles
Peabody, lieutenant ; Josiah Kimball, ensign ; Oliver Wood,
Joseph Foster, Tobias Davis, Abraham How, Nathan
Dresser, Seth Burnham, Samuel Perley, Jacob Dresser,
Henry Perley, Jonas Foster, Jacob Gould, Samuel Perley,
jun., Joseph Towne, Joseph S Peabody, Francis Peabody,
John Perley, Francis Perley, and Timothy F Stevens,
privates. Moody Foster and Nathaniel Long belonged to
it in 1815 ; Asa Perley, Daniel Andrews, Asa Stiles, Daniel
Gould, jun , Artemas Kimball, and Ancill Perley, in 1816 ;
Oliver Killam, Samuel Bixby, Joseph P. Gould, John Gould,
Peabody Russell, Oliver T. Peabody, and Joseph Daniels,
in 1817

Oct. 14, 1813, the militia met near Parker's Tavern in
Andover, and were reviewed by Gen Stickney of Newbury. Sept 29, 1814, they were inspected by Gen. Stickney and suite. Oct 18, 1814, the two companies, with
Capt Brocklebank's company from Georgetown, met at
Rufus Burnham's (the Batchelder place), where they were
trained in battalion by Col Low

Oct 12, 1815, the West Boxford company, then commanded by Amos Kimball, together with the East Boxford company, met with their regiment, which was then commanded by Lieut.-Col. Commandant Low, at the camp-ground near the late residence of C. C. Stevens, and joined the rest of the brigade, and were inspected by Major Scott of Newburyport.

Oct. 9, 1816, the regiment met, and were inspected by Col. Low. Oct. 9, 1817, the regiment met at the meeting-house in Georgetown, marched to Byfield, and joined the brigade, where they were inspected by Major Scott, and reviewed by Gov. John Brooks and suite. Oct. 16, 1818, the regiment met, and was inspected by Brig.-Major Scott of Newburyport, and reviewed by Major-Gen. Hovey. Oct. 7, 1819, the regiment was inspected by Major Scott. Oct. 5, 1821, the brigade met at Bradford, and were inspected by Brig.-Major Scott, and reviewed by Major-Gen. Stickney. Oct. 8, 1822, the regiment met, and were inspected by Brig.-Major Scott, and reviewed by Brig.-Gen. Low. Oct. 9, 1823, the brigade met at Eliphalet Chaplin's in Georgetown, and were inspected by Brig.-Major Low and Major-Gen. Stickney. Oct. 5, 1824, the regiment met in Andover, and were inspected by Brig.-Major Scott, and reviewed by Brig.-Gen. Low. Oct. 4, 1825, the brigade met at Eliphalet Chaplin's in Georgetown, and were inspected by Brigade-Inspector Joseph L. Low, and reviewed by Major-Gen. Stickney. Oct. 1, 1827, the brigade met in the West Parish in Bradford, and were inspected and reviewed as in 1825. Oct. 6, 1828, inspected by Major Low. Oct. 6, 1829, inspected by Major Parish. Oct. 3, 1830, met at John Poor's in Andover, and were inspected by Daniel Parish, and reviewed by Gen. Solomon Low. Oct 11, 1831, and Oct. 9, 1832, met in Bradford, and were inspected and reviewed as above. Oct. 2, 1833, met at the West Parish meeting-house in Bradford, where they were inspected by Major Stickney, and reviewed by Gen. Solomon Low.

Thus we have chronicled the historic days upon which the militia met, and passed the grand review. The members of these companies have nearly all passed over the river, and joined those gone before around the camp-fire in another world. Many are the anecdotes we have listened to regarding the training-days of our fathers; many are the times they have related the stories of their "heroic" sham-fights ; but ever-hurrying time bids us advance, and so we must pass onward to new scenes and later days.

Not much was done by Boxford to aid the government in carrying on the war of 1812, because of its unpopularity. The people believed that the several embargo acts passed by the government of the United States were uncalled-for and unnecessary, and that England had been compelled to make the declaration of war. They held "that the uniform system of restrictions and vexations upon our commerce, adopted and obstinately pursued in by our own government, their contemptuous rejection of every application of relief by the injured citizen, together with a base and dishonorable submission to the most wanton, unprovoked, and piratical outrage committed on our commerce by France, could not be reconciled by a declaration of war against Great Britain, as a friendly design to rescue and protect our commerce from British depredations, especially whilst that government, in their negotiations with the American government, continued to express friendly dispositions, and a strong desire that all differences existing between the two governments might be amicably adjusted." The war continued for a few years, though in a mild form. A treaty was signed at Ghent, Dec. 14, 1814, though a number of battles were fought afterwards, because of the armies being ignorant of the existence of the treaty. The most important of these was fought at New Orleans, La., Jan. 8, 1815. The return of peace was hailed with great joy

For several years from 1818, the First Church was in a
state of disunion, caused by a private disagreement between some of the members. The injured members left
the church, and erected a quite extensive building near the
meeting-house, in which they had preaching

This building had been built two stories in height, and
the second story was fitted up with settees for a school or
lecture room. In 1826 Major Jacob Peabody, a merchant
of Boston and a native of Boxford, was instrumental in turning it into an academy, which flourished for two or three
years in a marked degree. The first teacher was Professor
Leavenworth, who was followed by Pratt, Wyatt, and one
or two others. Some fifty scholars were in attendance.
Preaching was carried on on Sundays, sometimes by the
professors of the school, and by other "reverend gentlemen," among whom was one Robertson. They were very
liberal in their preaching, — their sermons partaking of the
Universalist, and, sometimes, of the Unitarian, belief. The
feeling existed for a few years only, and Parson Briggs'
sermons were again heard by the offended. The school-
building was afterwards occupied as a dwelling-house by
Major William Low and Mr. William G. Todd, and was
ultimately burnt on the night of Dec. 26, 1867.

By this reduction of the number of members of the
church, the minister's salary was hard to be obtained, and
the church was in great danger of an entire dissolution.
In this extremity they received a communication from
Enoch Perley of Bridgton, Me., expressing his good-will
to the people of this his native place, and offering one
hundred dollars towards establishing a fund "to secure the
permanent enjoyment of the preaching of the gospel here."
After passing through such a trial as they had recently
done, they immediately concurred in his views, and received the said amount through the hands of Thomas Perley, Esq., who had been authorized to pay it. In acknowl-

edgment of Mr. Perley's generosity the parish voted, "that they receive with becoming emotions the pious and liberal communication of the above named Enoch Perley, Esq. And when by various unfriendly occurrences it had become expedient to make extraordinary efforts to retain our existence as a religious society, by attempting to establish a fund for the support of the ministry, in this situation every aid seems to come with increased value ; and the truly helping hand, extended in this instance for our encouragement by one born and brought up with us, demands and receives our grateful acknowledgment; and we hereby wish to assure our generous benefactor that, although we are few in number, we continue to entertain a comfortable hope that by the blessing of God the institution of religion here established by our pious ancestors may be long enjoyed and blessed to us, their unworthy descendants."

A subscription-paper was circulated among the inhabitants of the parish, with excellent results.   The following is a copy of the paper, and a list of the several subscriptions :—

"EAST BOXFORD, Sept. 20, 1824

" We, the subscribers, in some measure sensible of the importance of the preaching of the gospel, to promote the present peace and future happiness of mankind, and to continue this inestimable blessing with us, we agree and promise to give the respective sums to our names annexed, to bear interest annually, from the first day of November next ensuing, to be secured by promissory notes with sufficient securities, one tenth part of the sum by each person subscribed to be paid in one year, and the remainder at nine equal annual payments, the interest on the whole sum to be paid annually, and to be applied towards paying the salary of Rev. Isaac Briggs, conformable to the conditions of his settlement in the First Parish in Boxford ; and after his decease, or removal from his ministerial relation to the parish, the annual interest of the sums hereby subscribed shall forever be paid and applied towards the support of a learned, pious, Trinitarian Congregational minister, settled in the said parish, with the concurrence of the church and congregation composing the said parish During all vacancies of a settled minister, in manner aforesaid, the annual interest arising in such vacancies shall be applied towards increasing the fund, till thereby, or by other means, the principal shall amount to $10,000.

"The sums to our names hereafter annexed we severally agree to secure and pay in manner and for the purpose aforesaid, provided the whole of the sum so subscribed and secured shall amount to $3,500, and not otherwise; and also, provided that the said parish shall within one year next ensuing obtain from the General Court an Act empowering them to appoint three suitable trustees, to receive, manage, and improve the same, and to apply the interest in manner aforesaid. And it is further provided, that whenever any part of the principal or interest of the sums hereby subscribed and secured shall be diverted and applied to any other than the purposes aforesaid, then the sums subscribed by each individual shall revert to them, and be recoverable by them, their heirs, executors, and administrators.

" Thomas Perley	.	.	$1,050	Joseph Smith	.	.	$25
Aaron Perley	.	.	500	John Gould	.	.	25
John Sawyer	.	.	125	Oliver T. Peabody	.	.	25
Daniel Gould	.	.	100	Amos Perley	.	.	20
Parker Spofford	.	.	100	Betsey Foster	.	.	20
Oliver Peabody	.	.	100	Anna Herrick	.	.	20
Josiah Kimball	.	.	100	Artemas W. Perley	.	.	20
Samuel Peabody	.	.	100	Joseph Foster	.	.	20
William H. Herrick	.	.	100	Daniel Gould, jun	.	.	15
Asa Perley, jun.	.	.	100	Charles Peabody	.	.	10
Ancill Stickney	.	.	100	Ruth Trask	.	.	10
Samuel Kimball, jun.	.	.	100	John Stiles	.	.	10
Isaac Briggs	.	.	100	Charles Perley	.	.	10
Enoch Perley	.	.	100	Henry Perley	.	.	5
Francis Curtis	.	.	90	John Hale	.	.	5
Jacob Peabody *	.	.	90	Daniel Chapman	.	.	5
Moses Dorman	.	.	70	Zaccheus Gould	.	.	3
Oliver Killam	.	.	55	Thomas R. Chadwick	.	.	2
Jacob Gould	.	.	50				
Nathan Dresser	.	.	50	Total	.	.	$3,400."
Samuel Killam	.	.	50				

Thus the parish fund came into existence. In less than two years after, by gifts, &c., it had increased to $5,074.93. In 1834 it amounted to $5,585.86; in 1840, to $6,149.17,

* This is a part of the original subscription of Charles Peabody, paid by his brother Jacob. — *Parish Clerk.*

in 1865, to $7,111 ; and in 1870 it had amounted to $7,772,* at which sum it has continued ever since.

The first hearse in town was purchased by the West Parish in 1821, and Daniel Harriman was appointed sexton. He was to have $2 35 for attending each funeral, and digging the grave, — payable by the family of the deceased. In 1823 Peter Pearl was chosen sexton, and, with the exception of the succeeding year, held the office until within a few years. The hearse of the East Parish was procured about a score of years later. It was little used, because of its ancient style, for several years before it was sold at auction, — house and harness included, — a few years since A new hearse was procured some years since by the West Parish; and the old one, it was recently voted, not to sell, but to destroy.

About 1830 Deacon Joshua T. Day of Bradford married and settled in Boxford He built the house in which he resided, and about 1844 erected the grist-mill that is situated near his late residence. The mill has been kept in running order ever since, although for the past few years it has remained idle. About 1852 some box-machinery was inserted, and box-boards were sawn out. The old building bears an antiquated look , but we are informed it is to be renovated, and the whir of the millstones are to be again heard

<blockquote>"Through the meadows soft and low "</blockquote>

In 1836 Capt. Jonathan J Porter erected his present mill-building as a carpenter's shop. About three years later he placed a dam across the brook, flowed the meadow above, and founded a grist-mill in his shop , in 1857 he made some improvements in the mill in the wheels, &c.

---

* In 1869 the parish received $200 from the estate of Miss Mary Kimball, and $94 from the estate of Miss Caroline E Peabody, both then deceased. The amount arising from leasing the "minister's farm" was also probably added : this amounted to some $1,500

In 1841 he also added a saw-mill, which is still doing service in connection with the grist-mill. In another department of the mill-building Mr. Porter incorporated a kind of repair-shop, with requisite machinery, that was adequate to the wants of a "jack-at-all-trades." Some of his original appliances are proof of considerable skill in the art of mechanical invention.

After Thomas W. Durant was done blacksmithing in the East Parish, in 1815, he removed to the West Parish, and opened a blacksmith's shop in what is now Mr. William E. Perley's front-yard. The late Moses Kimball bought out Mr. Durant on his removal to Canada in 1828, and hired Mr. Robert B. Anderson of Salem, N.H., a blacksmith, to teach him the trade. Mr. Anderson worked for Mr. Kimball until about 1845, when he (Anderson) built a shop for himself near his residence, and continued to work at his trade in this new locality until about 1874. When Mr. Anderson built his shop, Mr. Kimball sold out to Benjamin Woodbury from Londonderry, N.H., who, after carrying on the business till 1862, died. The place was then sold to John Harriman, who removed the shop, and erected Mr. Perley's residence.

In 1825 the question of founding a new county out of the northern part of Essex County, to be called the County of Merrimac, was agitated. April 3, 1826, the mind of the town regarding this idea was obtained in town-meeting, — the result being a unanimous negative vote.

CHAPTER XIII.

1830–1860.

FROM the scanty written remains — but still more from what we have learned of the doings and achievements — of those whom these places once knew, we can form only a favorable opinion of their mental qualities. Their spelling and syntax might not always conform to rule, — at least to *our* rule, — but they knew what they meant to say, and they *said* it. Their phraseology was often quaint, but it was not often senseless or impertinent. If they talked but little, we may feel sure that they talked quite as much to the purpose as the more ambitious and long-winded orators of the present day.

The erection of the small and rude red structures of the time of which we are writing, in which the generation anterior to our own obtained what little book-learning they had the honor of possessing, though seeming very old-fashioned and primitive to us, was nevertheless a grand stride toward the educational privileges which are now enjoyed by the youth. Our ancestors had too many things to contend with to give themselves much culture in the literary or scientific world ; and it is no reproach, but high praise, to say — as we must say of multitudes then — that the extent of their attainments scarcely exceeded that of the humble cottager, who, we are told,

"Just knew — and knew no more — her Bible true."

In addition to those bequests already mentioned, Ephraim Foster, Esq., bequeathed to the West Parish, in his will, dated Jan. 3, 1835, fifteen hundred dollars to the schools of that parish — the income of said amount to be applied to paying the several teachers in that parish. The money was placed in the hands of trustees, and the interest arising from the same has been paid to the present time. The school fund of the town as contained in the several bequests now amounts to $3,467.59, and consists of the following items: Wood fund, $2,186.95; surplus revenue, $1,029.64; Foster fund, $176 ; Kimball fund, $75 ; having an income of six per cent, which amounted for the year 1878 to $208.05.

Rev. Mr. Briggs continued in the ministry in the East Parish until 1833, a period of twenty-five years, during which time thirty-four persons had been admitted to the church. As we have noticed a few pages back, the parish had been struggling to support their minister. In March, 1833, but a short time prior to his dismission, to ease their burden Mr. Briggs entered into the conditions contained in the following letter : —

"To the Members of the First Parish in Boxford.

"*My Dear Friends,* — With you I have spent a large part of my days in peace and harmony — have been a sharer in your *joys* and in your *afflictions.* I have been afflicted — I believe that my joy has been the joy of you all. Never (till the cold clod shall lie heavy on my breast) shall I forget your uniform attention and kindness, and the kindness of all this people to me and my family, especially in scenes of trial and affliction. If I know my own heart, I have endeavored to promote your spiritual and temporal interest. Being informed that, notwithstanding liberal donations have been made for my support, your parish taxes are still high, I hereby express my desire that no tax for the present year be laid upon this people for my support. I shall make no other demand than the annual interest of the parish funds for my salary. Whatever may be given by free and willing subscription, I hope I shall gratefully receive.

"Your friend, &c.

"Isaac Briggs.

"Boxford, March 25, 1833."

· The reasons of Mr. Briggs' leaving Boxford have been many, and most of them ambiguously got up. For fifteen years previous to this time, the parish had been completely mixed up in matters pertaining to the conducting of the church affairs, and the probability is that Mr. Briggs was also mixed up in it. It does not become us to mention the origin of this derangement.

Rev. Mr. Briggs was born at Halifax, Mass., about 1775, and graduated at Brown University in 1795. He was first settled over the church in York, Mé., where his stay was brief. He resigned in 1807, and in the following year was settled over the First Church in Boxford, as we have just noticed. They had had no regular preaching since 1793, the year of the commencement of Mr. Holyoke's infirmities, a period of about fifteen years.

Mr. Briggs was known by the appellation of "parson"— Parson Briggs — far and near. He married, first, Sarah, daughter of Deacon Richard Sears of Chatham, who died April 29, 1812, at the age of thirty-two years. He married, second (pub. Oct. 16, 1813), Mehitable Sears, sister to his first wife, who died Aug. 1, 1814, at the age of thirty years. He married, for the third time, Henrietta Chester

FIRST CHURCH.

Before Mr. Whitney left the ministry here, steps had been taken to erect a new meeting-house, which were successfully carried out; and a new house was begun and finished, and was dedicated on the day of Mr. Coggin's ordination, May 9, 1838. The work was carried forward in such a business-like manner, that it was quickly done, and little said about it by the parish-clerk. A description of this church, which is the present East Parish edifice, would be taking up too much space for an object that is yet new and known to all that are interested in its history. In reference to its being furnished and fitted up for use, we have a word to say about the gifts of some things that are still used in it. The first of these that we would mention is the bell which has so often waked the slumbers of the neighbors at an early hour on the morning of Independence Day. This was a present from Gen. Solomon Low, the noted military officer of forty years ago. The elegant sofa which adorns the pulpit, and the table and chairs in the altar, were the gift of Mrs. Sarah (widow of Thomas) Perley, and the Bibles and hymn-books of Mrs. Aaron Perley.

Shortly after Mr. Whitney's departure, in August, 1837, Rev. Mr. Coggin preached for the first time in Boxford. He was then but twenty-four years of age, and was still pursuing his theological course of study at Andover. He was invited to settle in the ministry here shortly after, but declined on account of his "youth and insufficiency to take the position of a pastor and teacher," as he remarks in his anniversary sermon. Again they urgently requested him to retract his former decision; which he did, and thereupon came to Boxford, and preached as a candidate for settlement. At the close of his engagement he received a unanimous invitation to settle; but he at first declined, because he regarded the salary that was offered as hardly competent for his support, and no provision had

SECOND CHURCH.

shingled for the first time since its erection in 1774, a period of sixty years. However, the building endured but a few years longer, and in 1841 the people evinced an idea of having a new edifice erected for public worship. In accordance with this view, a committee was chosen to "sound" the parishioners about the erection of a new meeting-house. May 25, 1842, the committee reported that "there are within the limits of said society, as we have ascertained, thirty-one persons who are in favor of taking down the old house and building a new one, twelve in favor of altering and repairing the old one, most of which wish to alter it to modern style, and make it about as good as a new one, and nine opposed to doing any thing. We have found persons who will take twenty pews in a new meeting-house, and others who think they shall want to buy or hire."

On the 4th of the next April, the parish voted to take down the old meeting-house, and build a new one. This vote was executed the following summer, and on Wednesday, Nov 22 (1843), the new edifice was dedicated to its service. The old meeting-house contained at the time of its demolition forty-nine body-pews, and fourteen pews in the gallery, besides the singers'-seats. There were in the new meeting-house sixty-two body-pews. The cost of the new meeting-house was $4,917.62.

No provision had been made for a bell, when the following letter was received by Charles Foster, Esq, one of the deacons of the church : —

"ANDOVER, Aug. 26, 1843.

" DEA. CHARLES FOSTER.

"*Dear Sir*, — It is now twenty-three years that I have spent a considerable part of my time within the limits of the Religious Society, of which the Rev. Dr. Eaton is pastor ; and during that period I have formed many agreeable acquaintances with those who there attend worship. As this parish are now building a new meeting-house, and have no provision for procuring a bell, and as many of my friends are very desirous that so useful and agreeable an accompaniment should not be wanting, — which coincides with my own feelings, — I have taken the liberty of an old friend to address you on the subject, and to authorize you to make the following proposal to the parish on my behalf (if you judge proper): that they shall authorize an agent or agents to procure a bell, of suitable size for the house, on the best terms they can make, and with such inscription as is thought proper, and that I will pay for the same, the parish giving me a legal obligation to pay the interest of the money which it shall cost, annually, to me or my wife, so long as both or either of us shall live, and no longer, and that the vote be unanimous. I regret that my circumstances do not enable me to make a gift, without conditions, but as my income is limited, and what may happen cannot be foreseen, my motive, I trust, will be construed liberally. Probably in a few fleeting years my wife and self shall have passed away, but the bell will remain, with its solemn sound, to summon other generations to the house of God.

"Truly your friend,

"CHARLES SAUNDERS."

The parish graciously accepted of his proposal, and a bell was purchased of Henry N. Hooper & Co., 24 Commercial Street, Boston, for the sum of $254.98. Its weight was 1,159 pounds.

In 1840 Rev. Mr. Eaton was the oldest minister in office in the county, being in his seventy-fourth year; and had been longer in the ministry than any one then in office, having completed half a century.[*] Shortly after, his health began to fail; and in the early part of the year 1845, he sent the following communication to the society, asking his dismission: —

"To THE CHRISTIAN SOCIETY IN WEST BOXFORD

"*Beloved Brethren*, — I am admonished by advanced age, the infirmities of body and mind, and the feelings of some in this society, that it is time for me to withdraw from the active duties of my profession. It is therefore my desire to be exempted from the performance of parochial duties after the close of the month of March; and I request this Religious Society to adopt the necessary measures that the civil contract may be disannulled.

"Your affectionate pastor,

"PETER EATON."

[*] See Gage's *History of Rowley*, p. 44.

The parish had no idea of losing their beloved pastor,
if he *was* getting old, and his mind weak ; and at the two
succeeding parish meetings it was voted unanimously that
he should remain, which Mr. Eaton consented to.   April
22, 1845, the parish voted that he should preach when he
felt able, and to employ some other person when he was
not able   He again requested to be dismissed, and, Aug.
21, 1845, the parish voted that his connection with the
parish should be dissolved from and after the first Sunday
in the succeeding month , upon which the parish passed
the following resolves, viz. —

"*Resolved*, That in view of the contemplated separation between
us and the Rev Peter Eaton, our pastor, we tender an expression of
our unfeigned attachment to him as a Christian minister, and that we
sincerely regret any thing we may have done as individuals, or as a
body, which may have hindered him in the work of the ministry, or
in any manner have injured his feelings.

"*Resolved*, That we tender to him our ardent desires for his future
usefulness and happiness, assuring him that our prayer to the great
Head of the Church is, that he may be prospered in life, blessed in
death, and receive an abundant entrance into the joys which are the
reward of those who through grace endure unto the end.

"*Resolved*, That, as the crisis has arrived when the contract
between the parish and their aged and venerable pastor (who has for
nearly fifty-six years broken the Bread of Life) should be dissolved, it
is regretted that any division between any members of the parish and
their pastor exists, we therefore express a hope that a divine blessing
may be bestowed upon our reverend father in the ministry, through
his remaining days while here on earth, and that, when called to his
home in *Heaven*, his exit from earth may be peaceful and happy."

Notwithstanding all we have just said, Mr. Eaton was
not dismissed from the ministry, but another minister was
called to assist him in the work.   This colleague was Rev
Calvin E Park, who was installed Oct. 14, 1846.   The
following were the exercises of the installation, viz.: Invocation and reading of the Scriptures by Rev William S
Coggin; introductory prayer by Rev. L. F. Dimmick of

Newburyport; sermon by Rev.-Professor Park of Andover; installing prayer by Rev Calvin Park, D D., of Stoughton; charge to the pastor by Rev. Daniel Dana, D.D., of New-buryport; right hand of fellowship by Rev. Nathan Munn of Bradford; address to the people by Rev. Samuel C. Jackson of Andover; and concluding prayer by Rev. Jonathan F. Stearns of Newburyport

Rev Mr. Eaton lingered in his old age until April 14, 1848, when he quietly passed away at the mature age of eighty-three years. He was born in Haverhill, Mass., March 15, 1765; graduated at Harvard, 1787; and studied divinity with Phineas Adams of Haverhill He married, first, Sept. 2, 1792, Sarah, daughter of Rev. Elias Stone — for sixty years pastor of the church in Reading, — who died Jan. 15, 1824, aged fifty-seven years He married, second, (pub. Aug. 17, 1824), widow Sarah Sweet of Andover. His children, all by first wife, were 1. Sarah, b. 24 July, 1794; m. Daniel Flint, 11 Dec., 1820. 2. Mary, b 1796; d. 20 June, 1797 3 Peter Sydney, b. 7 Oct., 1798 (see his biography). 4. Francis Welch, b. 28 July, 1800; was lost at sea, 15 Nov, 1821. 5. Mary Stone, b 30 May, 1802; m Moses Kimball of Boxford. 6 Joseph Webster, b 1 May, 1804; d. 29 Oct., 1821. 7. John Hubbard, b. 12 April, 1806

Rev. Peter Eaton was of a large and generous spirit, with powers as a preacher of a superior order, and with a character for kindness of heart and moral worth not often surpassed. He secured, during his long and quiet ministry, the respect and love of his people, who, as a memorial of their affection, erected a monument to his memory. — *Monument.*

Few ministers can be found in any age or country who have occupied the same pulpit for so long a period as did Mr Eaton For fifty-seven long years he was almost constantly in the pulpit, attending to his duties

He saw ministers grow up and die around him; he saw his young friends, who, when he was settled over the society, were yet in their teens, grow up, and become grandfathers; new generations were born into the world; new manners and customs took the place of the old-fashioned mode of living; and at last, aged, infirm, and with silver locks floating where, in his boyhood days, the golden curls grew, no wonder he felt like a pilgrim and a stranger whenever he thought of the scenes of his youth, his beloved wife, and most, if not all, of his children left him to wander alone He was dearly beloved by his flock, and deeply lamented when he died.

Several of Dr. Eaton's sermons were published, and are now extant.   Through the kindness of N W Hazen, Esq., of Andover, two of them now lie before us.   One of these was delivered at Topsfield, June 20, 1815, before "The Moral Society of Boxford and Topsfield," * at their first regular meeting.   The text was . "They returned, and corrupted themselves more than their fathers" (Judg. ii. 19). It contains much information concerning the morals of that time.   The other sermon is entitled, "Test of Christian Character," and was written upon the text: "Not every one that saith unto me, Lord, Lord, shall enter into the kingdom of heaven ; but he that doeth the will of my Father that is in heaven" (Matt. vii 21), — delivered on an exchange at North Andover, March 9, 1834.   Both show soundness and clearness of teaching.

After Mr. Eaton's death Mr Park continued to occupy the pulpit.

May 14, 1850, the following Articles of Faith and Cove-

---

* This society was formed, as its constitution professes, for "the suppression of immorality of every description, particularly intemperance, sabbath-breaking, and profanity ; and the promotion of piety and good morals " This was the introduction of the more narrow temperance organizations of the present day In this sermon the development of immorality, and the steps taken to prevent its spread, are clearly and skilfully divulged.

nant, which are those that are now used by the church, were adopted : —

ARTICLES OF FAITH.

" 1st, You believe in the one loving and true God — the Father, Son, and Holy Ghost ; and that it is the duty of all men supremely to love and obey him.

" 2d, You believe that the scriptures of the Old and New Testament are the Word of God, written throughout by the inspiration of the Holy Ghost, and that they are a perfectly sufficient and infallible rule of faith and practice

" 3d, You believe that God created our first parents upright, that by eating the forbidden fruit they fell from that state of righteousness, and that in consequence of their apostacy, all their descendants were made sinners.

" 4th, You believe in the incarnation, obedience, suffering and death of Jesus Christ ; His resurrection and ascension ; that He alone by His sufferings and death has made atonement for sin, and that faith in Him is essential to salvation.

" 5th, You believe that the wickedness of every man's heart is such as to render necessary his being born again, that he may enter into the Kingdom of God, and that no one will ever perform the conditions of salvation but such as are made willing to do so by the special influence of the Holy Ghost.

" 6th, You believe that God has from the foundation of the world chosen those from among men who shall receive eternal life, through sanctification of the spirit and belief of the truth, and who shall through grace persevere in holiness unto the end.

" 7th, You believe that Christ has established a church in the earth composed only of such as have savingly believed in Jesus Christ, and that he has appointed two ordinances to be observed by the church, — the Lord's Supper and baptism, the latter to be received by believers and their households.

" 8th, You believe in the resurrection of the righteous and the wicked, in a universal final judgment in which all men will receive according to their deeds done in the body, and after which the righteous will go away into eternal life, and the wicked into a punishment that will never end. — This you profess and believe.

COVENANT.

" You do now humbly and penitently, asking the forgiveness of your sins through the blood of your Saviour, give up yourself to God in an everlasting covenant in our Lord Jesus Christ, and in the presence of God, angels, and men, you promise by the assistance of the Holy Spirit, that you will forsake the vanities of this world, and let your conversation be such as becometh godliness, consecrating all your powers to the service of Jesus Christ, and seeking the good of the church and the world. You covenant with this church to walk in love, to submit to its discipline and ordinances, and in all things to seek its peace and welfare so long as in the providence of God you shall be connected with it.

"And we, the members of this church, do now affectionately receive you to our communion and fellowship; and engage to watch over your spiritual interests, and to walk with you in all the ordinances of the gospel, as becometh saints. And may God in His infinite mercy enable us to be faithful to Him and to each other while we live, that we may be admitted at last, through the blood of Christ, to His everlasting kingdom."

In 1838 the land for the new cemetery in the West Parish was purchased, and improved for that purpose immediately. In 1863 an addition was made to it, lots, carriage-ways, and avenues laid out, together with other improvements.

About 1837 Major William Low built a building near the residence of Ancill Dorman, Esq., which he used for a carpenter's shop; but Jacob, brother of Rev. Mr. Coggin, wishing to keep a store in the village, Mr. Low removed it to its present position. Having been used for that purpose ever since, it is now, as it has been for a number of years, under the care of Mr. Frederic A. Howe, who has been the postmaster of the East Parish for several years.

A number of shoe-manufactories existed in the town at the time of which we are writing. In 1837 the estimated value of shoes manufactured here was $52,975. One of these manufacturers was Samuel Fowler, in the West Parish. Some twenty years since, several shoe-manufactories were in vogue; among which were those of Marion Gould, John Hale, Isaac Hale, and Edward Howe. Marion Gould continued in the business but a short time. John

Hale erected his elegant factory-building about 1857, and began the manufacture of shoes. He failed during the war, but afterwards for a few years did a little business. Isaac Hale built his manufactory in 1859, and did business about three or four years. The last mentioned, however, had manufactured shoes a few years previous to the erection of his factory-building. Edward Howe began shoe-business in 1838; built his present shoe-manufactory in 1845, and entered into a larger enterprise. Uninterrupted by the fluctuations of business, he has kept his workmen busy to the present time. In 1876 his son William W. Howe became a partner in the business, and the firm-name from that date has been "Edward Howe & Son." Their trade is mostly confined to the Southern and Middle States, and, as their goods are of good stock and standard make, they have a regular sale. They now manufacture about six thousand pairs annually.

We pass onward with the history of the militia companies. In 1832 the two companies were joined together, and trained as *one* company until the spring of 1840, when all the militia throughout the State were disbanded. We insert the roll of the company, which was still a part of the Third Regiment, Second Brigade, Second Division, of the State militia, as corrected on the first Tuesday of May, 1838, viz. : —

Hosea C Killam, *Captain,*
John Peabody, *Lieutenant,*
Isaac Hale, *Ensign,*
Augustus Perley, *Clerk,*
Arro Bly, *Drummer,*
Oliver T Peabody, *Drummer,*
Daniel Bixby, *Fifer*

Privates.

Samuel Andrews,
Daniel Andrews,
Dean Andrews,
William Atherton,
Samuel Adams,
Levi Bartlett,
Charles Bixby,
Charles H. Bixby,
William Bly,
James Carleton,
Samuel B. Carleton,
Amos Chaplin,
Amos Davis,

Joshua T. Day,
John Day, jun.,
Moses Dorman, jun.,
Ancill Dorman,
Bradstreet E. Davis,
William Fegan,
John Fegan,
Richard K. Foster,
Warren Gage,
Francis Gould,
Elijah Gould,
Samuel Goodale,
Augustus Hayward,
John Hale,
Joseph Hale,
Israel Hale,
Daniel Hosmer,
Benjamin Hood,
Allen G. Hood,
Joseph Killam,
Joseph E. Killam,
Oliver Killam, jun.,
Amos Kimball,
Samuel Morse,
Jefferson Nichols,
Horatio Pearl,
James M. Peabody,
Stephen Peabody,
John Prescott,
Timothy Phillips,
Parker B. Perley,

Samuel Perley, 3d,
Stephen P. Perley,
Henry E. Perley,
Leonard Perley,
Charles Perley,
Hiram Perley,
Moody Perley,
Leander Perley,
Jesse Reynolds,
Benjamin Robinson, jun.,
Jeremiah Rea,
Samuel P. Russell,
Johnson Savage,
Elijah Stiles,
Israel Stiles,
Nathaniel G. Spiller,
John Spiller,
Calvin L. Smith,
Nathaniel Smith,
Charles Smith,
Simeon Spofford,
Solomon Spofford,
Samuel H. Towne,
Henry A. Towne,
Phineas P. Tyler,
Jeremiah Tyler,
William Tyler, jun.,
Daniel Wells,
Joseph Waterhouse,
William Wentworth.

Total number, 81.

The above company would have been much larger, but for the organization of the *Boxford Washington Guards* two years before (1836). Many of the old joined the new and dashing company, which was an intensely popular organization.

The old company, as we have before said, was disbanded in the spring of 1840. Aug. 10 of the same year the town voted that they would furnish an armory for the use of the

Guards, at an expense not exceeding $300, including land
for its site. On the 13th of the following November $70
more was voted to be expended in its completion, thus
making its cost $370. The armory was built by David
Dwinnell, and was situated near the residence of Mr. Jeremiah Rea. A few years later it was sold to the late
Mr. Joseph N. Pope, who removed and fitted it up into
the dwelling-house which he occupied till his death.

After flourishing for about ten years, the *Guards* dis-
united, never to meet as a company again. This is the
last company of militia that Boxford has had.

In 1852 steps were taken by the people living on its
line to build a railroad from Danvers to Newburyport, passing through the east part of Boxford. The Boxford people
invested much money in the shares of the capital stock,
from which little advantage was derived, except from the
convenience of the railroad The work of building the railway was accordingly begun in the summer of 1852; and in
October, 1853, the trains began to run. Three trains a day
each way was then the rule, — one at morning, the others
at noon and night. In 1859 the company sold the road to
the Boston and Maine Railroad, who have since owned and
controlled the road, which they have extended to Wakefield
to unite with their line. The Boxford dépôt is situated
in the extreme eastern part of the town, and Mr. William
J. Badger is, and has been for sixteen years, the popular
and efficient station-agent. The station-agents before Mr.
Badger were S. Page Lake, John Hale, jun., and Samuel
McKenzie, respectively.

The practice of "boarding out" town paupers was continued up to the time of purchasing the farm of Capt.
Jacob Towne in 1847. The farm-buildings were repaired,
improvements made, and every thing was prepared for
the reception of the paupers. Mr. Jonathan Martin —
now living, and postmaster at Byfield, being upwards of

eighty years of age — was the first master of almshouse. Various men have occupied that position during the three decades that have elapsed since the purchase of the farm; some of them staying a number of years. Since coming into the possession of the town, the farm has been much improved, both in its appearance and fertility; and we congratulate the town in obtaining the services of such able men for masters.

March 7, 1846, the western extremity of the town of Ipswich was annexed to Boxford. The annexation contained about fifteen acres, and included the residences of Messrs. Edward and Leverett S. Howe.

A small village having sprung up in the southern part of the town of Groveland, those families that resided on an adjacent corner of Boxford desired to be set off to Groveland, and thus form a portion of the rising village of South Groveland. A petition was sent to the General Court, who granted their request, providing "that the inhabitants and land thus set off shall be holden to pay, and shall pay, to said town of Boxford, the sum of one hundred and ten dollars and fifty cents; the said sum being their part of the town-debt of said town of Boxford: and provided further, that all paupers who have gained a settlement in said town of Boxford by a settlement gained or derived within said territory shall be relieved or supported by said town of Groveland, in the same manner as if they had a legal settlement in said town of Groveland." In choosing representatives to the General Court, the voters in that district were ordered to vote with the town of Boxford until the next decennial census (1860). The act was approved by the governor, March 21, 1856.* The part set off was that enclosed by the following lines, viz.: "Beginning at a stone monument at the north-westerly corner of the town of Georgetown, and north-easterly corner of said town of Box-

* *Acts of General Court*, 1856, chap. 61, sects. 1–3.

ford, thence running, ten degrees thirty minutes west, three hundred and eleven rods and five links, on a line between said towns of Georgetown and Boxford, to a stone monument, at an angle between said towns; thence running on an angle with the first-mentioned line, containing forty-six degrees thirty minutes, five hundred and fifty-eight rods and twenty links, north-westerly, and between the houses of William Ross and John C. Foot, and across Johnson's Pond, to a stone monument between the towns of Bradford, Boxford, and Groveland; thence running easterly, on a line between said towns of Boxford and Groveland (which is the present dividing line between said towns), to the point first begun at."

In 1857 the number of school-committee was reduced to three. The same number is still chosen annually, — one being chosen for three years, one for two, and one for one year, by which arrangement one of the committee leaves, and a new one enters the office, each year. In 1858 it was voted to have a "prudential" committee, consisting of one person in each district, to hire their own teacher. This arrangement continued for a number of years, and was then abandoned.

The present school system is very advantageous, accommodating itself to the scholars by its summer, fall, and winter terms, continuing in the aggregate some six or seven months out of the twelve. The younger children, that could not attend the winter term on account of the inclemency of the season, can avail themselves of the summer months. Also, the young men that are employed at home upon the farm during the summer season can attend the winter term. Many of the higher branches of study have been introduced into the schools, so that our younger population can obtain a good education without leaving town, although we have no high schools or academies.

CHAPTER XIV.

THE REBELLION.

E now enter upon a period which bereaved many families of their main support, and brought sorrow to every household in the loss of a son, a father, a husband, or some near kindred. It was a period that tried the patriotism of the Northern States, and which proved that they would sustain the Union, cost what it might. Among the many towns and cities of the old Commonwealth, Boxford made known to the world that her share of the conflict would be sustained ; and she kept her word by sending into the service several soldiers more than had been called for.

The question of slavery — the cause of the strife — need not be agitated, as every American home has been thrilled with its discussion, and all well understand its alliance with the South.

At the national election in 1860, Abraham Lincoln of Illinois, the Republican nominee, was elected President of the United States. Disdaining to accept the result of the election, because of Lincoln's aversion to slavery, a number of the Southern States seceded, and attempted to set up a government of their own, choosing Jefferson Davis president, and Alexander H. Stephens vice-president, and calling themselves the Confederate States of America The United States immediately began measures to suppress the attempt of disunion, but on a very limited scale.

At half-past four on the morning of April 12, the first shot was fired from Fort Moultrie, — in which the South had placed seven thousand men under the command of Gen. Beauregard, — upon Fort Sumter, which contained only seventy of the Union soldiers under the command of Major Anderson Thus commenced this strange, unequalled battle, in which no lives were lost on either side. Fort Sumter, after withholding fire three hours, opened her guns with vigor. The battle continued without result during the day, and Beauregard kept up his fire at intervals during the night The next day the woodwork of Fort Sumter was set on fire by shells, and the men were forced to leave the guns to arrest the flames. At noon the whole roofing of the barracks was on fire, and there was imminent danger of an explosion of the magazine. At last, worn out, suffocated, and almost blinded, the garrison capitulated. The telegraph conveyed the tidings to all parts of the country; it excited everywhere the greatest amazement, few persons having believed hitherto that the South would ever proceed to extremities. It was also met with the determination on the part of nine-tenths of the people of the North, that the rebellion should be suppressed, no matter how much human life, or how much time and money, its suppression might require. President Lincoln issued a proclamation on the 15th, calling for seventy-five thousand volunteer soldiers.

On the 6th of May, the selectmen of Boxford called a town-meeting, at which it was voted "to furnish each of those persons who have volunteered, or who may volunteer, into the service of their country from this town, within the

present year, with such clothing and other things as they
may need , also, to pay them during their elementary
drill as much per month as their pay will be when in
regular service." The number, names, &c., of the men
that volunteered this year, as well as those that enlisted
during the whole five years that the war continued, will be
found by referring to the table given a few pages ahead.

The events of the first year, 1861, aroused the North to
more extensive operations. The first battle of Bull Run,
which was fought this year, was the most disastrous to
both armies, about two thousand being killed on each side.

July 22, 1862, to further encourage men to volunteer
into the service, the town voted "that a bounty of two
hundred dollars be offered to any person being a citizen of
this town who may enlist into the service of the United
States for the term of three years, to be paid them when
they are sworn into said service, until the town's quota is
full. They must enlist within twenty-one days from this
date " (July 22, 1862). Also, voted "that the recruiting
officers be authorized, after the expiration of twenty days,
to recruit from any other source approved by law, offering
a bounty of one hundred dollars."

Aug. 22, the town voted "that they will pay to each
person that is a resident of this town, who will enlist into
the Federal army, and be duly enrolled under the last call
of the President for three hundred thousand men for nine
months service, until the quota for Boxford shall be filled, a
bounty of two hundred and fifty dollars."

Mr. Samuel K. Herrick of Boston was recruiting agent
for Boxford, 1864.

March 5, 1864, the selectmen were ordered to keep on
recruiting soldiers " *without one day's delay.*"

Boxford acted a conspicuous part in the Rebellion.
Ninety-two of the young and middle-aged men of the town
volunteered to go to the front, and help sustain the union

of the United States. Of these, two died while imprisoned at Andersonville ; two more were imprisoned in
the Libby Prison, one of whom died there. Twenty of the
brave young spirits succumbed to the deadly effects of
rifle-balls and Southern diseases ; the bodies of most of
them now mouldering in the soil of the sunny regions
of the South, in graves unknown and unhonored, with no
memorial-stone but the cenotaph at home, on which their
names are engraved. Thirteen were wounded in battle, or
contracted diseases of which they died soon after arriving
home In addition to these volunteers, thirty were drafted,
five more entered the navy, and faithfully served their
country until they died or were discharged.

Entering the army, most of them, at the beginning of
the strife, Bull Run, Cedar Mountain, and other battle-
fields, witnessed the death-struggle of more than one
Boxford boy. Others were wounded, some fatally, in the
battles of Port Hudson, Blunt's Creek, Antietam, Spottsylvania, Mechanicsville, Bull Run, Gettysburg, Lookout
Mountain, and other fierce conflicts of the Rebellion.
Under the command of Gen. Joe Hooker, some of them
were numbered with the Army of the Potomac. Death by
starvation in the rebel prisons, on the battle-field, by fatal
diseases ; inconveniences, discomforts, — all stared them in
the face ; but with unwavering patriotism they fought
until their end was gained, till the Union was restored :
then they laid down their muskets, to take them no more
up until another threatening storm of disunion should
sweep over the land.

In connection with the Rebellion the old Morse house,
situated among the hills of the West Parish, is of more
than common interest It was built in 1799 by Jacob
Parker, who afterward resided in it till his death. After
his death, until a few years since, it was occupied by his
son, Aaron L. Parker, and Samuel Morse, who married his

OLD MORSE HOUSE.

daughter Mary Parker. These two families had nine sons, all of whom volunteered into the service of their country; and one of them was starved to death in the rebel Libby Prison. It is truly, as the mother of five of those soldiers remarked, "a soldier house."

The following table has been prepared to aid the reader by a more comprehensive view of the various dates of enlistment, in what regiment, company, &c., — the footnotes giving information regarding their services, &c. : —

NAMES	ENLISTED AND MUSTERED INTO SERVICE	PERIOD OF SERVICE	REGIMENT	COMPANY	ENLISTED POSITION
Martin L. Ames,*	Drafted July 15, 1863 M. 1863	3 yrs	32	G	Priv
David M. Anderson,†	E. M.	9 mos	48	B	"
Edward G. Batchelder,‡	E. Jan. 20, 1862 M. Jan. 20, 1862	3 yrs	29	I	"
John Q. Batchelder,§	E. Jan. 16, 1862 M. Jan. 16, 1862	"	"	"	"
Samuel H. Batchelder,‖	E. Aug. , 1862 M. Sept. 19, 1862	9 mos.	50	K	"

* He was born in Ossipee, N.H., Feb. 22, 1838. Worked out for Mr. John Hale. Was in delicate health; was sent to Rendo, Long Island. Was taken prisoner about May 30, 1864, and died at Andersonville Prison, Sept. 8, 1864.

† Born in Boxford, Oct. 29, 1843. Son of Robert B. and Irene Anderson. Enlisted as one of the quota of West Newbury, and received his bounty from that town. Went in Gen. Banks' division, — detailed from the regiment as teamster. Was in the battle at Port Hudson, May 27, 1863. Arrived home Aug. 23, and mustered out of service Sept. 3, 1863. Died March 8, 1869.

‡ Born in Danvers, Oct. 19, 1822. Son of Jacob and Mary C. Batchelder. Was on guard-duty May 14, 1862, and fell into a pit or hole, and injured his ankle so that he was unfit for duty afterwards. Came home June 22, 1862. Discharged Dec. 16, 1862. Died May 7, 1879.

§ Born in Lynnfield, Jan. 22, 1815. Brother to the above. Was in battle at Savage's Station, June 29, 1862. Died of typhoid-fever on board the hospital-ship *Euterpe*, Oct. 17, 1862; buried in Soldiers' Cemetery, near Mill-Creek Hospital.

‖ Born in Lynnfield, June 2, 1819. Brother to the above. Promoted to a sergeantcy. Went in Gen. Banks' division to New Orleans; from there to

NAMES	ENLISTED AND MUSTERED INTO SERVICE	PERIOD OF SERVICE	REGIMENT	COMPANY	ENLISTED POSITION
Frank Brady,*	E. 1861 M. July 22, 1861	3 yrs.	17	I	Priv.
Jacob D. Brown,†	E. April 26, 1861 M. July 22, 1861.	"	"	F	"
Samuel H. Brown,‡	E. Aug. 1, 1862 M Aug 6, 1862.	"	35	F	"
Frank A. Burrell,§	E. April, 1861 M	"	41	I	D'r.
D. Butler,‖	E. M				
George E. Carleton,¶	E. Aug 1, 1862 M. Aug. 1, 1862.	"	35	F	Priv
John R. Chadwick,**	E M Oct 8, 1862	9 mos	50	K	"
Charles W. Cole,††	E 1862 M 1862	3 yrs.	35	F	"

Baton Rouge. Was in battle at Port Hudson, May 27 and June 14, 1863. Arrived home Aug. 11, and mustered out of service Aug 24, 1863. Lives in Methuen, Mass.

* Born in Brooklyn, N Y., July 4, 1845. Son of Michael and Susan Brady. Was in battle at Kinston Dec 15, and Goldsborough Dec. 20, 1862. Promoted to the rank of corporal, March, 1863

† Born in Boxford, Nov. 9, 1837. Son of John W and Mary E. Brown. Left camp in Lynnfield, Aug. 22, and arrived in Baltimore, Md., Aug. 24, 1861. Embarked on board the steamer *Merriam* for Newbern, N.C., March 27, 1862, where he remained till May 28, 1863. Was in four battles: at Kinston, Dec. 15, Whitehall, 17th, Goldsborough, 20th, 1862; and battle of Blunt's Creek, April 9, 1863. Dismissed by reason of disability, May 28, 1863.

' ‡ Born in Boxford, Feb 2, 1846 Brother to the above. Was in battle of Antietam, Sept 17, 1862 Taken sick soon after, went into hospital at Keidsville, and died there of typhoid-fever, Oct. 23, 1862.

§ Born in Salem.

‖ Died Sept. 13, 1864.

¶ Born in North Andover, March 28, 1842. Son of Robert E. and Maria E. Carleton. Was in battle of South Mountain, Sept. 14, and Antietam, 17th; left the regiment, and was carried to the hospital in Alexandria, Nov. 8; transferred to the hospital in New York, Dec. 22, 1862; remained there until discharged, Feb. 22, 1863. Died Jan. 27, 1875.

** Born in Bradford, Mass., Aug. 23, 1824. Son of Jonathan and Eunice Chadwick Service, same as Samuel H. Batchelder's Died Sept. 15, 1863, thirty-five days after his arrival home.

†† Born in Boxford, April 2, 1844 Son of Ephraim F. and Sarah S Cole. Enlisted as one of the quota of North Andover, and received bounty from

NAMES	ENLISTED AND MUSTERED INTO SERVICE.	PERIOD OF SERVICE.	REGIMENT	COMPANY	ENLISTED POSITION
John F. Cole,*	E. July 27, 1862. M. July 29, 1862	3 yrs	35	F	Priv.
Francis Curtis, jr ,†	E. Aug 15, 1862 M. Aug 18, 1862.	"	40	"	"
Oscar F. Curtis,‡	E. July, 1861. M. 1861	"	14	I	"
Isaac C. Day,§	E. July 27, 1862. M. July 29, 1862	"	35	F	"
John A. Day,‖	E. Sept 18, 1861 M. Sept 20, 1861	"	22	H	"

that town Taken sick March 1, and died March 3, 1863, of fever, at Newport News, Va. Buried in West Boxford, March 26, 1863

* Born in Boxford, Jan. 20, 1841. Brother to the preceding Was in battle of South Mountain, Sept 14, and Antietam, Sept 17, 1862 At capture of Jackson, Miss , May 14 ; surrender of Vicksburg, July 4 ; and battle at Knoxville, Tenn , Dec 1, 1863. Was wounded in left shoulder in battle of Spottsylvania Court House, May 18, and died June 14, 1864, at McLellan Hospital, Philadelphia. Buried in West Boxford

† Born in Boxford, July 11, 1836. Son of Francis and Lorintha (Davis) Curtis Enlisted as one of the quota of Topsfield, and received bounty from that town Lives in Topsfield

‡ Born in Boxford, Jan 2, 1839 Brother to the above Wounded in battle at Spottsylvania, May 19, 1864, and died at Washington, D C , in consequence of his wound, June 8, 1864. Buried in Topsfield, June 22. Credited to Topsfield on State records.

§ Born in Boxford, June 2, 1843 Son of Joshua T and Elvira K Day. Was in battle at South Mountain, Va., Sept 14, 1862 , wounded by a bursting shell at battle of Antietam, Sept. 17 , sent to hospital at David's Island, N Y., where he remained six weeks. Dec. 6, 1862, had a furlough for thirty days , came home, and was married to Miss Harriet M. Jaques, Dec. 11, who died Feb. 7, 1863. Left home to join his regiment Jan. 13, 1863 Went in Gen. Burnside's division. Was at capture of Jackson, Miss , May 14, at surrender of Vicksburg, July 4, and the battle of Knoxville, Tenn , Dec. 1, 1863. Wounded in stomach in passing through the gap made by the explosion of the mine in front of Petersburg, September, 1864 ; was transferred to the Lincoln General Hospital at Washington, D C., got a furlough of thirty days to come home ; then returned to Washington, where he (Feb. 23, 1865) had charge of a hospital-team. Lives in Boxford.

‖ Born in Boxford, Jan. 24, 1837. Son of John, jun , and Emily K. Day. Left Lynnfield, Oct 8, 1861 ; arrived in Washington, 11th ; camped on Hall's Hill, 13th , was taken sick so as to be unfit for duty, March 1, 1862. Went to Fort Corcoran with the sick, March 25 ; left the hospital 31st, and joined

NAMES	ENLISTED AND MUSTERED INTO SERVICE	PERIOD OF SERVICE.	REGIMENT.	COMPANY	ENLISTED POSITION.
Joshua G. Day,* George S. Dodge,†	{ Drafted July 15, 1863 } { M 1863 } { E. April 19, 1861 } { M. April 19, 1861 }	3 yrs 3 mos.	32 5	I D	Priv. "

his regiment at Hampton, Va., April 2; left Hampton next day to go to Yorktown, where they arrived the 5th. Staid there doing duty until evacuated, May 8, and went up York River to West Point, left there 13th, and marched to Whitehouse, arrived there 15th; left there 19th, and marched to Tanstall's Station; left there 23d, went to Keid's Mills, and encamped; left, and went to Gaines' Mills, then went to Hanover Court House, and was in battle there the 27th; was sick, or doing light duty, from that time till June 26, when he went with the regiment, and was in the battle of Mechanicsville and the seven-days' battle in front of Richmond, Va. Got to Harrison's Landing July 2; was sick, and went to Mill-Creek Hospital, Fortress Monroe, Va., Aug. 11, 1862. Was sent from Fortress Monroe, Oct. 27, to Long-Island College Hospital, Brooklyn, N Y., where he was discharged Nov. 12, 1862.

* Born in Boxford, June 13, 1845. Son of Joshua T. and Elvira K. Day. Sent to Rendo, Long Island. Was in battle at Bristow Station, Oct. 14, and at battle of Mine Run, Va., Nov. 27, 1863. Wounded in right arm at the battle of Mechanicsville, May 30, and died in hospital at White-House Landing, June 8, 1864, where he now lies buried.

† Born in Newburyport, Feb. 1, 1837. Son of Robert and Betsey (Bragg) Dodge. Belonged to Haverhill Light Infantry. The company's orders were received at noon, April 19, 1861, and, as they had been drilling daily, they were ready to rush to the rescue of Washington and their country. He marched in Company D, Capt. C P. Messer, Fifth Regiment (which was before known as Company G, in the Seventh Regiment), as a three-months' volunteer, and is said to have been the first one in Boxford to respond to the call of Lincoln in the beginning of the eventful struggle. During his first period of service he was in the first battle of Bull Run, July 21, 1861, and his time expired immediately after. He enlisted, second, Aug. 4, 1862; mustered same day, for the service of three years in Company F, Capt. Samuel Oliver, Thirty-fifth Regiment, and received a corporal's warrant, and was in battles of South Mountain, Sept. 14, Antietam, Sept. 17, and at Fredericksburg, Dec. 13, 1862. Was at the capture of Jackson, Miss., May 14, and surrender of Vicksburg, July 4, 1863. Aug. 18, 1863, was obliged to go into a hospital in Ohio; was transferred from there to Portsmouth Grove Hospital, R.I. Nov. 5, 1863, had a furlough of seven days to come home. Was

NAMES	ENLISTED AND MUSTERED INTO SERVICE	PERIOD OF SERVICE	REGIMENT	COMPANY	ENLISTED POSITION
Edwin T. Ehrlacher,*	E. June 18, 1862 / M.	3 yrs.	41	H	Priv.
Murdock Frame,†	E. Aug. 11, 1861 / M.	"	2	C	"
Albert A. Frye,‡	E. Aug. , 1861. / M. 1861.	"	17	F	"
Isaac E. Frye,§	E. Aug. , 1861 / M. 1861	"	14	D	"
Charles H. Frye,‖	E. 1861 / M. 1861.	"	14	D	"
Isaac Frye,¶	E. Sept. 17, 1861 / M. Sept. 17, 1861.	"	22	G	"
Benjamin Fuller,**	E. Jan. 3, 1865 / M. Jan. 3, 1865	1 yr.			
Daniel Fuller,††	E. Sept. 16, 1861. / M. Oct. 1, 1861.	3 yrs.	23	G	"

sent to McDougal Hospital, Fort Schuyler, N Y., Dec. 21, 1863. June 7, 1865, he was promoted to a sergeantcy in Company H, Nineteenth Regiment of Veteran Reserve Corps. Lives in Boxford.

* Born in Newburyport, Mass., Feb. 10, 1847. Son of —— and Frances Ehrlacher. He enlisted in the Forty-first Regiment (afterwards Third Cavalry Regiment), Company H. Went in Gen Banks' division to New Orleans. Was in battle at Irish Bend, La., April 13, 1863 ; at Port Hudson, May 27 and June 14, 1863 , and at Jackson, La , June, 1863. Discharged by reason of surgeon's certificate of disability, Jan. 18, 1864.

† Born in Stewiacke, N S. Son of Robert W. and Mary Frame. Killed in battle of Cedar Mountain, at Culpepper, Va , Aug 9, 1862. Credited to Topsfield on State records.

‡ Born in Boxford, July 16, 1844. Son of Isaac and Charlotte B. Frye. Died in Baltimore, Md., of typhoid-fever, Dec. 27, 1861. Buried in Louden Park Cemetery, Baltimore, Dec. 29, 1861. Credited to Haverhill on State records

§ Born in Topsfield, April 20, 1841. Brother to the above.

‖ Born in Topsfield, Feb 15, 1839. Brother to the above. Discharged by reason of re-enlistment in the First Heavy Artillery, as a veteran volunteer, Dec. 17, 1863, for three years. Had a furlough of thirty days, commencing Dec 17, 1863, to come home and visit his friends.

¶ Born in Andover, March 31, 1809. Son of Enoch and Mary Frye. Was in battle at Hanover Court House, May 27, 1862, and in the seven-days' battle before Richmond. Sick and discharged from service, Dec. 3, 1862

** Born in Middleton, Nov. 13, ——. Son of Benjamin and Esther Fuller. Enlisted in the Twenty-seventh Company of Heavy Artillery (unattached)

†† Born in Danvers, Sept 3, 1842. Brother to the above. Promoted to the rank of corporal, March 1, 1862 ; and to sergeant, Aug 19, 1862. Discharged by reason of physical disability, Oct. 6, 1863.

NAMES	ENLISTED AND MUSTERED INTO SERVICE		PERIOD OF SERVICE	REGIMENT	COMPANY.	ENLISTED POSITION
Enos Fuller,*	E.		1 yr			Priv.
	M.					
Thomas Fuller,†	E Sept 16, 1862.		9 mos	48	D	"
	M Sept 25, 1862					
George H. Gage,‡	E Aug 6, 1862		3 yrs.			
	M					
Charles A. Goodale,§	E Oct. 2, 1862.		9 mos.	50	K	"
	M Oct 9, 1862					
Samuel D. Goodale,‖	E Aug 25, 1862		"	"	"	"
	M. Sept. 19, 1862.					
Henry G. Gore,¶	E Aug 22, 1862		"	"	"	"
	M Oct 8, 1862					
Eben Gould,**	E Sept 24, 1862		"	48	B	"
	M Sept. 24, 1862.					
Marion Gould,††	E. Sept. 24, 1862.		"	"	"	2d S
	M. Sept. 24, 1862					
William H Greenleaf,‡‡	E June 12, 1861		3 yrs	11	G	Cor.
	M June 21, 1861					

* Born in Danvers, July 15, 1844 Brother to the preceding. Enlisted in the Twenty-seventh Company of Heavy Artillery (unattached).

† Born in Danvers, Feb 13, 1840. Brother to the above. Went in Gen Banks' division to New Orleans, La. Was in battle at Port Hudson, May 27 and June 14, 1863. Arrived home Aug. 23, and discharged Sept. 3, 1863.

‡ Born in Pelham, N H Son of Joseph B and Hannah Gage Enlisted in the First Rhode-Island Cavalry, Company C Was in battle of Fredericksburg, Dec. 14, 1862 Wounded in battle of Gettysburg, July 1, 1863, and sent to hospital at Fort Schuyler, N.Y. Died May 10, 1864.

§ Born in Boxford, April 30, 1848 Son of Samuel and Nancy (Boardman) Goodale Service, same as S H Batchelder's.

‖ Born in Boxford, Aug. 16, 1845 Brother to the above. Service, same as S. H Batchelder's.

¶ Born on Isle of Antigua, Sept 26, 1845 Son of Henry G. and Anna S. Gore. Service, same as S H. Batchelder's

** Born in Middleton, March, 1842. Son of Moses Gould. Re-enlisted for three years, as a veteran volunteer, in the Second Heavy Artillery, Twelfth Company, in 1863 Jan 1, 1864, was stationed at Fort Pickering, Salem, Mass.

†† Born in Baltimore, Md., March 7, 1841. Son of Dr. Moses and Lydia A Gould

‡‡ Born in Haverhill, Dec. 22, 1821 Son of Samuel and Dolly Greenleaf. Was in first battle of Bull Run, July 21, 1861; and in battles of Yorktown, Williamsburg, Fair Oaks, and four days in the seven-days' battle before Richmond. Discharged Aug 18, 1862, and re-enlisted as one of the quota of Boston, Oct 27, 1862, for nine months, in the Forty-eighth Regiment, Company B. Went in Gen Banks' division to New Orleans ; was detailed

NAMES	ENLISTED AND MUSTERED INTO SERVICE	PERIOD OF SERVICE.	REGIMENT	COMPANY	ENLISTED POSITION.
Frederic A. Griffin,*	E Aug , 1862 M 1862	3 yrs.	33	H	Priv.
Edward E Gunnison,†	E Nov 16, 1863 M Nov 26, 1863	"			
William A Gurley,‡	E M Oct 8, 1862	9 mos	50	K	"
William O Gurley,§	E Aug 2, 1862. M 1862.	3 yrs.	33	H	"
Harrison Hale,‖	E 1862 M 1862	"	"	"	"
John Hale,¶	E 1862 M Aug 7, 1862.	"	"	"	"
Matthew Hale,**	E Aug 22, 1862. M Oct 8, 1862	9 mos	50	K	"
Chandler B. Hardy,††	E Jan 19, 1862 M Jan 19, 1862	3 yrs.			
George P Hobson,‡‡	E Aug 15, 1862. M Aug 18, 1862	"	40	F	"

to help take care of the sick in the hospital. Arrived home Aug. 23, and discharged Sept 3, 1863

* Born in Newburyport, June 9, 1844. Son of James and Lydia Griffin.

† Born in Boxford, April 7, 1837. Son of William and Hannah Gunnison Enlisted in the Twelfth Company, Second Heavy Artillery Jan. 1, 1864, was stationed at Fort Pickering, Salem, Mass Lives in Topsfield

‡ Born in Boxford, Dec 18, 1817. Son of William and Betsey Gurley Went in Gen Banks' division to New Orleans, La. Detailed from the regiment as one of a signal corps at Baton Rouge, Dec., 1862 Taken sick in March, and died at Baton Rouge, May 22, 1863.

§ Born in Boxford, Nov. 13, 1844 Son of William A. and Hannah Gurley. Wounded in the shoulder in battle near Lookout Mountain, Va., Oct. 29, 1863. Dec 13, 1863, had a furlough of thirty days to come home. He had furloughs from time to time until April, 1864; then went to Readville, where he was March 1, 1865.

‖ Born in Boxford, Oct. 8, 1840. Son of John and Matilda Ann (Bailey) Hale. Died in Falmouth, Va., of typhoid-fever, Feb 6, 1863 Buried in Boxford, Feb. 15, 1863

¶ Born in Boxford, Aug. 22, 1831 Brother to the above.

** Born in Boxford, April 16, 1828 Brother to the above. Went in Gen. Banks' division to New Orleans, La. Was unfit for duty most of the time. Was in battle of Port Hudson, May 27, 1863 Died at Mound City, Ill., on his way home, Aug 15, 1863

†† Born in Groveland, Feb 10, 1821. Son of John B and Lavinia H Hardy Enlisted in Third Rhode-Island Artillery, Company L.

‡‡ Born in Rowley, Oct 26, 1837. Son of Prescott and Dorothy Hobson Enlisted as one of the quota of Topsfield Taken sick after he went to the

NAMES	ENLISTED AND MUSTERED INTO SERVICE	PERIOD OF SERVICE	REGIMENT	COMPANY	ENLISTED POSITION
Albert P. Hovey,*	E. April , 1861. / M. 1861.	3 yrs	12	F	Priv.
Williard P. Howe,†	E. 1862 / M. Sept 19, 1862	9 mos.	50	K	"
Horace A. Killam,‡	E. April 21, 1864 / M. April 21, 1864.	3 yrs.	59	"	"
Thomas A. Masury,§	E. Nov. , 1861. / M. 1861	"	30	E	"
Herbert C. C. Morse,‖	E. April 20, 1861 / M. June 26, 1861	"	12	F	"
Edwin A. C. Morse,¶	E. Sept 19, 1862 / M.	9 mos	50	K	"
Sylvester G. P. Morse,**	E. Aug 17, 1862 / M.	"	35	G	"
Henry M. H. Morse,††	E. July 25, 1862. / M.	"	17	F	"

seat of war, and died in the hospital at Georgetown, D C , Oct. 25, 1862. Buried in Topsfield, Nov. 18, 1862.

* Born in Boxford, Nov. 23, 1828. Son of Thomas S. and Sarah (Parker) Hovey. Lives in Boxford.

† Born in Ipswich, July 22, 1824. Son of Abel and Margaret (Bixby) Howe. Service, same as S II. Batchelder's.

‡ Born in Boxford, Sept 3, 1845. Son of Oliver P. and Catharine C. Killam Left Readville, April 26, 1864. Was in several battles. Taken prisoner May 24, 1864, at the battle of North Anna River; was carried to Richmond; in hospital there three months, then paroled, and sent to Annapolis, Md.; remained there until Oct. 4, 1864, when he died with typhoid-fever. Buried in West Boxford.

§ Born in Salem, Aug. 16, 1845. Son of Thomas B and Maria L. Masury. Went in Gen. Butler's division to New Orleans, La. Died of chronic diarrhœa in United States barrack hospital, New Orleans, April 6, 1862 (State records say Feb 6, 1863).

‖ Born in Boxford, Sept. 17, 1840. Son of Samuel and Mary (Parker) Morse. He served in all the active service of the regiment until he was taken prisoner by the rebels at the battle of Gettysburg, July 1, 1863, and imprisoned in Libby Prison, Richmond, Va., where he died, March 13, 1864.

¶ Born in Boxford, June 17, 1825. Brother to the above. Discharged at the expiration of term of service, Aug. 27, 1863. Lives in Georgetown, Mass.

** Born in Boxford, Aug 5, 1829. Brother to the above. Was in battles of South Mountain, Sept. 14, and Antietam, Sept. 17, 1862. In the battle last mentioned, he was severely wounded in the knee, and, for that reason, was discharged from service Jan 24, 1863. Lives in Bradford, Mass.

†† Born in Boxford, June 2, 1833. Brother to the above. He was discharged because of disease contracted in the service, Jan. 30, 1863. Lives in Pueblo, Col.

NAMES ·	ENLISTED AND MUSTERED INTO SERVICE	PERIOD OF SERVICE	REGIMENT	COMPANY	ENLISTED POSITION
S. Gardner S. Morse,*	E April 26, 1861. M July 22, 1861	3 yrs.	17	F	Cor.
William H. Newhall,†	E. Oct. , 1862. M. Oct. 6, 1862	9 mos.	50	K	Priv
Chandler L. Parker,‡	F June 12, 1861. M	3 yrs.			Mus.
Gilman P. Parker,§	E. April 20, 1861. M June 26, 1861	"	12	F	Priv
Thomas B. Parker,‖	E. Aug 20, 1864 M.				Cor

* Born in Boxford, Oct. 14, 1837. Brother to the preceding. Promoted to sergeant, Oct 1, 1863, and was "color-sergeant" of the regiment for one year. Was in battles of Kinston, Whitehall, Goldsborough, and Winton, all in North Carolina. Wounded in the shoulder by a shell, at battle at Blount's Mills, April 9, 1863 Had a furlough of twenty-five days, commencing Sept. 25, to come home. Arrived home 30th, was taken sick soon after, and was not able to return to his regiment Jan. 1, 1864. Served until discharged at the expiration of his term of service, Aug. 3, 1864

† Born in Lynn, Mass., Jan. 23, 1821. Son of Samuel and Mary Newhall Service, same as S. H. Batchelder's.

‡ Born in Boxford, Feb. 13, 1837. Son of Aaron L. and Priscilla (Buzzell) Parker. Enlisted in the Second Regiment of the Rhode Island Infantry, as musician Was in first battle of Bull Run, in all the battles and skirmishes of the "seven-days' fight," at Williamsburg, and other battles, and was discharged Aug 11, 1862. He re-enlisted in Fiftieth Regiment of Massachusetts Infantry, as musician, Sept. 19, 1862, and served until expiration of term of service, and was discharged Aug 27, 1863. After the close of the war, Mr Parker received a commission as "band-master" of the Eighth Massachusetts Regiment, in which capacity he served for the period of two years. Lives in Haverhill, Mass.; leader of the Groveland Brass Band.

§ Born in Boxford, July 21, 1839 Brother to the above. Was in first battle of Fredericksburg, last battle of Bull Run, and in all the active service of the Twelfth Regiment until the winter of 1862-63 Was wounded in the breast at Bull Run. Was stricken with paralysis in winter of 1862-63, and, soon after, was transferred to the Invalid Corps, in which he served as Commissary Sergeant until expiration of term of service, and was discharged July 8, 1864 Lives in Bradford, Mass.

‖ Born in Boxford, July 29, 1826. Brother to the above. Enlisted in Company M, Fourth Regiment, Massachusetts Heavy Artillery, Aug 20, 1864, and served as corporal until the close of the war; and was discharged June 17, 1865. Lives in Georgetown, Mass.

NAMES.	ENLISTED AND MUSTERED INTO SERVICE	PERIOD OF SERVICE.	REGIMENT.	COMPANY.	ENLISTED POSITION
John B. Parker,*	E Feb , 1864. M.		58	F	Priv.
George W. Peabody,†	E , 1861. M June 11, 1861	3 yrs.	11	I	Ser.
Joseph B. Perkins,‡	E Sept 22, 1861 M Sept 22, 1861	"	23	G	Priv
Albert E. Perley,§	E 1862 M Sept 25, 1862.	9 mos.	48	D	"
Asa K. Perley,‖	E 1862 M Sept 19, 1862	"	50	K	"
Thomas P. Perley,¶	E 1862 M Sept 19, 1862	"	"	"	"

* Born in Boxford, Jan 13, 1834 Brother to the preceding. Was in active service at the front for only twenty-eight days; but, during that time, was under fire for ten days, and was in battles of the Wilderness, Spottsylvania, North Anna River, and Cold Harbor In the last battle he was shot through the leg, seriously injuring the bone, and was obliged to lie in the hospital until May 17, 1865, when he was discharged (by order of the War Department) for disability caused by his wound. Lives in Brockton, Mass.

† Born in Boxford, Feb 26, 1836. Son of John and Henrietta S. (Baker) Peabody. Was in fourteen battles. Was appointed standard-bearer at the first battle of Bull Run, July 21, 1861 , carried the colors until the last battle of Bull Run, Aug. 30, 1862, when he was wounded by a piece of shell in his side. Transferred to Company D, First Regiment Invalid Corps, Oct. 27, 1863. Jan 1, 1864, had the command of five corporals and twenty-eight privates, guarding Aqueduct Bridge at Georgetown, D C Lives in Chelsea, Mass.

‡ Born in Middleton, Feb 27, 1826 Son of Berry and Betsey (Ray) Perkins Was sick and unable to do military duty most of the time. Was employed as nurse in the hospital at Fortress Monroe, Va, and Newbern, N C Discharged by reason of physical disability, June 2, 1862.

§ Born in Boxford, June 8, 1845 Son of Albert and Hannah (Hayward) Perley. Went in Gen Banks' division to New Orleans; from thence to Baton Rouge. Wounded in right arm in battle at Port Hudson, May 27, 1863. Arrived home Aug. 23, and mustered out of service Sept. 3, 1863. Re-enlisted in the Heavy Artillery, Aug. 26, 1864. Died in Danvers, April 21, 1877.

‖ Born in Georgetown, Mass., April 4, 1837 Son of Elbridge and Sarah (Kimball) Perley Service, same as S H Batchelder's Died of fever, Aug 16, 1863

¶ Born in Boxford, Aug. 19, 1840. Brother to the above Went in Gen. Banks' division to New Orleans; was sick and unfit for duty ever after he left New York on his passage out Died on the Mississippi River, on his way home, Aug. 3, 1863, near Helena, Ark., where he was buried.

NAMES	ENLISTED AND MUSTERED INTO SERVICE	PERIOD OF SERVICE	REGIMENT	COMPANY	ENLISTED POSITION
William E. Perley,*	E. Aug 2, 1862 M. Aug. 2, 1862	3 yrs.	35	F	Priv.
Thomas A. Perley,†	E. Aug. 24, 1862 M. Sept 15, 1862	9 mos.	50	A	"
Enoch K. Robinson,‡	E. Aug , 1862 M. Aug , 1862.	3 yrs.	35	F	"
William H. Rugg,§	E. M June 26, 1861	"	12	"	"
Leonard C. Savage,‖	E. Nov. 19, 1861. M Nov 19, 1861.	"	30	C	"
John Sawyer,¶	E. July 28, 1862 M July 28, 1862	"	33	F	"
Charles L. Smith,**	E. Sept. 20, 1862 M Sept. 24, 1862.	"	48	B	"

* Born in Boxford, Oct. 2, 1842. Brother to the preceding. Was in battle at South Mountain, Sept. 14, and Antietam, Sept 17, 1862. Was at capture of Jackson, Miss., May 14, at surrender of Vicksburg, July 4, and in battle at Knoxville, Tenn, Dec, 1863.

† Born in New-York City, Sept. 15, 1845. Son of Augustus and Adeline Perley Service, same as S. H Batchelder's.

‡ Born in Boxford, Nov. 16, 1842. Son of Benjamin and Rebecca F. Robinson. Enlisted as one of the quota of Newburyport Sick in the hospital most of the time. In June, 1863, was in Portsmouth Grove Hospital, R I Remained there until Dec. 31, 1863, was then removed to McDougal Hospital, Fort Schuyler, N.Y. Had a pass of three days to come home, June 2, 1863, and another in October Had a furlough of eight days to come home Nov. 25, 1863.

§ Born in Boxford, April 2, 1840. Son of William and Mary O. Rugg. from Lancaster, N H. Had been engaged in ten battles up to June, 1863, Taken prisoner by the rebels at battle of Gettysburg, July 1, 1863; and imprisoned on Belle Island Lives in California.

‖ Born in Boxford, April 27, 1839 Son of Johnson and Mary Savage Went in Gen. Butler's division to New Orleans. Died at Salisbury, N.H, Dec. 30, 1864

¶ Born in Boxford, June 5, 1843. Son of John and Elizabeth L Sawyer. Was detailed as one of the Ambulance Corps, 1863. Taken prisoner, and died at Andersonville Prison, Aug 7, 1864

** Born in Boxford, July 2, 1846. Son of Calvin and Elizabeth (Pearce) Smith Was sick and unable to leave Massachusetts with his regiment; went soon after as far as Fortress Monroe, Va., but was unable to go farther; went into the Hospital Chesapeake; staid eleven weeks; then sent home by the surgeon, June 8, 1863 Mustered out of service, Sept 3, 1863 Re-enlisted in 2d Heavy Artillery, 12th Co, Nov 16, 1863 (mustered ten days after), as a veteran volunteer; and Jan. 1, 1864, was stationed at Fort Pickering, Salem, Mass.

NAMES	ENLISTED AND MUSTERED INTO SERVICE	PERIOD OF SERVICE	REGIMENT	COMPANY	ENLISTED POSITION
George C. Smith,*	E. Sept. 23, 1861. / M. Sept. 23, 1861	3 yrs	23	G	Priv.
Sylvester C. Smith,†	E. Nov 19, 1861 / M. Nov 19, 1861.	"	30	C	"
Aaron Spofford,‡	E. June 11, 1861. / M. June 26, 1861	"	12	E	"
Daniel W. Spofford,§	E. Aug 9, 1861. / M. Aug 11, 1861	"	19	A	"
Hervey M. Spofford,‖	E. July 17, 1863. / M. Aug , 1863	"			"
David M. Sullivan,¶	E. Aug 2, 1862 / M. Aug 2, 1862	"	33	H	"

* Born in Boxford, March 17, 1836. Brother to the preceding. Was in all the battles that the Twenty-third Regiment was in, up to May 1, 1863. Was at Newport News, Va, Dec. 31, 1863 Was in front of Petersburg from April 13 to Aug. 15, 1864; then went to Newbern. Left for home, Sept. 27. Mustered out of service, Oct. 13, 1864.

† Born in Boxford, March 21, 1844. Son of Erastus and Judith A Smith Went in Gen. Butler's division to New Orleans, La. Was sick most of the time after he went out. Steward in United States Hospital, New Orleans, April, 1863.

‡ Born in Boxford, April 20, 1833. Son of Aaron and Betsey F. Spofford. Killed in last battle of Bull Run, Aug. 30, 1862.

§ Born in Boxford, Nov 30, 1834. Brother to the above. Was in battle on the Peninsula; in the seven-days' battle before Richmond, wounded in battle of Antietam, Sept. 17, 1862, and entered the hospital, where he remained until Oct 12, when he again joined his regiment. The following is an incident of the battle of Antietam: Phineas F. Spofford, an elder brother and a regimental officer in the Rebel army, acting colonel at the close of the war, was stationed in that portion of the Southern army that was in direct antagonism to the Nineteenth Massachusetts Regiment, in which his brother Daniel W. served. Learning the fact that his brother Daniel was one of his opponents, an interview was effected, and together they spent the night following the battle in a neighboring barn, reviewing the past and present situation, and recalling the memory of their brother who had previously fallen a victim to the fratricidal strife.

‖ Born in Boxford, April 9, 1843. Son of Charles A and Sarah H. Spofford. He enlisted in the Second Heavy Artillery, 8th Co, July 17, 1863; July 15, he was drafted, but the news of the draft did not reach him until after he enlisted Detailed to go to Alexandria as guard, September, 1863. Was stationed on Long Island, Boston Harbor, Mass, unfit for duty, Jan. 1, 1864.

¶ Born in Fall River, Mass, April 15, 1846 Son of Daniel Sullivan. Died at Lookout Valley, Tenn., of chronic diarrhœa, March 1, 1864.

NAMES.	ENLISTED AND MUSTERED INTO SERVICE.	PERIOD OF SERVICE	REGIMENT.	COMPANY	ENLISTED POSITION.
John N. Towne,*	E July 21, 1861. M 1861	3 yrs.	14	D	Priv
Samuel E. Twisden,†	E. Aug. 1, 1862 M. 1862.	"	33	H	"
Philip A. Welch,‡	E May , 1861 M. July , 1861	"	12	D	"
Henry Williams,§	E. April 22, 1861. M	"	2	C	Cor.

Only five men, as far as we have ascertained, were in the navy from Boxford, whose names, services, &c., we give, viz. : —

1. John Canavan. Entered service, Aug. 9. 1864, on steamer *Rhode-Island.*

2. Michael Doyle. Born in Boston. Entered service, July 4, 1861. Enlisted on board the receiving-ship *Ohio,* then went on board the *Pensacola,* in which ship he served till he was discharged at the expiration of two years

3. William Langdon. Entered service July 26, 1864, on the ship *Ohio.* Substitute for Mr. William P. Cleaveland. Discharged July 8, 1867.

4 Michael Ney. Entered service Sept. 15, 1864. Substitute for Mr. Horace Berry. Discharged Aug. 15, 1868.

5. Benjamin Stone Twisden. Born in Lynn, March 5, 1838. Son of Samuel and Hannah Twisden. Entered service, 1861. First served on steamer *Huron;* was trans-

---

* Born in Salem, Nov. 24, 1816. Son of Jacob and Hannah Towne. He was detailed from the regiment, July, 1863, as provost guard to take charge of the drafted men on Long Island, Boston Harbor, Mass. Lives in Georgetown.

† Born in Lynn, Dec. 1, 1844. Son of Samuel and Hannah Twisden. Went in Gen. Hooker's division in the Army of the Potomac.

‡ Born in South Berwick, Me., 1844.

§ Born in Pennsylvania. Was in Gen. Banks' retreat, 1862. Was in battle of Cedar Mountain , and Antietam, Sept. 17, 1862. Sick from Dec., 1862, to March, 1863.

ferred to steamer *Connecticut*, which plied between New York and New Orleans Taken sick, and sent to the hospital at Brooklyn, N.Y., where he died of disease of the throat, Nov. 24, 1862.

The following men were drafted at Lawrence, July 15, 1863, but never entered actual service. They, or most of them, were stationed for about a month at the fort in Salem. The facts regarding their discharge, &c , will be found in the footnotes. Some of them were already in the service, one was dead, two were non-residents, and one was replaced by a substitute.

Martin L. Ames, ‡ Charles R. Anderson,* John G. Bailey,† George E. Carleton,† Franklin E. Day,§§ Joshua G Day,‡ Joseph K. Farley,† Charles O Foster,† Roscoe W. Gage,† John Hale, jun.,†† John G. Harriman,† Alonzo J. Henly,‖‖ George P. Hobson,** Daniel H. Keezer,‖ Henry J. Kimball,† Herbert C. C. Morse,‡ Samuel G. Morse,‡ Gilman P. Parker,‡ John V. Robinson,§ Enoch K. Robinson,‡ David M. Spofford,†† Thomas L. Spofford,† Albert W. Stevens,†† William G Todd,‡‡ Oliver B. Welch,¶ and William H. Wood.†

The Rebellion is so recent, that the recital of the incidents connected with the various battles in which our volunteers took part is needless.

Adjutant-Gen. Schouler, in his *History of Massachusetts*

---

* Exempted by the Board of Enrolment, Aug 19, 1863.
† Exempted Aug. 20
‡ In service.
‖ Exempted Aug 3; non-resident.
§ Exempted Aug. 31.
¶ Exempted, Aug. 22.
** Dead.
†† Exempted
‡‡ Replaced by a substitute, Aug. 25.
‖‖ Commuted for Aug. 28.
§§ Exempted by the Board, Aug 7 , non-resident.

—Rebellion Record Boxford.

SOLDIERS' MONUMENT.

in the Civil War, says: "There were no commissioned officers from Boxford. Ninety-two men were in the service, a surplus of five over all demands."

The whole amount of money appropriated and expended by the town on account of the war, exclusive of State aid, was $10,756.35. State aid paid in 1861, $367.60, in 1862, $1,170; in 1863, $1,184; in 1864, $1,097.71; and in 1865, $1,150.

The ladies of Boxford were active all through the war, in adding to the comfort of the soldiers at the front, and forwarded through the Sanitary and Christian Commissions on several occasions underclothing, quilts, pillow-cases, dried apples, jellies, newspapers, and other comforts for the sick and wounded.

In 1874 Jonathan Tyler Barker, Esq., gave the West Parish $1,000 toward the erection of a soldiers' monument. Various persons in the town added the necessary amount of money, and a granite monument was erected in the spring of 1875. Its whole cost was $2,017.19. It was dedicated on Memorial Day, May 29, 1875, with appropriate ceremonies. The height of the monument is about twenty feet, and the base four and a half feet square.

The following is the inscription on the front face of the monument: —

IN MEMORY OF

OUR PATRIOT SOLDIERS.

WAR OF 1861.

ERECTED BY THE

MUNIFICENCE OF THE LATE

J. TYLER BARKER

OF NORTH ANDOVER.

1873.

The following inscription is on the right-hand side : —

WEST BOXFORD NAMES.

A. SPOFFORD JR DIED
                    AUG 30th 1862
S. H. BROWN   DIED   OCT 3d 1862
C. W. COLE   DIED MARCH 3d 1863
T. P. PERLEY   DIED   AUG 4th 1863
C. L. FOSTER   "   "   8th 1863
A. K. PERLEY   "   "   16th 1863
J. R. CHADWICK "   SEPT 5th 1863
H. C. C. MORSE   "   MAR 13th 1864
G. H. GAGE   "   MAY 10th   "
J. G. DAY   " |JUNE 8th   "
J. F. COLE   "   "   13th   "
D. BUTLER   "   SEPT 13th   "
H. A. KILLAM   "   OCT 14th   "
D. M. ANDERSON " MARCH 8th 1869

The West-Parish names are continued on the back, as follows :

WEST BOXFORD NAMES.

GEO. E. CARLETON DIED.
            JAN. 27th 1875.

The following is the inscription on the left-hand side, containing the names of the dead East-Parish soldiers : —

FIRST PARISH NAMES.

M. L. AMES   DIED SEPT. 8, 1864
J. Q. BATCHELDER " OCT. 17, 1862
O. F. CURTIS   " JUNE 8, 1864
A. A. FRYE   " DEC. 27, 1861
W. A. GURLEY   " MAY 22, 1863
M. HALE   " AUG. 15,   "
H. HALE   " FEB. 6,   "
T. A. MASURY   "   "   6,   "
J. SAWYER JR   " AUG. 7, 1864
L. C. SAVAGE   " DEC. 30,   "
D. M. SULLIVAN   " MARCH 1,   "
B. S. TWISDEN   " NOV. 24, 1862

It will be seen by these inscriptions that the names of the East-Boxford soldiers were also added.

At a parish-meeting held May 2, 1875, it was "*Resolved,* that the members of this parish will ever cherish a grateful remembrance of the generosity of the late Mr. Barker in thus making provision for the erection of a monument, in memory of the soldiers, resident in this parish, who fell during the recent civil war. Their hope is, that the daily sight of this monument, while serving to keep alive a sentiment of gratitude for Mr. Barker, and for the soldiers whose patriotism and bravery it commemorates, will also quicken their love for the common country, and the disposition to labor for its good." — *Records of Second Parish.*

During the beginning of the Rebellion a number of the regiments of the Massachusetts volunteers were quartered on the old training-ground near the past residence of Mr. Charles C. Stevens, their quarters being known as Camp Stanton. This fact has given Boxford more notoriety, perhaps, than any thing else of equal importance. The same ground has been used from time to time for more than a hundred years for the same purpose. In 1868, the annual muster was also held here; and, though the governor endeavored to obtain the use of the ground for the like purpose again, the town voted against it because of the soldiers' depredations upon their vegetable-gardens and hen-roosts.

William Dale, Surgeon-General of the State of Massachusetts, says, "Boxford is the most patriotic town in the Union, i.e., according to the number of inhabitants." By this reliable testimony, which is but another witness to the fact, it is proved that the law of hereditaments is true, and the feeling that put life into the acts of our patriot sires was prominent in their posterity to the third and fourth generation. Several of those who suffered and bled in the Rebellion are still with us; and that philanthropy and love of country which guided them in that hour of danger should be reverenced and blessed by those for whom they fought. Loyal indeed were those hearts that first conceived the celebration of Decoration Day, and noble will be those who will assist in the annual anniversary, as generation after generation passes along old Time's path.

CHAPTER XV.

1860–1879.

Rev. Mr. Coggin's Pastorate. — His Dismission and Ministry. — First-Church Covenant — Rev. Mr. Gammell settled. — New East-Parish Parsonage — "Mary Ann Peabody Sunday-School Library." — Rev. Mr. Park's Dismission and Ministry. — Rev. Charles M. Peirce settled — His Dismission and Ministry. — Tyler's Bequest to the Second Parish — High-School Bequest. — United-States Circuit Court Jurymen. — Kimball and Sawyer's Mill — West-Parish Parsonage. — Rev. James McLean settled — His Dismission — Rev. Charles L. Hubbard settled. — Second-Church Sunday School. — Ordination of a Deaf-Mute. — Harriman's Hall, Store, and Post-Office — Parkhurst's Store — Public Library. — Musical Talent. — Boxford Brass Band — New Business Places. — Occupation of the Inhabitants — Politics. — Population.

AS pastor of the First Church, Mr. Coggin saw its numbers and spirituality augmented. Retaining the love and confidence of his people, the twenty-fifth anniversary of his settlement was observed May 9, 1863, with appropriate exercises The neighboring ministers, special friends of the pastor, and many others were present, and assisted in making it an interesting and happy day The audience was large and appreciative The memorial address delivered by the pastor upon that day was published, and forms the only published production of his pen that we have seen. After this time his health began to fail, and, when two or three years more of service had passed, he felt that he must not be confined to the pulpit and the other duties incumbent upon a pastor's life. Therefore, Nov. 3, 1867, he sent in a formal letter expressing his desire to be dismissed from his position. Mr. Coggin was accordingly granted his dismission, which was to take effect on the 9th of the following May (1868). His farewell sermon was preached May 3, 1868. During his ministry of thirty years, one hundred and seventy-four persons united with the church.

Among the resolutions passed by the church on account of Mr. Coggin's leaving the ministry is the following : —

"*Resolved*, That in reviewing the thirty years' ministry, now nearly closed, we have abundant reason for gratitude to the great Head of the Church, for sending us one who has labored so earnestly and faithfully to promote the temporal and eternal good of this people, and for crowning his labors with so good a degree of success ; and, in the prospect of parting with our pastor, we pledge our best wishes and earnest prayers, that his health may be strengthened and confirmed, so that he may yet for many years be useful in the Church and in the world ; that his last days may be his best days, and that he may finally be gathered with those who, having 'turned many to righteousness, shall shine as the stars forever.'"

The following are extracted from the resolutions passed by the parish to the same purport as the above : —

"*Resolved*, That we recognize in our beloved pastor, our spiritual guide and teacher, a man who has ever been faithful in his Master's service, not failing to declare the whole counsel of God, whether men hear or forbear. In his pastoral relations with this people we shall ever cherish the most grateful and pleasant recollections of him as a Christian gentleman. His ever-ready sympathy and his uniform urbanity is most aptly expressed by the poet, —

'In his duty prompt at every call,
He watched and wept, he prayed and felt for all.'

"*Resolved*, That, while reviewing the pleasant relations between our pastor and his flock, we would especially recognize in his beloved partner one who, by her active co-operation with her husband, has been greatly instrumental in producing results so felicitous.

"*Resolved*, That the Rev Mr. Coggin and his excellent partner will ever retain a strong hold upon the love and respect of this people; and it is our earnest desire and prayer that life's evening with them both may be crowned with Heaven's richest blessings."

We would not add to the above resolutions. They contain a plain description of the character of Rev. Mr. Coggin as a minister and as a gentleman. Content to live with the people of his charge, he still remains among them, sometimes officiating in the pulpit, and pursuing his pastoral visits, though under the name of friendly calls, the same as in the past.

Rev. William Symmes Coggin was son of Rev. Jacob Coggin of Tewksbury, where he was born, Nov. 27, 1812. His mother was Mary Symmes, a lineal descendant of the first minister (Rev. Thomas Symmes). He graduated at Dartmouth College in 1834, at the age of twenty-two years. He married Miss Mary Clark ; and, having no children of their own, they adopted their young nephew, Samuel Kidder Coggin (son of his brother David Coggin), who was drowned while skating, Dec. 16, 1857.

Feb. 19, 1868, the following confession of faith and covenant, which is yet in use, was adopted by the First Church :—

"CONFESSION OF FAITH.

"Recognizing the unity of the Church of Christ in all the world, and extending to all true believers the hand of Christian fellowship, we confess with them our faith in these great fundamental truths in which all Christians should agree

"We accept the Scriptures of the Old and New Testaments as the Word of God, composed by holy men of old, as they were moved by the Holy Ghost.

"We profess our faith in one God, the Father, the Son, and the Holy Spirit, — the Creator, Preserver, and Ruler of all.

"We confess the common sinfulness and ruin of our race, and acknowledge that it is only through the life and expiatory death of Christ that any are justified before God, receive the remission of sins, and, through the presence and power of the Holy Comforter, are delivered from the power of sin, and perfected in holiness

"We believe in an organized and visible Church ; in the ministry of the Word , in the sacraments of baptism and the Lord's Supper ; in the resurrection of the dead , and in a future judgment, the issues of which are eternal life and everlasting punishment.

"COVENANT.

" Accepting this faith, you do now, in the presence of God and this assembly, solemnly avouch the Lord Jehovah to be your God, the supreme object of your affections, and your portion forever ; you confess with sincere contrition your sins against his law and love, you trust alone in the Lord Jesus Christ, his only Son, for pardon and redemption , and, relying upon the promised help of the Holy Spirit to keep you to the end, you consecrate *yourselves* unreservedly to a life of love to God and man "

Shortly after Mr. Coggin's resignation, the parish extended an invitation to Rev. Sereno D. Gammell of Charlestown, which was accepted July 1, 1868.

Rev. Mr. Gammell was accordingly ordained over the society, Sept 9, 1868. The following were the exercises of the ordination : Invocation, and reading of the Scriptures, by Rev. Anson McLoud, of Topsfield; sermon, by Rev. J. E. Rankin of Charlestown ; ordaining prayer, by Rev. E. N. Kirk, D.D., of Boston ; charge to the pastor, by Rev. William S. Coggin ; right hand of fellowship, by Rev. B. F. Hamilton of North Andover ; address to the people, by Rev. C. B. Rice of Danvers ; and concluding prayer, by Rev. David Bremner.

Rev. Sereno Dwight Gammell, born in Charlestown, Mass., March 2, 1842, was son of Rev. John and Susan W. (Mayhew) Gammell His mother belonged to the family of that name whose missionary life on Martha's Vineyard is well known. Mr. Gammell entered Amherst College at the age of eighteen years, in 1860, and graduated in 1865 ; then entered the Theological Seminary at Andover, and graduated in 1868 His collegiate course was somewhat broken by his service in the Rebellion. He

EAST-PARISH PARSONAGE.

at first enlisted as a sergeant in Company E, Forty-seventh Regiment, M V., and was afterwards first lieutenant in Company F, Fourth Regiment, M.V., Heavy Artillery

Rev. Mr. Gammell still occupies the pulpit, with the prospect of years' continuance in the future. During his ministry to Jan. 1, 1879, sixty-two persons have been admitted to the church, a large part of them by profession. May his ministry of the truth redound with glory to the Deity!

For the convenience and necessity of a parsonage, steps were taken in 1869 for procuring a fund with which to build one in the East Parish. The money was quickly subscribed, and a nice, commodious, and substantial dwelling, with other necessary buildings, were built the next year. The following is a copy of the subscription-list (many others, whose names are not included, lent their own manual labor and teams to the work) : —

Mrs. Sarah Sawyer	$500 00	Deacon John K. Cole	$75 00
William N Cleaveland	360 00	Samuel Andrews and sis-	
Capt. Samuel Kimball	350 00	ters	50 00
Moses Dorman and wife	300 00	Solomon W. Howe	50 00
Deacon Julius A. Palmer	300 00	Edward Howe	50 00
John Sawyer	300 00	Jacob P. Palmer	50 00
Charles Sawyer	100 00	Samuel N. Ayers	50 00
Deacon Samuel Bixby	100 00	Major William Low	50 00
Daniel Andrews	100 00	William Sawyer	50 00
Benjamin S. Barnes	100 00	Isaac Hale	50 00
Jefferson Kimball	100 00	Henry Newhall	26 24
Augustus E. Batchelder	100 00	Leverett S. Howe	25 00
Daniel Gould	100 00	Charles C Stevens	25 00
Israel Herrick	100 00	William A. Howe	25 00
Messrs. Byam and Carl-		William E. Killam	25 00
ton	100 00	Peter Strout	12 50
Major Samuel Perley	100 00	Total	$3,723 74

The Sunday school connected with the First Church have a library of two hundred and fifty volumes. It was the gift of Mary Ann Peabody, an earnest Christian worker, daughter of Samuel and Mary (Bradstreet) Peabody, who died Jan 22, 1865 ; and is known as the "Mary Ann Peabody Library."

April 9, 1859, Rev. Mr. Park resigned his charge over the Second Church and Society. A council was convened May 4, when, on account of the inability of the society to pay more than a mere nominal salary, his request was granted. He preached his farewell sermon on the first sabbath in June, 1859. Mr. Park's labors were judicious, faithful, and unremitting ; and under his hands the church had been materially enlarged and strengthened. The circumstances under which he found it, on account of the age and infirmity of Dr. Eaton, were disadvantageous ; and, under the severe embarrassments with which his pastorate had been prosecuted, his measure of success is evidence of "rare devotion, zeal, and patience, as well as wisdom." *
The people were reluctant to dissolve the connection between them, but necessity compelled them to do so. He continued to occupy the pulpit some time after, and has ever since occasionally preached there. He still continues to reside near to the church, where he has a private school for young men, and is also engaged in literary labors.

Rev. Calvin Emmonds Park was born in Providence, R.I, Dec. 30, 1811. His parents were Rev. Calvin and Abigail (Ware) Park. Mr. Park was ordained over the church at Waterville, Me, Oct 31, 1838; he was dismissed in 1844, and two years later, as already stated, was settled as colleague with Dr. Eaton, in Boxford.

Thus the society was left without a settled minister. April 9, 1861, the church voted to extend a call to Rev. Lucius Root Eastman, jun., of Needham ; but he declined the invitation the following August. March 24, 1863, the church voted to invite Rev. Charles M Peirce of Hinsdale,

* *Church Records.*

Mass., who was still pursuing his studies at the Theological Seminary at Andover, to become their pastor. Mr. Peirce consented, and his ordination took place Sept. 2, 1863. The exercises of the occasion were as follows, viz.: Invocation, and reading of the Scriptures, by Rev. E. C. Hooper of Newburyport; prayer, by Rev. L. Thompson of West Amesbury; ordaining prayer, by Rev. S. C. Leonard of Andover; charge to the pastor, by Rev. Anson McLoud of Topsfield; right hand of fellowship, by Rev. William M. Barber of South Danvers (Peabody); address to the people, by Rev. William S. Coggin of the First Church; concluding prayer, by Rev. L. H. Cobb of North Andover, and the benediction, by the pastor.

Rev. Mr. Peirce continued in the ministry a few years, when, his wife being desirous of removing, and the salary small, he resigned his pastoral office June 23, 1867. In his letter of resignation he expresses his sorrow at the proposed separation. He says, "Here are the hallowed associations of my first pastorate, and tender ties bind my heart to those for whom I have labored."

At his request, a council of pastors and delegates from the neighboring churches was convened July 17, when it was voted to dissolve the connection, as asked by Mr. Peirce. By the dissolution of this connection, the church lost an able and faithful pastor; one who cared much for his Master's glory, and who sought to be his faithful servant in the Christian's work. He was of sound discretion and Christian zeal, endowed with a fine scholarship, and rich ministerial gifts. Mr. Peirce was soon after settled in Middlefield.

John Tyler of West Boxford died in November, 1872. In his will he bequeathed as follows: —

" And all of the rest, residue, and remainder of my estate, after the payment of the legacies aforenamed, and my funeral charges, and the charges and expenses of the settlement of my estate, I give and bequeath to the religious society in West Boxford, where I usually worship, to be held as a perpetual fund, the income of which to be appropriated annually for the support of the gospel in said society forever."

After the settlement of his estate, the fund was found to amount to about thirty thousand dollars. On receiving this bequest, the parish, April 8, 1873, passed the following resolutions : —

"*Resolved,* That the parish of West Boxford accept with sentiments of unaffected thankfulness the legacy bequeathed to them by the late Capt. John Tyler.

"*Resolved,* That the parish recognize in this act of Capt. John Tyler a sign of the same liberality and the same cordial interest in the religious welfare of the parish which was ever manifested by him during his unusually protracted life ; and they rejoice that he felt himself prompted to crown a long life of honest industry and well-doing by such an act of liberality, which they trust will continue to be fraught with great good to the parish, and will be gratefully remembered by all coming generations."

The want of funds, which had been the cause of the irregularity of their preaching, by this bequest was annulled. This fund is sufficient to support the ministry, and leave a margin for the increase of the principal, which places the society in an independent position for the future.

Jonathan Tyler Barker of North Andover died in May, 1872. The following is an extract from his will : —

" As my brothers and sisters are well supplied with property, I have therefore concluded to give my estate for the benefit of the youth. I therefore give, devise, and bequeath all my estate to establish and support a free school in the West Parish in the town of Boxford in said county of Essex. Said school is to be located northerly from the West Parish meeting-house, and as near the house where the late Thomas Hovey formerly lived as may be convenient. After defraying the expenses of building and furnishing a suitable house for said school, the remainder of my estate is to be kept in trust, and the income thereof is to be appropriated for the benefit and support of said school."

The estate amounted to about fifty-eight thousand dollars. The will being contested by the heirs, a compromise was made between them and the trustees, the trustees receiving thirty thousand dollars for the school-fund. As soon as this fund is large enough, the school will be founded, and then our youth can receive a high-school education without going out of town.

The first juryman from Boxford to the United-States Circuit Court, held at Boston for this district, was Franklin Jacques, who attended the winter session of 1873–74. The next winter, S Porter Peabody attended. These are all the jurymen, we believe, that ever attended that court from Boxford.

About twenty years since, the manufacture of pegs was an important enterprise of several of our business men. Capt. Samuel Kimball was undoubtedly the first one to originate the business in this vicinity. About 1860, he raised the road (where the brook crosses it just north of his residence) high enough to form a dam, so as to be able to flow the meadow above. He was laughed at for his pains , and, when the people spoke of his proceedings, they called it " Kimball's Folly." Nevertheless he finished his work, and, on the south side of the road, erected a building in which machinery was placed by one Jordan, its inventor, for the manufacture of pegs. Mr. Kimball entered upon the business, and turned out about twelve bushels a day. In 1862 he was joined by Mr. William Sawyer They unitedly carried on the business till 1865, when they introduced the manufacture of box-boards, in connection with their peg-business. After this time, because of the introduction of more modern machinery, which would turn out pegs with greater celerity, and the numerical increase of manufactories, the peg-business of Messrs Kimball and Sawyer gradually came to an end They still pursued the box-business until the mill was burned in the spring of

1875. Pegs were also manufactured at the match-factory, and at the sawmill of Jacob Batchelder, where considerable business was done. Numerous ruins mark the sites of his dry-houses, &c.

After Rev. Mr. Peirce's departure from the Second Church, the following successive "calls" were extended and refused, viz.: to Rev. Hilary Bygrave, who was then preaching there, March 25, 1873; Rev. F. D. Sargent of Brookline, N.H., Dec. 25, 1873; Rev. Theodore L. Day of Holyoke, Mass., June 10, 1874; Rev. Edward S. Huntress of Waltham, Jan. 3, 1875; and to Rev. Granville Yager of Boston, Feb. 20, 1876.

In 1875 the West Parish built an elegant parsonage upon an eminence north-east from the church. It is in the Gothic style of architecture, and a handsome and commodious residence, doing honor to the tastes of the parish. The cost was about five thousand dollars.

The Second Church, April 9, 1876, extended a call to Rev. James McLean of South Weymouth. Mr. McLean came, and preached the rest of the year to the entire satisfaction of the church, and was installed on Wednesday, Feb. 20, 1877, with the following exercises, viz.: Invocation by Rev. William S. Coggin of the East Parish; reading of the Scriptures, by Rev. Rufus C. Flagg of North Andover; introductory prayer by Rev. D. T. Fisk, D.D., of Newburyport; sermon by Rev. George E. Freeman of Abington; installing prayer by Rev. C. E. Park (former pastor); right hand of fellowship, by Rev. S. D. Gammell of the First Church; charge to the pastor, by Rev. David Bremner of Plaistow, N. H.; address to the people, by Rev. J. D. Kingsbury of Bradford; concluding prayer by Rev. Alfred F. Marsh of Georgetown; and benediction by the pastor.

Rev. Mr. McLean was the first occupant of the new parsonage. He was a native of Scotland, and had been settled at South Weymouth, Mass., and several other places. After being settled here in the ministry one year, Mr. McLean tendered his resignation. A council, consisting of pastors and delegates from the First Church in Boxford, two churches in Haverhill, church in North Haverhill, Bradford, Byfield, and the Memorial Church in Georgetown, met May 17, 1878. Rev. W. S. Coggin was chosen moderator, and Rev. D. D. Marsh, scribe. After a prolonged examination and hearing of the facts, the council came to the unanimous conclusion that the connection had better be dissolved the 1st of July following. The use of the parsonage was granted to Mr. McLean till the 1st of October ensuing. He has since been preaching in Groveland, as the unstated pastor of the Congregationalist church there.

On Wednesday, Jan. 15, 1879, one of the coldest days during the winter, Rev. Charles L. Hubbard of Merrimac, N. H., was installed over the Second Church. The exercises were as follows · Rev. Mr. Gay of Georgetown invoked the divine blessing ; Rev. Mr. Barnes read the Scriptures, and Rev. Mr. Park offered prayer. The sermon was preached by Rev. E. Seldon of Manchester, N. H., on the subject of " The Human Side and the Supernatural Side of the Great Christian Doctrine." Rev. Mr. Kingsbury of Bradford offered the installing prayer ; Rev. George H. Ide of Lawrence gave the charge to the pastor ; and Rev. D. D. Marsh of Georgetown gave him the right hand of fellowship. Rev. Mr. Bremner of Boxford gave the charge to the people of the parish ; Rev. Mr. Paine of Groveland offered the closing prayer ; and the pastor installed pronounced the benediction. With the best wishes of his parish, Mr. Hubbard commences upon his pastorate.

Rev. Charles Lawrence Hubbard, born in Candia, N. H., July 4, 1839, was son of Joshua P. and Adeline (Eaton) Hubbard. He was ordained over the church at Merrimac,

N. H., Sept. 1, 1868, and dismissed Nov. 17, 1878, with the regrets of his parish.

The Sunday school — in connection with the Second Church — has a library of about two hundred volumes.

In 1878 Mr. Samuel Rowe, a deaf-mute, and a resident of West Boxford, was ordained to the gospel ministry at the Second Church. This is said to be the first Congregational deaf-mute ordained in this country. His field of labor comprises the State of Maine, and principally the vicinity of Portland.

In 1870 Mr. D. Francis Harriman built a store near his residence in the West Parish, the second story of which is a hall, known as Harriman's Hall, in which entertainments are often held. This is the only store in the West Parish. The post-office was also incorporated there at the same time, Mr William F. Harriman being postmaster. As no railroad is very near, the mail is transported by a mail-stage, which runs from Georgetown to Lawrence.

In 1877 Mr John Parkhurst, at the match-factory, founded a grocery-store for the accommodation of his employees. This makes three stores, all grocery, now in the town.

In 1873 the Public Library was founded in the East Parish. The first contributions were made by A. E. Batchelder, Esq., of Boston, who manifested much interest in its welfare. The library now contains about six hundred volumes of works of various authors and subjects and character, and is under the supervision of a board of trustees.

For its musical talent, Boxford is especially noted. Nearly every family that is able is supplied with an organ, piano, or some such musical instrument. It would be improper not to mention, in connection with this part of our history, James Hamilton Howe, a native of the town, and a graduate of the New-England Conservatory of Music, and who is destined to become a prodigy in the art. Mr Elvin French, also a native of the town, noted as a musical director and teacher, returned to his old home, and, noticing the talents of the young men, conceived the idea of founding a brass-band. Rehearsals were weekly held ; and, the aspects becoming promising, a band of eighteen pieces was regularly organized Jan. 3, 1874, with Solomon W. Lowe as musical director and leader. During the ensuing summer they fulfilled numerous engagements with great satisfaction to their employers. Praised by the press and people for their *recherché* executions, they were encouraged to persevere in their exercises the following winter, at which time they were joined by four or five musicians from Topsfield.

The present and comparatively recent business incorporations, not before mentioned, are: Alonzo J. Henly, J. Horace Nason, Henry Newhall, Perley Brothers, and Frederic Thomas, blacksmiths; J. Horace Nason, Perley Brothers, and Frederic Thomas, wheelwrights. A. J. Henly does business in the West Parish, his shop being situated near the church. J. Horace Nason runs the saw and grist mill of Jonathan J. Porter, near the Second Church, and has also near by a blacksmith's shop, and a department in the mill-building, where wheelwrighting is carried on. Henry Newhall's shop is in the East Parish, near the church. Some twenty-five years since, Mr. Jefferson Kimball built the shop nearer to the post-office, commenced the business, and continued in it till his removal from the town, when it was sold to Mr. Newhall, who removed it to its present position. In 1873 Perley Brothers erected their place of business, which is situated near by the dépôt on the Boston and Maine Railroad, in the East Parish. Their business is carriage-building and carriage-repairing ; machinery is also repaired by the requisite skill, and their numerous machines are driven by steam-power. Frederic Thomas, whose shop is situated near the church in the West Parish, carries on blacksmith's, wheelwright's, and painting departments of carriage-repairing.

From the earliest settlement of the town to the present time, the principal occupation of the inhabitants has been that of agriculture; and from the primitive soil of our rocky hillsides they have ever drawn, by their industry and well-adapted labor, an independent livelihood, while many of them have prospered so well that they have become comparatively rich. Not only has agriculture, in its general term, been carried on, but its various branches — market-gardening, fruit-raising, &c. — have been indulged in during the past few years; Haverhill, Lawrence, and Salem furnishing ready markets for the produce. According to the State census for 1875, there were 125 farms in the town. We give an illustration of the manse of one of these farms on the opposite page. It is the residence of Mr. Isaac C. Day, and originally the old Ross place. The enterprise of Mr. John T Day of Boston has caused new buildings and extensive repairs to be made, and by other outlay has made it one of the finest farming-seats in the town.

The political history of Boxford is a monitor that would well instruct the enthusiastic and tumultuous politicians of the present day. The outbursts of political fevers, though sometimes occurring in a limited degree, are exceptions to the movements of the people of this staid old town. The steady Republican principle has been a ruling power here for many years. The Democrats have been few in number, but are on the increase; and the new Greenback movement has won a few proselytes to its support.

The population of Boxford for the last century has always been more than it is at present. In 1765 the population was 851; in 1776, 989; 1790, 925; 1800, 852; 1810, 880; 1820, 906; 1830, 935; 1840, 942; 1850, 982; 1860, 1,020; 1865, 868; 1875, 834, — 421 males and 413 females. The

DAY PLACE.

last census gives a further division of the present inhabitants: unmarried persons, 219 males and 208 females; married, 184 males and 174 females; widowed, 18 males and 31 females. The families average four persons each, and there is none containing more than ten persons. The average age of the inhabitants of Boxford at the present time is thirty-five years.

CHAPTER XVI.

DISTINGUISHED AND PROFESSIONAL NATIVES.

Rev. Oliver Peabody. — Rev. Moses Hale. — Rev. James Scales. — Rev John Rogers. — Major Asa Perley — Hon. Aaron Wood — Col. Thomas Knowlton. — Rev. Stephen Peabody. — Rev. David Jewett. — Rev. Benjamin Chadwick — Aaron Porter, M.D — Major-Gen Amos Hovey. — Rev. Humphrey C. Perley — Samuel Holyoke, A.M. — Nathaniel Perley, Esq — William Peabody, M.D. — Samuel Peabody, Esq. — Joseph Hovey, Esq — Gen Solomon Lowe. — Rufus P. Hovey, Esq. — Rev. Peter S. Eaton. — Hon. Ira Perley — Dr. Daniel Perley. — Rev. John H. Eaton. — Joseph E. Bartlett, M.D. — Walter H. Kimball, M D. — Charles I. Adams, Esq — Henry O. Peabody. — Rev. Albert B. Peabody. — Cyrus K Bartlett, M.D. — William A. Herrick, Esq

OXFORD has probably given birth to more enterprising persons than any other town of its size in the Commonwealth. They can be found in the busy business circles of the large towns and cities, engaging in manufacturing, home trade, and commerce, institutions of learning in distant parts of the country have asked their assistance ; heathendom has called to them to bring the light of Christianity to its darkened lands; invention has cried, "We need you to show to the world some new appliance," pulpits and offices of trust have been filled; the court-room has re-echoed with their voice, and not a few have assisted, and are assisting, in building up the distant West with towns and cities, and

346

turning the rank virgin soil of the prairies into grain-fields and fruit-farms. Thus it has ever been with the young men of Boxford Leaving the old, dull home of their fathers, they enter the busy scenes, and soon become involved in the fortunes or misfortunes of a business life. But, thanks to their parents and the morality of the place, most of them have succeeded in their career, and made themselves an honor to the dear old home of their boyhood.

REV. OLIVER PEABODY.

Mr. Peabody was born May 7, 1698, and was son of William and Hannah (Hale) Peabody. Entering Harvard College at an early age, he graduated in 1721. There was an Indian church at Natick, which was dissolved about 1720; and the commissioners of the society in England for propagating the gospel in New England deputed Mr. Peabody to preach in that town. He delivered his first sermon there Aug. 6, 1721, when there were but two white families in the town After preaching there eight years, a church was gathered, composed partly of Indians and partly of English, over which he was ordained pastor, Dec. 7, 1729. He discharged his pastoral office with great renown for thirty years, ministering to the people of Natick, especially to the aborigines, in the cause of sacred learning. He was a model in social life, and in benevolence and hospitality pre-eminent. He took great delight in theological investigations, as well as in all needful learning. He taught the Indians temperance, the English language, and the use of agricultural implements. Though naturally of a slender and delicate constitution, he consented to go on a mission to the *Mohegan* tribe of Indians, which caused a final decline in his health. He died Feb. 2, 1752. His last words were: " I have fought a good fight, I have finished my course, I have kept the faith : henceforth there is laid up for me a crown of righteousness, which the Lord, the righteous Judge, shall give me at that day" (2 Tim. iv. 7, 8). (See Bacon's *History of Natick*, p. 61.)*

REV. MOSES HALE.

Mr. Hale was born Dec. 5, 1701, and was son of Joseph and Mary (Watson) Hale. He graduated at Harvard College, 1722. Oct. 20, 1731, he was ordained over the church that had just been gathered in Chester, N.H. He was, at times, afflicted with insanity, and for this reason was dismissed June 4, 1735. His life terminated in 1760.

REV. JAMES SCALES.

Mr. Scales was born, near the residence of the late Mr. Ephraim F. Cole, May 31, 1707, and was son of James and Sarah (Curtis) Scales. He graduated at Harvard College, 1733, and was ordained, Nov. 23, 1757, at the age of twenty-four years. Was settled at Hopkinton, N.H. He died July 26, 1776.

REV. JOHN ROGERS.

Mr. Rogers was born Sept. 24, 1712, and was son of Rev. John and Susanna (Marston) Rogers. He graduated at Harvard College, 1732. He was ordained as the first pastor at Leominster, Mass., Sept. 14, 1743. In his pastorate Mr. Rogers met with great difficulties ; but, before his death, matters were Christianly adjusted. "Mr. Rogers was a man of intellectual powers," says Dr. Bancroft, in his half-century sermon, "and an inquisitive spirit, possessed of a name fitted to make a man independent of his

---

* Mr. Peabody married Hannah, daughter of Rev. Joseph Baxter of Medfield, a lady distinguished for her piety and good sense. The result of this union was the birth of twelve children · Catherine, Oliver, William, Rebecca, Mercy, Joseph, Hannah, Susanna, Susanna, Elizabeth, Thomas, and Sarah. Hannah married Rev. Elizur Holyoke of Boxford. Oliver graduated at Harvard College, 1745, and was pastor of the First Church in Roxbury from 1750 to his death, May 29, 1752, aged twenty-six years.

opinions, and prepared to encounter every difficulty in defence of religious truth." He was strictly an honest man. His moral character was never impeached. In conversation he was frank, even to bluntness, and sometimes gave offence to, or wounded the feelings of, his friends unintentionally. He was tenacious of his own opinion; perhaps he thought too highly of the name But no man is perfect, and his greatest fault was a want of prudence. He died Oct. 6, 1789; and in 1845, under the direction of the First Congregational Society of Leominster, a marble monument was erected to his memory. (See Wilder's *History of Leominster.*)

MAJOR ASA PERLEY.

Mr. Perley was born Oct. 10, 1716, and was son of Thomas and Sarah (Osgood) Perley. Mr. Perley erected the residence of Mrs. Isaac Hale (at the Old Elm-Tree), married, and settled down on the land which had been bequeathed to him by his father's will, in the immediate vicinity of his birthplace, where he continued to reside during his life of almost ninety years. Mr. Perley was one of the most prominent men in the town, where he held at various times the highest offices. In 1758, 1764, 1767-69, 1771, 1774, 1777, 1778, and 1782, — ten years in all, — he held the office of selectman. In 1771, 1772, 1780, and 1781, he was chosen representative to the General Court. In 1775, — that noted year in the history of the nation, — he was chosen a member of the Provincial Congress, in which Congress, as its records inform us, he held prominent positions. Seven of his sons served in the War of Independence. He died April 10, 1806.

HON. AARON WOOD.

Mr. Wood was born Nov. 20, 1719, and was son of John and Ruth (Peabody) Wood. He resided on the Stevens place in the East Parish, and probably built that house, which has since been burned. Mr. Wood was a senator in 1781; representative to the General Court, 1761–1770, 1773, 1774, 1776–79, sixteen years in all; and was also employed in the councils and conventions of the Commonwealth of Massachusetts with gratification to the people. Mr. Wood died Jan. 20, 1791, after having faithfully served his country for many years previous to, and during, the long conflict with Great Britain, securing a name for integrity, justice, and judgment, and leaving an untarnished reputation.*   The following is the inscription on his gravestone : —

ERECTED
In Memory of the
Honᵒ Aaron Wood Efq
Who died Janʳ 20ᵗʰ
1791 :
Aged 71 years.

Yet my fond hope would hear him speak again
Once more at leaft one gentle word & then
Aaron aloud I call in vain I cry
Aaron aloud, for he muft ne'er reply
In vain I mourn & drop thefe funeral tears
Death & the grave have neither eyes nor ears.

* Mr. Wood's first wife was Jane, widow of Dr. Eliphalet Kilborn of Rowley, who died June 15, 1775, aged sixty-eight years.   When the British drove the General Court from Boston in 1775, Mr. Wood and some of the representatives boarded with Mrs. Lydia Barnard, — daughter of Phineas and Grace (Hastings) Warren of Waltham, Mass., and widow of David Barnard — (who was born Jan. 18, 1745), in Watertown, where, it will be remembered, many of the members of the General Court took refuge.   Mr. Wood fell in love with his buxom hostess, married, and brought her to Boxford. After the death of Mr. Wood, who died childless, she married Benjamin Spofford of Boxford, Nov. 14, 1792.   She was a woman of strong mind and body, weighing over two hundred pounds, and died Sept. 6, 1839, aged ninety-five years.   When the British retreated after the battle of Lexington, they passed by her house.   One of the privates stole a horse, and was making his retreat in better style.   He said something to Mrs. Barnard that was not acceptable to her patriotic mind, and she pulled him from his horse, and took him prisoner; and, it is said, this was the first prisoner taken during the Revolution.

COL. THOMAS KNOWLTON.

Mr. Knowlton was born in November, 1740, and was son of William and Martha (Pinder) Knowlton. At the age of eight years he removed with his father to Ashford, Conn. Thomas attended the common schools, whose narrow routine was the limit of his literary education. As he grew older, he developed into a manly form, six feet in height, erect and elegant in figure, and formed more for activity than strength. In addition to his fine appearance, his complexion was light, his hair dark, and his eyes of deep spiritual beauty. He entered the French war when scarcely fifteen years of age, and continued in its service till the war ended, when he left the army in the rank of lieutenant, having been promoted three successive times during the campaign. He was prominent in the battle of Bunker Hill, where he commanded a company, and, with Col. Stark, defended the rail-fence from the trinal attack of Lord Howe. For his gallantry in this engagement, he was promoted to the rank of major. Passing over numerous events, in one of which he was promoted to the rank of colonel, we approach the closing scene in the life of the brave Knowlton. At Harlem Heights Col. Knowlton was sent to watch the enemy's movements. Two of his soldiers, who were reconnoitring their lines, approaching within gunshot, and yielding to a mad desire, fired upon them, and then hurried back to the camp followed by six hundred Britishers. A hot fight ensued, in which Col. Knowlton was mortally wounded, and survived but an hour. His eldest son, a lad aged fifteen years, was in the same battle, and fired several rounds before he received the sad intelligence. When word was brought that his father was dying, he hurried to his side, when he was thus addressed: "You see, my son, I am mortally wounded; you can do me no good: *go, fight for your country.*" Col.

Reed, an eye-witness of the scene, says, "All his inquiry was, whether we had driven the enemy." In the general orders of the next day, Washington says that Col. Knowlton would have been "*an honor to any country.*"

He was the intimate and trusted friend and companion of Gen. Putnam and other leading officers in the army. Col. Burr, a keen judge of men, and a brilliant officer, notwithstanding the odium cast upon him by the later transactions of his life, became acquainted with Knowlton, and was singularly captivated both by his military talent, and the qualities of his open and fearless nature.

The possession of an intellect naturally bright, and quick to profit by the experiences and associations of military life, caused his companionship to be sought by the most cultivated. He was courteous and affable in manners, and wholly free from ostentation and egotism. Ever willing to bestow on others the praise due to their merits, he received the applause due to himself without a murmur of dissent. Calm and collected in battle, and, if necessity required, ready to lead where any could be found to follow, he knew no fear of danger. The favorite and superior officer, the ideal of his soldiers and fellow-townsmen, he fell universally lamented. Col. Knowlton was buried with military honors near the road leading from Kingsbridge to the city. A monument, planted by the hand of affection, has been erected to his memory in the cemetery at Ashford, Conn.

REV. STEPHEN PEABODY.

Mr. Peabody was born Nov. 11, 1741, and was son of John and Sarah Peabody When about nine years of age, his father removed to North Andover, where Stephen was reared. He graduated at Harvard College, 1769. He was ordained over the church in Atkinson, N. H., Nov. 25, 1772, where he was the first minister. Taking a great interest in the war of the Revolution, he served as chaplain in the regiment of Col. Poor, which was stationed at Winter Hill. He died May 23, 1819, aged seventy-seven years.*

REV. DAVID JEWETT.

Mr. Jewett was born Nov. 6, 1743, and was son of Ezekiel and Martha Jewett. He graduated at Harvard College, 1769. Ordained Sept. 1, 1771. Settled over the church at Candia, N. H. The hard times of the Revolution coming on, and the town being small, they could not pay his salary, and he was dismissed about 1780. He was immediately re-settled as the first minister at Winthrop, Me. He died Feb. 28, 1783.

REV. BENJAMIN CHADWICK.

Mr. Chadwick was born March 26, 1745, and was son of Thomas and Mary (Porter) Chadwick. He graduated at Harvard College, 1770 We know little concerning his life, character, or abilities. He died in 1819.

AARON PORTER, M D.

Mr Porter was born March 28, 1752, and was son of Moses and Mary (Chadwick) Porter. He was a physician of eminence He was first settled at Biddeford, Me, and afterwards at Portland, Me. Died at Portland, June 30, 1837, aged eighty-five years.†

---

* Mr. Peabody married, first, Polly Hazeltine, Jan 19, 1773, who died Sept. 19, 1793, at the age of fifty-one years, leaving two children, Stephen and Mary. Stephen was judge of the Court of Common Pleas, Hancock County, Me Mr. Peabody married, second, Dec. 8, 1795, Mrs. Elizabeth, daughter of Rev William Smith of Weymouth, sister of the wife of the senior President Adams, and widow of Rev John Shaw of Haverhill, Mass. She died, at the age of sixty-five years, April 9, 1815.

† Mr. Porter married Paulina, daughter of Richard King of Scarborough, Me., — and sister of Hon. Rufus King, the first United-States senator from New York, minister to England, &c , and half-sister of Hon. William King, the first governor of Maine, — April 30, 1777, who was born March 1, 1759, and died Feb. 27, 1833 Their children were : Rufus King, Moses ; Mary

MAJOR-GEN. AMOS HOVEY.

Amos Hovey was born May 31, 1757, and was son of Deacon Joseph and Rebecca (Stickney) Hovey. In early life he entered with enthusiasm into the military service of his country during the Revolutionary War, and served in many arduous campaigns with great credit. On the restoration of peace in 1783, he settled in Salem, and was in the dry-goods business in Neptune Street, and subsequently in the Franklin Building. At one time he was a merchant on Union Wharf. The various offices, both civil and military, which had been conferred upon him by his fellow-citizens, indicate the high estimation in which he was universally held. He was lieutenant and captain of the Salem Artillery, major and colonel of the Artillery Regiment, and brigadier and major-general in the Second Division of the Massachusetts Militia. He died Oct. 17, 1838, at the age of eighty-one years, leaving no issue.

REV. HUMPHREY CLARK PERLEY.

Mr. Perley was born Dec. 24, 1761, and was son of Capt. William and Sarah (Clark) Perley. Entering Dartmouth College at the age of twenty-five years, he graduated in 1791 with the degree of A.M. He studied divinity with Rev. Ebenezer Bradford of Rowley, and Rev. Ebenezer Dutch of Bradford, two eminent divines of his time. He was approbated to preach July 3, 1794, by the Essex Middle Association. On the 2d of December, in the following year, he was ordained over the church in Methuen, where he continued to officiate till his dismission, May 24, 1815. He was next settled over the North Society in Beverly,

(mother of the wife of Rev. Charles Beecher of Georgetown, Mass) ; Richard King ; Paulina (mother of wife of Rev. Edward Beecher of Brooklyn, N.Y.) ; Isabella Blagdon , Harriet, married (second wife) Rev Dr. Lyman Beecher, and became the mother of Rev Thomas Beecher of Elmira, N.Y , Almira , Rufus King; Lucy, Elizabeth ; and Lucy Elizabeth.

Dec 2, 1818, where he had been preaching a while previously. Here he continued in the ministry till he was dismissed, June 13, 1821. This was his last pastorate. He preached in several pulpits at times during the few following years. His abilities were meagre, and his principles of religion rather inclined to Unitarianism. Several of his sermons were published, and are yet extant. He died in Georgetown, May 10, 1838, at the age of seventy-six years.

SAMUEL HOLYOKE, A M.

Mr. Holyoke was born in the old Holyoke house, Oct. 15, 1762, and was son of Rev. Elizur and Hannah (Peabody) Holyoke. He graduated at Harvard College, 1789. He was a popular musician, and became renowned as a music-composer. The first of the tunes which he composed was *Arnheim,* and, although he was but sixteen years of age at the time, this is the only one of his productions that remains popular at the present time.

In 1790 he prepared the copy of his first collection of sacred music, which made its appearance in January, 1791. This book is entitled "*Harmonia Americana.* Containing a concise Introduction to the Grounds of Music With a variety of Airs, suitable for Divine Worship and the use of Musical Societies. Consisting of three and four parts. By Samuel Holyoke, A B " It was "Printed at Boston, *Typographically,* By Isaiah Thomas and Ebenezer T. Andrews, at Faust's Statue, No. 45, Newbury Street — MDCCXCI." This book was published by subscription; and, at the time of its publication, the author had received subscribers for two hundred and sixty copies. In the preface of this volume he discards the general use of *fugue* in sacred music.

Mr. Holyoke was extensively and favorably known as a teacher and composer of both vocal and instrumental music In 1806 he published at Exeter, N H, vol i. of

The Instrumental Assistant, a quarto of eighty pages ; and in 1807 was published, at the same place, vol. ii. of that work, containing one hundred and four pages, quarto. In these two volumes were given "rules for learning music, and complete scales of all the instruments used," and about two hundred pieces of music for instruments, arranged in parts from two to eight. In 1809 appeared *The Columbian Repository of Sacred Harmony.* This was the most extensive collection of sacred music ever published in this country. It contained four hundred and seventy-two quarto pages, and about seven hundred and fifty pieces of music, including the whole of Dr. Watts' psalms and hymns, to each of which a tune was adapted, and some additional tunes suited to the particular metres in Tate and Brady's, and Dr. Belknap's collection of psalms and hymns. The volume is a very good specimen of printing, and from it have been selected a large number of tunes which help to make up the various collections of church music which have since appeared. This work was published by subscription, the price per copy being three dollars. Mr. Holyoke was also concerned in the publication of *The Massachusetts Compiler*, with Oliver Holden of Charlestown, Mass. ; and, at the time of his death, was engaged in preparing for publication a third collection of instrumental music. In early life he possessed a remarkably good voice ; but in his latter years it had become so harsh that he was obliged to use a clarionet in his vocal schools.

At a social gathering of his musical friends, at the house of Jacob B. Moore, Esq., in Concord, N. H., Feb. 2, 1820, at the close of the exercises Mr. Holyoke requested them to sing *Arnheim*, remarking that perhaps he would never meet with a choir on earth so well calculated to do justice to his first composition. It was sung twice, and Mr. Holyoke was affected to tears. He never sang again.

He had been teaching at Concord, N. H., during the

winter, and died Feb. 7, 1820, of an attack of lung-fever, at Lang's Tavern, East Concord, after a short illness of four days. He died poor, but highly respected and esteemed by those who knew him.*

NATHANIEL PERLEY, ESQ.

Mr. Perley was born March 22, 1763, and was son of Nathaniel and Mehitable (Perley) Perley. Mr. Perley graduated at Dartmouth College, 1791, and was a lawyer in Hallowell, Me. ; but was more noted for his wit — which sometimes turned the gravity of the court-room into uncontrollable hilarity — than for his pleas. He was unsurpassed for sound judgment, and possessed of every personal quality, if properly employed, to have made him one of the great men of our country. He died in 1824.

DR. WILLIAM PEABODY.

Mr. Peabody was born in the old mansion occupied during the summer by William A. Herrick, Esq., of Boston, Jan. 10, 1768, and was son of Richard and Jemima (Spofford) Peabody. He practised the medicamental art for several years at Frankfort, Me., and afterward removed to Corinth, Me. He bore a good reputation as a physician.

SAMUEL PEABODY, ESQ.

Mr. Peabody was born in the old mansion occupied during the summer by William A. Herrick, Esq., of Boston, Jan 30, 1775, and was son of Richard and Jemima (Spofford) Peabody He graduated at Dartmouth College, 1803. Was an attorney and counsellor at law. Resided at different times in Sandwich, Epsom, and Tamworth, N. H., and from 1842 to 1859 in Andover, Mass. His death occurred Oct. 17, 1859. He was a gentleman of the

* A part of our information has been gleaned from Moore's *Encyclopædia of Music.*

highest moral and social qualities, and much general culture and professional attainment *

JOSEPH HOVEY, ESQ.

Mr. Hovey was born Oct. 31, 1776, and was son of
Joseph and Mary (Porter) Hovey. Graduated at Harvard
College, 1804. Was a lawyer at Haverhill, Mass. He
died in 1816.

GEN. SOLOMON LOWE.

Mr. Lowe was born April 9, 1782, and was son of Nathan
and Lucy (Lord) Lowe. He served in the militia of the
State many years, and held the office of general of the
Second Brigade, Second Division, from September, 1820,
until April, 1840, when all the general officers were discharged, preparatory to a re-organization of the militia. He
represented the town of Boxford in the Legislature of the
State during the years 1823, 1827, 1828, and 1841, and
was selectman for many years. Lived in Boxford till about
1857, when he removed to West Newbury, where he died
April 3, 1861. In 1836 he was vice-president of the Essex
Agricultural Society.†

---

* Mr. Peabody married Abigail, daughter of Jonathan Wood, Oct. 7,
1813, by whom were born Charles A., Abby Hale, William Frederic, George
Samuel, Enoch Wood, Sarah Jane, David Wood, John Tyler, Mary Spofford, and Ellen Eliza. Charles A., the oldest child, was a lawyer in New-
York City, judge of New-York Supreme Court. President of United States
appointed him judge of the United-States Provisional Court for Louisiana,
at New Orleans, in 1862 ; chief justice of the Supreme Court of Louisiana, —
the appellate court of last resort in that State, — 1863-64, and afterwards
United-States attorney for the Eastern District of Louisiana.

† Mr. Lowe married, first, Huldah Kimball of Boxford, 1806, who died
Sept. 24, 1808, aged twenty-eight years, having given birth to two children,
twins. One died in infancy, and the other was Major William Lowe. Mr.
Lowe married, second, Dolly Wood of Boxford, 1813, who died May 10,
1817, aged thirty-one years, having given birth to another pair of twins.
One died in infancy, and the other was Mary Ann, who was the first wife of
Mr. Edward Howe. Mr. Lowe married, third, May 14, 1849, Martha, daugh-
ter of Thomas and Hannah Eastman of Sanbornton, N. H., and widow of

RUFUS PORTER HOVEY, ESQ.

Mr. Hovey was born Feb. 5, 1790, and was son of Joseph and Mary (Porter) Hovey. He graduated at Harvard College, 1813. Was an attorney at Lynn, Mass. His death occurred in 1820.

REV. PETER SYDNEY EATON.

Mr. Eaton was born Oct. 7, 1798, and was son of Rev. Peter and Sarah (Stone) Eaton. He fitted for college under the supervision of his father; and graduated at Harvard in 1818, and at the Theological Seminary at Andover in 1822. He was licensed to preach by the Presbytery of Londonderry, in the spring of 1822. He was settled over the church at Merrimac (then West Amesbury), Mass., Sept. 20, 1826, and was dismissed May 10, 1837. He retired from the ministry, and for some years resided in Chelsea, where he died March 13, 1863. Those of his former charge who yet survive remember him with sincere respect and affection.

Of his religious life he says: "My attention was first called to an earnest consideration of the subject of religion while a teacher in Phillips Academy, Andover, through the awakening of a favorite pupil, remarkably amiable and intelligent, but who exhibited the most pungent convictions of sin. Quite a revival followed. I had been greatly perplexed by the doctrine of man's entire depravity; but now, after a course of thorough self-examination, am satisfied of its truth."

Fred. J. Merriam of Topsfield, who died July 24, 1855, aged fifty years. Mr. Lowe married, for his fourth wife, Caroline H. Chase of West Newbury, who survived him, and married, secondly, a Mr. Chase of West Newbury, where she is still living. The remains of Gen. Lowe lie in his tomb in Harmony Cemetery. The tomb has attracted many visitors, because of the pictures of himself and his four wives, which are engraved on marble tablets, and placed upon the face of the tomb.

HON. IRA PERLEY.

Mr. Perley was born Nov. 9, 1799, and was son of Samuel and Phebe (Dresser) Perley. Ira's father was a farmer in not affluent circumstances, though his family was far from being in an indigent condition. When Ira was eight years of age, his father died, and the farm was left to the care of the widow and three sons, aged respectively eight, four, and three years. By the widow's hard labor, with what little help the young children could render, the farm was carried on, and a part of its income laid by. Ira, as well as the doctor, whose biography follows, early evinced a desire for knowledge. At odd hours of the day, when not employed in labor, he would be found with book in hand ; and on the long winter evenings, by the light which the fire on the hearth afforded, he pored over his Latin grammar, and other works which formed the elements of his after-study. At an early age he entered Bradford Academy, when Benjamin Greenleaf was preceptor. At the age of eighteen, in 1818, he entered Dartmouth College, where he graduated in 1822. He then read law with B. J. Gilbert, Esq., of Haverhill, Mass., and commenced the practice of the profession in Concord, N.H. He also afterwards practised law with great honor at Hanover, N. H. He was a representative to the Legislature of New Hampshire from Concord and Hanover, respectively ; treasurer of Dartmouth College ; vice-president of the New-England Historic-Genealogical Society for a number of years ; and was for several years chief justice of New Hampshire. In 1866 Mr. Perley delivered, before the Association of the Alumni at Dartmouth College, the eulogy on the death of Rufus Choate, and also of the Hon. Daniel Webster, Dartmouth's two most distinguished sons. Mr. Perley died in Concord, N. H., where he resided, Feb. 26, 1874, aged seventy-four years.

A classmate in college has kindly furnished us some prevailing traits of Mr. Perley's character. He says : —

"I entered the sophomore class in Dartmouth College at the commencement in the year 1819. I then first became acquainted with Ira Perley. He had been in college one year, and had established, beyond all controversy, his title to the first appointment in his class, which in number was second only to that of 1811. Not only so : I think he was considered, from that time until we finished our course in 1822, the best general scholar in the college. He had not the brilliancy, the imagination, nor the fascinating power of Rufus Choate, who graduated when I entered, nor had he, probably, the same extent of classical learning; but, after Choate left, no one remained that could compete with Perley in all the college studies.

"Ira Perley was modest and unassuming. Conscious of his own abilities, he had no occasion to assume any factitious importance. As he was beyond the reach of rivalry in college, he excited no one's envy. The same position he held among his classmates in college, he readily obtained at the bar and upon the bench ; I mean as a learned lawyer and an accomplished judge.

"He was an active and an honest man. He passed a long life in the discharge of various important duties, — civil, professional, political, and judicial. They were all performed with integrity and ability, without a stain upon his character. Perley was not a marked man, either in his personal appearance, or in his manner of address. He was not a natural orator or poet ; but, as a lawyer, to collect the law of the case, arrange and apply it, he was excelled by few.

"He was not a politician, according to the common acceptation of the word. When the Rebellion broke out, Perley's voice gave no uncertain sound. He sympathized fully with the North, believing that the national life should be preserved ; and, as he felt and believed, so he spoke.

"In the profession which Judge Perley selected, a good memory is of the utmost importance. This faculty he possessed and cultivated to an extent beyond most men. Did a principle of law require to be elucidated or established ? he would readily name the case, quote the book, and frequently the page, where the authority could be found. This faculty made him of great value to the other members of the court. He was, in fact, their legal dictionary. This power of recollection was not confined to the law. He was an extensive reader of miscellaneous works of fiction, travel, and the various productions of modern literature ; and he seemed not only to devour, but to digest thoroughly, whatever he had read This faculty was cultivated to such an extent, that, in summing up his cases to the jury, he made little use of his notes of the evidence, and frequently astonished the bar and the jury at the minuteness, accuracy, and fulness of his recollection of the names and testimony of the witnesses.

"Another trait in Judge Perley's character was independence. As he was self-reliant, he was not disposed to accept the results of the investigation of others, without examination.

"His literary labors were chiefly confined to the law. He indeed delivered eulogies upon two of Dartmouth's most distinguished sons, Daniel Webster and Rufus Choate; but his reputation as a lawyer and jurist must rest finally upon his record in the Reports of the Judicial Courts of New Hampshire." (See *Alumni of Dartmouth College*, and other documents)

On the opposite page is an engraving of Mr. Perley's birthplace. It is also of interest because of the gigantic elm-tree The tree is one of the largest, and the most symmetrical and beautiful, of any to be found in this section of the State. It was set out about 1760, by Major Asa Perley, grandfather of Hon Ira Perley, whose young sons brought it from the woods when a sapling.

DR. DANIEL PERLEY.

Mr. Perley was born in the house (an engraving of which is here given) where his elder brother, the Hon Ira Perley, was also born, March 24, 1804, and was son of Samuel and Phebe (Dresser) Perley He prepared for and entered Dartmouth College in 1824, from which institution he graduated with honor in 1828. He took up the study of medicine, and began to practise in the Second Parish of Rowley, — now Georgetown, — where he continued several years. He at length removed to Lynn, in which place he continued in the duties of his profession. During twenty-five months of the Rebellion, he was surgeon of the Board of Enrolment of the Fifth District of Massachusetts He still resides at Lynn, in the seventy-sixth year of his age. (See *Alumni of Dartmouth College*)

BIRTH-PLACE OF HON. IRA PERLEY.

Yours truly,

Joseph E. Bartlett.

REV. JOHN HUBBARD EATON.

Mr. Eaton was born April 12, 1806, and was son of Rev. Peter and Sarah (Stone) Eaton. He was fitted for college by his father, at the age of twelve years He graduated at Harvard College, 1827. He preached several years, but, on account of ill health, was never settled in the ministry. He died in New-York City, where he had been engaged with the Tract Society.

JOSEPH ELBRIDGE BARTLETT, M.D.

Mr. Bartlett was born Feb. 16, 1819, on the farm bordering upon Ipswich River, which had been owned and occupied by his ancestors for many generations. He was son of Samuel and Lois (Holt) Killam. He labored upon the farm, and attended the public schools, till eighteen years of age, when he engaged in teaching. Afterwards he attended Topsfield Academy for three years, fitting for, and prosecuting the studies usually pursued in, college. He then began the study of medicine with George Cogswell, M D., of Bradford, Mass. In 1844 he was a member of the medical department of Dartmouth College. In 1845 his surname was legally changed from Killam to Bartlett. In 1845 and 1846 he was a member of the medical department of the University of the City of New York, from which institution he graduated with the degree of M.D. in the last-named year. He began the practice of his profession in Somerville, Mass., and continued it in that town and the adjoining cities of Charlestown and Boston, for eighteen years. In 1853 he was chosen president of the Mystic-river Corporation, a company organized for the purpose of constructing wharves, quays, and docks, and for making other improvements, in Boston Upper Harbor, near the mouth of Mystic River In 1864 he retired from the practice of his profession, and has since given exclusive attention to the official and other duties connected with the above-named work.

DR. WALTER HENRY KIMBALL.

Mr. Kimball was born June 20, 1820, and was son of Amos and Lucy (Foster) Kimball. He graduated at Dartmouth College, 1841. Resides in Andover, Mass., where he is a physician.

CHARLES ISRAEL ADAMS, ESQ.

Mr. Adams was born Dec. 21, 1823, and was son of Isaac and Sophia (Spofford) Adams. He graduated at Dartmouth College, 1852 ; and, after teaching school in Gloucester for several years, he commenced the study of law in Boston, where he afterward had a law-office. In his legal profession he continued but a few years, his constitution not admitting of such close application to business. He contracted a fatal illness, of which he died about 1863.

HENRY OLIVER PEABODY.

Mr. Peabody was born May 13, 1826, and was son of Oliver Tyler and Sarah A. (Towne) Peabody. Mr. Peabody being of an ingenious turn of mind, his thoughts were early directed to the invention of a better breech-loading rifle. Several years after conceiving the plan of his invention, he spent in perfecting and completing the "Peabody-rifle," which is said by the best judges to be superior to the other rifles of this class. The small-arms committees of Austria, Prussia, Belgium, Holland, and Denmark have pronounced this gun as "meeting every requirement of a military weapon." Other governments have made similar and equally satisfactory reports. Large orders have been executed by the manufacturers (Providence Tool Co., Providence, R.I.) for the Swiss Military Department, than whom no people are better instructed in the use of fire-arms, or are better judges of their merit. The Dominion of Canada also have these arms largely in use. A military small-arms commission in our own country closes its report by saying: "Having examined and tested all the breech-loading arms submitted for their consideration, the board recommends for adoption the breech-loading arm known as 'Peabody's.'" Mr. Peabody is a resident of Boston.

REV. ALBERT BRADSTREET PEABODY.

Mr. Peabody was born Nov 1, 1828, and was son of Samuel and Mary (Bradstreet) Peabody. His childhood was spent at Boxford at school and at work upon the farm ; later he studied at Pembroke Academy, N H., and at Phillips Academy in Andover. For several years he was a teacher, part or all of the year, at Bow and Raymond, N.H., Ipswich, West Newbury, and Boxford, Mass., and for a year at Tarrytown, N.Y. After this he became a Christian, and felt it his duty to leave the farm, to which he had returned from teaching, and study for the gospel ministry, this being his mother's expressed desire before her death. He studied a year in connection with Topsfield Academy, and entered Andover Theological Seminary in the autumn of 1856, and graduated there in 1859. For a part of the following year he was a resident licentiate at Andover. He accepted a call to settle from the Congregational church in East Longmeadow, Mass, in April, and was ordained there May 24, 1860. He continued in the ministry there with happy relations and marked success, for above seven years, when he resigned, and for about two years was acting pastor for the church at Seabrook, and at Hampton Falls, N. H. In November, 1869, he received a second call — an unsuccessful call having been extended to him in February, 1860 — from the Congregational church at Stratham, N.H., which he accepted, and was thereupon installed Nov. 25, 1869, and continues there with good success to this time.

Mr. Peabody has had his share of the work that usually falls to ministers, — on school-committees, councils, committees of the several associations; secretary of County Conference, president of County Bible Society, secretary of County Missionary Society, &c. He was a delegate to the National Council of the Congregational Churches, that met at Detroit in the fall of 1877. During the summer of 1879 Mr. Peabody made the voyage to Europe, travelling, with great pleasure and profit, through Scotland, Ireland, England, Belgium, Germany, Switzerland, France, and Italy.

CYRUS KILLAM BARTLETT, M.D.

Mr. Bartlett was born Jan. 23, 1829, and was son of Samuel and Lois (Holt) Killam. He labored upon the farm and attended the public schools, till about eighteen years of age. Afterwards he fitted for, and prosecuted the studies usually pursued in, college, at the academies in Topsfield, ·Mass., and Pembroke, N H., Bradford Seminary, and with a private tutor, — Rev. William S. Coggin. He was engaged in teaching for a season. He studied medicine with Dr George Cogswell of Bradford, and with his brother Joseph E, and then had his name legally changed from Killam to Bartlett. He was a member of the Berkshire Medical School one term, and then of the medical department of Harvard College, from which he graduated with the degree of M D in 1852. He practised his profession in Newton and Charlestown, Mass, six years, when he was appointed assistant physician at the Asylum for Insane, Northampton, Mass, where he remained ten years. In 1868 he was appointed superintendent and physician of the Minnesota State Hospital for Insane, at St Peter, where he is still in office.

WILLIAM AUGUSTUS HERRICK, ESQ.

Mr. Herrick was born Jan. 6, 1831, and was son of William Hale and Lois (Killam) Herrick. He prepared for college at Phillips Academy, Andover, and graduated at Dartmouth College in 1854 He read law in Boston with Esquires Harvey Jewell and A. A. Ranney, and, at the same time, attended the Cambridge Law School. He commenced the practice of law in Boston in 1857, and practised at the same time, for a short period, at Andover. He has continued in his practice in Boston and vicinity, until the present time, and has always borne the reputation of being a shrewd, learned, and honorable legal adviser. His legal compositions are numerous, and honored by the profession. He edited *Kerr on Injunctions*, and, with Judge Redfield, also prepared for publication several other prominent works. In 1870 he published the first edition of his *Town Officer;* another edition is ready for the press. This is the standard work of its kind at the present time.

APPENDIX A.

LIST OF TOWN-CLERKS OF BOXFORD.

1686–1710. John Peabody, sen
1711. Thomas Hazen.
1712–1723. Thomas Perley, jun.
1724–1729. Joseph Hale.
1730 Thomas Redington.
1731. Joseph Hale.
1732 Thomas Redington.
1733–1735. Joseph Hale.
1736–1742. Joseph Symonds.
1743–1749. William Foster
1750–1751. Thomas Redington.
1752–1757 Thomas Perley.
1758 Aaron Wood.
1759–1760. Thomas Andrews.
1761–1779. Aaron Wood.
1780–1788. Thomas Perley.
1789–1790. Aaron Wood.
1791–1792. John Dorman
1793–1796. Jonathan Wood.
1797–1798. Parker Spofford.
1799–1811. Moses Dorman.
1812–1813. Amos Kimball.
1814. Moses Dorman.
1815. John Kimball.
1816. Moses Dorman.
1817. Amos Kimball.
1818. Moses Dorman.
1819 John Tyler, 3d.
1820. Moses Dorman.
1821. Amos Kimball.
1822. Moses Dorman.

1823. John Bacon.
1824 Moses Dorman
1825. John Bacon.
1826. Charles Peabody.
1827. George Pearl.
1828. Phineas Barnes.
1829. Benjamin Robinson.
1830. Phineas Barnes.
1831. Benjamin Robinson.
1832. Phineas Barnes.
1833. William Farnham
1834. Samuel Kimball.
1835 William Farnham.
1836. Samuel Kimball.
1837. Moses Kimball
1838 Samuel Kimball.
1839. Joshua T. Day.
1840. Samuel Kimball.
1841. Joshua T. Day.
1842. Samuel H. Batchelder.
1843. George Pearl.
1844. Samuel H. Batchelder.
1845 George Pearl.
1846. Moses Dorman, jun.
1847. William R Cole.
1848 William Lowe
1849. William R. Cole.
1850. Moses Dorman.
1851 John F. Kimball.
1852 William E Killam.
1853. Joshua T. Day.

1854. William Lowe.
1855. William H. Wood.
1856. William E. Killam.
1857. William H. Wood.
1858. William E. Killam
1859. William R. Cole.
1860. William E. Killam.
1861. William H. Wood.
1862. William E. Killam.

1863. William H. Wood.
1864. William E. Killam.
1865. William R. Cole.
1866–1868. Roscoe W. Gage.
1869–1870. William R. Kimball.
1871–1872. Thomas P. Dorman.
1873–1877. Ancill Dorman.
1878–1879. Benjamin S. Barnes.

APPENDIX B.

LIST OF SELECTMEN OF BOXFORD.

As will be seen, the number of selectmen chosen annually in the early part of our history was generally five. Since 1822 the number has been three. The following is the list, viz. : —

1687.*

John Peabody, sen ,
William Watson,
Daniel Wood,
John Andrews,
Abraham Redington, jun.

1688.

John Chadwick,
Thomas Andrews,
Daniel Wood,
Abraham Redington, jun ,
Thomas Hazen,
John Peabody, sen.

1689.

Joseph Bixby,
Thomas Hazen,
William Foster, sen.,
Joseph Andrews,
William Peabody.

1690.

John Peabody,
Nathaniel Brown,
Joseph Peabody, sen.,
Thomas Redington,
Thomas Perley.

1691.

John Perley,
Moses Tyler,
Thomas Andrews,
Samuel Symonds,
John Kimball

1692.

Samuel Symonds, sen.,
Thomas Hazen,
Joseph Peabody, sen.,
John Andrews,
Robert Eames, sen.

1693.

John Peabody, sen.,
John Chadwick,
Zaccheus Curtis,
Daniel Wood, sen ,
Joseph Bixby.

1694.

Thomas Perley,
Thomas Hazen,
Moses Tyler,
William Foster, sen.,
Ephraim Curtis.

* See page 87.

373

1695.

John Perley,
Moses Tyler, '
Joseph Bixby,
John Andrews,
Joseph Peabody.

1696.

John Peabody,
William Peabody,
Thomas Andrews,
Jonathan Foster,
Jonathan Bixby.

1697.

Joseph Bixby,
Joseph Andrews,
William Peabody,
John Chadwick,
Thomas Perley, jun.

1698.

John Peabody,
John Andrews,
Samuel Symonds, sen.,
Joseph Hale,
Moses Tyler

1699.

Thomas Perley,
John Peabody,
John Andrews,
John Eames,
William Peabody.

1700.

John Perley,
Joseph Bixby,
Joseph Andrews,
Josiah Bridges,
Joseph Peabody.

1701.

Samuel Symonds,
Thomas Perley,
Thomas Redington,
John Kimball,
Samuel Smith.

1702.

Samuel Symonds,
Daniel Wood,
Joseph Hale,
John Andrews,
John Stiles.

1703.

John Peabody,
Thomas Hazen,
Jonathan Foster,
Samuel Symonds,
Timothy Dorman.

1704.

Thomas Perley,
Joseph Bixby,
Abraham Redington,
Joseph Andrews,
Josiah Bridges.

1705.

John Peabody,
Joseph Peabody, jun.,
David Wood,
Nathaniel Perley,
Zaccheus Curtis.

1706.

Thomas Hazen,
David Wood,
Richard Kimball,
Samuel Symonds, sen ,
Jonathan Bixby.

1707.

John Peabody,
Thomas Perley,
Joseph Hale,
Samuel Foster,
Thomas Wilkins.

1708.

Thomas Hazen,
Abraham Redington,
Zaccheus Curtis,
Luke Hovey,
Jacob Perley.

1709.

Thomas Perley,
John Andrews,
Joseph Bixby,
Luke Hovey,
Samuel Fisk.

1710.

Samuel Symonds, sen.,
Thomas Jewett,
Jonathan Foster,
Daniel Kenney,
Samuel Fisk.

1711.

John Peabody,
Daniel Wood,
Timothy Foster,
Cornelius Brown,
Thomas Jewett.

1712.

John Andrews,
Samuel Symonds, jun.,
Samuel Foster,
Moses Tyler,
Jacob Perley.

1713.

Jonathan Foster,
Nathaniel Peabody,
Thomas Cummings,
David Peabody,
John Andrews.

1714

Joseph Bixby,
John Tyler,
Jeremiah Perley,
Jacob Smith,
Thomas Perley, jun.

1715.

Joseph Hale,
Timothy Dorman,
Samuel Symonds,
John Chadwick,
Thomas Spofford.

1716.

Thomas Jewett,
Jonathan Bixby,
Job Tyler,
John Symonds,
Daniel Kenney.

1717.

Thomas Perley, jun.,
Thomas Perley, sen.,
John Andrews,
John Howe,
Joseph Eames.

1718.

Joseph Bixby,
Cornelius Brown,
Joseph Peabody,
Samuel Symonds,
Ephraim Dorman.

1719.

Joseph Hale,
Thomas Killam,
Luke Hovey,
Joseph Symonds,
John Wood.

1720.

Thomas Perley, jun.,
Joseph Bixby,
Thomas Wilkins,
Nathan Eames,
John Andrews, jun.

1721.

Joseph Bixby,
Thomas Jewett,
Thomas Cummings,
Richard Peabody,
Nathan Peabody.

1722.

Timothy Dorman,
Jeremiah Perley,
John Chadwick,
Thomas Redington,
Samuel Symonds.

1723.

Joseph Bixby,
Stephen Peabody,
Samuel Symonds,
Thomas Perley,
John Kimball.

1724.

David Peabody,
Stephen Peabody,
Daniel Kenney,
Timothy Stiles,
Nathaniel Perkins.

1725.

Stephen Peabody,
John Stiles, sen.,
John Symonds,
Joseph Hale, jun.,
Jonathan Tyler.

1726.

Thomas Jewett,
David Peabody,
Robert Andrews,
Jacob Hale,
Thomas Redington.

1727.

Thomas Perley,
Joseph Hale,
Samuel Pickard,
Nathaniel Symonds,
John Howe.

1728.

Joseph Hale,
Thomas Cummings,
Jacob Smith,
Timothy Stiles,
Moses Tyler.

1729.

Stephen Peabody,
James Curtis,
Jacob Smith,
Jacob Perley,
John Stiles, jun.

1730.

Joseph Hale,
Joseph Symonds,
Thomas Perley,
Thomas Andrews,
John Wood.

1731.

Joseph Symonds,
Stephen Peabody,
Thomas Cummings,
Jacob Smith,
Samuel Foster.

1732.

Jacob Perley,
Robert Andrews,
Joseph Hale, jun.,
Zebediah Foster,
John Bixby.

1733.

Stephen Peabody,
Nathaniel Symonds,
Jeremiah Perley,
Jonathan Foster,
Samuel Gould.

1734.

John Symonds,
Joseph Hale, jun.,
Thomas Redington,
Timothy Stiles,
Zebediah Foster.

1735.

Joseph Hale,
Jacob Smith,
Jonathan Foster,
Timothy Stiles,
Amos Perley.

1736

John Symonds,
Luke Hovey,
Jonathan Foster,
Stephen Peabody,
John Killam.

1737

Joseph Symonds,
John Kimball,
Joseph Hale,
Thomas Peabody,
Jeremiah Foster.

1738..

Joseph Symonds,
Thomas Peabody,
Robert Andrews,
Benjamin Porter,
Gideon Bixby.

1739

Robert Andrews,
Benjamin Porter,
John Andrews,
Thomas Peabody,
John Dorman.

1740

Thomas Andrews,
Joseph Hale,
Jonathan Sherwin,
Samuel Gould,
Nathan Kimball.

1741.

Robert Andrews,
Zebediah Foster,
Thomas Peabody,
Nathan Peabody,
Thomas Perley, jun.

1742.

Robert Andrews,
John Kimball,
Thomas Andrews,
Luke Hovey, jun.,
Jeremiah Foster.

1743.

Robert Andrews,
Benjamin Porter,
Joseph Symonds,
Luke Hovey,
Thomas Redington.

1744.

Robert Andrews,
Benjamin Porter,
Joseph Hale, jun.,
Thomas Redington,
Job Tyler.

1745

Joseph Symonds,
Zebediah Foster,
Nathaniel Perkins,
Thomas Peabody,
John Dorman.

1746.

Joseph Symonds,
Thomas Peabody,
Amos Perley,
Jonathan Foster,
Jeremiah Foster.

1747.

Jonathan Foster,
Thomas Redington,
Nathaniel Symonds,
Thomas Peabody,
Thomas Perley.

1748.

Benjamin Porter,
Joseph Symonds,
Luke Hovey, sen,
Gideon Bixby,
Joseph Hale, jun.

1749.

Thomas Redington,
John Hovey,
Nathaniel Symonds,
Aaron Kimball,
Isaac Adams.

1750.

Thomas Redington,
Jonathan Foster,
John Peabody, jun.,
Luke Hovey, jun,
John Hale.

1751.

Jonathan Foster,
Joseph Hale, jun.,
Aaron Kimball,
Joseph Hovey,
Jacob Cummings.

1752.

Thomas Peabody,
John Dorman,
Francis Perley,
Richard Kimball,
John Hale.

1753

Jonathan Foster,
William Foster,
Richard Kimball,
John Peabody,
Solomon Wood.

1754.

Thomas Peabody,
Thomas Perley,
Job Tyler,
Thomas Andrews,
Paul Prichard.

1755.

Thomas Perley,
Isaac Adams,
Jacob Cummings,
Joseph Hovey,
Solomon Wood.

1756.

John Peabody,
Luke Hovey,
Solomon Wood,
Nathan Barker,
Samuel Fisk

1757.

Thomas Perley,
Joseph Hovey,
Aaron Kimball,
Moses Porter,
Jacob Cummings.

1758.

Jonathan Foster,
Asa Perley,
Ebenezer Killam,
Richard Kimball,
Solomon Wood.

1759.

Jonathan Foster,
Francis Perley,
Samuel Fisk,
John Chadwick,
Nathan Wood.

1760.

Thomas Perley,
Luke Hovey,
Aaron Kimball,
Gideon Tyler,
Jacob Cummings.

1761.

Thomas Perley,
Luke Hovey,
Aaron Kimball,
Gideon Tyler,
Jacob Cummings.

1762.

Aaron Wood,
Luke Hovey,
Jacob Cummings,
Isaac Adams,
James Andrews.

1763.

Aaron Wood,
Luke Hovey,
Israel Adams,
Jacob Cummings,
James Andrews

1764.

Aaron Wood,
Isaac Adams,
Aaron Kimball,
John Chadwick,
Asa Perley.

1765.

Aaron Wood,
Joseph Hovey,
Jacob Cummings,
Moses Porter,
Ebenezer Killam.

1766

Thomas Perley,
Samuel Runnells,
Abraham Redington,
Jonathan Foster,
Paul Prichard.

1767.

Asa Perley,
Richard Kimball,
Nathan Andrews,
Nathaniel Peabody,
James Peabody.

1768.

Asa Perley,
Joseph Hovey,
Ebenezer Killam,
Stephen Runnells,
Paul Prichard.

1769.

Asa Perley,
Isaac Adams,
Richard Foster,
Moses Porter,
Nathaniel Perley.

1770.

John Hale,
Samuel Runnells,
Nathan Andrews,
Nathaniel Peabody,
Jacob Cummings.

1771.

Asa Perley,
Isaac Adams,
Jacob Cummings,
Joseph Hovey,
Paul Prichard.

1772.

Nathan Wood,
Isaac Adams,
William Perley,
Jonathan Foster,
Richard Peabody.

1773.

Nathan Andrews,
Isaac Adams,
Moses Putnam,
John Cushing,
William Perley.

1774.

Asa Perley,
Isaac Adams,
John Curtis,
John Robinson,
Benjamin Perley.

1775.

Nathan Andrews,
Isaac Adams,
Nathan Wood,
John Cushing,
Moses Putnam.

1776.

Nathan Andrews,
Isaac Adams,
Nathan Wood,
John Cushing,
Richard Peabody.

1777.

Asa Perley,
John Chadwick,
Benjamin Perley,
Samuel Spofford,
Jacob Andrews.

1778.

Asa Perley,
John Cushing,
Benjamin Perley,
Asa Merrill,
John Wallit.

1779.

William Perley,
Isaac Adams,
Benjamin Perley,
Lemuel Wood,
John Dorman.

1780.

Nathan Andrews,
Lemuel Wood,
John Curtis,
Bradstreet Tyler,
Asa Peabody.

1781.

Aaron Wood,
Isaac Adams,
Benjamin Perley,
Lemuel Wood,
Moses Peabody.

1782.

Asa Perley,
Asa Merrill,
John Dorman,
Lemuel Wood,
Francis Perley.

1783.

Nathan Wood,
John Robinson,
Stephen Symonds,
Jonathan Foster,
Francis Perley.

1784.

Nathan Andrews,
William Porter,
Francis Perley,
Samuel Carleton, jun.,
Asa Peabody.

1785.

Francis Perley,
Lemuel Wood,
Jonathan Wood,
William Porter,
Thomas Perley, jun.

1786.

Francis Perley,
Samuel Carleton, jun.,
Thomas Perley, jun.,
Lemuel Wood,
Samuel Kimball, jun.

1787.

Nathan Andrews,
Jonathan Foster,
Samuel Kimball, jun.,
Thomas Adams,
Amos Perley.

1788.

John Dorman,
John Robinson,
Francis Perley,
Ivory Hovey,
Aaron Perley.

1789.

Richard Foster,
Lemuel Wood,
Samuel Kimball, jun.,
Moses Carleton,
Daniel Nurse.

1790.

Nathan Andrews,
Lemuel Wood,
Richard Foster,
Moses Carleton,
Stephen Peabody.

1791.

John Dorman,   ·
Ivory Hovey,
James Chute,
Parker Spofford,
Simeon Stiles.

1792.

John Dorman,
Ivory Hovey,
James Chute,
Parker Spofford,
Simeon Stiles.

1793.

Francis Perley,
Lemuel Wood,
David Kimball, jun.,
Parker Spofford,
Simeon Stiles.

1794.

Francis Perley,
Lemuel Wood,
David Kimball,
Moses Carleton,
Parker Spofford.

1795.

Francis Perley,
John Tyler,
David Kimball,
Samuel Chadwick,
Moses Dorman.

1796.

Thomas Perley,
John Tyler,
Timothy Dorman,
Samuel Chadwick,
Moses Dorman.

1797.

Thomas Perley,
Enos Runnells,
Samuel Perley,
Samuel Spofford, jun.,
Moses Dorman.

1798.

Thomas Perley,
Enos Runnells,
Moses Dorman,
Samuel Spofford.

1799.

Thomas Perley,
Israel Adams,
Nathan Andrews, jun ,
Israel Foster,
Amos Perley.

1800.

Thomas Perley,
Israel Adams,
Nathan Andrews, jun.,
Israel Foster,
Amos Perley.

1801.

Thomas Perley,
Moses Carleton,
Jacob Andrews,
John Kimball,
Joseph Symonds.

1802.

Thomas Perley,
Moses Carleton,
Jacob Andrews,
John Kimball,
Joseph Symonds.

1803.

Thomas Perley,
Lemuel Wood,
Jacob Gould, jun.,
Israel Adams,
Israel Herrick

1804.

Thomas Perley,
Enos Runnells,
Joseph Symonds, jun.,
Thomas Spofford,
Israel Herrick

1805

Thomas Perley,
Isaac Barker,
Joseph Symonds, jun.,
John Kimball,
Israel Herrick.

1806.

Thomas Perley,
John Kimball,
Joseph Symonds, jun.,
Enos Runnells,
John Dorman

1807.

Moses Dorman,
John Kimball,
Stephen Spofford,
Samuel Carleton,
Amos Perley.

1808

Jonathan Foster, jun.,
Moses Dorman,
Stephen Spofford,
Jonas Runnells,
Jacob Gould.

1809.

Moses Dorman,
Jonathan Foster,
Parker Spofford,
Daniel Adams,
Daniel Chapman.

1810.

Moses Dorman,
Jonathan Foster, jun.,
Parker Spofford,
Daniel Adams,
Daniel Chapman.

1811.

Moses Dorman,
Samuel Spofford,
Stephen Spofford,
Samuel Kimball,
Abraham Perley.

1812.

Stephen Spofford,
John Kimball,
Simeon Pearl,
Parker Spofford,
Joseph Symonds, jun.

1813.

Moses Dorman,
John Kimball,
Joseph Symonds, jun.,
Simeon Pearl,
Jacob Gould.

1814

Moses Dorman,
John Kimball,
Joseph Symonds, jun.,
Simeon Pearl,
Jacob Gould.

1815.

Moses Dorman,
John Kimball,
Israel Foster.

1816.

Moses Dorman,
John Kimball,
Amos Perley,
Simeon Pearl,
Solomon Lowe.

1817.

Moses Dorman,
Israel Foster,
Amos Perley,
John Tyler,
Artemas Kimball.

1818.

Moses Dorman,
Amos Kimball, jun.,
Jacob Gould,
Simeon Pearl,
Abraham Perley.

1819.

Moses Dorman,
Amos Kimball, jun.,
Jacob Gould,
Simeon Pearl,
Abraham Perley.

1820.

Moses Dorman,
Amos Kimball, jun.,
Jacob Gould,
Simeon Pearl,
Abraham Perley.

1821.

Moses Dorman,
Seth Burnham,
Charles Peabody,
Simeon Pearl.

1822.

Moses Dorman,
Jonathan Foster,
Simeon Pearl,
John Tyler, jun.

1823.

Moses Dorman,
Aaron Spofford,
Josiah Kimball.

1824.

Moses Dorman,
Simeon Pearl,
Aaron Spofford.

1825.

John Bacon,
Solomon Lowe,
Asa Foster.

1826.

Josiah Kimball,
Daniel Wood,
Benjamin Pearl.

1827.

Samuel W. Clement,
Josiah Kimball,
Charles Peabody.

1828.

Samuel Kimball,
Samuel W. Clement,
Edmund Barker.

1829.

Samuel W. Clement,
Samuel Kimball,
Phineas Barnes.

1830.

Samuel Kimball,
George Pearl,
Benjamin Robinson.

1831.

Thomas S Hovey,
Samuel Kimball,
Moses Dorman, jun.

1832.

Moses Dorman, jun.,
Simeon Pearl,
Amos Kimball.

1833.

Amos Kimball,
Moses Dorman, jun.,
Phineas Barnes.

1834.

Moses Dorman, jun.,
Amos Kimball,
William Farnham.

1835.

Amos Kimball,
Moses Dorman, jun.,
George W. Sawyer.

1836.

Moses Dorman, jun.,
Amos Kimball,
Thomas S. Hovey.

1837.

Joshua T. Day,
Charles Peabody,
George W. Sawyer.

1838.

George W. Sawyer,
Joshua T. Day,
Amos Kimball.

1839.

Joshua T. Day,
Samuel Andrews,
John Sawyer.

1840.

Moses Dorman, jun.,
Joshua T. Day,
George Pearl.

1841.

Joshua T. Day,
Moses Dorman, jun.,
William H. Herrick.

1842.

Moses Dorman, jun.,
Samuel W. Clement,
George Pearl.

1843.

Joshua T. Day,
William H. Herrick,
John K. Cole.

1844.

Moses Dorman, jun.,
George Pearl,
William R. Kimball.

1845.

Joshua T. Day,
William H. Herrick,
Ancill Dorman.

1846

Moses Dorman, jun.,
William R. Kimball,
S. W. Jenkins.

1847.

George Pearl,
Ancill Dorman,
Moses Dorman, jun

1848.

Moses Dorman, jun.,
George Pearl,
William R. Cole.

1849.

Joshua T. Day,
Ancill Dorman,
William Lowe.

1850.

Ancill Dorman,
Joshua T. Day,
Benjamin S. Barnes.

1851.

William R Cole,
Ancill Dorman,
Benjamin S. Barnes.

1852.

Ancill Dorman,
William R. Cole,
John F. Kimball.

1853.

John F. Kimball,
Moses Dorman,
Benjamin S. Barnes.

1854.

Moses Dorman,
Oliver P. Killam,
John F. Kimball.

1855.

John F. Kimball,
William Lowe,
Leonard Perley.

1856.

Moses Dorman,
George Pearl,
William R. Cole.

1857.

John F. Kimball,
William E. Killam,
William H. Herrick.

1858.

William E. Killam,
John F. Kimball,
William R. Cole.

1859.

William R. Cole,
William E. Killam,
Benjamin S. Barnes.

1860.

William E Killam,
William R. Cole,
Joshua T. Day.

1861.

William R. Cole,
William E Killam,
John K. Cole.

1862.

William E. Killam,
George W. Chadwick,
Thomas L. Spofford.

1863.

John F. Kimball,
William E. Killam,
Israel Herrick.

1864.

William E. Killam,
Joshua T. Day,
William R. Cole.

1865.

John F. Kimball,
Benjamin S. Barnes,
Edward Howe.

1866.

Ancill Dorman,
John F. Kimball,
Oliver P. Killam.

1867.

John F. Kimball,
Ancill Dorman,
Roscoe W. Gage.

1868.

Roscoe W. Gage,
Joshua T. Day,
John Pearl.

1869.

George W. Chadwick,
William E. Killam,
John K. Cole.

1870.

Ancill Dorman,
George W. Chadwick,
Joshua T. Day.

1871.

George W. Chadwick,
Ancill Dorman,
John K. Cole.

1872.

Thomas P. Dorman,
George W. Chadwick,
William R. Kimball.

1873.

Oliver P. Killam,
Ancill Dorman,
John K. Cole.

1874.

Ancill Dorman,
George W. Chadwick,
Israel F. Spofford.

1875.

George W. Chadwick,
Ancill Dorman,
John K. Cole.

1876.

Ancill Dorman,
George W. Chadwick,
Isaac W. Andrews.

1877.

George W. Chadwick,
John K. Cole,
Ancill Dorman.

1878.

Ancill Dorman,

George W. Chadwick,
James Henry Nason.

1879.

George W. Chadwick,
Benjamin S. Barnes,
John K. Cole.

APPENDIX C.

SENATORS AND REPRESENTATIVES FROM BOXFORD.

SENATORS.

Two senators only have been furnished by Boxford, viz. : —

1781. — Aaron Wood (1719–1791), b. in Boxford, son of John and Ruth (Peabody) Wood. (See his biography.)

1869. — Julius Aboyneau Palmer * (1803–1872) ; b. in Little Compton, R.I., son of Thomas and Susanna (Palmer) Palmer.

* Hon Julius A. Palmer, son of Thomas and Susanna (Palmer) Palmer, was born in Little Compton, R.I, June 14, 1803. His parents were both descendants of William Palmer, — who came over in the ship " Fortune," and landed at Plymouth, Mass, in 1621, — though distantly related to each other. He went to Boston in 1819, and was, at the time of his death, the senior member of the firm of Palmer, Batchelder, & Co, jewellers, in that city. He was an uncle of Rev. Charles R. Palmer of the Tabernacle Church, Salem ; and he delivered the address at the dedication of the new Tabernacle chapel, in 1870. He was an ardent temperance man, and was several times selected as the temperance candidate for mayor of Boston. He was a representative to the Legislature from Boston in 1843 and in 1851. Retiring to Boxford on account of his age and health, he was elected to the Senate from Essex County in 1869 This was his last public office. Mr. Palmer was connected with many charitable, religious, and reformatory organizations, where he exercised marked influence on account of his intelligence and high personal character. He was an active member and deacon of the Mount Vernon Church, Boston. Deacon Palmer, though living much of the time and doing business in Boston, was nevertheless closely identified with this town, where he held, occupied, and improved a valuable estate, and where he gave his encouragement to all good local undertakings. He died in Boston, on Thursday, Feb 15, 1872, and was buried from the Mount Vernon Church the following Saturday. Mr Palmer married Lucy Manning Peabody, daughter of Major Jacob Peabody, a descendant of Capt John Peabody, one of the early settlers, who resided in the old mansion that was razed to the ground by Deacon Palmer.

389

REPRESENTATIVES.

It seems that no representative was sent to the General Court until the "Old Government" was resumed after the downfall of Sir Edmund Andros in the spring of 1689. The first session convened May 8 of that year. Until 1693, four sessions were held annually; after this time an annual session convened in May, each year. The quarterly sessions commencing Oct. 24, 1689, May 28, 1690, April 14 and May 20, 1691, March 8 and May 4, 1692, were convened without a Boxford representative. Of the annual sessions, Boxford was not represented in the years 1693, '94, '96, '97, 1701, '05, '06, '08, '33, 1739–60 (why for so long a period we have never learned), '82, 1789–91, 1818, '22, '24, '25, '26, '29, '30, '37, '42, '44, '45, '48, 1851–56. In 1858 the State was divided into representative districts, from two to four, or more, towns constituting a district, and one representative being annually elected in each district; the towns furnishing the representatives in turn. The fifteenth district is composed of Boxford, Ipswich, and Rowley. Boxford is in the sixth Congressional district of Massachusetts. The following is a list of representatives from Boxford, viz. : —

1. JOHN PEABODY (1642–1720); b. in Topsfield; son of Lieut. Francis and Mary (Foster) Peabody. Was representative for the quarterly sessions commencing May 8, 1689, Oct. 8 and Dec. 10, 1690, Oct. 14 and December, 1691, and (with Thomas Perley) June 8, 1692; and of the annual sessions, 1695, '98, '99, (with Thomas Perley) 1700, and 1710–13.

2. JOHN PERLEY (1636–1729); b. in Ipswich; son of Allan and Susanna (Bokeson) Perley. Was representative for the quarterly sessions commencing Feb. 12, 1690, and Feb. 3, 1691.

3. THOMAS PERLEY (1641–1709); b. in Ipswich; brother to the preceding. Was representative (with John Peabody) for the quarterly session commencing June 8, 1692.

4. THOMAS PERLEY (1668–1745); b. in Rowley; son of Thomas (the above) and Lydia (Peabody) Perley. Was representative, (with John Peabody) 1700, '02, (with William Foster) 1703, '07,' 09, '18, and '19.

5. THOMAS PERLEY (1668–1740) ; b. in Ipswich ; son of John (above) and Mary (Howlet) Perley. Was representative, (with Stephen Peabody) 1727.

6. WILLIAM FOSTER (1670–1755) ; b. in Boxford ; son of William and Mary (Jackson) Foster. Was representative, (with Lieut. Thomas Perley) 1703.

7. SAMUEL SYMONDS (1638–1722) ; was representative, 1704.

8. JOSEPH HALE (1671–1761) ; b. in Newbury ; son of Thomas and Mary (Hutchinson) Hale. Was representative, 1714–17, 1720–25, 1728–32, and 1735.

9. STEPHEN PEABODY (1685–1759) ; b. in Boxford ; son of William and Hannah (Hale) Peabody. Was representative, 1726, (with Lieut. Thomas Perley) 1727.

10. JOHN SYMONDS (1674–17—) ; b. in Boxford ; son of Samuel (above) and Elizabeth (Andrews) Symonds. Was representative, 1734, 1736–38.

11. AARON WOOD (1719–1791) ; b. in Boxford ; son of John and Ruth (Peabody) Wood. Was representative, 1761–70, '73, '74, 1776–79.

12. ASA PERLEY (1716–1806) , b. in Boxford ; son of Thomas and Sarah (Osgood) Perley. Was representative, 1771, '72, (member of the Provincial Congress) '75, 1780–81.

13. ISAAC ADAMS (1713–1797) ; b. in Rowley ; son of Isaac and Hannah (Spofford) Adams. Was representative, 1783–86, '88.

14. NATHAN ANDREWS (1726–1806) ; b. in Boxford ; son of Robert and Deborah (Frye) Andrews. Was representative, 1787.

15. THOMAS PERLEY (1746–1831) ; b. in Boxford ; son of Thomas and Eunice (Putnam) Perley. Was representative, 1792–1810, — nineteen years in all.

16. PARKER SPOFFORD (1755–1837) ; b. in Boxford ; son of Samuel and Mary (Poor) Spofford. Was representative, 1811–14.

17. ISRAEL FOSTER (1765–18—) ; b. in Boxford ; son of Jonathan and Rebecca (Dorman) Foster. Was representative, 1815–17.

18. MOSES DORMAN (1765–1850) ; b. in Boxford ; son of John and Hannah (Jackson) Dorman. Was representative, 1819–21.

19. SOLOMON LOWE (1782–1861) ; b. in Boxford ; son of

Nathan and Lucy (Lord) Lowe. Was representative, 1823, '27, '28, and '41.

20. CHARLES PEABODY. Was representative, 1831–34.

21. MOSES DORMAN (1803–1877) ; b. in Boxford ; son of Moses (above) and Huldah (Gould) Dorman. Was representative, 1835–36.

22. JOSIAH KIMBALL (1803–1878) ; b. in Boxford ; son of David Kimball. Was representative, 1838.

23. MOSES KIMBALL (1798–1879) ; b. in Boxford ; son of John and Ruth (Eastman) Kimball. Was representative, 1839–40.

24. BENJAMIN PEABODY (1789–1879) ; b. in Boxford ; son of Ebenezer and Sarah (Pearl) Peabody. Was representative, 1843.

25. WILLIAM LOWE (1807–1870) ; b. in Boxford ; son of Gen. Solomon (above) and Huldah (Kimball) Lowe. Was representative, 1846–47.

26. ENOCH WOOD (1797) ; b. in Boxford ; son of Jonathan and Abigail (Hale) Wood. Was representative, 1849, '50, and '58.

27. GEORGE PEARL (1798–1878) ; b. in Boxford ; son of John and Mehitable (Hall) Pearl. Was representative, 1857, — the last under the old system.

28. JOHN KIMBALL COLE (1814) ; b. in Boxford ; son of Kimball and Abigail (Runnells) Cole. Chosen representative, 1861.

29. JEFFERSON KIMBALL (1808–1879) ; b. in North Andover ; son of Thomas Kimball. Chosen representative, 1864.

30. ROSCOE W. GAGE (1839–1869) ; b. in Pelham, N.H. ; son of Abel and Anna Gage. Chosen representative, 1868.

31. CHARLES PERLEY ; b. in Dunbarton, N.H. ; son of Benjamin and Ruth (Mills) Perley. Chosen representative, 1873.

32. WILLIAM SYMMES COGGIN (1812) ; b. in Tewksbury, Mass. ; son of Rev. Jacob and Mary (Symmes) Coggin. Chosen representative, 1878.

APPENDIX D.

MORTALITY, ETC.

Boxford has always been noted, on account of its rural advantages, temperance, and simple manner of living, as one of the most healthful places that can be found anywhere in our northern latitude. It has been a current remark, and one that is exceedingly full of meaning, that Boxford is without a doctor. The reason of this is, there is little for a doctor to do. Dr. George Moody, who was settled here for a few months, said. "I might as well practise in heaven." The inhabitants live generally to extreme old age. The prevalence of fatal diseases is almost unknown. Small-pox was first known in 1722 ; and it prevailed to a slight extent in 1760, and resulted in the deaths of Lydia, wife of Dr. Foster, Jan 17, and Richard, son of Richard Pearl, Dec. 7, both of the West Parish. In a letter dated Aug. 26, 1776, Eunice, wife of John Pearl, says, "The small-pox has been at Richard Tyler's for several weeks past , those who have had it are likely to get well." Again, in 1854, we were visited by this dire disease ; this time resulting, Dec. 17, in the death of James Leach, a native of Taungend, Eng., and a laborer in the cotton-factory In order to prevent the prevalence of this disease, Cornelius Gould, Stephen Peabody, and Israel Adams were appointed a committee April 15, 1811, to superintend inoculation.

Deaths by casualty have been very few, most of them being occasioned by drowning Samuel Sessions, an old man of seventy years of age, was drowned Dec 6, 1750, "in the brook near the house of John Chadwick." Amos, son of Samuel Spofford, was drowned in Hovey's Pond July 1, 1814, aged seven years. William Runnells and Isaac Peabody were lost at sea about October, 1818. Mark Genness of the West Parish was drowned Jan. 15,

1833, aged twenty-nine years. Within the last quarter of a century, several cases of drowning have occurred among our young men, — Samuel K. Coggin, Frank F. Russell, and others. Mr. John Foster, jun., was killed by lightning, July 24, 1772. A few cases of suicide have occurred, most of them by hanging, among which are those of Moses Wood, Joseph Adams, Mrs. Tyler, Edward G. Batchelder, Edward Hussey, and Dudley Cummings.

The following is a list of those persons that have died in Boxford at an age exceeding ninety years. —

1. JOHN PERLEY, widower; d. 15 Dec., 1729, a. ninety-three years, b in Ipswich, Mass, 1636, son of Allan and Susanna (Bokeson) Perley; buried in Boxford.

2. MARY DURIN, widow, d. 14 Feb., 1749, "between ninety and a hundred years old, as is supposed."

3. SUSANNA HOVEY, widow; d. 22 Dec., 1767, a. ninety years, ten months, twenty-one days, b. 1 Feb., 1677; dau. of Moses Pillsbury; widow of Luke Hovey of Boxford. (See No. 8.)

4. HANNAH ADAMS, married; d. 3 Sept., 1775, a. ninety-three years.

5. SUSANNA COLE, widow; d 29 July, 1785, a. ninety-five years, widow of Samuel Cole of Boxford

6. HANNAH KIMBALL, widow, d. 16 April, 1786, a. ninety-nine years.

7. MARY SMITH, married; d. 23 May, 1792, a. ninety-two years. "Sarah Smith, widow; d. 9 July, 1792, a. ninety-three years." Is this the same?

8. DORCAS FOSTER, widow; d — Aug., 1793, a. ninety-two years, three months; b. in Boxford, 10 May, 1701; dau. of Luke and Susanna (Pillsbury) [No 3] Hovey; widow of John Foster

9. RICHARD PEARL, widower, d. 20 Dec., 1793, a. ninety-one years, seven months; b. in Bradford, 20 May, 1702; son of John and Elizabeth (Holmes) Pearl.

10. THOMAS PERLEY, widower, d. 28 Sept., 1795, a. ninety years, seven months, six days, b. in Boxford, 22 Feb., 1704–05, son of Thomas and Sarah (Osgood) Perley of Boxford, buried in Boxford.

11. MARY CHADWICK, widow; d. 4 Oct., 1798, a. ninety-three years

12. PRUDENCE TYLER, d. 23 July, 1804, a. one hundred years

13. MOSES PORTER, widower, d 3 Nov, 1811, a. ninety-one years, eleven months, fifteen days; b in Boxford, 18 Nov, 1719; son of Benjamin and Sarah (Tyler) Porter of Boxford.

14. MOLLY SMITH, "Mrs.," d — Oct, 1814, a. ninety years.

15. —— BARKER, widow, d 21 Dec, 1814, a. ninety years, widow of John Barker of Andover

16. MARY PORTER, widow; d. 1 Jan., 1818, a. ninety-six years.

17. REBECCA YOUNG, married; d. 1 June, 1819, a. ninety-four years. She was of Wellfleet when she died; buried in Boxford.

18. ASA PARKER; d. 29 May, 1820, a ninety years.

19. —— CHADWICK, widow, d. 8 Nov., 1824, a. ninety-eight years, widow of Ephraim Chadwick.

20 MARGARET WOOD, widow; d 10 Feb, 1830, a. one hundred and one years, ten months; b in Topsfield, 29 April, 1728; dau. of —— Perkins; widow of Thomas Wood of Boxford. (See No. 29.)

21 JANE ANDREWS, widow; d 24 Feb, 1837, a. ninety years, seven months, twenty-four days, b. in Topsfield, 30 July, 1746, dau. of Simon and Jane (Palmer) Gould, widow of Jacob Andrews of Boxford.

22. LYDIA SPOFFORD, widow; d. 6 Sept., 1839, a. ninety-five years; b. in Waltham, 18 Jan., 1745, dau. of Phineas and Grace (Hastings) Warren of Waltham, widow of Benjamin Spofford of Boxford; buried in Boxford

23. BRADSTREET TYLER, widower, d. 5 April, 1842, a. ninety-six years, seven months, eight days; b in Boxford, 27 Aug, 1745, son of Job and Elizabeth (Parker) Tyler. (See No. 37.)

24 SAMUEL CARLETON, widower; d. 18 March, 1843, a. ninety-two years, six months, one day, b in Boxford, 17 Sept., 1750; son of Samuel and Rebecca (Goodridge) Carleton of Boxford.

25 MARY DOLE, widow; d. 26 Feb, 1844, a. ninety-two years.

26 MARY WOOD, widow; d. 21 Nov., 1844, a. ninety-two years.

27. —— BARKER, widow; d. 30 April, 1845, a ninety-one years; widow of John Barker.

28. MARY SMITH, widow; d. 21 Nov., 1846, a. ninety-four years.

29. MEHITABLE PERLEY, widow; d. 15 March, 1853, a. ninety-one years, three months, nineteen days; b. in Boxford, 26 Nov., 1761; dau. of Thomas and Margaret (Perkins) [No. 20] Wood; widow of Aaron Perley; buried in Boxford.

30. JOHN CHAPMAN, unmarried; d. 9 March, 1861, a. ninety-one years, seven months, nine days; b. in Boxford, 1 Aug., 1769; son of Daniel and Hepzibah Chapman of Boxford; buried in Boxford.

31. EUNICE WILDES, widow; d. 19 Sept., 1864, a. ninety-four years, eight months, twenty-four days, b. in Ipswich, 25 Dec., 1769; dau. of Lot and Eunice Conant of Ipswich, Mass.; widow of Dudley Wildes; d. of dysentery; buried in Topsfield.

32. HANNAH HOLYOKE, unmarried, d. 5 Dec., 1865, a. ninety-one years, one month, nineteen days; b. in Boxford, 16 Oct., 1774; dau. of Rev. Elizur and Hannah (Peabody) Holyoke; buried in Boxford.

33. WILLIAM TYLER, widower; d. "of old age and fever," 25 Aug., 1867, a. ninety-two years, ten months, fifteen days, b. in Boxford, 10 Oct., 1774; son of Abraham and Abigail (Stickney) Tyler of Boxford; buried in Boxford.

34. JOHN DAY, widower; d. "of old age," 3 Aug., 1868, a. ninety-one years, seven months, twenty-three days; b. in Brad-ford, 10 Dec., 1776, son of John and Elizabeth (Ingersol) Day; buried in Boxford.

35. MARY BATCHELDER, widow; d. of old age, 22 June, 1871, a. ninety-one years, nine months, twenty-two days; b. in Tops-field, 31 Aug, 1779; dau. of Joseph and Annie Cummings; widow of Jacob Batchelder; buried in Boxford.

36. MARY GOWEN, widow; d. 6 Feb., 1872, a. ninety-two years, three months; b. in "Boxford;" dau. of Bimsley Peabody; buried in Boxford.

37. JOHN TYLER, unmarried; d. 12 Nov., 1872, a. ninety-one years, seven months, b. in Boxford, son of Bradstreet [No. 23] and Mary (Foster) Tyler; buried in Boxford.

38. SALLY CLEMMENT, widow, d. of apoplexy, 2 Dec., 1877, a. ninety years, three months, eight days, b. in Boxford, 24 Aug, 1787; dau. of Simeon and Polly (Smith) Cole of Boxford; widow of Samuel W. Clemment, buried in Boxford.

39. MEHITABLE BLANCHARD, widow ; d. 3 Feb., 1878, a ninety-two years, nine months, twenty-eight days ; b. in Boxford, 5 April, 1785 ; dau. of Daniel and Sarah (Bradstreet) Gould , widow of Rev. Abijah Blanchard ; buried in Boxford.

40. HANNAH FRIEND, unmarried ; d. 25 March, 1878, a. ninety-three years, five months, five days ; b. in Dracut, 20 Oct. 1784 ; dau. of John and Hannah (Wells) Friend of Wenham ; buried in Wenham.

41 NANCY R. FOWLER, widow , d. 15 June, 1878, a. ninety years, eleven months, fifteen days ; dau. of Jonathan Kavitt.

APPENDIX E.

LIST OF COLLEGE GRADUATES FROM BOXFORD.

NAMES	NATIVE PLACE	WHERE GRADUATED	WHEN
Chandler Braman Adams .	Boxford.	Union.*	1855
Charles Israel Adams	"	Dartmouth	1852
George W Atherton . .	Newburyport.	{ Yale	1863
		{ Amherst	
Benjamin Chadwick . .	Boxford.	Harvard	1770.
John Cushing . . .	"	"	1761.
John Hubbard Eaton . .	"	"	1827
Peter Sydney Eaton . . .	"	{ Harvard	1818.
		{ Theo Sem., Andover	1822.
Moses Hale . . .	"	Harvard.	1722.
William Augustus Herrick	"	Dartmouth	1854
Samuel Holyoke	"	Harvard.	1789.
Joseph Hovey . .	"	"	1804
Rufus Porter Hovey. . .	"	"	1813.
David Jewett	"	"	1776
Walter Henry Kimball .	"	Dartmouth.	1841.
Albert Bradstreet Peabody	"	Amherst	1859
Augustus Peabody . .	"	{ Dartmouth	1803
		{ Harvard (Laureate).	1809
Oliver Peabody . . .	Boxford.	Harvard	1721.
Samuel Peabody . . .	"	Dartmouth.	1803
Stephen Peabody . .	"	Harvard	1769
William Peabody. . . .	"	Dartmouth.	179-.
Daniel Perley	"	"	1828.
Humphrey Clark Perley .	"	"	1791.
Ira Perley	"	"	1822.
Nathaniel Perley . . .	"	"	1791
Asa Porter	"	Harvard	1762.
John Rogers	"	"	1732
Francis Savage . .	"	Dartmouth	
James Scales	"	Harvard	1733
Stephen Symonds . .	"		
Dean Tyler	"	Harvard.	1776
Jacob Wood	"	Dartmouth	

398   * Schenectady, N.Y.

APPENDIX F.

NEW SETTLERS, 1700–1725.

AMMEY. — *John* m. Abigail Daland, 2 Feb., 1721–22, and had two children born here : Abigail, 1723, and Michael, 1726. She joined the church in 1728 ; and they probably went to Haverhill shortly after, as a John "Amey" was there in 1732.

ARCHER. —*Benjamin* came from Rowley, 1716. By his wife Anna, one child was born here, — Mehitable, 1717. He had other children : Sarah, Benjamin, and Josiah. Was in Boxford as late as 1720.

BALCH. — *Cornelius* came to Boxford, 1713. By his wife Mary, had two children born here : Mary, 1715, and Cornelius, 1717. Cornelius, jun., m. Martha Robinson of Topsfield, 1739, and settled in Topsfield.

BRADFORD. — *William*, by wife Grace, had several children ; first one born in 1723. He was here as late as 1740.

BROWN. — *Cornelius* was surveyor in 1707, and a selectman in 1711. Wife, Susanna. His dau. Susanna was admitted to First Church, 1705. He lived in the West Parish, and belonged to the church in Bradford till the Second Church was formed in Boxford. His wife d. in 1734, at the age of seventy-four years. He was in Boxford in 1737. *Aaron;* wife, Susanna, by whom he had ch.: Aaron, b. 1720; Daniel, 1722; and Abigail, 1724. He was taxed here, 1717 and 1718. He d. before 1731, when she m. William Lakeman of Ipswich. *Caleb* was deacon of the Second Church. Wife, Elizabeth. First child b. 1724. Ch.: Sarah, Mary, Hannah, Elizabeth, Caleb, Susanna, Clark, Hepzibah, David, and Maximilian. Removed to Harvard, spring of 1743.

BURBANK. — *Caleb*, b. in Rowley, 1 May, 1671, son of Caleb

and Martha (Smith) Burbank. Came to Boxford before 1711.
His wife was Hannah, by whom he had ch. b. in Boxford:
Timothy, Margaret, Asa, and David. He d. "very suddenly,"
1 Feb., 1749–50, a. seventy-nine years. *Ebenezer*, brother of
Caleb, b. in Rowley, 28 June, 1687. Was taxed here 1715, 1716.
Calls himself of Boxford, 1717, when he confirms to Samuel Cole
of Lynn the farm occupied by the late Manly H. Cole. Wife,
Sarah. Carpenter by trade.

BUTMAN. — *Matthew;* m., 1st, Faith Jewett, 1716, who d. the
following March, a. twenty-two years. He m., 2d, Hannah
Cummings, 1720, by whom he had: Hannah, b. 1721; Ebenezer,
1724; Elizabeth, 1730, Mary, 1734, and Asa. Was constable
in 1736.

CHAPMAN. — *William* m. Ann Jenks, 1704. Dau Elizabeth
baptized, 1706. "William Chapman, jun.," admitted to First
Church, 1704.

CLARK. — *William*. Weaver. Wife, Jean. Son John b 14
Feb., 1712; d 30 July, 1714 For several years Mr. Clark was a
pauper, and he was boarded out with different families until the
winter of 1742–43, when, living with Benjamin Porter, he was
taken sick, and was treated by Dr. Foster; he d. Feb 8, 1742–43.

CLEAVES. — *William*. Wife, Rebecca. Son William b. 2
April, 1712.

COLE — *John* of Lynn (*ante* of Malden), cooper by trade; m.
Sarah ——, and had ch: Samuel, b. 27 Dec., 1687, and Anna,
5 Aug, 1690. In 1717 Samuel came to Boxford with his father,
and, for one hundred and ten pounds, purchased of Ebenezer
Burbank the farm on which his posterity have resided until within
a few years (the farm of the late Mr Manly H Cole, in the
West Parish). This was the tract of sixty-seven acres laid out
to Thomas Leaver in 1666.* John Cole, the father, d "very
suddenly," 1737, a. sixty-eight years Samuel d 1765, and his
widow Susanna, 1785, a ninety-five years Samuel's children were:
Samuel, John, Rebecca, Susanna, and Mary. The last-mentioned
Samuel (who was great-grandfather of Mr. D. M. Cole) had a
family of fifteen children John removed to Amherst, N. H., about

* See page 42.

1763. *Jonathan* m. Judith Brown, 1724. Lived in Boxford in 1738, and removed to Harvard in 1746.

CUMMINGS. — *Thomas* was b. in Topsfield, 27 June, 1670, and was son of Isaac Cummings, who m. Mary, dau. of Robert Andrews of Boxford. He came to Boxford before his marriage. March 20, 1705, he m. Mehitable Porter of Salem. By her he had four children born, one of whom, Jacob, lived here, and had seven children, two of whom were Dudley and Thomas, — two queer characters, whose *non compos mentis* state is well known to our older inhabitants. They lived with Mr. John Sawyer — father of our present resident of that name — until their death. Thomas was b. 12 Oct., 1765, and d. 29 May, 1834, at the age of sixty-eight years. Dudley was b. 18 Feb., 1748, and hung himself in Willis' Woods, in the East Parish, at a locality known as "The College," June 25, 1815, a. sixty-seven years. His mode of self-execution was novel. He went to "The College," which lies a short distance from the house, to gather herbs, carrying with him a line with which to tie his bundle. Taking the line, he stretched it from one tree to another, several feet from the ground, near a large ledge whose perpendicular side rose up in close proximity to the trees. Letting his feet lie on the top of the ledge, he placed his neck upon the line, and there lay till death ensued.

DORMAN. — *Ephraim*, b. in Topsfield, 17 Sept., 1677; was son of Ephraim and Mary Dorman. He settled in Boxford, 1710; and died in 1724. By his wife Martha, six children were born here. *Jabez*, also from Topsfield, m., 1st, Hepzibah Perley, 1715; had a son, Jabez, b. 1716; and mother and son d. same year. He m., 2d, Abial Foster, 1716, and had another son, Jabez, b. 1717.

FISK. — *Samuel* was here, 1705. Wife, Sarah. Ch.: Hannah, b. 1707; Mary, 1710; Sarah, 1713; and Samuel, 1716. Was taxed here till 1718. *John* was taxed here as early as 1711. Wife, Abigail. He d. before 1727, when she m. Thomas Holt of Andover.

FOSTER. — *Benjamin* came from Topsfield about 1720. Father of Dr. Foster. Born in Ipswich, 1670. Weaver. Wife, Ann. Removed to Billerica about 1729, and d. at Lunenburg, 1735. Had several children.

FRAME. — *John* m. Elizabeth Stiles, 1719, and had ch.: Marcy and Mary (twins), b. 1720; John, 1723; and Lydia, 1726.

GALLUP. — *Thomas* was taxed here, 1716. By wife Love, he had children born in Boxford: Abigail, 1720; William, 1722; George, 1726; Jeremiah, 1728; Sarah, 1733; and Mary, 1739. Warned out of town in 1729, but came back again, and lived here many years afterwards.

GAR. — *Thomas.* By wife Ann, his son John was born, 1725.

GOULD. — *Samuel*, came from Topsfield, 1700. He was son of Capt. John and Sarah (Baker) Gould, and born in Topsfield, March 9, 1669–70. He married Margaret Stone, 1697, and had children Sarah, Samuel, Moses, Patience, Jonathan, Margaret, Zaccheus, and Hubbard. The sons ultimately settled in Brookfield and Lunenburg. Mr. Gould died, 1724. In 1714 his house was destroyed by fire, and the town abated his tax for that reason.

HARDY. — *Nathaniel.* By wife Prudence, he had children born here: "Roos," 1707; Elizabeth, 1709; Keziah, 1711; Zachariah, 1713; Abigail, 1715; Richard, 1718; and Martha, 1720. He died before 1725.

HOWE. — *John.* Lived in what is now Middleton. By wife Sarah Caves (whom he married in 1697, when they were both of Topsfield), he had children born here: Mark, 1701; Sarah, 1703; "—ey" (dau.), 1705–06; and Joseph, 1719.

ILES. — *William;* said to be a native of England; m. Elizabeth Curtis, 1719. Children born here: Elizabeth, William, John, Jacob, and Mary. William married, and lived here, as also another generation.

JEWETT. — *Thomas* was born in Rowley, 20 Sept., 1666, and was son of Ezekiel and Faith (Parrott) Jewett. He married Hannah Swan, 1692, and had children born in Rowley: Ezekiel, 1693; Faith, 1694; and Mehitable, 1698. Came to Boxford about 1703, having married a second wife, Faith. He died in 1731. He probably settled where these lines are being written, and where his posterity resided till they removed to New Hampshire, a century ago.

KENNEY. — *Daniel*, by wife Mary, had children born here: Daniel, 1705; Isaac, 1707; Israel, 1712; Mary, 1715; Ruth,

1717, and Eunice, 1719. He was selectman in 1724. *Jonathan*, by wife Rebecca, had children born here; Jonathan, 1712; Rebecca, 1714; and Thomas, 1716 Both of these settlers resided in that part of the town which was afterwards Middleton.

KILLAM. — *Samuel.* Came from Wilmington. Was taxed here many years. He married Grace Symonds, 1715, and had a son Samuel born in 1716. *Thomas* was taxed as early as 1711 By wife Sarah he had children born here · Ebenezer, 1714, and Sarah, 1716. Ebenezer also resided here. *John* married Abigail Symonds, 1725, and probably erected the "old Killam house;" had ch Abigail, b 1725; John, 1729, and Mary, 1731. He died, 1738 John, jun, was the grandfather of Samuel, George, Oliver P., and the late William E. Killam

KNOX — *Adam*, by wife Jane, had children born here: Jane, 1721, John, 1724; Elizabeth, 1726, William, 1730; Adam, 1732, and Mary, 1734

PERKINS — *Nathaniel* owned land, and was taxed here as early as 1714. It is thought by the writer, that he built and resided in the "old Hood house," lately occupied by Mr. Benjamin Hood, in the East Parish. He married Hannah Hazen of Boxford, 1716, by whom he had several children born here Nathaniel, Daniel, Israel, Mary, Benjamin, Hannah, Hepzibah, Eunice, and Jacob. The family were here as late as 1760

PICKARD — *Samuel.* He married Phebe Bixby, 1713, and his son Samuel was baptized in 1714. *Thomas.* He was here as early as 1714, and was chosen constable in 1740

PORTER — *Benjamin*, was born in Wenham in 1692, and was son of John and Lydia (Herrick) Porter. He married, 1716, and settled in Boxford He was the ancestor of the Boxford Porters He had children Mary, Moses, Benjamin, Sarah, Tyler, and Lucy. He died, 1778, aged eighty-six years. Moses and Benjamin (great-grandfather of Capt J. J. Porter) settled in Boxford. Among the descendants of this settler are Rufus King Porter, Bowdoin College, 1813, lawyer at Machias, Me., forty years; John Cooper Porter, banker of St. Louis, Mo.; George Thatcher Porter, physician at Calais, Me., John C Porter, professor of mathematics at New-York Central College, Thomas W. Porter, lawyer in Boston, member of Massachusetts Legislature; Byron Porter, physician of Newport, Me., member of Maine Legislature; and Parker Cleaveland Porter, graduate Maine Medical School, 1863, surgeon in the Rebellion.

SCALES. — *James* was b. in Rowley, 30 March, 1679, and was son of James and Sarah (Curtis) Scales. He m. Sarah Curtis (his cousin) of Boxford, 1703, and settled in Boxford. He resided near the residence of Mr. Oliver P. Killam. Although they were in humble circumstances, one of the sons entered the ministry, after passing through the collegiate course at Harvard. The children of this settler were : Mary, James, Moses, Hannah, John, Nathan, Mercy, Joseph, and Oliver. The family removed to Wilmington about 1740.

SPOFFORD. — *Thomas* was b. in Georgetown (then Rowley), 6 June, 1678, and was son of Samuel and Sarah (Birkbee) Spofford. He m. Bethiah Hazeltine, 1701, and settled in Boxford. Ch.: —— (son), Bethiah, Mehitable, Hannah, Dorothy, Thomas, Elizabeth, and Abraham. *Samuel*, brother to the above, was b. in 1690, and came to Boxford upon his marriage with Sarah Stickney of Bradford, 1717. He was taxed here as early as 1714. Ch : Bethiah, b. 1719; Sarah, 1721; Samuel, 1722; Thomas, 1726; Amos, 1729. Through the last-mentioned Amos, and *his* son Thomas, Samuel was the great-grandfather of the late Richard and Capt. Aaron Spofford.

STEWART. — *James*, by wife Elizabeth, had a son, Moses, b. here 12 July, 1712. This settler was here in 1716.

APPENDIX G.

LIST OF DEACONS.

FIRST CHURCH. — Thomas Perley was a deacon in 1708, and he died next year. Abraham Redington was one in 1710, and continued in office till 1713, Dec. 22, when he died. Daniel Wood was deacon in 1714, and was also styled deacon in 1718. Timothy Foster was deacon in 1718, and continued in office until a new set of deacons were chosen in 1759, on the settlement of Rev. Mr. Holyoke. Jonathan Foster was a deacon in 1717, and probably continued in office to his death, May 21, 1730. Nathan Peabody was chosen in November of that year to take his place. Deacon Peabody died March 4, 1733, at the age of fifty years. Thomas Redington was then chosen in December, 1734, who continued in office till a new set of deacons were chosen in 1759, as above stated, on account of the mixed matters of the church during the long interval that it had been without a settled pastor.

The deacons chosen in April, 1759, were Aaron Kimball and Joseph Hale. Deacon Kimball was in office as late as 1774, and was probably followed by Joseph Symonds, who was in office in 1778. He was followed by John Dorman, who is first found in office in 1782. Deacon Dorman died in 1792, and Moses Peabody was chosen in his stead in September of that year. Deacon Peabody died in January, 1826, and his son, Oliver Tyler Peabody, was appointed in his stead in June, 1827. Deacon Peabody resigned in 1853; and the present deacon, John K. Cole, was chosen in his stead in June of that year. Deacon Joseph Hale, above mentioned, resigned in 1765, and died Oct. 5, 1778, aged eighty-six years. In December, 1765, Stephen Symonds was appointed to take his place. Deacon Symonds died April 9, 1808, at the age of eighty years. He was followed in October,

1795, by Jonathan Wood, who died two years later; and he was followed in May, 1798, by Parker Spofford, who married the widow of his predecessor in office. Deacon Spofford died in 1836; and in June, 1838, Josiah Kimball was chosen to take his place. Deacon Kimball removed to Lawrence in 1852, and in August of that year Samuel Bixby, who is still in office, was chosen to fill the vacancy. Deacon Kimball died in Boston, where he had resided for some years, in 1878.

SECOND CHURCH — After the church was incorporated in the West Parish, two deacons were chosen. These were John Woster and Caleb Brown. Deacon Woster removed to Leicester in 1745, and was dismissed from his office Oct. 7 of that year. Thomas Chadwick was appointed his successor the following April 21. Deacon Chadwick was succeeded by Asa Parker, April 8, 1790, and Parker served till March 20, 1806. The other original deacon, Caleb Brown, removed to Harvard in the spring of 1743, and David Foster was chosen in his stead June 15, 1743. Deacon Foster served till his death in 1759, when Lieut. Joseph Hovey was chosen to succeed him, Aug. 24 of that year. Deacon Hovey died in 1785, and in April of the following year John Chadwick was chosen to fill the vacancy. Deacon Chadwick resigned Nov. 19, 1795, and died in 1797. Deacon Chadwick was succeeded by John Robinson, Esq., who was appointed Nov. 19, 1795, and continued in office till he resigned, March 20, 1806.

March 20, 1806, a new pair of deacons were chosen, namely, Bradstreet Tyler and Charles Foster. Deacon Tyler declined serving longer, April 13, 1814, and thanks were voted to him for his "acceptable services." John Day was appointed Deacon Tyler's successor on the same day. Deacon Day continued in office till June 2, 1848, when both he and Deacon Foster resigned.

June 2, 1848, a new pair of deacons were again chosen, namely, Joshua T. Day and Daniel K. Gage. Deacon Day served till his death, Feb. 12, 1873, when he was succeeded by Dane Foster, who is now in office. Deacon Gage served till his death in the spring of 1875. He was succeeded, June 16 of that year, by Isaac W. Andrews, who is now in office. Several of the deacons have been residents of North Andover.

INDEX OF SURNAMES.

CPSIA information can be obtained
at www.ICGtesting.com
Printed in the USA
LVHW080919211219
641337LV00015B/179/P